VICTORIAN LITERA
THE ECOLOGICA

Reading Victorian literature and science in tandem, *Victorian Literature, Energy, and the Ecological Imagination* investigates how the concept of energy was fictionalized – both mystified and demystified – during the rise of a new resource-intensive industrial and economic order. The first extended study of a burgeoning area of critical interest of increasing importance to twenty-first-century scholarship, it anchors its investigation at the very roots of the energy problem, in a period that first articulated questions about sustainability, the limits to growth, and the implications of energy pollution for the entire global environment. With chapters on Charles Dickens, John Ruskin, Robert Louis Stevenson, Joseph Conrad, and H. G. Wells, Allen MacDuffie discusses the representation of urban environments in the literary imaginary, and how those texts helped reveal the gap between cultural fantasies of unbounded energy generation and the material limits imposed by nature.

ALLEN MACDUFFIE is Assistant Professor in the English Department at the University of Texas, Austin.

CAMBRIDGE STUDIES IN NINETEENTH-CENTURY
LITERATURE AND CULTURE

General editor
Gillian Beer, *University of Cambridge*

Editorial board
Isobel Armstrong, *Birkbeck, University of London*
Kate Flint, *Rutgers University*
Catherine Gallagher, *University of California, Berkeley*
D. A. Miller, *University of California, Berkeley*
J. Hillis Miller, *University of California, Irvine*
Daniel Pick, *Birkbeck, University of London*
Mary Poovey, *New York University*
Sally Shuttleworth, *University of Oxford*
Herbert Tucker, *University of Virginia*

Nineteenth-century British literature and culture have been rich fields for inter-disciplinary studies. Since the turn of the twentieth century, scholars and critics have tracked the intersections and tensions between Victorian literature and the visual arts, politics, social organization, economic life, technical innovations, scientific thought – in short, culture in its broadest sense. In recent years, theoretical challenges and historiographical shifts have unsettled the assumptions of previous scholarly synthesis and called into question the terms of older debates. Whereas the tendency in much past literary critical interpretation was to use the metaphor of culture as "background," feminist, Foucauldian, and other analyses have employed more dynamic models that raise questions of power and of circulation. Such developments have reanimated the field. This series aims to accommodate and promote the most interesting work being undertaken on the frontiers of the field of nineteenth-century literary studies: work which intersects fruitfully with other fields of study such as history, or literary theory, or the history of science. Comparative as well as interdisciplinary approaches are welcomed.

A complete list of titles published will be found at the end of the book.

VICTORIAN LITERATURE, ENERGY, AND THE ECOLOGICAL IMAGINATION

ALLEN MACDUFFIE

CAMBRIDGE
UNIVERSITY PRESS

CAMBRIDGE
UNIVERSITY PRESS

University Printing House, Cambridge CB2 8BS, United Kingdom

One Liberty Plaza, 20th Floor, New York, NY 10006, USA

477 Williamstown Road, Port Melbourne, VIC 3207, Australia

4843/24, 2nd Floor, Ansari Road, Daryaganj, Delhi - 110002, India

79 Anson Road, #06-04/06, Singapore 079906

Cambridge University Press is part of the University of Cambridge.

It furthers the University's mission by disseminating knowledge in the pursuit of education, learning and research at the highest international levels of excellence.

www.cambridge.org
Information on this title: www.cambridge.org/9781107668089

First published 2014
First paperback edition 2017

A catalogue record for this publication is available from the British Library

Library of Congress Cataloging in Publication data
MacDuffie, Allen, 1975–
Victorian literature, energy, and the ecological imagination / Allen MacDuffie.
pages   cm. – (Cambridge studies in nineteenth-century literature and culture ; 93)
Includes bibliographical references and index.
ISBN 978-1-107-06437-9 (hardback)
1. English literature–19th century–History and criticism.   2. Literature and science–England–History–19th century.   3. Conservation of natural resources in literature.   4. Ecocriticism.   I. Title.
PR461.M25 2014
820.9'356–dc23
2013050833

ISBN 978-1-107-06437-9 Hardback
ISBN 978-1-107-66808-9 Paperback

Contents

Acknowledgments

I owe an enormous debt of gratitude to Elaine Scarry and Robert Kiely, the co-advisors of the dissertation that eventually became this book. Their unfailing generosity, patience, and critical insight sustained me at every stage, and their example continues to shape my scholarship and pedagogy. I would also like to thank Leah Price, who graciously joined the committee in the later stages and provided invaluable guidance.

It has been a sincere pleasure to work with Linda Bree and Anna Bond at Cambridge University Press. I am especially grateful to Linda for her steadfast support of the project throughout the entire process.

I thank the editors of *Representations* and *ELH* for their kind permission to publish revised versions of pieces that first appeared in those journals. A version of Chapter 6 appeared in *Representations* 96.1 (© 2006 The Regents of the University of California): 1–20. A version of Chapter 7 appeared in *ELH* 76.1 (© 2009 Johns Hopkins University Press): 75–98.

This book benefited tremendously from the feedback of a number of patient, perceptive readers. I would like to thank Joe Childers, Kathleen Frederickson, Claire Jarvis, and Elsie Michie, all of whom read chapter drafts and offered suggestions, insights and encouragement.

I am grateful to my colleagues at the University of Texas, past and present, whose friendship and support made Austin feel like home from the first day I arrived. There are too many to mention all by name, but I would like to acknowledge Samuel Baker, Coleman Hutchison, Neville Hoad, Douglas Bruster, Elizabeth Scala, Elizabeth Cullingford, Alan Friedman, Daniel Birkholz, Carol MacKay, Mia Carter, Frank Whigham, Martin Kevorkian, Brian Bremen, Janine Barchas, Wayne Rebhorn, Oscar Casares, Brian Doherty, Lance Bertelsen, Ann Cvetkovich, Julia Lee, Lindsay Reckson, J. K. Barret, Lisa Moore, and Heather Houser. I would also like to thank Lisa and Heather for their incisive comments on my *Bleak House* chapter.

My family encouraged my interest in literature from the first Richard Scarry book through Tolkien, Shakespeare, Eliot, and Dickens. I am able to pursue this incredibly rewarding academic life only because of their unconditional love and support, and I can never sufficiently express my gratitude. I would also like to think of the time my mother ran out of gas on the Toms River bridge with me in the backseat (age four) as a formative moment in what has become a lifelong concern about energy.

Lastly, and at the risk of sounding inexplicably Nabokovian, I would say that this book, like everything else, is for Vera.

Introduction
Limited environments, fictions of escape

In a recent advertising campaign, the oil company Chevron raised concerns about mounting worldwide energy consumption and population growth. The problem we face, a narrator says in the opening of one of the ads, is that "there are six and a half billion people on this planet ... and every one of us will need energy to live. Where will it come from?" Shots of highways, city skylines, and oil derricks suggest impending crisis: population growing, consumption spiraling, and energy production struggling to keep pace with demand. But there is a solution to this crisis, the narrator says, and an answer to the question "Where will it come from?" There are vast reserves just waiting to be tapped from "the greatest source of energy in the world – ourselves." And with that, the ad's images of a teeming, overpopulated globe are transformed from a source of concern to a source of optimism: "this," the ad says, "is the power of human energy."[1]

Such a formulation is misleading in many ways, and one of the most striking is its inconsistent use of the word "energy." In the opening of the ad, energy is defined as a resource, the fuel needed to keep the world's cars, airplanes, ships, stoves, light bulbs, televisions, computers, offices, hospitals, farms, factories, and cities running. But when the discussion shifts to "human energy," the word takes on an almost entirely different meaning. Energy in the second sense, "human energy," suggests something like creativity, initiative, intelligence, and cooperation. Technological innovation, it seems, brought about by the "power" of the human mind (and spearheaded by Chevron), will allow us to engineer our way out of whatever crisis we face. The ad plays upon a common understanding of the word energy as a disembodied power, a force of will or spirit that humans seemingly summon from within, which allows them to overcome whatever limits brute matter would impose. Indeed, this sense of the word is emphasized by the ad's visual rhetoric, which provides us with footage of a wide array of natural and human-made formations: glaciers, oceans, refineries, transportation networks, sprawling conurbations; the camera ranges fluidly, seemingly at will, over the globe. Swept up in this panorama and sense of complete visual command, we may not remember – we are perhaps encouraged to forget – the helicopters needed to capture many of those shots, or the fuel those helicopters used in order to do so, or, indeed, any of the resources involved in producing the two-minute fantasy of mastery designed to inspire belief in the power of human energy. Energy the resource becomes energy the metaphor, and the very problem the ad claims to address – "the population needs resources" – is transformed into its own solution – "the population *is* a resource." In this space of verbal and visual fantasy, the thermodynamic problem of the irreversible trans-formation of energy is solved by means of the linguistic and visual trans-formation of "energy."

The energy problem our world faces is both material and representa-tional. It is material in the sense that many vital resources exist in finite quantities, and in the sense that energy-intensive practices have profound, measurable, and perhaps irreversible environmental consequences. It is representational in the sense that these issues are commonly distorted in our cultural imaginary, and through our inconsistent use of the word itself. In a recent book about sustainable energy practices, the physicist David Goodstein argues:

> We don't have to conserve energy, because nature does it for us. For the same reason, there can never be an energy crisis. That doesn't mean we don't have a problem; it just means we haven't been describing the problem in the correct terms. There is something that we are using up and that we need to learn to conserve. It's called fuel.[2]

Here, Goodstein focuses on a particular tension in the word, between energy defined as a usable resource, and energy defined as ambient agency circulating endlessly through the world. It is the latter definition that lies behind Chevron's claims about "human energy": the ad's imagery of cease-less activity and motion at first seems like a problem ("look how much energy we're using"), but soon comes to seem like the solution ("look at all this marvelous energy").

The failure to differentiate these two different uses of the word is an ongoing source of misprision and fuzzy thinking about resource con-sumption, but the conflict has its roots in the nineteenth century, and it is those roots this book is interested in investigating. Although, as Christopher Herbert notes, intellectual history requires "abandoning the fantasy of originary moments," we can locate a few pivotal junctures in the formation of these issues, and in the history of the representation of energy resources.[3] One is Thomas Robert Malthus's *Essay on the Principle of Population*, together with the work that, in part, prompted him to write it, William Godwin's essay "Of Avarice and Profusion." Although Malthus was not concerned with fossil fuels, he was focused, at heart, on the availability of energy, and the material limits to human growth. For him, those limits centered upon a point of equilibration between food supply and human energy demands: when the population exceeded available resources, famine and disease would cut it back down to a sustainable size, after which it would begin growing again. The problem for Malthus is that utopian texts like Godwin's represent energy as something derived from within the human mind or spirit, rather than something that needs to be harvested from the environment. Thus he critiques Godwin's arguments about the "power of the mind over the body," because they imply that energetic limits can be surpassed through will, attitude, or motivation. He quotes Godwin's comment: "I walk twenty miles in an indolent and half determined temper and am extremely fatigued. I walk twenty miles full of ardour, and with a motive that engrosses my soul, and I come in as fresh and alert as when I began my journey." Malthus concedes there is a "mysterious connection of mind and body,"[4] but argues that a stimulus like this represents only a temporary means of forgetting fatigue, not a material supply of fuel: "if the energy of my mind had really counteracted the fatigue of my body, why should I feel tired the next morning?"[5] For Malthus, there is no "effort of reason" that can engineer its way out of the energy problem – because any increase in productive power or efficiency will only cause a corresponding surge in population – but there are also no mysterious springs of energy intrinsic to, or generated by, the human spirit.[6]

Malthus was wrong about quite a lot, and his arguments about scarcity were inflected by his commitment to a ruinous *laissez-faire* economic doctrine. In his work, the burden and the moral responsibility fall upon the backs of the poor and almost nowhere else. The argument for the scarcity of resources, as Marx and Engels saw, served to disguise the problem of the *distribution* of resources, exploitative social relations, and the question of the ownership of the means of production. Moreover, the astonishing expansion of industry and the development of agricultural chemistry soon increased human productive power to levels Malthus could not have imagined in 1798. As Kathleen Tobin argues, it was common for Malthus's Victorian critics to reference "technological advances in agriculture as evidence that [his] claims could no longer be substantiated."[7] Lewis Henry Morgan, for example, argues that "mankind are the only beings who may be said to have gained an absolute control over the production of food,"[8] echoing Godwin's claim that "Man is to a considerable degree the artificer of his own fortune."[9] And Engels argued that "science increases at least as fast as population; the latter increases in proportion to the body of knowledge passed down to it by the previous generation, and science advances in proportion to the size of the previous generation, that is, in the most normal conditions it also grows in geometrical progression – and what is impossible for science?"[10] If Malthus imagined an entrapping world of struggle and want, new energy technologies seemed the key to emancipation: the natural world was nowhere near as tight-fisted as he would have us believe. As we shall see, the doctrine of the conservation of energy suggested to many Victorians a universe of almost infinite energetic plentitude just waiting to be tapped by human industry.

And yet, one can see behind Engels's comment an almost faith-based argument about the course of scientific development and the unstoppable upward march of technology. This was a common refrain about energy resources in the Victorian period (as it is in ours): science will always figure out a way to stay one step ahead of scarcity. In a sense, it is a version of Godwin's argument, a belief in technological advance and humanity's potential finally to master its environment. But as Malthus pointed out, there is an "essential difference ... between an unlimited improvement and an improvement the limit of which cannot be ascertained."[11] The enormous development of industrial and agricultural energy, the sudden (in historical terms) access to immense reserves of stored motive power in the form of fossil fuels made it easy to mistake the former for the latter. Malthus's predictions seemed misguided not because his basic principles were necessarily wrong, but because he could not have predicted that the amount of energy available for human purposes would spike in such dramatic fashion, or that human civilization would begin running through it so quickly.[12]

Malthus left a decidedly mixed legacy for Victorian thinking about energy. On the one hand, his theory provided a powerful means of conceptualizing crucial questions about environmental limits and resource scarcity. On the other hand, the ideologically offensive elements of his theory, the way it seemed to naturalize an unfettered, weak-to-the-wall brand of free-market economics, made it (understandably) toxic to left-wing and radical Tory critics of capitalism alike. Economist Michael Perelman argues this was a pivotal problem for Marx, who wanted to critique capitalist production as environmentally reckless and unsustainable, but did not want to cede an inch of ground to Malthus or to the notion that scarcity was a natural, rather than a social, phenomenon. Thus for Marx "shortages reflected the inability of capital to master the environment": a problem that would be rectified in the future Communist state.[13]

Open and closed systems

Not only does Malthus insist that the "power" of the human mind is not an avenue of escape from resource scarcity, he paints a bleak vision of the earth as a single enclosed system, where there are no fuel supplies or geographical spaces that can relieve the conflict between population growth and environmental limits.[14] Introducing one of his thought experiments, he writes: "To make the argument more general and less interrupted by the partial views of emigration, let us take the whole earth, instead of one spot."[15] His argument actually requires a vision of the earth as a single totality; otherwise, the processes of emigration and the cultivation of other lands suggest there are "elsewheres" – vents for excess population, sources of additional energy – that can mitigate or disguise the basic problem of overpopulation and resource depletion. But when imagined as a totality, the earth clearly has only limited space for people (or any species), and only so much arable land. Thus what appears to be development is merely a very long process – punctuated by periods of starvation and misery for the poor – of discovering how much human consumption the earth can sustain. Malthus fills his pages with the vocabulary and imagery of entrapment, enclosure, and thwarted escape: "Necessity, that imperious all-pervading law of nature, restrains them within the prescribed bounds. The race of plants, and the race of animals shrink under this great restrictive law. And the race of man cannot, by any efforts of reason, escape from it."[16] Possible routes out of this dilemma are ruthlessly foreclosed, especially in the *Essay*'s first edition. This image of a single, inescapable world-environment would become a significant component of twentieth- and twenty-first-century discourse on ecological destruction and sustainable development. It appears perhaps most famously in the English-American economist Kenneth Boulding's metaphor of "spaceship earth." Popularized in the 1960s, the idea of the earth as a spaceship conjures a small, tightly bounded world that must subsist on its stored resources and carefully manage its waste products. For Boulding, an ecological vision that can meet the challenges of modernity requires coming to terms with new kinds of imaginative models for human life on the planet. It means recognizing that there are no "elsewheres," no unspoiled zones to move to if we ruin the one we're living in. He writes:

> We are now in the middle of a long process of transition in the nature of the image which man has of himself and his environment. Primitive men, and to a large extent also men of the early civilizations, imagined themselves to be living on a virtually illimitable plane. There was almost always somewhere beyond the known limits of human habitation, and over a very large part of the time that man has been on earth, there has been something like a frontier. That is, there was always some place else to go when things got too difficult, either by reason of the deterioration of the natural environment or a deterioration of the social structure in places where people happened to live. The image of a frontier is probably one of the oldest images of mankind, and it is not surprising that we find it hard to get rid of.[17]

Malthus may be living at the dawn of empire, but he is already beginning to imagine the end of new frontiers.

As both writers suggest through their imagery – and as Boulding was well aware – one of the key conceptual models for the discourse of energy resources, waste, and the environment is the *closed system*. As we will see, the idea of the closed system is at the very heart of Victorian thermodynamic discourse, and its formulation of the entropy concept. Although modern physics uses the term somewhat differently, we will follow the Victorians and define a closed system as one that does not receive any inputs of energy from outside itself. As Daniel Hall puts it in a Victorian physics primer: "in any closed system the energy present is a constant quantity."[18] But "constant," paradoxically, does not mean "unchanging" – and here we run into Goodstein's distinction between energy and fuel. The second law of thermodynamics states that, in a closed system, energy always moves from an available to an unavailable state. So the total amount of energy remains constant, but the amount of fuel, or usable energy, decreases. The cosmos itself was often imagined in these terms: as T. E. Young puts it, "the Solar Universe is a closed system receiving no supplies of energy from external sources."[19] Such a bounded cosmic model gave rise, in the middle decades of the nineteenth century, to fears of the ultimate "heat death" of the sun, which we will discuss in more detail in Chapter 2. An open system, in contrast, is defined by an incoming flow of energy that counteracts whatever dissipation occurs. Eric Schneider and Dorion Sagan call this "metastability" and liken it to the way a ping-pong ball can be made to hover suspended on a column of air coming out of a tube.[20]

But whether a system can be understood as closed or open depends on where representational boundaries are drawn: whether the system is defined in such a way that there is energy coming from an "elsewhere" that is not counted as part of the system. A wound-up watch may be conveniently imagined as a closed system, but it becomes open as soon as we include the owner who can pick it up and wind it again. The solar system appears closed if we imagine the sun contains a limited supply of fuel that it uses up over time; but it appears open if we imagine (as some Victorians did) that the sun keeps receiving fresh supplies of energy through collisions with comets or meteors.[21] But this introduces an important complication when we turn to the representation of the earth itself. Since it receives a continuous stream of solar energy, the earth's biosphere is most assuredly *not* closed. Why, then, the emphasis on "spaceship earth" and other images of a bounded planet? In some ways, this imagery betrays deeply anthropocentric biases. As a natural energy system, the earth is not closed. But as an energy system that can continue supporting human life with its current patterns of growth and consumption, it may well be. This is the point of Malthus's rhetoric of inescapability, and why his theory is often called the Malthusian "trap": the human need for energy presses up against the limits of the environment, and the ability of the earth to supply it. It is not energy that is limited, but *available* energy. While the rise of a fossil-fuel-driven industrial order seemed to some to provide a release from Malthusian fears, it only changed the shape of the problem. An energy system that runs on fossil fuels is, for all intents and purposes, closed. Coal and oil, once converted into heat, smoke, and mechanical motion, will not return to their earlier energy-rich condition, and, as far as anyone knows, there are no more supplies on the way. Moreover, as we are increasingly coming to discover, the irreversible consumption of fossil-fuel resources creates its own irreversible environmental effects. The earth does not immediately vent all the waste heat we produce; instead, much of it remains trapped, altering the makeup of the biosphere itself. The biologist and demographer Paul Ehrlich describes the double bind in which this puts industrial civilization. The laws of thermodynamics:

> make it clear that *all* the energy used on the face of the Earth ... will ultimately be degraded to heat. Here the laws catch us both coming and going, for they put limits on the efficiency with which we can manipulate this heat. Hence, they pose the danger that human society may make this planet uncomfortably warm with degraded energy long before it runs out of high-grade energy to consume.[22]

The earth remains an open system, continually fed by the sun, and nothing we do will change that. But it may cease being a place that can support our current population numbers and patterns of energy consumption.

In other words, the biosphere is open, but our resource-intensive industrial system, which increasingly comes to shape the global environment, is not. The nineteenth century had trouble with this distinction, and this is seen most clearly in its representations of the city. Like the biosphere, a city is also not a closed system; in fact, a city wouldn't be able to exist if it couldn't draw resources from beyond its boundaries. Ilya Prigogine and Isabelle Stengers write:

> When we examine a biological cell or a city, however, the situation is quite different: not only are these systems open, but also they exist only because they are open. They feed on the flux of matter and energy coming to them from the outside world … cities and cells die when cut off from their environment. They form an integral part of the world from which they draw sustenance, and they cannot be separated from the fluxes that they incessantly transform.[23]

This idea of the city as an organism that must feed continually on its external environment in order to survive was a familiar one to the Victorians. London was often represented as "an immense open-mouthed body," as Lynda Nead puts it, and there are endless examples of the city-as-consumer in Dickens, Ruskin, Mayhew, and other writers.[24] And yet, oddly, the city was *simultaneously* imagined as a kind of closed system in which usable energy was inexorably running down, and entropy mounting uncontrollably. In a recent book on the Victorian city Richard Lehan writes:

> The first two laws of thermodynamics explain the nature of entropy: first, the amount of energy in the universe is fixed, and energy can never be increased or diminished, only transformed; second, every time energy is transformed from one state to another, there is a loss in the amount of energy available to perform future work. Entropy is that loss of energy in a closed system. In an open system, negative entropy supplies an added source of entropy; plants, for example, absorb energy from the sun. A city is a closed system: nothing provides it energy outside itself.[25]

My point is not that Lehan is wrong; it's that he's *right*, in a way. That is, although in thermodynamic terms, that last sentence is incorrect, it speaks to a crucial feeling about, and a common mode of representation of, the city in the nineteenth-century imaginary – that it was a bounded space irreversibly consuming its own energy and suffocating in its own detritus and waste heat. For what makes widespread energy waste a problem, what makes the city *seem* like a closed system, is the development of an urban-industrial complex that depends, increasingly, on fuels drawn from the earth's limited resource base. Not the city itself, but a mode of production and social organization *embodied* in the city creates a closed system of non-renewable resource dependence, where the consumption of energy outpaces the intake. As William Stanley Jevons notes, "A farm, however far pushed, will under proper cultivation continue to yield for ever a constant crop. But in a mine there is no reproduction, and the produce once pushed to the utmost will soon begin to fail and sink towards zero."[26] A city does not grow like a field; as the Victorians knew well, it depended, increasingly, on coal for its heat, its light, its commerce, even for its water. An economic system premised on the use of finite stocks of resources has limits – what we would today call the "limits to growth" – and the city, overcrowded, saturated with pollution, expending energy in prodigious, even spectacular fashion, made these limits imaginatively available to novelists, critics, scientists, economists, artists, and others.

As twentieth-century ecological economist Nicholas Georgescu-Roegen argues, "There is … a difference between returns in mining and returns in agriculture. In mining, we tap the stocks of various forms of low entropy contained in the crust of the planet on which we live; in agriculture, we tap primarily the flow of low entropy that reaches the earth as solar radiation."[27] There is a fundamental asymmetry between solar and terrestrial sources of energy: the former flows from the sun at a rate that we have no control over, but it flows, for our purposes, indefinitely; the latter, in contrast, flows at a rate that is, to a growing extent, determined by human capacities and wants – as Georgescu-Roegen notes, we could theoretically harvest all of our coal and burn it all at once if we chose.[28] But terrestrial energy will *not* flow indefinitely; it burns irreversibly, and once it is gone, it will not come back. For Malthus, population and resources oscillated around the flow of energy in a dynamic but essentially stable equilibrium. There was room for historical development in Malthus's world, but it was determined by the rate of flow and by the continual push-and-pull of consumption and reproduction. Dependence upon terrestrial stocks of energy introduces a new dynamic, one defined not by equilibration but by unidirectionality.[29] With our hand on the proverbial spigot, there is an illusion of control over the energy of the planet, and that sense of control is sustained by a faith in ever-increasing technological perfectibility. But it is also haunted by the question of irreversible depletion, by the knowledge that the tap leads to a reservoir that is not being refilled. The dependence upon fossil-fuel resources (and chemical fertilizers) thus introduces a very different relationship between human growth and the energy of the natural world, and that new relationship was most evident at the mouth of the spigot – the nineteenth-century urban environment.

This at the root of Lehan's remark: it suggests a common vision of the city as a stand-in for the entire industrial order, enclosed in its dependence upon finite terrestrial resources. George Levine makes a similarly telling comment in his discussion of *Little Dorrit*: "While the total energy remains the same, the total available energy diminishes so that within any closed system (like the world) the movement is always toward increased cooling and increased disorder and decreased energy available to do work."[30] To see the world as a closed system, as a domain in which usable energy is constantly decreasing, is, in fact, a sign of the way in which urban-industrial logic surreptitiously comes to structure the representation of *everything*. The "world" in this case is not distinguishable from London: just as there is no escape from the Marshalsea for Mr. Dorrit even when he is outside its walls, there is no escape from the totalizing system of energy relations represented in and through the city. The city, the world, the cosmos – all of these seem analogously "closed," with entropy mounting and energy sinking towards zero, because each subsists on a finite supply of resources. Thus, as I will discuss at greater length in Chapter 2, visions of solar decay become intimately tied to visions of urban collapse.

Anxiety about environmental limits, whether in the form of overpopulation, industrial contamination, energy exhaustion, or some combination of these (interlocking) problems, shaped the representation of urban centers in the nineteenth century, because cities could suggest, in their seemingly unstoppable growth patterns, a future in which the entire globe would be given over to the demands of a fully urbanized civilization. We see such imaginings in some of H. G. Wells's science fiction – the totalized future city of *When the Sleeper Awakes*, or, as I will discuss in some detail in the final chapter, the covertly urban landscapes of *The Time Machine*. We see it in mid-century works, in the suffocating London of later Dickens, the contaminating reach of which always extends into unexpected, non-urbanized locations: Chesney Wold in *Bleak House*, or the marshes in *Great Expectations*. We even see it in John Stuart Mill, who contemplates:

> the world with nothing left to the spontaneous activity of nature; with every rood of land brought into cultivation, which is capable of growing food for human beings; every flowery waste or natural pasture ploughed up, all quadrupeds or birds which are not domesticated for man's use exterminated as his rivals for food, every hedgerow or superfluous tree rooted out, and scarcely a place left where a wild shrub or flower could grow without being eradicated as a weed in the name of improved agriculture.[31]

This, Mill cautions, is the logical endpoint of an economic system that posits unending growth on a finite base of land and resources. John Ruskin comments on this passage:

All England may, if it so chooses, become one manufacturing town; and Englishmen, sacrificing themselves to the good of general humanity, may live diminished lives in the midst of noise, of darkness, and of deadly exhalation. But the world cannot become a factory nor a mine. No amount of ingenuity will ever make iron digestible by the million, nor substitute hydrogen for wine.[32]

The question all of these writers face in various ways is where the processes of urbanization *end*. To respond to Mill's concerns, Ruskin invokes the basic biophysical limits to human development. But while it is certain that such limits do exist, it is far from certain (as Mill clearly recognized) that the process of reaching them won't be a moral and environmental disaster. This, as I discuss in Chapter 5, is the conclusion Ruskin also reaches in his late lecture *The Storm Cloud of the Nineteenth Century*, which imagines energy-intensive practices leading to ruinous global consequences. For Ruskin, the *entire atmosphere* seems to be becoming urbanized, the global climate transfigured by the effects of spiraling energy consumption. The city makes such profound and unceasing demands upon the resources of the natural world, and visits such obvious damage upon surrounding environments, that it would, if allowed to continue expanding, eventually threaten the entire planet. We find in Mill, Ruskin, Dickens, and others, the stirrings of an imaginative apprehension of what the chemist Paul Crutzen has termed the "Anthropocene": a new geological epoch defined by humankind's status as a global "environmental force."[33] Just as climate scientists investigate polar ice to find evidence of atmospheric changes beginning in the eighteenth and nineteenth centuries, so can we find in the imaginative literature of an earlier period traces of these new environmental realities beginning to enter the cultural imaginary.

An "open-mouthed" consumer of energy resources; a fog-enclosed world of dust heaps, river sludge, and spent fuel; a world groaning under the pressures of population and its demands: the city was a Malthusian nightmare for the dawning fossil-fuel age. As we will see in the next two chapters, writers on "the coal question" found in the city a unique and growing threat to natural resources and the environment. The sense of threat is present in the discourse of urban sanitary reform, even among those optimistic about the future. Take, for example F. C. Krepp's vision of waste recycling in London:

> By a judicious use of the immense resources placed at our disposal by modern science, in the shape of such acknowledged practical appliances as pneumatic force, steam-power, and agricultural chemistry, Captain Liernur has shown that this may be effected by practically transforming filth into food. Thus a peaceful, moral, and social revolution will be effected such

as the world has hardly seen before! What hitherto was only a most pro-
lific source of constant annoyance, of disease and death, behold, it is now
a most valuable specific for nourishing and stimulating vegetable growth,
a fertiliser of surpassing power, giving bread to millions; a source of such
boundless plenty, that, instead of the misery and strife which the "struggle
for life" always engenders, peace and good-will will more generally reign
upon earth; in short, an agent of happiness and a blessing to all![34]

The Malthusian (and now Darwinian) "struggle for life" – the intra- and
inter-species competition for scarce resources – lurks here as the menace
that technology is called upon to neutralize. Krepp is confident it will do
so, but the stakes here are quite high if the superabundant waste cannot
be converted into superabundant fertilizing power. Moreover, while his
system entirely depends upon "steam-power" to fuel the process, he does
not count those inputs as a *cost*. Here we have the situation in a nutshell:
the problem of resource consumption, waste, and struggle is on vivid display in the city, and the solution to it depends upon the consumption of
even *more* resources that are themselves available in only limited quantities. By gesturing vaguely towards the "immense resources" of science
but neglecting to count their cost, Krepp founds a vision of a self-pow-
ering, fully sustainable capitalist economy on the back of an unsustainable, resource-intensive industrial order. Throughout this book, we will
repeatedly encounter such representational games with energy, as well as
attempts to confront squarely the problem of resource depletion and the
environmental limits to human consumption.

Thermodynamic narratives

This book seeks to investigate the nineteenth-century roots of our contemporary discussion of energy at a time when a rising industrial civilization
first began representing its own energy-intensive life to itself. It is about
how Victorian culture, like ours, found various ways to warp, bend, and
otherwise misrepresent the relationship between human development and
the resources of the natural world. But it is also about the different ways
in which the Victorians confronted the problems of increasing energy
consumption, and first articulated grave concerns about what we would
now call the "sustainability" of a fossil-fuel-driven order. In the nineteenth
century, then, we see both the dawn of a robust ecological imaginary that
first mapped the contours of our ongoing energy crisis, *and* the emergence
of highly mystifying fantasies about energy, which persist today and have
helped make that crisis as intractable as it is. This book maps the complex,

volatile, sometimes contradictory, discursive terrain in which the under-standing of energy resources took shape.

In what follows, I discuss the emergence of "thermodynamic narra-tives" – stories about the way energy travels through social, natural, and cosmic systems. In doing so, I draw on the work of some pioneering lit-erary scholars in this field, including George Levine, Gillian Beer, Ted Underwood, Catherine Gallagher, Barri Gold, and Tina Young Choi. All of these critics, in different ways, have helped to establish the deep con-nections between thermodynamic science and the nineteenth-century lit-erary imaginary. The novel has been especially fertile territory for locating such connections, in part because of its interest in representing large sys-tems of organization – cities, courts, bureaucracies, imperial networks – that seem to operate by means of aggregated, impersonal forces. In the Victorian imagination, such human systems are imagined as potential analogues for the natural world or for the cosmos itself; thus Chancery in *Bleak House* is disturbing not just because of how it wastes energy, but because its operations seem to provide a glimpse into more fundamental wasting agencies. Moreover, as Choi and Gold argue, the Victorian novel was *itself* imagined as an energy system, one that manages, expends, and recycles the various energies of its characters, and frames them as part of a totalized network of reactions and transformations. This is more than mere metaphor: both critics show how both the conservation and dissipa-tion of energy provided templates for narrative structure, conceptions of temporality, and forms of narrative closure.

This book draws on the work of these scholars, and tracks further con-nections between literary and scientific imaginaries. But it is even more interested in locating the places where these discourses *diverge*, where the stories of energy they tell seem to paint discrepant and even conflicting pictures of the use, waste, and availability of natural resources. I contend that the canonical account of energy in Victorian scientific discourse often distorted the *ecological* significance of the energy concept, in part because many of the first generation of British thermodynamic scientists focused their attention on the theological and cosmological significance of the laws of thermodynamics. As Prigogine and Stengers argue, Victorian ther-modynamics trafficked in "mythic and religious archetypes" rather than the biological (and ecological) tropes of "progressive complexification and diversification."[35] This is nowhere more evident than in the emphasis some Victorian energy scientists placed on the eventual "heat death" of the sun. As I discuss in more detail in Chapter 2, the prediction of the ultimate extinction of solar light and heat discussed by William Thomson, Balfour

Stewart, and others encoded a picture of *nature* as a deeply flawed and inefficient energy system. Although the second law of thermodynamics emerged from the investigation of the waste generated by industrial technology, it was quickly used to paint a picture of energy waste as natural, universal, and inevitable. The emphasis placed on energy dissipation as a cosmic inevitability, rather than the outgrowth of wasteful human practices, helped shift the burden and the responsibility for waste away from an entropy-producing industrial order, and onto the natural world itself. Where (as Beer demonstrates) Darwin's work is deeply invested in the processes and texture of the natural world, evincing wonder and even a kind of love for the very materiality of nature, Victorian thermodynamics often tends to denigrate material nature as flawed, transitory, and, ultimately, unreal. Whereas Darwin attempted to shift his language and his concepts decisively away from those of natural theology, energy scientists were avowedly interested in using the laws of thermodynamics to provide support for their own theological worldview. Despite the popular belief that evolution and the second law of thermodynamics are somehow incompatible, they are, as scientific principles, perfectly reconcilable. There are, however, crucial differences in the way in which they were discussed, propounded, and framed in the nineteenth century.

In some ways, this may seem surprising, since thermodynamics is such a staple of modern ecological thought. Contemporary work about sustainability and the limits to growth invariably point to both the first and second laws of thermodynamics as indispensable analytical tools. Paul Ehrlich writes:

> One illustration of the power of the laws of thermodynamics is that in many situations they can be used to predict the maximum efficiency that could be achieved by a perfect machine, without specifying any details of the machine! ... Thus, one can specify, for example, what *minimum* amount of energy is necessary to separate salt from seawater, to separate metals from their ores, and to separate pollutants from auto exhaust without knowing any details about future inventions that might be devised for these purposes. Similarly, if one is told the temperature of a source of thermal energy – say, the hot rock deep in Earth's crust – one can calculate rather easily the maximum efficiency with which this thermal energy can be converted to applied work ... In other words, *there are some fixed limits to technological innovation, placed there by fundamental laws of nature.*[36]

As Ehrlich notes, the laws of thermodynamics can be used to debunk fantasies about technology's miraculous properties and potential, and thus function as powerful tools of demystification. That they must be continually called upon to do so testifies to the persistence of such fantasies. Although much of this demystifying potential was present in the laws of thermodynamics from the start, the cosmological and natural-theological arguments in which the laws were often embedded made their ecological significance difficult to see at first.

But that doesn't mean such significance wasn't accessible through other discourses and modes of representation. In Chapters 3 through 8, I show how literary texts by Dickens, Ruskin, Stevenson, Conrad, and Wells attempted to come to grips with the problem of energy as a resource, and with energy consumption as a pressing environmental issue. If Victorian thermodynamics fashioned nature as an unsustainable energy system, these writers focused on the unsustainable patterns of *human* energy use. I describe these texts as *alternative thermodynamic narratives* – narratives that are deeply invested in questions about energy, work, waste, transformation, and systematicity, but that depart in important ways from some of the ideological and theological assumptions present in canonical thermodynamic discourse. The importation of thermodynamic tropes into the domain of the literary allows writers both the ability to draw on these powerful metaphors, and freedom from the disciplinary restraints and discursive practices that structured the scientific conversation about energy. The literary texts I examine in this book ground their representation of energy not in cosmic abstractions or in close-focus accounts of engine technology, but in specific locations: skies, fields, rivers, streets, houses, slums, and cities. Cities especially. As I argue in the first two chapters, the Victorian city was not only imagined as a kind of energy system – fueled continuously by coal, corn, and other raw materials from the countryside and imperial domains; it became, for some writers, *the quintessential vision of the industrial-capitalist motor*. As such, the city could expose the besetting contradictions within the logic of development: in the hands of writers like Dickens and Ruskin, the urban environment appears as a zone in which the economic fictions of exponential growth collide with the material pressures of environmental contamination and resource exhaustion. To imagine economic development as unlimited is to imagine nature as a commodity that can be manipulated and transformed at will; but the obvious environmental disorder of the city, the mounting presence of noxious gases, effluvia, soot, smoke, ash, and all the other unrecoverable by-products of aggregated energy consumption, were a reminder of what could *not* be manipulated or transformed, of what could only be carted away, scraped off, hidden, buried, or flushed. Urbanization, like population growth, was a process that had no internal "brakes" – no self-checking mechanism that would cause it to slow down on its own – but the manifest disorder of the Victorian city made it clear that there were, in fact, biophysical limits to growth, imposed by the irreversible direction of resource consumption, and the experience of entropy in the form of pollution.

The book, however, does not construct an easy binary between a blinkered scientific discourse and a more ecologically responsible approach to the environment found in the novel and other works of imaginative literature. Instead it argues that if the novel opened up possibilities for alternative stories about energy, it also often remained committed to reassuring structures of Providential patterning, and worked to transform wasted energy into forms of symbolic value within narrative systems. In the introduction to *Darwin's Plots*, Beer discusses the curious power of Victorian prose to push the boundaries of the thinkable through its deployment of figurative language: "Symbol and metaphor, as opposed to analysis, can allow insight without consequences because perceptions are not stabilised and categorised."[37] Such flights into unstabilized and uncategorized territory, I would argue, allow Victorian fiction access to crucial ecological insights about sustainable energy practices; but they also mean that such insights are *themselves* unstable, and thus liable to be both robustly imagined and incompletely articulated. Just as Victorian thermodynamic discourse simultaneously mystified and demystified the workings of energy by encumbering its insights about natural limits with ideological and metaphysical baggage, the Victorian novel could offer a potent vision of the unsustainable fictions of urban-industrial development while also sidestepping or even undermining some of the more radical implications of its insights. This book examines a number of fictional texts – including *Bleak House*, *Dr. Jekyll and Mr. Hyde*, and *The Secret Agent* – in great detail, since it is only by means of a thorough exploration of the various tensions and fissures in these texts that we can appreciate the profound difficulty in coming to terms with the unfolding environmental crisis brought about by the consumption of fossil fuels. I range over a fairly broad period of English literary history – from the early 1850s to the opening of the twentieth century – because my aim is, to borrow a phrase from Patricia Yaeger, "to chart some coordinates for an energy-driven literary theory."[38] This book attempts to provide some of those coordinates, and thus some sense of the diverse and divergent ways in which the problem of energy consumption and sustainability was articulated in the period. I see this book as a necessary first step in establishing the terms through which we might begin to understand the ways in which energy was – and continues to be – *fictionalized*.

In making this argument, I draw upon the methods of scholars like Levine and Beer, who trace connections between science and literature not so much in terms of the influence of the former upon the latter, but in terms of a shared cultural context and a multi-directional traffic of metaphors, conceits, rhetorical structures, and narrative methods. As James Mussell puts it: "Victorian science, in other words, was part of Victorian culture, and Victorian culture in turn shaped Victorian science. It was not unusual for literary authors to engage with scientific ideas in their work; nor did scientists ignore the concerns, forms, or techniques of literature."[39] Indeed, the nineteenth century is especially ripe for this kind of investigation, as Vanessa Ryan has recently argued.[40] Thus James Secord can discuss the debt Robert Chambers's evolutionary text *The Vestiges of the Natural History of Creation* owed to Walter Scott's novels; Nancy Paxton, meanwhile, can treat George Eliot's fiction as a serious theorization of scientific topics.[41] To make such arguments, as Ryan points out, is not to say that the practices of literature and science were indistinguishable to the Victorians, but that they often functioned as complementary forms of knowledge production.[42]

This complementarity is especially important to the development of thermodynamic science. As we will see, many of Britain's leading energy scientists in the nineteenth century owed a debt to Romantic literature and the emphasis it placed, in Iwan Rhys Morus's words, on "looking beneath the phenomena in an effort to capture the real underlying unity of nature."[43] As Morus argues, not only did this emphasis on unity deeply inform the scientific investigation of a wide array of energetic processes, it could also be used to borrow for the thermodynamic investigator something of the Romantic's claim to visionary, totalizing perception:

> For early nineteenth-century Romantic philosophers, natural philosophy required a particular kind of individual. Apprehending nature's hidden unities required someone with the innate capacity to look beneath the surface of events and see what others could not. Midcentury natural philosophers such as William Robert Grove suggested that the natural philosopher needed to be someone educated to look beyond the limitations of particular disciplinary preoccupations and see the wider picture of the correlation of forces. By the end of the century, proponents of energy physics argued that only those like them, deeply trained in the complexities of mathematical physics, could see the world as it really was.[44]

Indeed, the concept of energy demands an interdisciplinary approach, because questions about its use and waste can be fully addressed through neither quantitative nor qualitative analysis alone. As we will see throughout, deciding what even falls under the sign of "use" and "waste" is not at all straightforward, since such designations are always deeply (if sometimes covertly) value-laden. Energy moves through natural, industrial, animal, social, and even mental spheres in complex, ramifying, and overlapping ways; its expenditure has consequences that are cultural, personal, economic, and environmental. Thus when thermodynamic scientists like Thomson, Stewart, and Tyndall turn to metaphors, narrative archetypes, and apocalyptic stories to represent energy, they are not only trying to put their esoteric equations in a language the wider public can understand; they are necessarily working out the points of contact between those equations and the broader spheres of human and nonhuman existence that give energy use its meaning and significance in the first place. And thus we can also recognize how a novelist like Dickens, for example, who was, by and large, unschooled in the technical details of thermodynamic research, could have vitally important things to say about energy through his representation of complex, resource-intensive systems; the points of interchange between forms of natural, social, industrial, and bodily energy; and his acute insight into the possibilities and limitations of representation *itself*. Because of the way it connects both seemingly disparate phenomena and modes of experience, energy demands an ecological vision, and reckoning with representational boundaries.

The difficulty in representing energy, as I have been suggesting, still troubles us. This book views the understanding of energy through two distinct but mutually informing historical lenses. The first is a deep engagement with the specific discursive practices of the Victorian period through an examination of scientific texts, literary works, popular lectures, reviews, periodicals, and other cultural materials. Through this engagement, the book explores in some detail the historically specific inflections of the word "energy" during the period. But simultaneously, and more broadly, it argues that there are certain trends in the representation of energy that are continuous between eras, and that transcend many of the particularities of historical and cultural difference. This latter, I acknowledge, is the more dubious historical claim, and I offer it provisionally and with due concern about the problems of courting anachronism and ahistoricity. But here I would borrow a page from Rick Rylance, whose formulation of the continuity between eras nicely captures something of the guiding spirit of this book: "certain deep conceptual problems ... are, if not 'timeless' (because their forms are historically produced and specific), tenaciously persistent ... In a real way, for all their difference, we are still in active conversation with Victorian ideas."[45] The geologist

M. King Hubbert argues the rise of a civilization built on the exploitation of fossil fuels offers an alternative model of periodicity: in his words, "the two-hundred year period from 1776 to 1976 marks the emergence of an entirely new phase in human history ... It is the period during which there has occurred a transition from a social state whose material and energy requirements were satisfied mainly from renewable resources to our present state that is overwhelmingly dependent upon nonrenewable resources."[46] As the chemist Frederick Soddy writes, humanity's shift from a dependence upon energy flow (from the sun) to dependence on energy stocks (fossil fuels) marks a decisive shift in human history and argues for the deep structural continuities between the Victorian period and our own:

> One point seemed lacking to account for the phenomenal outburst of activity that followed in the Western world the invention of the steam engine, for it could not be ascribed simply to the substitution of inanimate energy for animal labour ... The profound change that then occurred seemed to be rather due to the fact that, for the first time in history, men began to tap a large capital store of energy and ceased to be entirely dependent on the revenue of sunshine ... The flamboyant era through which we have been passing is due not to our own merits, but to our having inherited accumulations of solar energy from the carboniferous era, so that our life for once has been able to live beyond its income.[47]

This "flamboyant era" is what Crutzen would later theorize as the "Anthropocene," although Soddy is focused less on global environmental effects than on historical shifts in social relations and modes of economic organization. The economic metaphors Soddy uses are, as we will see, crucial to the Victorian conception of energy, but the key point is that the structural problem of "living beyond our income" defines the economic and productive logic of our era as well as theirs. Soddy was writing in the early decades of the twentieth century; since then, the dependence on fossil fuels has only grown, and the energy "capital" accumulated in the early carboniferous era has been consumed at an ever-accelerating rate. It seems to me such insights are liable to be lost when we speak of the late twentieth and early twenty-first centuries as "post-industrial"; or when we stress the remarkable potential in alternative fuel sources, green energy, wind turbines, clean coal, cold fusion, solar-powered cars, and the like; or when we describe the internet revolution as enabling civilization to transcend material constraints by moving activity into a bloodless, virtual realm. Implied in such rhetoric is a notion that we have left the dirty, smoke-filled, "Victorian" world of fossil-fuel consumption behind.[48]

The technologies that will purportedly carry us into this next stage of energy often reveal themselves to be deeply dependent upon the very non-renewable fuels they seek to replace. Corn-based ethanol, for instance, is often touted as an alternative to gasoline, but the process of converting corn into a biofuel *itself* requires inputs of energy from fossil fuels and other sources. As Goodstein (and many others) have argued, ethanol is, for this reason, a net energy *loser*: the process consumes more energy than it produces.[49] Again, we return to questions of representation: if you describe how ethanol can power a car just like gasoline, it seems like a viable alternative to fossil fuels. But once you widen the picture to take into account all of the energy inputs that make its production possible, it seems little more than a pipe dream, or worse. There are echoes of Krepp's argument here, where an alternative to wasteful contemporary practices secretly depends upon those very practices, and visions of a sustainable energy economy are themselves built upon unsustainable foundations.

Indeed, the irony is that in our own claims for being or becoming "post-industrial" or "post-Victorian," we recapitulate the very same arguments that the Victorians themselves made about their own energy future. Nineteenth-century discussions of the unsustainable path of fossil-fuel consumption almost inevitably included some kind of consoling gesture towards the promise of new technologies and energy supplies that would rescue civilization from pollution and exhaustion. The astronomer Richard Proctor, in a discussion of "Britain's Coal Cellars" in 1871, ends on this note:

> What the vegetable world did for us unconsciously during the Carboniferous Epoch, the scientific world of our epoch must do for our remote descendants. While we are consuming the stores of force laid up in past ages for our benefit, we must invent the means for obtaining directly from the solar rays fresh and inexhaustible supplies of motive energy.[50]

As we will see throughout this book, fears of future depletion are consistently referred to vaguely imagined technological breakthroughs, which will at last produce clean and "inexhaustible" power. Then, as now, the ability to harness directly the immense amount of energy in sunlight was the holy grail of technological development; then, as now, the ability to imagine such a utopian future always outpaced the ability to figure out how actually to do it.[51] Then, as now, technological rescue is imagined as a necessary part of a meaningful historical narrative, underwritten, in implicit and explicit ways, by Providential narratives. The geologist Joseph Holdsworth, discussing the exhaustion of coal in the 1860s, says: "we have the fullest faith, that the Power which made this wonderful provision [coal] for our manifold contingencies has, so to speak, amply provisioned us for triumphantly carrying out our glorious world-wide mission of humanising usefulness."[52] Some 150 years later, we find similar patterns in the discussion of energy. This is from a recent front-page article in *The New York Times*:

> Still, many people in the natural-gas industry believe a new era is at hand, and a rising chorus of Wall Street analysts and Congressional lawmakers supports that notion. Competition among companies for the rights to the new gas has set off a frenzy of leasing and drilling.
> "It's almost divine intervention," said Aubrey K. McClendon, chairman and chief executive of the Chesapeake Energy Corporation, one of the nation's largest natural gas producers. "Right at the time oil prices are skyrocketing, we're struggling with the economy, we're concerned about global warming, and national security threats remain intense, we wake up and we've got this abundance of natural gas around us."[53]

Cleaner, abundant energy is always right around the corner: it must be, because otherwise history might seem a record of profligacy and waste, rather than a story of meaningful growth. Such fantasies are persistent and recurrent, as historian of technology George Basalla argues:

> [A]ny newly discovered source of energy is assumed to be without faults, infinitely abundant, and to have the potential to affect [*sic*] utopian changes in society. These myths persist until a new energy source is developed to the point that its drawbacks become apparent and the failure to establish a utopian society must be reluctantly admitted. That is to say, the myths persist until skies darkened by coal smoke must be acknowledged as a problem or until the real threat of a nuclear accident (Three Mile Island) forces society to concede that coal or uranium are not the miraculous substances they were once thought to be.[54]

The wildly optimistic claims made for radium at the turn of the twentieth century (which I shall consider at the end of this book) are echoed in the claims now being made for clean coal, hydrogen, biofuels, cold fusion, thorium, and other seemingly "miraculous" substances. This is not to say that the pursuit of new kinds of technology is *merely* quixotic, or that "green" energy is nothing more than a mirage. It is not to denigrate or disregard the very real advances that have been made in solar and wind technology, many of which do, indeed, represent promising, healthier alternatives to our current fossil-fuel-intensive infrastructure. The problem is not so much with the technologies themselves, but (as Basalla argues) with the way in which they are represented. To hail solar energy (for example) as a panacea is to obscure the tremendous thermo-dynamic difficulties involved in making this technology viable on a large scale; it is to understate just how profound our dependence on fossil fuels is, and how difficult that energy is to replace; it is to argue, or at least imply, that scientific progress will allow us to maintain our current mode of consumption, just with a new motor swapped in. While it is possible that some new technology will unlock an inexhaustible, clean, alterna-tive energy source, until then it is of utmost importance, I would argue, to recognize the larger pattern of exuberance and retrenchment in which these various stories about energy occur and reoccur. The price for our utopian dreams of boundless energy is exacted from the natural environ-ment – from the oceans, forests, rivers, fields, and skies of our planet – but the manifold crises and fears thus engendered only prompt an even deeper commitment to the dream. In this way, a story about development that ends in an energy-abundant future and a fully sustainable capitalism is itself embedded in a very different narrative pattern of repetition and for-getting that is itself entirely unsustainable.

This book, then, attempts to trace some of the first threads of that pattern, and examine the way in which energy was fictionalized in the Victorian period. In this introduction, I have dwelt on our contemporary issues and technologies both to suggest the continuities between our era and theirs, and also to insist that we do not view the Victorians through a kind of smug present-ist lens. Again, Basalla is helpful:

> [I]t is much easier to recognize the myths clustering about older energy sources than it is for us to acknowledge that such myths are a part of the way we respond to currently fashionable ones. Hence, it is less difficult for us to find fault with the naïve progressive ideas the nineteenth century held about coal and the steam engine than it is to admit that we might be simi-larly infatuated with solar energy today.[55]

While I am interested in excavating the various ways in which energy was mystified and misperceived by the Victorians, I do so not to "find fault" with a blinkered worldview, but to suggest that the difficulties in coming to terms with natural limits and unsustainable practices persist, and that, on some level, their myths are ours.

PART I

Thermodynamics and its discontents

CHAPTER I

The city and the sun

In his essay "On the Formation of Coal" published in the *Contemporary Review* in 1870, T. H. Huxley sketches the chemistry and history of coal formation in striking terms. The article is worth quoting at some length because it gathers a number of significant strands of Victorian thinking about the relationship between fossil-fuel energy and the natural environment. Huxley writes:

> Let us suppose that one of the stupid, salamander-like Labyrinthodonts, which pottered, with much belly and little leg, like Falstaff in his old age, among the coal-forests, could have had thinking power enough in his small brain to reflect upon the showers of spores which kept on falling through years and centuries, while perhaps not one in ten million fulfilled its apparent purpose, and reproduced the organism which gave it birth: surely he might have been excused for moralizing upon the thoughtless and wanton extravagance which Nature displayed in her operations.
>
> But we have the advantage over our shovel-headed predecessor – or possibly ancestor – and can perceive that a certain vein of thrift runs through this apparent prodigality. Nature is never in a hurry, and seems to have had always before her eyes the adage, "Keep a thing long enough, and you will find a use for it." She has kept her beds of coal many millions of years without being able to find much use for them.
>
> ...
>
> Thus, all this abundant wealth of money and of vivid life is Nature's interest upon her investment in club-mosses and the like, so long ago. But what becomes of the coal which is burnt in yielding this interest? Heat comes out of it, light comes out of it; and if we could gather together all that goes up the chimney, and all that remains in the grate of a thoroughly-burnt coal-fire, we should find ourselves in possession of a quantity of carbonic acid, water, ammonia, and mineral matters, exactly equal in weight to the coal. But these are the very matters with which Nature supplied the club-mosses which made the coal. She is paid back principal and interest at the same time; and she straightway invests the carbonic acid, the water, and the

25

ammonia in new forms of life, feeding with them the plants that now live. Thrifty Nature! Surely no prodigal, but most notable of housekeepers![1]

This is a strange passage in many ways, the most remarkable of which is its attempt to represent the burning of coal as a clean, economical process that participates easily and automatically in the harmonious cycles of nature. While Huxley is right, of course, that the elements released during the combustion of coal return to the environment, an enormous number of Victorians would have experienced that return in the form of blackened skies, soot-covered buildings, filthy waterways and streets, and respiratory ailments directly attributable to the toxic atmosphere. Not only does waste not seem to be a problem in Huxley's accounting, coal-combustion actually appears to *support* the natural environment by contributing to the growth of "new forms of life." This is coal imagined, amazingly, as a "green" energy source. The point is not that Huxley was somehow unaware that coal produced noxious by-products; rather, it is that he is arguing for the capacity of the natural world *automatically* to transform those by-products back into healthful materials. In Huxley's formulation, not only is nature designated as our "housekeeper," burning coal itself is our way of paying her. Nature's work for us *is* her compensation.

We could take this a step further and note that, in its faith in automatic cyclical processes of expenditure and "reinvestment," the passage – written almost twenty years after the establishment of the second law of thermodynamics – entirely ignores the question of fossil-fuel burning as an irreversible process. That is, while it's true that the elements produced in the combustion of coal do return to nature, *they don't return as coal.* Huxley discusses the breakdown and recombination of elements in terms of a financial transaction, but he fails to note that the value of coal as a high-quality form of energy is lost when it is converted into "carbonic acid, water, ammonia, and mineral matters" through combustion. Indeed, in order to make his transaction seem to balance, Huxley quietly alters his terms halfway through the passage: the original "investment" of "vivid life" that nature has stored in coal deposits is energy. But when he discusses how the elements produced are "exactly equal in weight" to the original lump of coal that was burned, he switches from energy to matter. There is a similar mismatch between the temporalities in question: the formation of coal and its eventual combustion at human hands involve a timeline that stretches over millions of years, and follows an irreversible path. The process of organic decay and regrowth that Huxley also describes occurs on a more limited, seasonal timeframe, and operates in regular cycles. In this passage, the first kind of formation gives way to the second, but without any hint that the framework has been changed.

Huxley is writing in the wake of both the establishment of the second law of thermodynamics and the publication of W. S. Jevons's *The Coal Question* (1865), an influential treatise on England's diminishing coal supplies. The Victorians were well aware of the properties of coal, the irreversible nature of its combustion, and, of course, the havoc it could wreak on natural environments. Indeed, in many ways they were more aware of these things than we are. This is what is, to me, so interesting about Huxley's essay: it reveals the strange disconnect between certain established scientific facts about fossil-fuel energy, and the persistence of paradigms that apply to different kinds of energy sources. The solar energy accumulated and stored by plants is, in important ways, simply not the same as the energy contained in fossil fuels. The supply of the former is essentially limitless – at least as far as humans are concerned – and it is self-renewing. It flows from the sun at a constant rate that is not subject to change, and it makes possible the cycles of growth, decay, and regrowth Huxley discusses. The supply of fossil-fuel energy, on the other hand, is limited. It is extracted from terrestrial deposits at a rate determined by history, subject to the technological capacities and demands of human civilization.

This is not a blind spot of Huxley's alone, but his essay illustrates the peculiar tenacity of certain assumptions about the natural world. Even in the hands of "Darwin's Bulldog," an agnostic, materialist, and (elsewhere) bracing critic of anthropocentric thinking, fossil-fuel energy is subject to a mystifying, metaphysical faith in the perfect "economy" of the natural order. As we will see, the time-worn axiom Huxley draws upon – that nature never wastes anything – was a pillar of early-nineteenth-century natural-theological thinking, one that persisted long after both natural selection and the second law of thermodynamics had unraveled it. Henry Adams, discussing the endurance of the notion of a perfectly conservative natural economy, comments: "had planets gone off like comets, and never returned, the scholar of 1860 would still have feared to question the scientific dogma which asserted resolutely, without qualification, the fact that nothing in nature was lost."[2] It is this cognitive dissonance that we will see in the attempt to square the new world of fossil-fuel resources with the circle – or cycle – of a balanced natural economy. In what follows, I discuss the clash of these two distinct energy paradigms, and the way the development of the concept of energy in the nineteenth century – which resulted, finally, in its modern thermodynamic definition, as a measure of work – served both to create and to obscure this crucial distinction.

Natural theology

Despite his well-known agnosticism and mistrust of a-priori reasoning, Huxley's argument about coal clearly borrows a page from natural theology. In William Paley's seminal *Natural Theology: or, Evidences of the Existence and the Attributes of the Deity* (1802), as well as the nine Paley-inspired *Bridgewater Treatises* that followed, the arguments for design hinged on adducing evidence for the existence of God based on the "beauty and perfection in the arrangements" of natural formations, whether descried in animal bodies, jungle ecosystems, or planetary rotations.[3] The critic James Moore summarizes the argument: "God works all things together for good. His providence in nature and history is orderly and harmonious; nothing is without purpose, nothing is done in vain. In physical nature, in organic matter, and in political society the divine principle is *economy*."[4] The theodicy that was premised upon this, propounded in various guises by natural theologians coming from a variety of denominational positions, held that anything seemingly wasteful or disorderly was actually, seen rightly, "beneficence in disguise."[5] William Buckland writes:

> [T]he physical history of our globe, in which some have seen only Waste, Disorder and Confusion, teems with endless examples of Economy, and Order, and Design; and the result of all our researches, carried back through the unwritten records of past time, has been to fix more steadily our assurance of the Existence of One supreme Creator of all things, to exalt more highly our conviction of the immensity of his Perfections, of his Might, and Majesty, his Wisdom, and Goodness, and all sustaining Providence.[6]

A common natural-theological gambit was to take something that seemed wasteful and reframe it to showcase the intricacy of the Providential system – the fact that in no corner of the natural creation would one fail to find an illustration of the care of the ordering hand. Thus Buckland writes about the existence of carnivores: "to the mind which looks not to general results in the economy of Nature, the earth may seem to present a scene of perpetual warfare and incessant carnage: but the more enlarged view … resolves each apparent case of individual evil, into an example of subserviency to universal good."[7] We are but a short step here from a defense of free-market capitalism, where the ruthlessness and waste of competition are justified through a belief in their necessary place in a larger system of order. As Frank M. Turner argues, "natural theologians functioned as much as defenders of contemporary social arrangements and their underlying values as they did of science."[8] In a line of reasoning we will encounter repeatedly, it is industrial technology that rescues nature from the waste of its "apparent purpose" by revealing its true purpose as fuel.

While Darwinian biology is often said to have fatally punctured the natural-theological armature, we can see in Huxley's essay how even evolution (although perhaps not natural selection) could be accommodated within this paradigm. Indeed, for Huxley, evolution, human intelligence, and technology form a kind of closed system of reciprocal explanation and justification. Intelligence evolves until it can master technology, which, in turn, helps reveal the various uses to which nature can be put, which justifies the seeming waste involved in evolutionary history, which justifies the use of technology: "The eighteenth century arrived, and with it James Watt. The brain of that man was the spore out of which was developed the modern steam-engine, and all the prodigious trees and branches of modern industry which have grown out of this."[9] Mind and technology are extensions of nature, but – even more significantly for Huxley – they also provide means of transcending its limits. Spores become coal or they become mind, and both are sources of energy. The release of the productive power of nature through industrial technology provided natural theologians and others with an important argument against Malthusian alarms of natural scarcity, which seemed to open up questions of "an apparent inconsistency between the permanence of human happiness, and the natural action of the laws established by Providence," in the words of Richard Jones.[10] The idea that the development of energy allows for a triumph of mind over the ordinary limits nature imposes is one we will repeatedly encounter in the following pages.

Huxley's essay echoes early nineteenth-century natural theology not just in its waste-disposal methods, but in its framing of coal as the agent of an unfolding progressive narrative. Here is Buckland again:

> However remote may have been the periods, at which these materials of future beneficial dispensations were laid up in store, we may fairly assume, that, besides the immediate purposes effected at, or before the time of their deposition in the strata of the Earth, an ulterior prospective view to the future uses of Man, formed part of the design, with which they were, ages ago, disposed in a manner so admirably adapted to the benefit of the Human Race.[11]

Statements like this, imagining the hand of God quietly planting coal beneath the ground for a sleeping nation to discover someday, were extraordinarily common throughout the nineteenth century. "Coal was formed," wrote Robert Hunt in 1861, "doubtless, with a design, and placed deep in the Earth with a purpose … to promote the great effect of spreading over the world those Divine principles which lead to 'Peace on Earth.'"[12] Such resources represented a perfect harmonization of the divine plan with the historical forces of industrialism and the grand self-conceptions of England as a rising world power.[13] This Providential narrative obscured the much stranger temporalities of fossil-fuel energy, in which coal might seem not the fulfillment of history, but as an unstable accelerant.[14]

Nowhere is the blending of industrialism and theology more evident than in the writings of Charles Babbage, author of the so-called *Ninth Bridgewater Treatise*. His 1827 text *An Essay on the General Principles which Regulate the Application of Machinery* works to square the ordered natural-theological paradigm with the emergent world of fossil-fuel energy use. Describing a steam engine in terms strikingly similar to Huxley's, he argues that the by-products of combustion are rendered innocuous by the restorative cycles of nature:

> The chemical changes which thus take place are constantly increasing the atmosphere by large quantities of carbonic acid and other gases noxious to animal life. By what process nature decomposes or reconverts these elements into a solid form, is not sufficiently known. The absorption in large quantities of one portion of them by vegetation is stated to take place; but if the end could be accomplished by Mechanical force, it is probable the power necessary to produce it would at least equal that which was generated by the original combustion.[15]

Ted Underwood argues that Babbage makes his case about perfect conservation "blithely" here, and that the "only basis for this claim is his model of Nature as a constant dynamic equilibrium, which rests … on the assumption that the earth is designed as a stable home for human beings."[16] Indeed, what is remarkable about this passage is how exposed – and thus vulnerable – this assumption is. Babbage admits his own ignorance of the chemical process; argues, rather weakly, that the reabsorption of elements "is stated to take place"; and describes the perfect energy balance as "probable." In one sense, Babbage can afford to make such hazy claims about the cyclical economy of energy expenditure since the absolute proscription of waste in nature could simply be assumed as axiomatic. On the other hand, the fuel he is discussing here is coal, a substance that, once burned, does not return to its original state. It is telling that, in discussing the way nature "reconverts" these by-products, he has recourse to the vague expression "a solid form" to describe the result (the move is akin to Huxley's switch from matter to energy). Like Huxley, Babbage is discussing an irreversible process as if there is a way to reverse it; unlike Huxley, he seems troubled by the move. There is thus a buried chain of slightly anxious reasoning in this passage: we *think* that nature will take care of this, but, if not, the cost of restoring the environment will demand whatever power we gained from the process to start with. If that is the case, one might wonder what the point of expending the energy would be in the first place.

The mix of anxiety and overconfidence continues in the passage that directly follows:

> Man, therefore, cannot create power; but, availing himself of his knowledge of Nature's mysteries, he applies his talents to diverting a small and limited portion of her energies to his own wants; and, whether he employs the regulated action of steam, or the more rapid and tremendous effects of gunpowder, he is only producing, in small quantity, compositions and decompositions which Nature is incessantly at work in reversing, for the restoration of that equilibrium which we cannot doubt is constantly maintained throughout even the remotest limits of our system. The operations of man participate in the character of their Author; they are diminutive, but energetic during the short period of their existence; those of nature, acting over vast spaces, and unlimited by time, are ever pursuing their silent and resistless career.[17]

While nature was often imagined as a reservoir of energy for human industry to tap, it is here imagined on the opposite end of the metabolic process: as a zone in which waste can be restored to its vital condition. Again, there is somewhat hesitant rhetoric ("we cannot doubt" in this context sounds provisional), but more importantly, there is an excessive insistence on the insignificance of industry and its energy expenditure when compared to the sheer size of the natural order: "small and limited portion," "small quantity," "diminutive," "short period." Even "diverting" suggests a minor modification in the flow of energy, a much more innocuous term than, say, "expending" or "consuming." The idea of reversing what industry is doing both to natural resources and to the environment is founded very openly on a *belief* in automatic conservation; but in case that isn't convincing, some further consolation can be found in the notion that the disarrangements are, in the grand scheme of things, pretty minor.

As he does elsewhere, Babbage treats waste or disorder as merely a perceptual problem, stemming from a lack of information or the proper perspective. In his *Ninth Bridgewater Treatise*, he posits a counting machine that adds one plus one plus one. If, he says, in the hundred millionth iteration of its summing operation, the machine suddenly yields an unexpected number, if it begins adding ten thousand to each successive number instead of adding one, it is not that the machine is faulty. Rather, he says, its contriver, like God the creator, has set it to working out a pattern of such complexity and magnitude that the contours of its design will only slowly be revealed, and perhaps the full pattern will remain ultimately unavailable to finite minds.[18] In his schema, the metaphor of *counting* describes the fundamental operation of the universe, for it is an order in which everything is *ac*counted for. For Babbage, the connection between mundane activity and transcendent ledgers was mediated through both the ideal model and the actual application of technology. But the reliance on machinery as the grounds of analogizing introduces certain fissures in the discourse that Babbage is not entirely in control of. Although the machine was initially idealized into a model for precision and balance, and, thus, an analogue for the harmonious design of the universe, the rise of the combustion engine as the quintessential piece of machinery radically altered this comparison. Historians of science M. Norton Wise and Crosbie Smith argue that, at this moment, "heat, and heat engines, were supplying a new epitome for scientific explanation in natural philosophy as in political economy," and thus made irreversible processes and waste fundamental to the understanding of the natural economy.[19]

What both Babbage and Huxley founder on is the growing conflict between two different understandings of energy. The first is energy as a pervasive, indestructible agency that moves freely between industry and nature. The second is energy understood as a resource, limited in quantity, subject to irreversible dissipation, and potentially toxic in its after-effects. In Babbage's passage about combustion, the two will simply not cohabitate as amicably as he seems to want them to. The problem of waste is actually two-pronged: it appears as the pollution, the "noxious" by-products and "decompositions" caused by energy expenditure, *and* it appears as the irreversible use of something limited and scarce. This latter version of waste only troubles the passage implicitly: as the undescribed lump of coal whose reconstitution is vaguely described. There is a tendency throughout the century, and in writers as diverse as Carlyle, Spencer, William Thomson, and even Marx, to turn resource waste into a necessary component of some sort of overarching teleological narrative, and thus, in a sense, *not really wasted*. The explicit references to divine Providence may drop away, as they do in Huxley, but technological development and human ingenuity more than pick up the slack.[20] By pointing this out, I do not mean to minimize the very real differences between and among these various thinkers; indeed, I would point to those very differences as *evidence* for the peculiar power and pervasiveness of the tendency to rationalize the waste of resources by appeals to *some kind* of conserving master narrative. As suggested by Huxley's arguments, an analogous dynamic can be seen in the discussion of Darwin's theory of evolution by natural selection following publication of *On the Origin of Species*. As Peter Bowler and others have argued, the wasteful, radically non-teleological natural world Darwin described was often downplayed or ignored altogether even by those flying under the banner of "Darwinism." [21] For many, including Huxley (and occasionally Darwin himself), the most challenging implications of natural selection were blunted by a reassuringly progressive and anthropocentric evolutionary *telos*.

Productivism

Natural theology's ability to accommodate industrial practices in its depiction of an orderly natural world is part of a wider set of beliefs about the relationship between society and nature that Anson Rabinbach has termed "productivism." In his book *The Human Motor*, Rabinbach defines productivism as, "the belief that human society and nature are linked by the primacy and identity of all productive activity, whether of laborers, of machines, or of natural forces"; as a result, "the cosmos was essentially a system of production whose product was the universal *Kraft* necessary to power the engines of nature and society, a vast and protean reservoir of labor power awaiting its conversion to work." [22] As he makes clear, productivism defines a set of beliefs about energy that cuts across the usual kinds of ideological, theological, national, and chronological dividing lines. [23] While Rabinbach argues that productivism was made possible by the emergence of the laws of thermodynamics in the middle decades of the century, Ted Underwood convincingly reverses the chain of development: the laws of thermodynamics, he argues, were a scientific formalization of productivist concepts already in wide circulation by the 1840s and 1850s. [24] Both productivism and early thermodynamic writing based their arguments on metaphysical axioms: energy could change from one form to another – from chemical bonds to heat to mechanical motion – but it was indestructible. Before the quantity of energy could be measured experimentally, it was simply assumed that the amount of energy in the universe always remained constant despite whatever changes of form it underwent. The convertibility of energy seemed to suggest the *endless* convertibility of energy. As Thomas Kuhn has argued, such metaphysical assumptions were necessary to the consolidation of the law of conservation of energy, the first law of thermodynamics. [25]

But there is a distinction to be drawn here between two overlapping but distinct ideas of what we would call "the conservation of energy" – the argument for the interconvertibility and the indestructibility of all energy forms. In the early nineteenth century, thanks to practical experiments with heat and mechanical motion; the development of industrial technology; and a middle-class social ethic that, as Underwood argues, strove to encode certain forms of middle-class industry as "natural," industry and nature were imagined to be powered by the same "thing" – energy. Heat could be converted into mechanical motion, and chemical reactions into electricity, and electricity into heat, irrespective of the distinctions between organic and mechanical bodies, industrial or natural processes. The dissolution of such distinctions in the unity of energy relations is what allowed the social ethic of productivism to arise. But it was still just an article of faith, a metaphysical presupposition, that all transformations of energy were equivalent, that nothing was ever "lost" in these transactions, and that the sum total of the universe's energy remained constant. At the root of this was another axiom: *Ex nihilo nihil fit*. Nothing comes from nothing. There is no production of anything without a corresponding cost elsewhere, because only God can make something from nothing; conversely, there can be no destruction either. Humans can effect transformations of energy, but cannot augment or diminish the sum total. As we saw, this is at the heart of Babbage's arguments. It was not until the 1840s when James Joule, among others, worked to determine a common metric between mechanical energy and heat that such assertions of equivalence could be experimentally verified and expressed in quantitative terms.[26] This resulted in the formalized "conservation of energy," the first law of thermodynamics, about which we will have more to say in a moment.

Productivist discourse essentially naturalized industry through the unity of the energy concept. If all forms of energy were interconvertible and indestructible, then it seemed impossible to draw firm distinctions between the operations of industry and those of nature, both of which were part of the same energetic economy. An important component of this was arguing for the participation of coal in natural cycles of expenditure and reintegration. We have seen this already in Babbage's text, which focuses on the environment's perfect reabsorption of industrial by-products. Far more frequently, productivist writers stressed the other side of the story: the fact that coal, like all forms of energy, has its origins in sunlight. In an oft-quoted passage from *The Life of George Stephenson*, Samuel Smiles describes Stephenson's enthusiasm for this idea:

> "Now, Buckland," said Stephenson, "I have a poser for you. Can you tell me what is the power that is driving that train?" "Well," said the other, "I suppose it is one of your big engines." "But what drives the engine?" "Oh,

very likely a canny Newcastle driver." "What do you say to the light of the sun?" "How can that be?" asked the doctor. "It is nothing else," said the engineer: "it is light bottled up in the earth for tens of thousands of years – light, absorbed by plants and vegetables, being necessary for the condensation of carbon during the process of their growth, if it be not carbon in another form – and now, after being buried in the earth for long ages in fields of coal, that latent light is again brought forth and liberated, made to work as in that locomotive, for great human purposes."[27]

Note the term "liberated," which occurs frequently in popular and scientific descriptions of energy use during the century.[28] It conveys implicitly something of what writers on England's Providentially bestowed coal supplies were arguing explicitly: natural resources realize their purpose only through use at human hands. Until then, they are either (seemingly) wasted, as in Huxley's formulation, or imprisoned, as in Smiles's. A bit more eccentric, but cut from the same conceptual cloth, is the metaphor of "bottled" sunlight, which imagines the natural world existing as a kind of manufactory *already*. Fossil-fuel energy is not only thoroughly commodified before it even enters the economy; it is pre-packaged, as if announcing its destiny through the convenience of its form. Indeed, in his bottle metaphor Stephenson touches on what makes coal so useful – it is dense, stable, storable, and transportable; but this is precisely what makes it irreplaceable and *unlike* other forms of energy. The energy density of coal is a function of millions of years of pressure on prehistoric organic material, an immensity the easy anthropomorphism of "bottling" does not attempt to capture, but that represents the very basis of its energetic value.

By emphasizing the solar origins of coal, productivist discourse leveled the distinction between natural and mechanical processes, agricultural and industrial production, arguing that these were all simply different expressions of a basic universal working power. Astronomer John Herschel writes:

> The sun's rays are the ultimate source of almost every motion which takes place on the surface of the earth. By its heat are produced all winds, and those disturbances in the electric equilibrium of the atmosphere which give rise to the phenomena of terrestrial magnetism. By their vivifying action vegetables are elaborated from inorganic matter, and become, in their turn, the support of animals and of man, and the sources of those great deposits of dynamical efficiency which are laid up for human use in our coal strata. By them the waters of the sea are made to circulate in vapour through the air, and irrigate the land, producing springs and rivers. By them are produced all disturbances of the chemical equilibrium of the elements of

nature, which, by a series of compositions and decompositions, give rise to new products, and originate a transfer of materials.[29]

Although Herschel would later discuss the alarming and unsustainable path of modern fossil-fuel exploitation, here he argues for the essential sameness of all energy forms as different expressions of solar power.[30] Note the way the rhetoric of the passage itself communicates a world of easy transformability and flux, as energy seems to circulate freely through air, water, land, and human industry in a continual cycle of "compositions and decompositions."

Although it is obviously true that coal is "natural," and the working power it produces is in some senses the "same" as the working power that can be found in vegetable matter, or the action of wind or water, the representation of nature and industry as contiguous zones of energy transformation obscures what is distinctive about fossil-fuel energy: it produces pollution not easily absorbed by the natural world, and its expenditure is unidirectional. Fossil-fuel use involves not simply a mere "transfer of materials" but an irreversible reconfiguration of them. When, in the same section of Smiles's narrative, Stephenson discusses the oneness of all productive energy forms, we can see how his comparison of meat and coal flattens out these distinctions:

> George went off into his favorite theory of the sun's light, which he said had fattened the pig; for the light had gone into the pease, and the pease had gone into the fat, and the fat pig was like a field of coal in this respect, that they were, for the most part, neither more nor less than bottled sunshine.[31]

Missing from the picture, because obscured by the insistence on a fundamental solar identity, is the respect in which a fat pig is not at all like a "field" of coal. To say they are both "bottled sunshine" is to ignore the temporal dimension that defines fossil fuel. Smiles pokes fun at Stephenson's single-minded attention to unity, but it is, in a broader sense, a single-mindedness – and an insistence on singularity – that runs through productivist discourse as a whole. As H. G. Wells would comment: "nobody seems to have realised that something new had come into human life, a strange swirl different altogether from any previous circling and mutation, a swirl like the swirl when at last the lock gates begin to open after a long phase of accumulating water and eddying inactivity."[32] Wells here gets at the newness of fossil-fuel energy by imagining a crucial distinction between temporalities, between the endless "circling and mutation" of an earlier epoch, and the uni-directional flow of energy released after a long process of build-up.

Thermodynamics

The development of thermodynamics in the 1840s and 1850s simultaneously challenged and reinforced the productivist picture. For one thing, the conservation of energy was translated into more rigorous mathematical terms. By establishing the mechanical equivalent of heat, and comparing different forms of energy by means of a common metric – the ability to do work – Joule, Robert Mayer, and other scientists were able to translate a metaphysical axiom into something experimentally quantifiable. What had been a loose idea of complete universal conservation was now put on solid footing, since it was now possible to measure, rather than simply assert, the interchangeability of different energy forms. For another, the dissipation of energy observed in the operation of industrial technology, formalized in the second law of thermodynamics, made the problem of irreversibility and waste impossible to ignore; indeed, it installed those things at the very center of a seemingly radical new cosmology.

We will look more closely at the second law in the next chapter. For now I want to note that the first law of thermodynamics, as it was articulated in the middle decades of the century, had mixed implications regarding the conceptualization of fossil fuels. On the one hand, it emphasized and, indeed, formalized, the strict economy of energy that writers like Babbage had drawn upon. The first law of thermodynamics established a set of rules about what could and couldn't be done with energy, and made it clear, in a mathematically rigorous way, that you cannot get something for nothing. This was a common refrain in both scientific and popular discussions of the first law; Balfour Stewart writes, "the world of mechanism is not a manufactory, in which energy is created, but rather a mart, into which we may bring energy of one kind and change or barter it for an equivalent of another kind, that suits us better – but if we come with nothing in our hand, with nothing we shall most assuredly return."[33] The law thus established working limits and helped rein in fantasies about the endless malleability and exploitability of the material world.[34]

On the other hand, the conservation of energy also depended upon many of the metaphysical assumptions and rhetorical devices that structured the treatment of fossil fuels in precursor productivist texts. We can hear echoes of natural theology in the work of Joule, credited by many as the first to put the conservation of energy on firm scientific footing: "Indeed the phenomena of nature, whether mechanical, chemical or vital, consist almost entirely in a continual conversion of attraction through space, living force, and heat, into one another. Thus it is that order is maintained in the universe, – nothing is deranged, nothing ever lost, – but the entire machinery, complicated as it is, works smoothly and harmoniously."[35] Victorian scientists writing on the thermodynamic concept of energy, especially those writing for popular audiences, did not only try to disavow or conceal the metaphysical underpinnings of the first law; they emphasized them, routinely tracing the roots of energy conservation back to natural theology, German Romanticism, and classical philosophy and mythology. Fleeming Jenkin, for instance, argues that the work of Lucretius "foreshadows the doctrine of the conservation of energy."[36] Hermann von Helmholtz, one of the key "discoverers" of the first law, credited Goethe with anticipating thermodynamics,[37] and John Tyndall, the English scientific naturalist, claimed that Carlyle "poetically, but accurately, foreshadow[ed] the doctrine of the Conservation of Energy," citing a passage from *Sartor Resartus* that we will look at in more detail in a moment.[38] Such genealogies established a pedigree for the energy concept, convincing readers that their findings confirmed a picture of the universe and an experience of the physical world that were stable, familiar, and perhaps reassuring.

Indeed, one could enthuse over the marvelous new world of industrial energy use and the dizzying new vistas being opened by technology, while arguing that such a world was merely the latest expression of forces and laws already known, or anticipated, by preceding generations. Tyndall, especially, tends to walk an interesting rhetorical line between trying to startle his reader and trying to reassure him that he knew all of these startling things already. This is from his *Heat Considered as a Mode of Motion*, the most popular Victorian thermodynamic text:

> We pass to other systems and other suns, each pouring forth energy like our own, but still without infringement of the law, which reveals immutability in the midst of change, which recognizes incessant transference and conversion, but neither final gain nor loss. This law generalizes the aphorism of Solomon, that there is nothing new under the sun, by teaching us to detect everywhere, under its infinite variety of appearances, the same primeval force. To Nature nothing can be added; from Nature nothing can be taken away.[39]

Tyndall is actually making two related arguments. By stating that energy can be neither created nor destroyed, the conservation of energy establishes an invariant order beneath the seeming flux of reality: even radical physical transformations are simply different expressions of an eternal principle. But he also suggests that the conservation-of-energy *concept* ratifies certain time-honored experiences of reality – in this case, the aphoristic wisdom of the Bible. In this way, the development of human thought itself behaves like energy: it presents a multiplicity of outward forms that are all expressions of a deeper order and unity. As he argues in his famous "Belfast Address":

> The world embraces not only a Newton, but a Shakespeare – not only a Boyle, but a Raphael – not only a Kant, but a Beethoven – not only a Darwin, but a Carlyle. Not in each of these, but in all, is human nature whole. They are not opposed, but supplementary – not mutually exclusive, but reconcilable … the human mind, with the yearning of a pilgrim for his distant home, will turn to the Mystery from which it has emerged, seeking so to fashion it as to give unity to thought and faith.[40]

At the end of *Heat*, Tyndall marvels at the scale of the universe of energy with a palpable sense of wonder, and insists on the continuities, rather than the fissures, between his own scientific materialism and a spiritualized cosmos. Poised in an ontological grey zone between spirit and matter, energy finesses the divide between them:

> Waves may change to ripples, and ripples to waves, – magnitude may be substituted for number, and number for magnitude, – asteroids may aggregate to suns, suns may resolve themselves into florae and faunae, and florae and faunae melt in air, – the flux of power is eternally the same. It rolls in music through the ages, and all terrestrial energy, – the manifestations of life as well as the display of phenomena are, but the modulations of its rhythm.[41]

The problem, ecologically speaking, with Tyndall's claim that there is "nothing new under the sun" is that the "primeval force" of fossil fuels actually *was* new, at least as far as human civilization was concerned. Fossil-fuel use represented something other than "incessant transference and conversion," in the irreversible changes it visited upon the natural environment. Tyndall's book tends to leap from close-focus accounts of the way energy works in specific technologies and natural formations to grand visions of a stable universal order. He continually emphasizes the limitlessness of cosmic energy supplies and, implicitly, the inability of human activity to have any appreciable effect upon them:

> Look at the integrated energies of our world – the stored power of our coal-fields; our winds and rivers; our fleets, armies, and guns. What are they? They are all generated by a portion of the sun's energy, which does not amount to 1/2,300,000,000th of the whole … Measured by our largest terrestrial standards, such a reservoir of power is infinite; but it is our privilege to rise above these standards, and to regard the sun himself as a speck in infinite extension, – a mere drop in the universal sea.[42]

Although Tyndall emphasizes the microscopic smallness of human existence within an ocean of cosmic energy, it is not accompanied by any existential angst about the insignificance of life. Indeed, as the book makes
clear elsewhere, the development of industrial technology has allowed
humans access to this world of infinite power. If Tyndall seems to shrink
the human world, it is only in the service of striking a note of wonder at
the vastness of the energy reservoir awaiting use. As we saw in Huxley,
what looks at first like a paean to nature is really just another way of
aggrandizing the human. We may be small, but our intelligence endows
us with the "privilege to rise above."

Thus industrial technology allows access to both the power and the
eternal stability of nature. In such a context, one would be hard-pressed to
detect that there could be anything amiss with the way humans use energy.
The issue, in part, resides in Tyndall's very use of the word "nature," which
tends to signify a cosmic abstraction (as in "To Nature nothing can be
added; from Nature nothing can be taken away") rather than a limited
terrestrial environment, or material ecosystem. It is a very different concept of nature than the one found in Darwin, for example, whose famous
"tangled bank" metaphor, and many descriptions of the intricate, restless
network of living organisms in *On the Origin of Species* emphasized not
simply nature's changefulness, but the way in which a single change produces cascading effects throughout the system. Although transformation
was a common metaphor in both evolutionary and early thermodynamic
discourse, the latter tended to ground its vision of transformation on a
stable, invariant foundation. Nature is the guarantor of stability beneath
the flux of transformation, whereas in Darwin's work, nature *is* transformation. As we'll see, to lay such stress upon nature's eternal changelessness
is to obscure the ways in which human action can have an impact upon a
natural world understood as a functioning ecological system.

More importantly, though, Tyndall takes to new levels productivist
rhetoric about the unity and identity of all forms of energy, until industrial activity and resource exploitation seem not only thoroughly natural
but inevitable expressions of solar agency:

> He builds the forest and hews it down, the power which raised the tree,
> and which wields the axe, being one and the same. The clover sprouts and
> blossoms, and the scythe of the mower swings, by the operation of the
> same force. The sun digs the ore from our mines, he rolls the iron; he rivets
> the plates, he boils the water; he draws the train. He not only grows the
> cotton, but he spins the fibre and weaves the web. There is not a hammer
> raised, a wheel turned, or a shuttle thrown, that is not raised, and turned,

and thrown by the sun. His energy is poured freely into space, but our world is a halting place where this energy is conditioned. Here the Proteus works his spells.[43]

Such a lyrical description of the sun freely mixes the organic with the mechanical, the naturally forming with the industrially produced, until any meaningful distinction between growth and expenditure vanishes in the haze of a freely circulating energy. Here the development of a forest ecosystem and its demolition are both framed as different expressions of energy. The parallel drawn between building and hewing works to naturalize industrial processes – indeed the very language of a forest being "built" means it is *already* part of a manufactured world – but it also makes the wholesale exploitation of resources and environments seem a natural event. Obscured in the emphasis on this raw, unifying cosmic agency are the divergent temporalities at play; the easy syntactic balance of a phrase like "He builds the forest and hews it down" conceals the deeper mismatch between the chronologies of building and hewing. The first, the development of a forest, may take thousands of years; the second can be accomplished in weeks or months, but the sense of easy transformability levels such crucial ecological distinctions. It is a subtler example of the kind of mismatch we saw in Huxley and Babbage, where a sense of balanced cyclicality – here rendered in the biblical rhythms of growing and hewing, sprouting and mowing – is applied to actions and processes that belong to a very different temporal paradigm. In this world of pure verb, the distinctions between what is accomplished by human labor, by coal power, by water, and by other means disappear. What is drawn upon is not a finite resource base formed over millions of years, but simply another form of a ubiquitous principle already circulating through the world.

Tyndall's cosmic lyricism at the end of *Heat* represents a departure from the experimental rigor that characterized the development of the first law of thermodynamics, and, indeed, parts of his own descriptions of energy in the early chapters of his book. But the emphasis on the cosmological stakes of these ideas is also typical of the way in which the conservation of energy was discussed and disseminated during the period. Accompanying the interest in the regularity and lawfulness of the new energy laws is the implication that energy conservation is something nature *just does* automatically, and thus not something requiring human superintendence. As Herbert Spencer pointed out, this confusion was inscribed in the very terms employed. He argues in *First Principles* that his "persistence of force" is preferable to the "conservation of energy" because the latter suggests, misleadingly, "a con-server and an act of conserving."[44] In many respects, Spencer is as guilty as anyone of propagating misinformation about the workings of energy, and his preference for "force" over "energy," following Michael Faraday and W. R. Grove, just confuses the question further.[45] But he is right to be troubled by the implicit agency smuggled in by the term "conservation."[46] Although Spencer's argument is not motivated by concerns about resource use and sustainability, we can see how the notion of an implied "conserver," organizing all energy relations and rectifying imbalances, might obscure the effect of humans on the resources of the natural world.

This suggestion of automatic conservancy, and the emphasis placed on the cosmological picture, is, in a way, an odd development. If the discussion of the conservation of energy often wound up de-emphasizing crucial distinctions between energy forms, or overlooking the problems of efficiency and economy that characterized the actual use of energy, the irony is that thermodynamics would not have even existed as a science without a keen interest in such distinctions and such problems. Thermodynamics developed first and foremost out of an engineering tradition where conserving energy and avoiding waste were of paramount significance, where the value of energy as motive power for production encouraged researchers to understand its properties and limits in precise, quantifiable ways.[47] Tyndall's own investigations of heat touched on key ecological questions in rather striking ways. In 1859 he set out to understand the process by which the earth's atmosphere traps the sun's energy and keeps the planet from losing heat too quickly. Without this "atmospheric swathing," Tyndall realized, the earth would quickly be "render[ed] uninhabitable."[48] Through a series of experiments he discovered that complex molecules trap heat, while simpler molecules allow it to dissipate into space unimpeded. Writing in the *New Scientist*, Stephanie Pain notes that Tyndall discovered that "coal gas – a mix of carbon monoxide, methane and other hydrocarbons – turned out to be as much a barrier to radiant heat as a piece of wood," an insight, Pain notes, that effectively brought him to the doorstep of describing anthropogenic global warming.[49] We will see John Ruskin make this leap in an imaginative, if not fully scientific, sense, in Chapter 5. Tyndall's work thus illustrates the way the thermodynamic investigation of the behavior of heat could raise profound ecological questions about the relationship between human energy use and the global environment, even if, simultaneously, it relied on metaphors, rhetorical structures, and metaphysical assumptions that made such questions that much harder to articulate.

Energy resources and the city

If, as William Stanley Jevons would argue, "Coal in truth stands not beside but entirely above all other commodities," then productivism helped fortify a peculiar but common form of what Marx termed commodity fetishism – a tendency to obscure the actual natural sources of energy and the natural and human costs involved in its extraction in favor of a focus on its marvelous effects.[50] When Tyndall describes how "Proteus works his spells," he both echoes and reinforces a common tendency to frame energy in mythical or magical terms. Smiles writes about the growth of industrial transportation networks:

> As I look back upon these stupendous undertakings, accomplished in so short a time, it seems as though we had realized in our generation the fabled powers of the magician's wand. Hills have been cut down and valleys filled up; and when these simple expedients have not sufficed, high and magnificent viaducts have been raised, and, if mountains stood in the way, tunnels of unexampled magnitude have pierced them through, bearing their triumphant attestation to the indomitable energy of the nation, and the unrivalled skill of our artisans.[51]

Such a description suggests, like the natural-theological narrative about the purpose of coal, that the ability to harness energy represents the fulfillment of an unfolding historical narrative.[52] But it also illustrates another crucial problem with the discussion of energy resources, a vagueness in the term "energy" itself. In Smiles's passage, the "energy of the nation" may call to mind the collective resources of Britain, the actual motive power – including coal and human labor – that has been used to effect these wondrous transformations. But to call this energy "indomitable," and to link it with "the unrivalled skill of our artisans," suggests that Smiles here is also talking about energy as a national *quality*. That is, the actual source of energy is mystified not only through the imagery of magic and fable, but also through the way energy seems to be produced by, or to be a sign of, English character. Such a passage participates in the very same kind of thinking we saw in Buckland and others, where coal was imagined as a sign of Providential blessing upon the nation; it is as if the spectacle of energy use somehow redounds to the moral credit of the Englishman. The word "energy" allows Smiles to finesse this: he can gesture towards the actual material basis of the power used by industry while simultaneously keeping it rooted in a moral or spiritual quality that justifies it and makes it possible. The wonders of industry seem to arise not out of a material resource base, but from the national character. As with Tyndall's paean to the conservation of energy in *Heat*, there is a suggestion that this marvelous new world of energy use is simply another expression of a reassuringly familiar set of truths.

But the rapid population growth and energy consumption of urban centers are precisely where productivism's interest in the easy energetic interchange between nature and industry founders. We might take as an example Carlyle's depiction of Manchester in *Chartism*, where the industrial city is depicted as a magnificent expression of natural energy:

> Hast thou heard, with sound ears, the awakening of a Manchester, on Monday morning, at half-past five by the clock; the rushing off of its thousand mills, like the boom of an Atlantic tide, ten thousand times ten thousand spools and spindles all set humming there, – it is perhaps, if thou knew it well, sublime as a Niagara, or more so. Cotton-spinning is the clothing of the naked in its result; the triumph of man over matter in its means.[53]

This is the city cast in productivist terms. More sublime than Niagara, rushing powerfully like the Atlantic Ocean, Manchester also functions implicitly as a substitute sun, as the commencement of its activity is now what signifies the break of day. Carlyle makes clear elsewhere that this scene occurs in the springtime, further aligning the thrumming mills with natural cycles of solar renewal. Through this imagery, Carlyle suggests both the newness of Manchester, and its deep continuity with other forms of energy and natural rhythms. The main difference is that these mills also harness and organize energy in the ongoing human attempt, as he puts it in "Signs of the Times," to "war with rude nature."[54] The productivist account is not just about aligning industry and nature, it is about the conversion of nature into a source of motive power. As in Tyndall's account of the sun driving trains and digging ore, the simultaneous industrialization of nature and the naturalization of industry remove all reference to the factory workers, the machinery, the environment in which this is embedded, the natural resources expended, or any of the other specific agents that make such production possible.

The problem with this attempt to include the emergent urban world in the productivist frame is that, while the city may be likened to the sun, it is not a source of energy, nor does it run on solar power, nor does its massive energy use come without serious environmental cost. Although Carlyle wants to include the city and the newly unleashed power of industry in his metaphysical system, these phenomena present difficulties his productivist vision cannot easily accommodate. The question of waste, specifically, becomes an insoluble problem in the attempt to fold industrial processes within the cycles of nature. Notice, for example, the relationship between energy (which Carlyle calls "Force") and waste in this passage from *On Heroes, Hero Worship, and the Heroic in History*:

> Force, Force, everywhere Force; we ourselves a mysterious Force in the centre of that. "There is not a leaf rotting on the highway but has Force in it: how else could it rot?" Nay surely, to the Atheistic Thinker, if such a one were possible, it must be a miracle too, this huge illimitable whirlwind of Force, which envelops us here; never-resting whirlwind, high as Immensity, old as Eternity.[55]

Waste, the leaf rotting on the highway, is claimed here as a full participant in the matrix of force relations. Even rotting is an energetic action, part of the functioning of a fully integrated and living universe, in which, as he puts it in *Sartor Resartus*, nothing is "detached, separated" and everything is "indissolubly joined to the whole."[56] Carlyle here attempts to differentiate his own position from what he considered a narrow Cartesian materialism that would draw distinctions between dead matter and living force, and conceived of motion as discrete particles traveling through void space. In taking such a position, Carlyle made himself congenial to the rising generation of scientific materialists like Tyndall.

But the question of waste won't go away so easily. When it appears, as it does here, in limited, singular, organic form, like a leaf, he can easily accommodate it in his metaphysics of force relations: "Despise not the rag from which man makes Paper, or the litter from which the earth makes Corn. Rightly viewed, no meanest object is insignificant; all objects are as windows, through which the philosophic eye looks into Infinitude itself."[57] A leaf, a rag, the "litter" that participates in the natural cycles of agricultural production: these objects present a version of waste that can fit comfortably in an ecologically stable picture of organic growth and decay, and that, as a result, open up "windows" – just as Manchester did – into the singular force principle that binds the entire universe into a productive whole. "The withered leaf is not dead and lost, there are Forces in it and around it, though working in inverse order," he writes, suggesting an easy, energetic economy of complete reversibility.[58]

But other, large-scale, environment-altering forms of waste don't fit so neatly into this scheme. These Carlyle treats with metaphysical hazmat gloves, abstracting them into allegory, or into epiphenomena that are ontologically divided from "true" natural processes. In *Chartism*, he asks "what is injustice?," and then answers: "Another name for disorder, for unveracity, unreality; a thing which veracious created Nature, even because it is not Chaos and a waste-whirling baseless Phantasm, rejects and disowns."[59] Nature is not "waste-whirling," he says, and therefore waste, chaos, disorder have meaning in moral terms alone; they are merely questions of perception and thus, in some fundamental way, not *real*. He pursues a similar argument in *Past and Present*: "We took transient superficial Semblance for everlasting central Substance; we have departed far away from the *Laws* of this Universe, and behold now lawless Chaos and inane Chimera is ready to devour us!"[60] Carlyle does not specifically mention the city here, but clearly the swirling images of chaos and lawlessness bring it to mind. In fact, such passages fit well with a strain of urban representation that imagines the city as a kind of monstrous collective illusion.[61]

Carlyle's interest in consigning waste to the status of "phantasm" comes to the forefront in his discussion of Manchester:

> Manchester, with its cotton-fuz, its smoke and dust, its tumult and contentious squalor, is hideous to thee? Think not so: a precious substance, beautiful as magic dreams and yet no dream but a reality, lies hidden in that noisome wrappage; – a wrappage struggling indeed ... to cast itself off, and leave the beauty free and visible there! ... Soot and despair are not the essence of it [the city]; they are divisible from it, – at this hour, are they not crying fiercely to be divided?[62]

Clearly enough, waste here exists only as a perception, an outer semblance that can be divided from reality. Carlyle sees in energy possibilities for creating an almost magical productivity, but for Manchester to fit this scheme, the productive output, the "substance," has to be separated from its by-products, the "semblance," and waste has to be reduced to mere "wrappage." To see wastefulness in Manchester, he suggests, reflects an inability to discern "reality," and thus what appears to be a stand against wastefulness comes uncomfortably close to a denial of its existence. Like Buckland, Carlyle treats waste as something that "some have seen," not the deep truth of things. This dematerialization of waste is something we will encounter repeatedly, in different forms, in the following chapters.

Carlyle's representation of the city is interesting for this reason. While he seemed to find in the city the possibility for a new, heroic expression of natural energy, it was an ideal that was becoming increasingly difficult to maintain. To build a metaphysical system premised on productivity and the indestructibility of force meant that a place needed to be made for the productive forces actually at work and on display in urban centers. And yet it was hard to avoid the conclusion that such forces *necessarily* involved waste and pollution, and Carlyle's attempts to "cast off," "divide," and, perhaps most tellingly, "disown" such waste appeared as so much whistling in the dark. The city at morning may have resembled the rising sun in certain ways, but cities aren't actually energy producers; instead, they depend upon the massive importation of terrestrial energy stocks. The waste products they give off cannot simply be described as "Forces ... working in inverse order," since that kind of easy reversibility or cyclicality is precisely what the city's consumption patterns disrupt. We can see Carlyle's ambivalence about this in the fact that force and wasted force are described in very similar ways in his prose: nature is described as a "huge illimitable whirlwind of Force, which envelops us here," and a "never-resting whirlwind." But he uses the same imagery of "waste-whirling" chaos "ready to devour us" to suggest (among other things) the ecological breakdown occurring in England's population centers. Carlyle wants to enforce a moral separation between the two expressions of energetic movement, and while there clearly is a moral problem to be descried in the way energy was being used, it was also becoming clear that waste was unavoidably part of industrial production and urban life.

Because of this, Carlyle's celebration of Manchester is ultimately untenable and thus something of an anomaly in his works. Very often his descriptions of the seamless merging of natural and human energy forms require a retreat from urban centers:

> Here let us rest, and lay-out seedfields; here let us learn to dwell. Here, even here, the orchards that we plant will yield us fruit; the acorns will be wood and pleasant umbrage, if we wait. How much grows everywhere if we do but wait! Through the swamps we will shape causeways, force purifying drains; we will learn to thread the rocky inaccessibilities; and beaten tracks, worn smooth by mere traveling of human feet, will form themselves. Not a difficulty but can transfigure itself into a triumph.[63]

Causeways but no thoroughfares; tracks but no railroads; drains but no sewers; difficulties magically transfiguring themselves – the passage is a productivist ode to the seamless merging of industry and nature with all the usual imagery and settings subtracted. The forces at work disappear into an agentless verbal haze, not unlike Tyndall's rhetoric of solar agency. No questions of limited resources trouble such passages. And when Carlyle does turn to "Coal Force," as he does in the following passage from *Sartor resartus*, he removes it from the urban geographies that would make it problematic:

> As I rode through the Schwarzwald, I said to myself: That little fire which glows star-like across the dark-growing (*nachtende*) moor, where the sooty smith bends over his anvil, and thou hopest to replace thy lost horse-shoe, – is it a detached, separated speck, cut-off from the whole Universe; or indissolubly joined to the whole? Thou fool, that smithy-fire was (primarily)

kindled at the Sun; is fed by air that circulates from before Noah's Deluge, from beyond the Dogstar; therein, with Iron Force, and Coal Force, and the far stranger Force of Man, are cunning affinities and battles and victories of Force brought about; it is a little ganglion, or nervous centre, in the great vital system of Immensity.[64]

As Underwood argues: "The projection of the scene into Germany – and moreover into a remote rural area – distances the smith not just spatially but chronologically from the factories of Birmingham."[65] This, it should be pointed out, is the passage that Tyndall admired so much, and which he used as evidence that Carlyle had "poetically, but accurately, foreshadow[ed] the doctrine of the Conservation of Energy." Tyndall's genealogy is part of a broader dispute about who deserved credit for the first law of thermodynamics,[66] but it illustrates the elision of the conservation of energy and the Conservation of Energy; that is, between a metaphysical notion that energy is always automatically conserved, and the thermodynamic definition of energy as a measurable quantity of working power, a resource. George Levine argues that, for Carlyle, "the natural order will reassert itself against every artificial, mechanical contrivance which disguises the continuity of all experience and the source of life and meaning in the mysterious depths of irrational but divinely just energy. The city, in such a context of moral and religious force, is barely visible."[67] Although in this essay Levine does not explicitly discuss "energy" and "force" as historico-scientific signifiers, his use of such terms is suggestive of precisely this context. For Carlyle, energy is still an abstract agency, not a resource, which is the only reason he can reduce the city to a "barely visible" phenomenon.

If energy at first seemed to define the relationship between industry and nature as one of perfect, Providentially mandated, ecological wholeness, the process of urbanization, the growing dependence on, and daily experience with, massive energy expenditure helped introduce a rival discourse of energy exhaustion in the middle decades of the century. Beginning in the 1840s, and increasing in urgency in the 1850s and 1860s, the city's massive energy consumption stirred widespread concerns about the unsustainable dynamic of industrial development and resource use. Indeed, the size of such consumption seemed, in the minds of some commentators, to augur the eventual failure of everything from coal supplies to farmlands to the sun itself. As Christopher Hamlin argues, while cities may have maintained a "rough organic equilibrium" with their environs before the large-scale implementation of industrial practices and the urban population growth that followed, "this had surely vanished by the early 1840s when the Health of Towns Commissioners followed their noses into the back courts of British cities. There they found enormous accumulations of rotting matter – in stagnant sewers and cesspools, in heaps of garbage and excrement, in church-yards so packed with bodies that corpse-parts continually surfaced."[68] That this kind of organic refuse was linked, in the Victorian imagination, to energy, is an issue we'll discuss at length in the next section. For now, it's enough to note that the seamless energetic interchange between industrial and natural worlds that fired the productivist imagination was forced into crisis by the emergence of the modern city. While the Victorians were good at obscuring the materiality of waste from themselves by cloaking it in different kinds of metaphysical and moral garb, they had not yet learned how to remove it materially, from their lived experience.

The coal question

Anxieties about England's energy resources date back at least as far as John Williams's 1789 *The Limited Quantity of Coal in Britain*, but they took on greater urgency over the course of the nineteenth century as both population and per capita consumption increased. In works that discuss coal exhaustion, such as Robert Bakewell's *Introduction to Geology* (1813), John Holland's *A History and Description of Fossil Fuels* (1835), William Armstrong's opening address to the British Association at Newcastle-upon-Tyne (1863), Edward Hull's *The Coal-Fields of Great Britain* (1861), and William Stanley Jevons's seminal *The Coal Question* (1865), London's massive, ever-increasing coal consumption was invariably singled out as a focus for grave concern, and fashioned as a potent synecdoche for the nation's energy consumption habits. Holland quotes Bakewell approvingly: "This competent and ingenious observer says, – 'We cannot but regard the exhaustion of our coal beds as involving the destruction of a great portion of our private comfort and national prosperity. Nor is the period very remote when the coal districts, which at present supply the metropolis with fuel, will cease to yield anymore.'"[69] A writer in *The Times* uses the city to paint a bleak picture of the stakes:

> Coal is everything to us. Without coal, our factories will become idle, our foundries and workshops be still as the grave; the locomotive will rust in the shed, and the rail be buried in the weeds. Our streets will be dark, our houses uninhabitable … We shall be surrounded and overwhelmed by the unprofitable lumber of buildings and machinery that we cannot use, and even cities we cannot occupy. For who will care to live in Manchester? Who will be able to live in the Metropolis?[70]

Table 1 *Coal imported into London*

Year	Total quantity of coal imported into London (tons)	Increase in 50 years or as for 50 years (tons)	Rate % of increase as for 50 years
1650	216,000		
1700	428,100	212,100	98
1750	688,700	260,600	61
1800	1,099,000	410,300	60
1850	3,638,883	2,539,883	231
1865	5,909,940	7,570,190	404

Source: Jevons, *The Coal Question*, 232.

The apocalypticism of such a description prefigures post-industrial science fiction. The writer here does not simply argue that city life would be very different without fossil-fuel energy, he declares it would be impossible. But if urban life had come to seem dependent upon, and thus defined by, an influx of resources, this also meant that its vast and growing appetite for those resources made it the most significant threat to its own survival.[71]

This was the knotty situation described in *The Coal Question*, the book that, above all others, helped make the question of resource exhaustion a part of the national conversation. (His table showing the rate of London's coal consumption is represented above). It shows us not simply the rate of London's coal consumption, but the rate at which that rate itself was increasing. He comments: "We see that it is almost impossible to compare this and previous centuries, and that *the rate of multiplication is in recent years many times as great as during preceding centuries*"[72] (original emphasis). London in *The Coal Question* is not merely a massive consumer of coal, it represents the bottomlessness of the modern appetite for energy, the fact that nothing seemed to be checking this increasing expenditure.

Nothing, that is, except the coal supplies themselves. As Jevons took pains to show, these were not infinite, and no other known sources of energy could stoke the furnaces and run the locomotives that kept the city functioning. Even things that at first glance seemed to have little to do with coal, such as the city's water supply, were revealed to be part of an interlocking fossil-fuel system: "it is only the engine that can supply water for the manufacturing and domestic uses of our great towns like Manchester and London."[73] Urban life was *premised* on the availability of fossil fuels, and since they would not last forever, it looked to Jevons as though the continued growth of cities was unsustainable. The Malthusian problem of geometrical growth paired with finite resources returned here with a vengeance, and *The Coal Question* is essentially an updating of this logic for the fossil-fuel age. Malthus imagined a stable balance between the human population and nature: the land would only fail to support a population once its numbers had grown to a certain size; when those numbers decreased again, the land's available productive capacity would once again be sufficient. Coal, Jevons argues, revises this picture by dramatically augmenting the productive capacity of the nation and allowing it to support a much more sizable population: "Hence it is that, in our most crowded towns, we have, in the development of our manufacturing and coal-consuming system, means of subsistence which for the present remove Malthusian checks to increase."[74] The key to the passage is Jevons's ominous qualifier *for the present.* For while it might seem that unlocking the earth's energy reserves had provided an escape from the scarcity trap, Jevons took pains to show that it had merely delayed its springing. Now, instead of a continual balancing and rebalancing between population and resources, there was an irreversible historical trajectory of uncertain future length.

Jevons knew that the deep-set faith in technological improvement provided an almost reflexive counter-argument to warnings about the coal supply. Increased technological efficiency, that counter-argument went, would always recoup whatever loss was visited upon the raw quantity of resources. We can see such thinking in the *Cyclopaedia of Commerce* entry on "Coal":

> the only legitimate end to be aimed at by speculators on the duration of coal, is the prevention of all waste. If, to the best of our power, we husband our resources, we may safely leave to posterity the management of their own interest, – the task of compensating for a diminution of mineral resources by an increase of mechanical skill and ingenuity.[75]

Against such narratives, Jevons makes two claims. First, he insists not only that coal is a uniquely dense and transportable source of motive power, but that many of the alternatives themselves depend upon it. An electromagnetic engine, he says, requires metals that must first be smelted, and smelting involves burning coal.[76] The same is true he says, sounding eerily modern, with the production of hydrogen as fuel.[77] The question for Jevons is not whether a working hydrogen or electromagnetic engine is theoretically possible, but what its net energy cost is in a full working environment of production and consumption. In other words, what is at stake is where the boundaries are drawn in the representation of energy systems. Jevons was identifying something of an intellectual Ponzi scheme: people were counting on the development of science and the "natural" progress of things to make coal exhaustion irrelevant, when coal is actually the very reason such progress takes place. Indeed, a key part of the argument of *The Coal Question* is that England's greatness in the arts and manufactures depends upon the development of coal energy. Coal is, says Jevons, "the source of civilization,"[78] and he suggests throughout the book that England owes its success as a player on the world-historical stage to it. This may not seem like such a radical claim, but it is important to see that, too often, such a notion was obscured in discussions of energy and resource exhaustion, where appeals were made to the native sagacity, ingenuity, and "energy" of the English people. Here is Grant Duff, leveling his objection to both *The Coal Question* and W. R. Greg's similarly resource-minded *Rocks Ahead*:

> No reasonable man doubts that a time will come when our cheap coal will be exhausted, when we shall, in all likelihood, cease to be the great workshop of the world … Coal and iron are but instruments in the hands of that energy which is the true source of our national strength. Coal and iron did not defeat the Armada, did not conquer India, nor colonise America.[79]

This is, as we have seen, a hazard of the word "energy" itself, which could signify both a material quantity, and a personal (or national) *quality*. Here, Duff plays on the ambiguity, making England's national character seem like the source of its physical energy. Jevons insists upon English culture's dependence upon coal throughout the book, partially to combat such encomiums to some sort of native national "energy."

The more devastating critique of faith in technological innovation was what would become known as "Jevons's paradox." Jevons argued that increased efficiency actually makes the problem of exhaustion *worse* because it lowers the relative cost of a given resource, which tends to *increase* consumption and dependency. He writes: "Nor will the economical use of coal reduce its consumption. On the contrary, economy renders the employment of coal more profitable, and thus the present demand for coal is increased, and the advantage is more strongly thrown upon the side of those who will in the future have the cheapest supplies."[80] Again, Jevons here did something that was not often part of the scientific discourse on energy: he pushed the representational boundaries to consider the total resource environment in which a technology operates. For Jevons, progress itself was the problem. In this way, he provided a corrective to the widespread tendency to moralize key terms in the discussion of energy, like waste, dissipation, and efficiency.

Energy efficiency may or may not be a moral good; within the greater system it only serves to create more waste and worsen the problem. This paradox perhaps represents his most significant updating of Malthusian logic. Malthus's predictions were so grim because they pointed out how health and productivity contained the seeds of their own undoing. As Catherine Gallagher puts it: "The degeneration from one society to the next, moreover, is effected neither by inner corruption nor by external adversity. It is solely a product of the procreative vigor of the body itself. The spirited health and strength of the utopian body leads within two generations to social chaos, want, warfare, and, finally, starvation."[81] While Jevons never sounds the alarm in terms like this – his picture of resource exhaustion is characterized by slow decline and waning – the logic is the same. The faster industry expands, the faster it undermines the very sources of its power. Similarly, the very growth and activity of the city could seem to be a sign of its impending demise. More on this in a moment.

Jevons was no environmental hero. *The Coal Question* has avowedly nationalist concerns at its center, as he continually warns his audience that England's worldwide supremacy is what is at stake in the future of its coal deposits. Whether or not this is a rhetorical ploy to mobilize the reader's concern, the book focuses much attention on the rise of other coal-producing nations, like the United States and Germany, whose untapped supplies will soon allow them to overtake England as a world power. The appeal is made on these grounds, and not, for the most part, on overt concerns about pollution or ecosystem degradation. Nevertheless, these concerns do find expression in the text, as part of the larger picture of the unsustainable organization of the industrial economy. The book offers a Scylla–Charybdis dilemma, where economic stasis will result in severe hardship and retrenchment, but maintaining forward momentum will end in a crash. This has an environmental dimension as well: coal "is our last great resource – the one kind of wealth by the sufficient employment of which we might reverse every other trade, draw every other material from abroad until the kingdom was one immense Manchester, or one expanse of 'Black Country.'"[82] Jevons here suggests how coal leads to eco-catastrophe in either direction: the logic of development is such that, given sufficient coal, it would make the whole country a polluted wasteland. On the other hand, since coal is not available limitlessly, its exhaustion will lead to "misery and danger."[83]

"The coal question" – as articulated by Jevons and others – thus threatened to sever the well-established link between energy resources,

divine favor, and history. Perhaps coal did not provide a sign of industry's rightful, anticipated place in "a system of prospective design," in the
words of William Sidney Gibson, but illustrated humankind's profligacy,
and collective inability to refrain from squandering and despoiling.[84] In
light of this, the discovery of coal could seem less like the fulfillment of a
Providential narrative, and more like the prelude to a complete unraveling.
In this alternative narrative, the great energy expenditure of urban centers was not the glorious expression of divine favor made manifest, but an
immense riot of waste that would take future history straight into the trash
bin. In other words, *The Coal Question* threatened the reader with more
than just the future unavailability of coal: it quietly got to the root of some
of the most cherished ideas about English national life, faith in technology,
and Providential history.

But these ideas are redoubtable, if nothing else, and even the grimmest
predictions could be accommodated, with some adjustments, within consoling narrative structures. The geologist Joseph Holdsworth, conceding
that the questions Jevons raised were of "transcendent importance," turns
technological advancement into an article of faith:

> In this cosmopolitan view of our subject, we cannot fail to mark the import
> of the marvellous preparation made by Divine Providence, in the physi-
> cal conditions of our own land, for the unwonted progress and prosper-
> ity so remarkably characterising the present eventful times. And we have
> the fullest faith, that the Power which made this wonderful provision for
> our manifold contingencies has, so to speak, amply provisioned us for tri-
> umphantly carrying out our glorious world-wide mission of humanising
> usefulness. We do not believe, for reasons advanced, that this our national
> career will be cut short, as predicted, in little more than two centuries, by
> the exhaustion of our Coalfields.[85]

Holdsworth simply does not "believe" in the gloomy predictions put
forth in *The Coal Question* and elsewhere because, he says, "The time is at
hand for our new resources to reveal themselves." He also looks forward
to the time when "the requisite measures are adopted for the development
of the mineral."[86] It's not clear whether the "new resources" and "requisite measures" refer to the discovery of additional coal deposits and the
development of advanced techniques to harvest them, or an altogether
different resource and technology; the truth is it doesn't much matter,
since the point for Holdsworth is that *something* will take the place of
coal. In the passages above we see the way such a faith-based argument
is fused with an imperial narrative about England's special "mission" in
spreading civilization across the globe, and encoded with a pre-emptive

rationalization of whatever exploitation will take place in the event any new resources "reveal themselves." The irony, as we'll discuss further in Chapter 7, is that it was, in part, the insatiable demand for energy at home that drove England and other European powers into Africa, South America, and elsewhere in search of additional raw materials and energy deposits. That is to say, in logic worthy of Lewis Carroll, the belief that resources will continue to be available becomes a justification for whatever measures must be taken to ensure those resources will continue to be available.

Holdsworth's argument illustrates the durability of the faith in both technology and national exceptionalism, and the power of the rhetorical devices marshaled in their service. He writes: "the actual disclosure of these mighty treasuries would be hailed as a new and inexhaustible source of human advancement and happiness, a mighty strengthener of the right arm of British power and usefulness, and as an especial blessing to the millions of England's vast and rapidly-increasing METROPOLIS."[87] It is not clear what the word "actual" is doing here, except lending a feeling of substantiality to what is an entirely faith-based argument.

Even more telling is his use of the word "inexhaustible," which Holdsworth cagily brackets even as he uses it to stiffen the passage's rhetorical spine. These mysterious energy resources "would be hailed" as "inexhaustible" – he's not arguing they would actually *be* inexhaustible. The very language unwittingly recapitulates the entire problem with the discussion around fossil-fuel energy: the *belief* in its limitlessness seems to matter more than the actual material conditions of scarcity. The effect is a gauzy optimism that wishes away whatever problems *The Coal Question* has raised. But the passage is also troubled by a certain anxiety. The reference to the growing METROPOLIS conjures, albeit quietly, the grim implications if technology is *not* able to fix this situation. Urbanizing England, with its "rapidly increasing" population, would be in deep trouble: "industrial enterprise has daily become more and more largely developed, so, in a perpetually increasing ratio, has been the drain on the invaluable deposits of our great carboniferous storehouses – in fact, the consumption of Coal at the present period is altogether unprecedented."[88] London alone, he notes, "consumes about 6,000,000 tons annually."[89] Holdsworth then goes on to quote an authority on coal who argues that: "Coal districts which at present supply the Metropolis with fuel will cease to yield any more."[90] The stakes are great, and they are growing; by placing his faith in technology, Holdsworth is, in effect, doubling down on its ability to rectify a situation it has itself caused.

The agricultural question

Coal, along with its offspring, gas, were key signifiers in the growing concern about national energy expenditure, since they were the substances that made modern life possible, and were clearly connected to the production of city light and heat, as well as the stifling pollution blanketing the skies of England's population centers. But the discourse of energy included agriculture as well as industry, biological as well as mechanical activity; as we have seen, the energy concept, in its formalized thermodynamic guise, as well as in its more common usage, helped blur the distinction between industry and nature, mechanism and organism, by reconceiving both vegetable and animal bodies as machines within a matrix of energy relations. Thus concerns about the future of the soil and about the food supply formed a second key part of the Victorian discourse of energy exhaustion.

The agricultural question seems roughly parallel to, but also significantly different from, the coal question, since while both industrial life and biological life require energy, the agricultural harvest appears to be cyclical, self-regenerating, and directly powered by the sun. Although Victorian geologists may have differed on the precise amount of coal remaining, there was clearly a finite stock available. Not so for agricultural energy, which was seemingly limited only by the availability of arable land, and which was reconstituted with every new seasonal cycle.

But nineteenth-century urbanization disrupted this cyclical and self-regenerating dynamic by introducing unsustainable patterns of consumption. For Malthus, so much fertility sustained so much population, and any increase in aggregate fertility could only come about through the addition of arable lands. But the development of new energy resources changed this equation practically and theoretically. In the 1840s and 1850s the nascent science of agricultural chemistry helped dramatically improve the productivity of land through the investigation of "soil vitality" and chemical fertilizers. This seemed an escape from the Malthusian trap: more energy could be drawn out of existing farmlands, and thus the population could expand without suffering the corrective action of starvation and extinction.[91] As Marx noted, the fertility, and thus the agricultural capacity, of any given portion of land was not a constant, but a factor that humans could alter through technological innovation. Agriculture, like everything else, was historical.[92]

As with coal, the enormous magnification of harvested energy provided sustenance for a growing population and an industrializing world, but also meant that this supply needed to be sustained into perpetuity.

The land had been pushed beyond its "natural" carrying capacity through the importation of guano and other fertilizing agents, leading to questions about whether and how long such a state of affairs could continue. Richard Proctor, in an article about solar energy, describes how humanity has managed to escape the Malthusian trap, but has, by doing so, put increasing pressure (and unrealistic expectations) on the earth's capacities:

> We are accustomed to look upon the Earth as an inexhaustible storehouse whence all our wants may be supplied. Year after year we till the soil, and still there is no lack in the growth of all the vegetable productions needed by man; nor do our flocks and herds diminish, notwithstanding the enormous supplies of flesh-meat we are continually consuming. Taking the whole Earth, it is probable that the yearly produce of agricultural and pastoral labours increases at even a higher rate than that at which the human race is increasing, so that were man content, as in old times, to draw upon the Earth's stores for the supply of his ordinary wants, there would be little fear of that store being ever exhausted.[93]

To many observers, the most significant threat to the continued productivity of the soil was the enormous growth of cities. The German chemist Justus von Liebig, one of the first scientists to articulate the modern doctrine of the conservation of energy, argued forcefully in an open letter to the Mayor of London that the improper disposal of human waste from urban centers meant that necessary chemical compounds were being flushed out to sea and thus lost for future productive uses. As a result, imported resources like guano deposits were disappearing at alarming rates to keep agricultural lands fertile enough to feed the voracious city. Liebig argues:

> If the common "sewerage system" is retained, then the imported manures, guano, and bones make their way in to the sewers of the cities, which, like the bottomless pit, have for centuries swallowed up the guano elements of the English fields, and after a series of years the land will find itself in precisely the condition it was in before the importation of guano and bones commenced; and after England shall have robbed the cultivated lands of Europe even to complete exhaustion, and taken from them the power to furnish her longer with corn and manure, then she will not be richer than before in the means of producing corn and meat, but will from that time become even poorer in these means.[94]

Guano stocks, which had helped fuel the upsurge in agricultural production, were like coal in some respects: they were productive deposits amassed over millennia. The one-way flow of resources from the country to the city was, as Liebig himself notes, nothing new – the metaphor of

the city as a consumer, feasting on the countryside, goes back at least to
the Renaissance. What had changed was the global scale of the rift and the
potential irreversibility of the consequences – the fact that city consumption now threatened *all the fields of Europe* with exhaustion. Deeply influenced by Liebig's writings on energy, Marx argued that the concentration
and growth of an "urban population":

> disturbs the metabolic interaction between man and the earth, i.e. it pre-
> vents the return to the soil of its constituent elements consumed by man
> in the form of food and clothing; hence it hinders the operation of the
> eternal natural condition for the lasting fertility of the soil … In modern
> agriculture, as in urban industry, the increase in the productivity and the
> mobility of labour is purchased at the cost of laying waste and debilitating
> labour-power itself.[95]

Following Liebig, he focuses on the concept of metabolism to frame the
city–country dynamic as an energy system. The city had often been compared to a single organism, or body: here, that metaphor was retained, but
reframed, as bodies were at this time being reconceived in terms of thermodynamic energy flow. The city was a vast organic machine that required
a ceaseless influx of fuel supplies to function.[96]

Thus the public discussion about city waste that took place in the middle decades of the century was much more than a pragmatic discussion
about keeping cities clean and disease-free (although it was that too). It
was also a discussion about energy resources; about the future existence
of the nation; and, crucially, about the operations of divine Providence in
the affairs of humankind. We can see, for example, how much was at stake
in the writings of the sanitary reformer Thomas Hawksley, who, in 1866,
expressed despair over the insufficiency of the solutions thus far advanced
for the problem of massive city waste:

> Seeing the failure of so much scientific and engineering skill, to deal effec-
> tually with this first and great requirement of society, that, namely, of the
> safe and beneficial disposal of the refuse organic matter set free from life
> in the busy hives of mankind, we are tempted to ask, does this great diffi-
> culty arise out of any imperfection in the arrangement of Providence? Is it
> possible that the great system of nature, otherwise so full of harmony and
> provision, in this instance breaks down, and exhibits an unpreparedness
> and incapacity of action?[97]

Here the narrative is explicitly Providential, but the city's expenditure
seems to open up questions about its viability.[98] What's so fascinating
about the issue Hawksley articulates here is how close his reasoning comes
to expressing something akin to the second law of thermodynamics. As

we will see in the next chapter, for energy scientists, the energetic "flaws," the heat losses incurred by industrial production, were extrapolated into a vision of the "flaws" inherent in all natural processes, and a breakdown of the very order of things into enervation and chaos. Here the waste in cities leads Hawksley along a similar chain of thinking, as the failures of human technology raise troubling questions about the "incapacity" and "breakdown" of the eternal order of nature. Like the imaginary heat engine that could renew its own fuel, or the fabled "perpetual motion machine," the perfectly conservative, productive urban system was a technological ideal that seemed to founder on the realities of actual practice. Indeed, the language of agricultural spoliation in many ways resembled language about the thermodynamic inefficiency of engines, and the "loss" of energy as waste heat, or entropy. In similar fashion, the sanitary reformer Edwin Chadwick published an editorial in the *Sanitary Record* arguing that by not recycling urban waste, a large quantity of nitrogen would be irretrievably scattered into unusable particles. In this way, he says, the fertilizing power of the nitrogen would be effectively "robbed from the universe."[99] By using, as Liebig did, the word "robbed," Chadwick does not mean the nitrogen would be destroyed, but rendered permanently disorganized, and thus unavailable for future use. Nitrogen here is in the same position as entropy is in the discussion of heat engines: it is not annihilated, but, for all practical purposes, it is lost. Where thermodynamics would argue that waste heat is radiated into space, for sanitarians like Chadwick and Liebig, the void into which energy is dissipated is the ocean. Chadwick plots energy loss, as the thermodynamic scientists often did, on the scale of the "universe," moving in surprisingly short order from microscopic particles to the fate of the cosmos.

For Hawksley, the means by which the "arrangement of Providence" can be repaired is through the technological improvements that will restore the city to a symbiotic and balanced relationship with the rest of the natural world. The stakes were high, for a restoration of ecological balance was necessary if the modern city would appear as a necessary part of, not outcast from, a superintending Providential narrative. The argument he marshals for the ability of technological improvements to rectify the problem of urban waste rests, as Holdsworth's does, not upon any technical certainty in the efficacy of future engineering practices, but rather upon a deep belief that it *simply must be the case* that this situation can and will be ameliorated. Again, the problem of city waste requires a doubling down on the same technological narrative that it has repeatedly undermined. Hawksley's essay stages a narrative of wavering faith and doubt (he is "tempted to ask," he says) followed by an even firmer recommitment to a belief in technology. The way in which the Providential narrative makes its appeal to technology, and technology makes its appeal to the Providential, narrative itself resembles a kind of self-generating, perpetual-motion fantasy.

Energy resources and narrative

The need for a master narrative to make sense of the city's energy use, I would add, is not simply a product of capitalist apologetics. Marx, as we noted, drawing on Liebig's work, argues that the city introduced a "metabolic rift" that threatened the exhaustion of terrestrial resources: "all progress in capitalist agriculture is a progress in the art, not only of robbing the worker, but of robbing the soil; all progress in increasing the fertility of the soil for a given time is a progress towards ruining the more longlasting sources of that fertility."[100] But in the same section he also describes the city as an entity that "concentrates the historical motive power of society."[101] Here we see the narrative exchange that, for Marx, renders the city's massive energy expenditure useful: energy in the form of resources is transformed into energy in the form of "historical motive power" – a worthwhile transaction as far as he is concerned, because the wasted material energies are gathering elsewhere into a historical "force" of tremendous transformative potential. Engels, writing on "the great towns," and using a slightly different metaphorical complex, argues "we can but rejoice over everything which accelerates the course of the disease."[102] For both writers, the process of "wasting" – whether conceived as the spoliation of resources, or as the debilitating spread of a disease – is converted by means of a narrative in which agencies of rejuvenation gather at the very moments in which they seem to be squandered.

The question of urban energy consumption, then, is a question of what kind of story can be told to make sense of the city's massive and growing expenditure, and how that story can or cannot be squared with the more familiar teleological narrative of historical development and Providential design. The question hinges upon the ambiguous notion of "expenditure" itself, which suggests the employment and waste of energy simultaneously. The idea of energy as a material quantity framed any action in terms of its cost, and, theoretically, that cost could be strictly tabulated down to the last *calorie*: this was one implication of the thermodynamic research program. The fact that the costs of energy from coal were always being exacted from a finite fund meant that any use of it entailed some loss as well. What separates the use of a resource from the *waste* of a resource depends on what it's being used for. Is the expenditure of light and heat in the city being gathered into "historical motive power"? Or is it, perhaps, becoming "a beacon of hope – a radiant pharos towards which millions of straining eyes are turned for liberty," as Holdsworth would have it?[103] If the expenditure of fossil-fuel energy rendered it unavailable for future uses, the critical question was: what had the spending purchased?

On the level of the individual, this question is not so troubling: burning coal to heat a home or turning on a lamp for a night's reading seem to the individual in question a *use*, not a waste, of energy. The expenditure of limited natural resources simply does not appear under the sign of waste when understood as part of a coherent narrative. But the city's energy use, made up of thousands of such narratives collected together, is a different matter. When expenditure is taken in the aggregate, as it so often was in discussions of urban life, and viewed without reference to the individual narratives that make given acts of expenditure seem necessary or worthwhile, it is stripped of a context that would give it meaning. Without a larger Providential or technological or historical-materialist narrative to provide that meaningful context, the city's expenditure, understood in terms of alarming tallies of consumption, might appear as *mere* expenditure, and thus as a kind of profligacy. The endlessly burning lights could make the city appear to be a theater of waste in its light as well as in its darkness.

This crisis in narrative engendered by the city's massive expenditure can be seen in unexpected places. Take, for example, the representations of a popular Victorian pastime, the nighttime balloon ascent over London. Lynda Nead argues that "at night, the view of London from a balloon became more fantastic and took on a magical dimension … A night ascent was less concerned with a utopian sensation of absolute control than with the dazzling transmogrification of the city through the combined effects of elevation and light."[104] The opening pages of Henry Mayhew's *The Criminal Prisons of London* discusses the night balloon ride in such terms, turning the city into an aesthetic spectacle:

> Those who have seen London only in the day-time, with its flood of life pouring through the arteries to its restless heart, know it not in *all* its grandeur. They have still, in order to comprehend the multiform sublimity of the great city, to contemplate it by night, afar off from an eminence … Though the stars be shining in the heavens, there is another firmament spread out below with its millions of bright lights glittering at the feet. Line after line sparkles like the trails left by meteors, and cutting and crossing

one another till they are lost in the haze of distance. Over the whole, too, there hangs a lurid cloud, bright as if the monster city were in flames, and looking from afar like the sea at dusk, made phosphorescent by the million creatures dwelling within it.[105]

The idea of London as a second firmament was not an uncommon image; as we saw with Carlyle, the city's energy was commonly linked with the sun and the stars. But for Mayhew, while the sight of the bright, nighttime city is sublime, what lurks in the shadows of the fantasy is the troubling sense that this sight represents a profound cost in resources. Calling upon statistical representations of the metropolis, he pauses to note that London is "consuming as much as 13,000,000 cubic feet of gas every night,"[106] and that "for the purposes of heating and lighting, the Metropolis burns no less than 3,000,000 tons of coal" per year.[107] There is an instability in this vantage point: from this distance, removed from the individual narratives that would make any given act of energy consumption meaningful, the result is simply a spectacle of aggregated expenditure coming at a tremendous cost. It may be aesthetically pleasing, but without a context, that aesthetic pleasure looks grotesquely expensive and, perhaps, unsustainable. For Mayhew, the city is "in flames" – an image of self-consumption as well as illumination.

J. C. Platt discusses the illumination of nighttime London, seen "from some height" in a balloon, in the same conflicted terms. While he marvels at it as Mayhew does, the sight also triggers troubling thoughts about what Lewis Mumford calls "the invisible city": the vast energy infrastructure of pipes, conduits, and power stations, as well as the raw amount of resources flowing through it.[108] He quotes the statistical tabulations of a Mr. Hedley:

> For lighting London and its suburbs with gas, there are eighteen public gas-works; twelve public gas-work companies; 2,800,000*l.* capital employed in works, pipes, tanks, gas-holders, apparatus; 450,000*l.* yearly revenue derived; 180,000 tons of coals used in the year for making gas; 1,460,000,000 cubic feet of gas made in the year; 134,300 private burners supplied to about 400,000 customers; 30,400 public or street consumers (about 2,650 of these are in the city of London); 380 lamplighters employed; 176 gas-holders, several of which are double ones, capable of storing 5,500,000 cubic feet, 890 tons of coals used in the retorts, in the shortest day, in twenty-four hours; 7,120,000 cubic feet of gas used in the longest night, say 24th December; about 2500 persons employed in the metropolis alone in this branch of manufacture; between 1822 and 1827 the consumption was nearly doubled; and between 1827 and 1837 it was again nearly doubled.[109]

The invisible city brings the visible city into being. Indeed, the appearance of energetic grandeur is, for both writers, hard to separate from calculations of energy consumption, which means that waste could be signified not simply by the by-products of energy use – smoke, soot, and other pollutants – but by the appearance of *light and heat themselves*. For both writers the spectacle of aggregated energy use was impossible to separate from another kind of aggregation – the statistical – which reframed the sublime perception in terms of quantities, costs, and total units of consumption. As Nead points out, while the numerical tabulations were ostensibly attempts to fathom the city, they always also conveyed, through their sheer size, a sense of how truly *un*fathomable it was.[110] Both the city-as-spectacle and the city-as-statistical-table lack a coherent narrative to frame the enormous expenditure represented. Thus while Mayhew describes the majesty of the metropolis seen from above, he also notes in the same section that it looks like "a mere rubbish heap."[111] This is not a contradiction, but a product of the ambiguity of a decontextualized expenditure.

A panoramic perspective on the city always carries with it the danger of excessive abstraction from everyday life, but conceiving of the city in terms of its energy adds a new dimension. From such heights, not only can human actions seem minuscule and insignificant – the ceaseless motions of ants; or mites; or, as Mayhew has it, "animalcules" – they can also seem like the creators of a vast spectacle of waste.[112] Mayhew, it should be noted, seems aware of this dynamic. *The Criminal Prisons of London*, he tells us, is an attempt to see the city from a vantage point distinct from the one taken in *London Labour and the London Poor*. Whereas that earlier work was built around individual narratives, he explains, this work will attempt to represent the city panoramically, where "the dense fumes from the million chimneys" made it so "there was no distinguishing earth from heaven."[113] And yet, in its opening sections, Mayhew keeps trying to reconnect the great panoramic expenditure of the city to the individual purposes and life narratives that can give it meaning. Otherwise, he says, the various zones of London become "blent into one immense black spot."[114] When energy expenditure is seen as an aggregate, without reference to either individual purposes, or some kind of historical *telos*, it cannot but appear as a spectacle of waste. If, as Nead argues, mid-Victorian London was "defined through a semiotics of gas," that semiotics included an enhanced and altered consciousness of waste under the ambiguous sign of expenditure.[115]

I don't mean to suggest, however, that the account of the city that emerged in the Victorian period forced a permanent change in the understanding of urban ecology or the representation of resources. While the evident loss of energy in London, and the apprehension of energy *as* a resource, provided one model for configuring the workings of urban systems, it was by no means the only one. Just as T. H. Huxley could continue to write about coal as if *The Coal Question* had never been written, plenty of writers could and did continue to create visions of the city that mystified the way energy worked. Blanchard Jerrold's wildly popular *London: A Pilgrimage*, for example, published just a few years after *The Coal Question*, describes various London scenes using the imagery and vocabulary of energy and force relations, but in a way that insinuates that the city is a quasi-magical source and generator of that energy. The trajectory of the "pilgrimage," he writes at one point, is to take the reader "from the general surface that is brilliant, to the underlying force."[116] In true productivist fashion, he identifies this force principle, binding all of the activity of the London streets and shipyards as a principle of *work* – "work is the key to London".[117] But that work is continually mystified through aestheticizing gestures that efface human labor through the passive voice ("The water is churned with paddles and oars; and the tiny skiffs dance and plunge in the swell of the steamers"[118]); through the bestowal of agency upon industrial activities ("The mills are grinding the corn, by steam; the barges are unloading hastily, the passenger boats are bound on pressing errands – the train shoots over the river towards the Continent, and crosses another with the mail from India"[119]); and through an imagery that suggests a kind of disembodied principle working through the streets and commercial zones ("Energy and earnestness pervade London shops – and are of fiery intensity in the popular markets"[120]). Jerrold employs Dickens's technique of animating the inanimate, but does so without his corresponding interest in tracking the sources or costs of that animation. London appears, indeed, as a place of automatic, almost magical, production and self-generating motion; for Jerrold it is precisely this apprehension of disembodied and unsourced energy that allows the city to submit to his unifying aesthetic organization. To many observers, the city appeared not only a place of constant motion, but an entire world urged into growth by impersonal, extra-human agencies. As Nead argues, the growth of London was so unprecedented and rapid that it seemed to be happening "by enchantment."[121] The city was not simply a zone of energetic movement and activity; it seemed a manifestation or eruption of energy *itself*. This was a way of seeing the city that both harkens back to Carlyle's productivist Manchester and looks forward to modern forms of urban perception, including Benjamin's *flâneur*, where the expression of energy is divorced from its roots in any material source, as well as from its by-products.

Thus I want to stress that this book is not tracing a linear narrative, from some kind of mystified natural-industrial symbiosis in the early part of the century, to an unblinkered apprehension of resource waste and energy loss in the middle and later decades. The realities of massive fossil-fuel energy exploitation were then, as they are now, both revealed and obscured through the representation of the city. But the Victorian period does give us a glimpse into the way that some insistent features of urban experience, and the reckoning with the various ongoing ecological catastrophes taking place in urban areas, helped force into consciousness new ways of thinking about the use, and the waste, of the resources of the natural world.

CHAPTER 2

The heat death of the sun at the dawn of the Anthropocene

In *Open Fields,* Gillian Beer discusses the "heat death" of the sun, the thermodynamic prediction of solar collapse that became an object of popular fascination in the middle decades of the nineteenth century. Beer places this prediction in a broad context of concerns about the future of the cosmos during this period, arguing that, for example, Max Müller's solar mythography "was so powerful because it gave expression to covert dreads then current."[1] Beer describes such "dreads" in primarily religious or mythical terms – "the loss of faith in *recurrence,* the loss of any assurance of 'eternal return,' the recognition that oblivion is not only the matter of the past but of the future" – but in this chapter I want to shift the focus a bit, and stress the ways in which we may also understand this solar imagery bearing specifically upon contemporary productive practices, modes of economic and social organization, and a nascent environmental consciousness.[2] That is, to see concern about the death of the sun not as a signifier for cosmic anxieties (though it was that) but as an expression of unease about resource use, energy expenditure, and widespread environmental damage. Implicit in the fascination with the sun is the recognition that modern civilization itself had become an energy giant: utterly dependent upon a continual burning, and thus necessarily anxious about an inevitable burning-out.

The eschatological language that structured the Victorian conversation about the future of the sun thus simultaneously represents a swerve away from the discourses of social planning and natural resource husbandry discussed in the previous chapter, and an implicit rearticulation of those concerns in apocalyptic form. As we'll see in the discussion that follows, the apocalypticism associated with the second law of thermodynamics could serve to reframe nature as an inescapably wasteful system, and thus shift the focus away from the problem of human energy use. But the magnitude of the disaster, the description of global environmental changes, along with the unabashedly human-centered terms in which it was often described, also make the "heat death" a powerful trope for the new pressures and concerns about energy waste and environment instability arising at the dawn of a new era of human impact upon the biosphere.

The second law: continuities and discontinuities

As we saw in the previous chapter, although the first law of thermodynamics defined energy as a measurable quantity of motive power, it nevertheless depended upon metaphysical assumptions about the unity and the indestructibility of the universe's energy. The dictum that, in Joule's words, "nothing is deranged, nothing ever lost" was a crucial axiom of early thermodynamic research, and seemed confirmed by the principle of the conservation of energy, the first law of thermodynamics.[3] The first law discussed energy as a *quantity*, and transformations of energy as perfectly conservative: burning a lump of coal may change potential energy to heat, but it does nothing to the total amount of energy in the universe. But there was something the first law did not take into account. If burning a lump of coal does not change the quantity of energy in the universe, it does change the amount of *high-quality* energy available to humans; once a lump of coal is burned, it cannot be unburned. Through their work improving the efficiency of industrial machinery, engineers and scientists had noticed something crucial: energy could never be entirely harnessed in mechanical processes. When coal is burnt in an engine, some portion of it always winds up as wasted heat – in the form of friction, or in the heating of the engine compartment itself. This heat does not do anything useful, it is not converted into work; it simply radiates through the walls of the mechanism and into the surrounding environment. Dissipated heat is still energy, it still "exists," and thus does not violate the conservation law. But it is disorganized and thus unavailable. In short, it moves from usable to unusable, high to low quality. The difference in quality between a lump of coal on the one hand, and the heat, motion, and by-products it gives off through combustion on the other, is where the second law of thermodynamics enters the picture. If the discussions of the first law tended to emphasize the abstract universal "machinery" through which energy ceaselessly flowed, the second law arose from experience with the terrestrial machinery in which the quality of energy changed. If discussions of the first tended to imagine energy as a ubiquitous cosmic agency, discussions of the second often framed it as a *resource*.

And almost immediately, the second law was interpreted in cosmological terms. In a paper entitled "On a Universal Tendency in Nature to the Dissipation of Mechanical Energy" (1852), William Thomson (later Lord Kelvin) argued that since any mechanical system gradually but irreversibly loses its high-quality energy over time, the universe too must be running down. In time – though he wasn't yet prepared to offer an estimate – the sun and all the stars would burn out altogether. The heat loss and inefficiencies Thomson observed in engines, which would become central to constructing this new thermodynamic cosmology, had been known to engineers for a long time, but few imagined that the problem of energy waste could have such far-reaching consequences. It had generally been assumed that, if engines were inefficient, it was because human-made artifacts could only imperfectly approximate the perfect, divinely constructed natural order. The guiding assumption, as we have seen, was that nature never wasted anything. But Thomson essentially flipped this on its head. Rather than begin with the premise that nature was perfectly ordered and an engine could only very poorly mimic its operations, he imagined that existing engines, in all their wastefulness, provided a model for the inefficiency of all energetic transactions, including natural ones. Thomson thus quickly moved from noticing the small energy losses in industrial technology, to postulating the eventual extinction of the sun. It was, as Ilya Prigogine and Isabelle Stengers put it, "a dizzy leap from engine technology to cosmology."[4] This leap was authorized, in part, by the unitary nature of the energy concept, the fact it was understood to move through the great and small, the molecular and the galactic, the natural and the mechanical, in precisely the same way. For Thomson, that way traced a path of continual dissipation.[5]

It may seem that, in this re-engineered picture, the second law of thermodynamics represented a powerful argument against the dominant natural-theological vision of nature as a perfectly balanced, waste-free economy. A writer in *The British Quarterly Review*, discussing the second law in 1870, describes the way it makes the entire world seem a veritable spectacle of wasted energy. After considering all the untapped energy of natural formations like Niagara Falls and Mount Vesuvius, as well as all the sunbeams "which play so unprofitably" on the surface of the earth without being "impounded and harnessed" by machines, the author concludes that "ours is certainly a wasteful world."[6] The idea of ubiquitous energy dissipation seemed a decisive challenge to the efficient natural order depicted in Paley's *Natural Theology* and the *Bridgewater Treatises*.

But, as Rick Rylance has argued, "Natural Theology proved a resilient argument, partly because, in deft hands, it could retreat gracefully under pressure."[7] In subtle ways, the second law of thermodynamics was used to preserve and even *bolster* the natural-theological concept of nature as perfect economy. Although energy inevitably dissipated, it wasn't exactly "lost"; entropy was a theoretically conserved quantity, even if it was no longer of any use. Thomson thus could argue, paradoxically, that waste was not wasted: "As it is most certain that Creative Power alone can either call into existence or annihilate mechanical energy, the 'waste' referred to cannot be annihilation, but must be some transformation of energy."[8] The emphasis put on transformation is a consoling spin, grounded in the idea that waste exists only as a kind of appearance or fiction. This is a move straight out of the natural-theological playbook, where, as we have seen, waste was imagined to be merely a function of the limitations of human perception. Indeed, as Myers argues, Thomson "saw his function, as Professor of Natural Philosophy at Glasgow, proponent of Newton and successor of his own father, as that of finding 'overpoweringly strong proofs of intelligent and benevolent design.'"[9] In his *Treatise on Natural Philosophy* Thomson writes that "It is also impossible to conceive either the beginning or the continuance of life, without an overruling creative power; and, therefore, no conclusions of dynamical science regarding the future condition of the earth can be held to give dispiriting views as to the destiny of the race of intelligent beings by which it is at present inhabited."[10] In almost every one of Thomson's formulations of the second law there is an escape clause like this that makes space for the limitations of scientific understanding of the universe's contours, and a place for the consolations of Providential design.[11]

In *The Unseen Universe*, Peter Guthrie Tait and Balfour Stewart, two of the period's most prominent thermodynamic scientists, extend Thomson's conception of waste to fashion explicitly a new natural-theological vision. For Stewart and Tait, since the expended energy of the universe must exist *somewhere*, since it is only "wasted" as far as humans are concerned, it must be awaiting reactivation in the fullness of time. It was God's place, they argued, to keep track of this spent energy and gather it into the "unseen universe" where it would be revitalized. The idea of natural energy "accounts" helped preserve the notion of a final account-keeper, and nature could thus continue to resemble the perfect, Providential system described in an earlier generation of theological discourse. For these writers, the second law of thermodynamics provided a powerful lens through which the operations of the natural world could be viewed, but it was nevertheless imagined to hold a subsidiary status in the cosmic order: "There would be no permanent confusion of thought introduced if these laws should be found not to hold, or to hold in a different way, in the unseen universe. Nor can we regard the Dissipation as equally fundamental with that of the Conservation of Energy."[12] The second law might be an inescapable part of the material world, but the material world *itself* was not inescapable.

If, as the economist Nicholas Georgescu-Roegen argues, "from the epistemological viewpoint, the Entropy Law may be regarded as the greatest transformation ever suffered by physics," the implications of that transformation were often evaded, disguised, or ignored altogether, sometimes even in works that were ostensibly engaged with explaining it.[13] Economic historian Philip Mirowski writes: "the point we should focus upon is that the rise of thermodynamics drastically revised the meaning of energy and its conservation; and all the while various physicists were trying their hardest to deny anything fundamental had changed."[14] What I want to stress here is that while the equivocations about waste in the writings of Thomson and his circle were partly motivated by theological commitments, they had important ecological implications. The second law of thermodynamics, at least as it was initially articulated, actually encoded two pictures of "nature" simultaneously. Nature in its various material forms was profoundly wasteful and profligate. Nature as an ideal record-keeper, however – as a system of accounts embodied in the diligent "housekeeper" discussed in the previous chapter – was still a perfectly orderly, legible, and divinely economical system. These two pictures helped structure the thermodynamic narrative of energy by providing representational boundaries. Depending on the argument being made, the natural world could either be depicted as a reservoir of fuel leaking out everywhere, or as an abstract bookkeeping system tracking every drop. The philosopher Michel Serres has noted that many philosophers and scientists who employed thermodynamic models were nevertheless "averse" to the second law: "Almost all of them attempted to find some failing with it: they wished, I believe, that the motor would never stop."[15] This, then, is the paradoxical situation: in articulating a cosmology that had, at its very foundations, a conception of how the machine must "stop," Victorian thermodynamics nevertheless attempted to construct a social and theological discourse congenial to the expansion and development of industrial motive power. In the following sections, I want to discuss how the death of the sun can be seen as a key expression of these representational constraints and how the emphasis placed upon remote, cosmic concerns obscured crucial ecological issues at stake in Victorian energy consumption.

Thermodynamic narratives

The death of the sun is, obviously enough, a grand narrative of decline: a story about the cosmos moving from abundance to exhaustion. The arc of this story was, of course, shaped entirely by the inevitable endpoint and the imagery used to describe it. Thomson and Tait conjured an arresting future vision of the universe gone "uniformly hot – an undistinguishable mixture of all that is now definite and separate – chaos and darkness."[16] But the sun's death was also explicitly fashioned into human-scale narratives as well, through frequent recourse to anthropomorphic conceits in popular thermodynamic works by Tait, Stewart, Norman Lockyer, and others. Stewart and Lockyer open an essay on thermodynamics by noting that scientific concepts can be embodied in fictions if done carefully and "truthfully":

> Each branch of the tree of knowledge bears its own precious fruit, and yet there is a unity in this variety – a community of type that prevails throughout. Nor is this resemblance a merely fanciful one, or one which the mind conjures up for its own amusement. While it has produced a very plentiful crop of analogies, allegories, parables and proverbs, not always of the best kind, yet parables and proverbs are or ought to be not fictions but truths.[17]

The writers declare the commensurability of scientific truth and narrative – an important point for believing Christians who want to insist there is no discrepancy between "proverbs and parables" and the new pictures of the natural world being drawn by science. Here, they rule some fictions out and others in: amid the many narratives mentioned, some will prove to be "of the best kind" by being "truths." In other places, Stewart even borrows techniques from serial fiction. At the end of the first installment of his essay "What is Energy?," he describes the energy of a stone shot upwards that, on its way down, comes to rest on a house:

> Here, then, it remains at rest, without the slightest tendency to motion of any kind, and we are led to ask what has become of the energy with which it began its flight? Has this energy disappeared from the universe without leaving behind it any equivalent? Is it lost for ever, and utterly wasted? But the answer to this question must be reserved for another article.[18]

It's not exactly *The Woman in White*, but we can see in this "cliffhanger" that the tracing of cause-and-effect relations and the transformation of action to consequence under the auspices of the laws of energy aligned thermodynamic writing with certain staples of conventional narrative organization.

Perhaps the most revealing examples of thermodynamic storytelling occur in Stewart's enormously popular work, *The Conservation of Energy*. In his discussion of the second law of thermodynamics and the cosmic "death" it portended, Stewart writes that the sun is like "a man whose expenditure exceeds his income. He is living upon his capital, and is destined to share the fate of all who act in a similar manner."[19] This kind of anthropomorphization of the sun was common in the period, as Beer argues. Richard Proctor describes the sun's "companions" and "brother suns,"[20] and Max Müller vividly describes it as a "majestic ruler, this departing friend or dying hero."[21] Stewart's description engages this anthropomorphic tradition, but casts the sun not as brother, friend, or hero, but as unregenerate spendthrift, an antagonist. Stewart situates us by means of a familiar moral narrative, complete with a recognizable character – the man who lives beyond his means – and the generic conventions that insist such a person receive his due punishment. Stewart's readers might well think of Richard Carstone or Auguste Melmotte, or any number of fictional profligates or scoundrels who spend recklessly and suffer the consequences. But the key here is that nature itself is cast in this role, playing the prodigal "sun" descending into headlong bankruptcy. Such moral storytelling not only frames nature as culpable for its lavish ways, it resizes the issue of cosmic disintegration to signify on a human scale.

Thus while the death of the sun was sometimes framed as a distant cosmic inevitability, it was at other times given more immediate, and distinctly human, narrative horizons. If this were merely a heuristic device, used to make a remote event comprehensible to a lay reader, it might not merit much attention. But a few pages later, Stewart, curiously, maintains these foreshortened temporal dimensions, and turns the dissipation of the universe's energy into a kind of call to action: "We have been content very much to remain spectators of the contest, apparently forgetful that we are at all concerned in the issue. But the conflict is not one which admits of on-lookers, – it is a universal conflict in which we must all take our share."[22] What makes this passage so odd is that the "contest" and "conflict" are left ambiguous. As Greg Myers notes, readers "may have wondered what exactly they were supposed to do about the continuing dissipation of the energy of the solar system."[23] This is key, for it highlights the unstable way in which thermodynamics simultaneously – and not always coherently – used the concept of energy as an intermediary connecting distant, inescapable cosmic events and duties incumbent upon humans on earth. Stewart, along with Thomson, Tait, and Lockyer, was attempting to fashion a moral cosmology out of very unlikely materials: entropy, waste, and universal death.

If the foreshortening of time in the heat-death imagery tended to collapse distinctions between cosmic and terrestrial timescales, it also helped bring the second law of thermodynamics into seeming alignment with certain religious assumptions that informed the work of many prominent Victorian thermodynamic scientists. The image of an expiring sun resonated with many of them because it seemed like confirmation of the apocalyptic visions of scripture. Wise and Smith have shown that Thomson's work on energy dissipation was underwritten by his belief in biblical prophecy, specifically Isaiah 51.6: "Lift up your eyes to the heavens, and look upon the earth beneath: for the heavens shall vanish away like smoke, and the earth shall wax old like a garment."[24] The physical world is transitory, the spiritual world permanent. As Myers notes, "Thomson recalls the Old Testament vision of decline in order to preserve a conservative, natural theological sense of the power of the Creator over nature."[25] Although Thomson and Stewart would claim, as a matter of practical scientific calculation, that the sun had millions of years of energy remaining, they also used its death as a symbol of a theo- and anthropocentric nature, compatible with a morally structured universe where divine judgment was still rendered within the bounds of human time. Even the preferred term for energy loss – "dissipation" – came loaded with moral connotations. Thus while thermodynamics may have participated, as Beer has argued, in the more general Victorian scientific trend of widening temporal vistas and decentering humanity's place in the cosmos, its imagery, its terminology, and its narrative practices simultaneously pulled in the opposite direction. Bruce Clarke argues that, despite the emphasis on temporal irreversibility and cosmic timescales, "the linearity of thermodynamic time came forward precisely as mythic rather than historical time … Hypothetical thermodynamic causality was troped as a universal and seemingly imminent mythic fate."[26] In this way, thermodynamics helped to frame energy dissipation as a signifier within a human-scaled and moralized cosmic drama. If, as we have seen, the city's aggregated energy waste both threatened to reduce individual narratives into mere vectors of expenditure, and undermined the plausibility of certain familiar large-scale historical narratives, the sun's "heat death" was fashioned in such a way as to preserve the signifying power of the individual moral story, while simultaneously resonating with a grand religious narrative about the transience and even, perhaps, disposability of the material world.

Thus despite its seemingly radical departure from models of natural stability and economy, the second law of thermodynamics was nevertheless incorporated into a system of signification, a divine allegory written in the vocabulary of work and waste that produced a meaningful anthropocentric narrative. In the 1860s, thermodynamic research took on an additional anti-materialist cast in the role it played in the debate over Darwin's theory of evolution by natural selection. Thomson and his cohort used the first and second laws to calculate the duration of the sun's energy supply, and found (erroneously) that it had simply not been burning long enough for evolution to have occurred in the extremely slow, gradualist fashion Darwin had described. The calculations disturbed Darwin greatly, who believed they represented "one of the greatest objections yet advanced" to the evolutionary hypothesis.[27] The heat death of the sun, then, was conscripted into the anti-Darwinian camp as a powerful counter-narrative to the troubling, anti-teleological theory of natural selection. Where Darwin makes it clear that he is interested in the origin of species, *not* the origins of life, Thomson's heat-death narrative permits and even encourages metaphysical speculations about absolute beginnings. If Darwinian storytelling privileged the material over the abstract, the particular over the archetypal, the open-ended network over the closed system, the continuity and affiliations of organic life over the unique centrality of human experience, thermodynamic storytelling placed its emphasis on bounded temporality and linearity; on an anthropocentric, teleological cosmic order; and on a Providentially overseen natural economy. Where Darwin seems to delight in the textured irreducibility of material nature, Thomson works to convert the natural world into an abstract theater of waste.

Indeed, the devaluing of the material world was in some ways a key component of the early stages of the thermodynamic research program. The laws of energy were strict and inviolable: they helped paint a picture of a universe where every movement was governed by a most precise, energetic bookkeeping. As such, there was a real concern that thermodynamics could support a thoroughgoing, deterministic materialism.[28] This conclusion was something Thomson, Stewart, Tait, James Clerk Maxwell, and other members of this first generation of thermodynamic scientists wanted to avoid at all costs; they insisted instead upon the power of the mind and the spirit to remain distinct from, or transcend, or work somehow differently within, the physical laws that energy obeyed. Just as Thomson suggested the divine transformation of seemingly wasted energy, just as Stewart and Tait emphasized the "unseen universe" that stood beyond what was merely "seen," these writers also suggested that the world of thought represented another method of transcending the strictly material, where the immaterial world could supersede the strict parameters set down by the laws of energy.

This was a hazard of such an ontologically ambiguous concept as energy. In its disembodied physicality, or "dematerialized materialism" as Gaston Bachelard puts it, energy could seem like a mediator between the realms of mind, spirit, and matter.[29] Near the end of a popular article on solar energy, Stewart and Lockyer discuss the existence of "a machine of infinite delicacy of construction" that would transmit great amounts of energy through the impelling power of a very tiny – indeed, almost non-existent – energetic prompt. They write:

> We may, for instance, imagine an electric arrangement so delicate that by an amount of directive energy less than any assignable quantity a current may be made to start suddenly, cross the Atlantic, and (as far as physical results are concerned) explode a magazine on the other side. Indeed, the forces of nature appear to be such that an infinite delicacy of construction is not inconceivable.[30]

Here, technology and human will become almost coterminous, as the explosion on the other side of the globe arises at the behest of the merest flicker of desire (a frightening notion that became all too real in the following century). But there is scant attention paid to the wider networks in which this story must be embedded. The enormous energetic outlay involved in building and maintaining such a transatlantic apparatus, as well as the resources used to make the explosive charge, are left untallied. We are only asked to compare a "directive energy less than any assignable quantity" with the profound amounts of energy activated. In this way, Stewart and Lockyer are implicitly arguing for the staggering power of the human mind in a world otherwise tightly restricted by thermodynamic laws. This has a theological component: on one level, they are clearly positioning themselves against the deterministic implications of the laws of energy. They write: "A living being is not only a machine capable of producing motion, but of producing it discontinuously, and in a great variety of ways which cannot be calculated upon except to a very limited extent."[31] But the writers also verge on arguing for the power of the technological imagination to overcome entirely the limits of the material world:

> [T]he transcendent power of steam as a motive agent has, let us imagine, been grasped by the human mind. Presently the scene widens, and as we proceed, a solitary engine is seen to be performing, and in a laborious way converting heat into work; we proceed further and further until the

prospect expands into a scene of glorious triumph, and the imperceptible streamlet of thought that rose so obscurely has swelled into a mighty river, on which all the projects of humanity are embarked.[32]

This passage stages a complicated braiding of mental and material levels: the human mind has the power to conceive of the steam engine, which then itself becomes a metaphor for the power of the mind, which then allows the writers to apotheosize the act of thinking *itself* into a kind of irresistible motive power.[33] As we have seen, this kind of thinking was, and continues to be, a continual source of mystification about energy: it lends credence to the idea that resource scarcity is not a problem because human ingenuity will always figure out how to produce greater and greater energetic effects from smaller and smaller energetic outlays. This is, in fact, nothing more than an article of faith, although one that is embedded very deeply in the Victorian (and modern) imagination.

We might once again draw a useful contrast between the thermodynamic research project as spearheaded by Thomson, and the research into evolutionary biology as articulated during this period by Darwin. For Darwin, the metaphor of the "laws" of nature was deeply problematic precisely because it came loaded with theological baggage. To imagine the universe functioning according to "laws" seemed to reinscribe a model of divine governance and intentionality.[34] George Levine argues that this metaphor troubled Darwin even if it also allowed him, at times, to soften some of the more radical implications of his chance-driven theory of natural selection. He writes: "Darwin's predicament was aggravated by the irony that scientists' recognition of an ideally organized and thus humanly intelligible world gave support to the view that intelligence itself was exempt from the rules that governed inorganic nature. It was itself the governor."[35] In contrast, Thomson, Stewart, Maxwell, and other physicists were less concerned about the metaphorical status of their own "laws" – the first and second laws of thermodynamics; indeed, the fact that the term "law" imported theological meaning was entirely congenial to their outlook, which sought congruence between science and scripture. But more importantly for our purposes, there was thus inscribed in thermodynamic research precisely the implication Darwin had sought to avoid: the idea that mind was somehow more than material, and thus, to use Levine's term, "exempt" from natural processes.

This sense of exemption, I would add, was not just held by those who explicitly promoted a theological-cum-scientific cosmology. Even a non-theist like Huxley argued that the human mind had a unique, superintending role to play in the universe of energy relations: "Fragile reed as he may be, man, as Pascal says, is a thinking reed: there lies within him a fund of energy, operating intelligently and so far akin to that which pervades the universe, that it is competent to influence and modify the cosmic process. In virtue of his intelligence, the dwarf bends the Titan to his will."[36] Human intelligence is its own "fund" of energy, a supply that is simultaneously continuous with the other forms of energy in the cosmos, and independent from them. The word "energy" lets Huxley occupy a materialist position with regard to human life, while still reserving a special, cosmically significant place for human intelligence. Such a sense of exemption has profound ecological consequences for the understanding of energy, because it suggests there is a way for human ingenuity – specifically technological ingenuity – to escape from natural limits. In Chapter 6, we will see how Robert Louis Stevenson uses this sense of exemption to structure Jekyll's downfall in *Dr. Jekyll and Mr. Hyde.*

The cosmic theological narratives fashioned through the idea of "heat death" thus did more than aggrandize the divine at the expense of the natural. They also helped stake a claim for techno-scientific development as a moral good within a universe of inevitable energy waste. Wise and Smith write: "decay opened up new vistas for natural theology. If mechanical laws conserving the eternal oscillations of a balance had suggested the goodness of God's rationality, a slow decay from a beginning to an ending suggested the goodness of moral choice."[37] This, indeed, is what is at stake when Stewart issues his call to action in the "universal conflict." It was not enough to wait for the ultimate "transformation" of nature's wasted energy; instead something needed to be done while some still remained usable. Wise argues:

> It is a mistake to imagine the second law as having to do only with dissipation. In the interpretation of its founders in Britain, it was just as much about the conditions for the progress of civilization and the moral duty of man to maximize the utility of the productive forces available in nature. Left to themselves, these forces would necessarily dissipate, to no purpose ... The historical progress of civilization, with more urgency now than ever, depended on directing this decline into productive work.[38]

Wise encodes here in his own imagery the pervasive sense that wasting solar energy would somehow be felt on earth, within the bounds of human history. He also suggests why the popular image of Thomson and his circle as apostles of gloom and disintegration misses an important component of their agenda. The death of the sun was an awe-inspiring vision of grim cosmic inevitability, but it was also meant as a moral justification for the expansion of energy-intensive practices in the face of a down-running world. In the work of the Victorian thermodynamic scientists, we are continually reminded of the way an unruly universe of energy can be brought to heel through the imposition of human intelligence. Stewart and Lockyer, drawing on the same imagery we saw Tyndall using in the previous chapter, write:

> There are several varieties of energy in the universe, and, Proteus-like, it is always changing its form. Had it not been for this habit we should have understood it long since, but it was only when its endeavours to escape from the grasp of the experimentalist were of no avail, that it ceased its struggles and told us the truth.[39]

Industrial technologies developed by "experimentalist" engineers like Thomson, Joule, and Carnot are the window into the "truth," and the means of imposing order. In analogous fashion, the frequent recourse to social metaphors in thermodynamic writing to describe energy suggests a similar investment in the human control and regulation of energy. "Energy in the social world is well understood," Stewart and Lockyer write, painting a picture of social stability and comprehensibility that could bring the seemingly less understood (and less organized) energy of nature into line.[40] Such social-physical analogies not only naturalize a certain picture of current social relations, as Myers has argued, they also locate in those social relations a kind of order that nature, left to its own devices, would mindlessly degrade. Indeed, implied in Stewart's vision of the sun as a profligate spender is an idea of a social world that is stable and morally legible, where reckless spendthrifts ultimately meet their fate.

The thermodynamic cosmology, then, that moralized human energy use through reference to the inevitable waste of nature, seems built upon a rather straightforward narrative, where the unsustainable natural energy system meets a deserved end in the form of a dead sun. And yet, because this cosmology is actually working with two vastly different, almost incommensurable temporalities – the cosmic and the human – it requires a continual manipulation of timescales that works against the "realist" narrative premised on stability, causation, and temporal legibility.[41] At some moments, as we have seen, cosmic events were reduced to thinkable narrative parameters, bringing the loss of solar energy within human bounds. At other moments, however, the vastness of the temporal horizons, and the sheer immensity of remaining energy reserves, were emphasized. At one point in *The Unseen Universe*, for example, Stewart and Tait seek to impress upon their readers a sense of the orders of magnitude under discussion: "the present potential energy of the solar system is so enormous, approaching in fact possibly to what in our helplessness we call infinite, that it may supply for absolutely incalculable future ages what is required for the physical existence of life."[42] This emphasis on the infinitude of energy supplies sits somewhat uneasily with the way the heat death of the sun is depicted elsewhere, as an urgent concern. It is thanks to energy's ability to mediate, and thus collapse, distinctions between the scalar dimensions of various systems, that the writers can move without explanation between local and cosmic visions of expenditure.[43]

The key to this tension between different timescales resides in the emphasis of human "helplessness" before the "infinite," since it evokes an almost religious feeling about the awesome power and plentitude of the universe's energy. This is precisely what Victorian thermodynamics, as a discourse both born out of applied engineering and freighted with cosmic religious significance, was interested in calibrating: what about energy use could be "helped," and what about it leads us to contemplate our own "helplessness." Energy dissipation was natural, inevitable, and the heat death of the sun stood as a terrifying symbol of a fore-ordained fate at the hands of the iron laws of thermodynamics. But along with this came a sense of the grand vistas of power awaiting those efficient and hardworking enough to understand those laws, and to use them to turn nature's wasted energy to advantage. Victorian thermodynamics could be a pretty grim discourse – there is some truth in this common impression – but it also contained a certain spirit of triumphalism, a sense that the secrets of a universe of energy had been unlocked, and that this universe was now waiting to be tapped. The devaluing of nature that occurred through the privileging of the immaterial over the material has its counterpart in a drive to view it as a massive reservoir available through the intercession of technology for human applications.

So the energy supply is finite, and the supply is infinite; the time is short, but the time is incalculably long; there is room for us to intervene, the conditions are absolutely fixed and beyond our capacity to change them. These are not so much a bundle of contradictions as a prism of perspectives, made possible by a continual shift of time signatures, and the selective application of deeply anthropomorphic metaphors to the realm of the non-human. Moving in and out of orders of infinitude, between straightforward caricatures of solar energy and awe-inspiring vistas of the fathomless universal reservoir, thermodynamic discourse worked to calibrate what was *thinkable* about energy. The thermodynamic narrative was a cosmic story of unstoppable decline and dissipation embodied by the death of the sun; it was a moral narrative of the free, purposive energy use that defined the human realm; and it was a guide to the continued development of industrial technology. Through these different visions of energy and energy dissipation, an unstable point of view emerges, but it is one that treats large-scale, systemic conditions as fixed and unchangeable, while regarding action within the bounds of that system a matter of urgent moral duty. In structuring what was thinkable and what was not thinkable about the uses and purposes of energy, Stewart, Thomson, and this first generation of thermodynamic scientists were working to create a cosmology of evangelical capitalism.[44]

The heat death of the sun, then, helped construct a discourse and a cosmology that were ecologically problematic. We can see all of the issues we've been discussing encapsulated in a remark by Stewart: "Universally diffused heat forms what we may call the great waste-heap of the universe and this is growing larger year by year. At present it does not sensibly obtrude itself, but who knows that the time may not arrive when we shall be practically conscious of its growing bigness."[45] Where Helmholtz, in his discussion of the death of the sun, would describe the universe as an "infinite ocean of time," and claim that, therefore, "we have nothing to fear" from predictions of stellar collapse, Stewart's emphasis on an energy loss felt "year by year" inflects the question with urgency.[46] But also notice the arresting metaphor he employs. By using a trope like "the great waste-heap," Stewart doesn't merely shrink the scale down to thinkable parameters, he attempts to transfer the negative, ecologically disastrous properties of industry onto nature. Massive energy loss, heaps of waste and debris, universally degraded landscapes: these things *just happen*, they are part of the sadly inescapable order of nature. The industrial world can thus be cleansed and refashioned as the agent of efficiency and organization. In this view, industry appeared to be the sole means of putting a universe running to waste to some use, rather than what it was: the *cause* of "waste-heaps" and widespread environmental degradation.

This truly is a strange state of affairs. While *The Conservation of Energy* may shadow forth the figures and plots of realist narrative, as well as the picture of the stable and orderly social world from which such narratives arise, the book's sudden, unexplained collapses of time, its dramatic warps and bends of scale, would seem to owe something more to Lewis Carroll than to Anthony Trollope. The thermodynamic cosmology that emerges around and through these stories of a dying sun presents a startlingly through-the-looking-glass picture of the relationship between nature and industry. Although thermodynamics arose from the investigation of the inefficiencies in industrial technology, although it helped to consolidate the conception of energy as a limited resource, although it described in scientific terms how the burning of fossil fuels was an irreversible process, it was nevertheless used to paint a picture of *industry* as the answer to wastefulness, and *nature* as a dangerously unsustainable system. Amazingly, the engine, the very technology whose flaws were hypostasized into a model for the wasting universe, was imagined to be the means of efficiently and heroically organizing human civilization. But such a strange move could only be realized by means of these highly suspect narrative practices.

Thermodynamics and fossil-fuel resources

We might return, then, to the death of the sun, and to the peculiar forms of narrative compression Stewart employed to make energy waste seem an urgent problem. It is precisely that kind of compression – the dramatic concentration of millions of years of solar energy into an expenditure that can be measured within the "year by year" bounds of human history – that is *embodied* in the energy of coal deposits. As George Hodgins noted in 1915, in burning coal, "what took years upon years to produce may be reclaimed in an hour as radiant heat."[47] If we imagine, then, that the phenomenon of fossil-fuel energy use informed – indeed, even *underwrote* – the compressed narrative temporalities we find in the work of Stewart and his cohort, we might imagine the death of the sun signifying something very different from what the thermodynamic scientists emphasized. Although the dying sun may have been fashioned as the ultimate embodiment of a wasteful nature, it had perhaps its peculiar power as a focus for Victorian "dreads," in its implicit suggestions of a rapidly self-expending industrial order, and the degraded environments such an order produced. Indeed, a trope like Stewart's "great waste-heap," and his suggestion that the running-down of the universe is almost palpable, were effective rhetorical tools *precisely because* readers had experience with such phenomena, and perhaps could and did feel the remnants of spent energy – in the form of industrial air pollution, slag heaps, coal dust, river effluents – "sensibly obtruding" upon their everyday experience. The heat death of the sun, as Stewart himself acknowledges elsewhere, was still some millions of years off, making it extremely unlikely that "we" are going to have any first-hand experience of the "growing bigness" of energy loss, unless it is in the form of the actual waste heaps and other noxious by-products currently pressing upon the environment. In other words, although the passage does not seem intended to be taken this way, it almost cannot help but connect the heat death of the sun with contemporary environmental conditions. Despite its commitments, implicit and explicit, to industrial development, thermodynamic writing contained within it the seeds of an ecologically conscious discourse about resource waste and unsustainable *human* energy practices. As Clarke notes: "An apocalyptic concept of heat death [was] the ur-form of 'energy crisis.'"[48] Even if thermodynamic apocalypticism cast temporal irreversibility in mythic, as opposed to historical, terms, it was also broadly expressing the sense of "crisis" that would inform an ecologically minded approach to human energy consumption.

In other words, the anthropomorphism so often used to describe the death of the sun cuts both ways. On the one hand, it plainly suggests an anthropo- and theocentric moral universe in all the ways I've described. On the other hand, however, it also suggests a potent hyperbole for the profound extension and imposition of human codes and structures of meaning into all corners of the cosmos. If the "Anthropocene" is the epoch in which humans become, in Crutzen's terms, an "environmental force," an actor in realms (the geological, the meteorological) hitherto shaped only by decidedly non-human agencies, then the death of the sun carries with it the stirrings of an awareness that this new epoch has begun.

As Beer argues, the heat-death narrative reached the heights of popular attention in the 1860s, following the publication of Thomson's "On the Age of the Sun's Heat" in 1862. This interest was fed by a number of phenomena: the growing acknowledgment of the centrality of thermodynamics, the wider circulation of thermodynamic concepts in the popular press, and the role Thomson's predictions played in evolutionary debates. But if we can also see in the "heat death" of the sun a powerful narrative of "unsustainable" development – explicitly the unsustainable direction of natural systems and, implicitly or unconsciously, perhaps, the unsustainable direction of industrial practices – then we might also frame the interest in the second law of thermodynamics as part of a wider, ecologically anxious discourse about resource exhaustion and environmental damage. It is no accident that the heat-death narrative and concerns about the universe's future energy supplies were becoming a part of the popular imaginary at the very same moment that "the coal question" was provoking a national debate about the future of England's own resources. Indeed, the coal question and the heat death of the sun both involve narratives of exhaustion based in imbalanced energy budgets, the irreversibility and inevitability

of energy loss, the future availability of fuel supplies, and the dire consequences in store. In its popular metaphorical elaborations, thermodynamics also drew upon the imagery of industrial machinery to describe the
operations of the universe. "The visible universe may with perfect truth
be compared to a vast heat-engine," Stewart and Tait write, describing the
sun as the "furnace" of the solar system.[49] As we have seen, productivism
connected sunlight and coal supplies, frequently imagining the latter as
the stored and buried embodiment of the former. But, as Ted Underwood
has shown, the comparison worked in the other direction as well: the sun
was often framed in distinctly mechanical and industrial terms. Reframing
the traditional opposition, he writes that, in many nineteenth-century
works, "pastoral sunlight is largely a reflection of industrial fire."[50] While
some thermodynamic writing collapsed the industrial and the cosmic in
the service of an apocalyptic, dematerialized cosmology, we can read in the
descriptions of down-running machines and furnaces running out of fuel
an expression of the kinds of anxieties about natural resource exhaustion
that Jevons and others were describing. Indeed, when Stewart and Tait
write that "heat is par excellence the communist of our universe, and it
will no doubt ultimately bring the present system to an end," the distinction between metaphorical levels, between the micro- and macrocosms,
threatens to give way.[51] As Myers notes, the term "present system" conflates
the entire cosmos with the industrial-capitalist order.[52]

The two phenomena were explicitly connected in the public imagination. In an article on "Sensationalism in Science" published in *Belgravia*
in 1868, R. H. Patterson writes:

> Besides predicting a speedy exhaustion of our coal-fields, and picturing a
> state of matters which must infallibly occasion the flight of half our popula-
> tion, and leave the other half dependent on our woods for fuel … Science,
> as represented by its present hierarchs, startles us with the prospect of a far
> wider calamity. The sun itself, they say, will soon be used up.[53]

Although Patterson had a highly idiosyncratic idea of how energy works,
and his object here, ultimately, is to mock these two exhaustion narratives
as "sensationalistic," he also suggests the deep imaginative connections
between them as nested calamities. The fleeing, energy-scavenging population, attempting to cope with a national fuel scarcity, will, "Science"
tells us, "soon" find itself confronted with the very same problem on the
cosmic level. Patterson is himself being sensationalistic in his description,
but clearly the collapse of temporal scales has made itself felt in the public
perception of heat death.[54]

In a more rigorous vein, an anonymous writer in *The Times* of London in 1866 discusses the coal question as part of the larger narrative of exhaustion framed by energy science:

> We may dislike to contemplate these gloomy consequences [the depletion of coal supplies] yet come they will, as surely as sunrise tomorrow … Some philosophers say that our whole solar system, like a clock wound up, is running down apace, and will one day be jumbled into one lightless, lifeless, inert, chaotic mass. If this be so, we have no reason to grumble at the prospect of our own decline, which it is a consolation to this generation to know is not likely to happen in their time. But how long will our coal last? That is the question.[55]

The winding-down clock is a metaphor that unites the two discourses, appearing in both Thomson and Tait's descriptions of solar decay ("as surely as the weights of a clock run down to their lowest position, from which they can never rise again, unless fresh energy is communicated to them from some source not yet exhausted, so surely must planet after planet creep in, age by age, toward the sun"[56]), and Jevons's imagery of waning coal supplies ("Coal has all the characteristics which entitle it to be considered the best natural source of motive power. It is like a spring, wound up during geological ages for us to let down."[57]). This shared image is *itself* a way of compressing time, joining both coal question and heat death, despite the vast difference in scales, in a figure that places both within the temporal horizons of ordinary experience. But where thermodynamics employed such compression to emphasize natural wastefulness, the writer in *The Times* does so to emphasize the wastefulness of industry and the urgent need to address the unsustainable human practices that will result in ruin. Instead of pinning the imagery of urban decay and disintegration on nature, *à la* Stewart, he uses the heat-death imagery of chaos and lifelessness (recalling Thomson's warnings of "chaos and darkness") to intensify the picture of an impending, human-wrought. ecological catastrophe: "our soot-begrimed Manchesters and Birminghams shall have crumbled into ruins and the plough shall pass over their sites."[58]

We might also note that the 1860s saw the publication of another key document in the literature of the "Anthropocene." In 1864, the American conservationist George Perkins Marsh published *Man and Nature*, the first major work to argue for the shaping influence of human activity on geomorphology. "We are even now," he writes, "breaking up the floor and wainscoting and doors and window frames of our dwelling, for fuel to warm our bodies and seethe our pottage.[59] For Marsh, the "dwelling" at risk was not simply the structure of modern civilization established on energy-intensive practices, but the earth itself. If, for Thomson, the cooling of the sun would one day render the earth "unfit for the habitation of man," Marsh identified the ways in which man was doing that to his own habitation: "the earth is fast becoming an unfit home for its noblest inhabitant, and another era of equal human improvidence ... would reduce it to such a condition of impoverished productiveness, of shattered surface, of climatic excess, as to threaten the depravation, barbarism, and perhaps even extinction of the species."[60] The imagery is similar, and both writers describe the dynamics of self-consuming energetic phenomena. But Marsh brings that imagery squarely into the domain of the human, to describe the far-reaching ecological impact of human activity upon the entire biosphere.

The heat death of the sun was thus an unstable ecological signifier. Initially imagined as the centerpiece of a cosmology dedicated to the continued expansion of industry and the harvesting of natural resources, it came to look more and more like the opposite: a powerful "green" trope that could vividly, if hyperbolically, represent the sheer scale of environmental damage being produced through human energy use. The entire cosmos, it seemed, was being remade by industry. If the relentless anthropomorphism with which the heat death of the sun was often depicted ostensibly served to frame cosmic processes within a coherent moral narrative, it also suggested the way in which the human had become a profound shaping force upon large-scale environments. If Thomson, Stewart, and the other leading thermodynamic scientists did not make explicit the connection between thermodynamic concerns and urban ecology, others did. Images of the dying, energyless sun occur almost exclusively in the skies above urban worlds: in everything from *In Memoriam* to *Bleak House* to *The City of Dreadful Night* to *The Storm Cloud of the Nineteenth Century* to *The Time Machine*. Poets, novelists, and critics offer a unique – if sometimes tentative or equivocal – window into the growing consciousness of energy loss and widespread environmental damage. In the next chapter, I want to consider this trope as it appears in the opening of Dickens's *Bleak House*. In that novel we see the roots of a discourse about unsustainable energy use and waste that, by connecting local behavior with unplanned, widespread effects, helped imagine how collective human actions might have "universal" consequences. This too involves a manipulation of time signatures – the sun, obviously enough, is not affected one way or another by anything humans do – but where thermodynamic writers like Tait and Stewart tend not to acknowledge their sudden shifts in scale, or what is at stake in the metaphors they employ, Dickens's repurposing of this trope in the service of what we might think of as proto-environmentalist concerns was accompanied by an awareness of new epistemological pressures.

PART II

Unsustainable fictions

CHAPTER 3

Energy systems and narrative systems in Charles Dickens's Bleak House

Over the long history of Dickens's criticism, everyone from G. K. Chesterton to J. Hillis Miller to Alex Woloch has used the word "energy" to describe the peculiar quality of his fictions.[1] It has no doubt become such a common critical metaphor because of how capacious it is. "Energy" seems to capture so much that is distinctive about Dickens: his industrious rise from the lower-middle classes; his furiously active professional schedule; his great imaginative generativity; his exuberant and teeming fictional worlds; and, of course, his great subject – life in the world's first energy-intensive economy. On the level of character, "energy" brings together two crucial understandings of the Dickensian personality. Up close, it captures the way his characters seem animated by an idiosyncratic life-force all their own; from a distance, it describes how all these idiosyncratic lights form a larger network of relationships – what W. J. Harvey calls the "complex field of force" of his fictions.[2] The distinct and separate existences of Dickens's characters – the "solitariness" that V. S. Pritchett called their "distinguishing quality" – are in fact bound together by invisible currents of influences and effects.[3] Of course, it is not only people who are unusually animated in Dickens's novels, but trees, hats, glasses, door knockers, buildings, paintings, tables, shoes. This "fanciful mingling of the animate and inanimate" implies that, as E. D. H. Johnson puts it, "a reciprocal relationship exists between beings and their surroundings."[4] In short, the word energy suggests what we might loosely call an "ecological" vision, a sense that character, event, and environment are mutually shaping, reciprocally expressive, and systematically interconnected.

Of course, we can't talk about the energy of Dickens's worlds without talking about the energy of his language – its abundance, its dynamism, the way it possesses both force and amplitude. Above all else, perhaps, Dickens's language is metamorphic – it traffics in transfiguring comparisons, in elaborate counter-factuals, in multi-layered puns. It creates a world of ubiquitous transformation, where fires tick like clocks, houses stare each other into stone, and the entire city rings like a "vast glass, vibrating."[5] Not only does Dickens's style grant even the most minor personages and inert things their own kind of incandescence, it suggests a shared existence within a thick and ubiquitous medium: that medium is both the material environment within which everything dwells, and the writing that shapes, and enlivens, and binds that environment.

As I've discussed in the previous two chapters, thermodynamic discourse also described the interconnections between seemingly disparate phenomena, and the transformations that bound the animal and the mechanical, the organic and inorganic, nature and industry, into one complex system of force relations. The thermodynamic imaginary, like the Dickensian, is motion-filled and metamorphic. And because thermodynamics was emerging as both a scientific and a popular discourse in the middle decades of the nineteenth century, the very vocabulary that we so often reach for to describe Dickens's novels was itself coming into being while he was writing them. *Bleak House* (1853) has been acknowledged by a number of important critical voices – J. Hillis Miller, Ann Wilkinson, and Barri Gold – to be deeply concerned with the thematics and atmospherics of energy and entropy.[6] The novel's imaginative landscape is filled with descriptions of energetic processes – dying lights; guttering candles; waning embers; "unsteady fire[s]"; and "misdirected energy" of all shapes and varieties, including, of course, "spontaneous combustion."[7] This pattern of imagery comes to seem like a systemic issue, rather than merely a generic convention, because the operations of the Court of Chancery soon teach us to read the disparate localities and characters we encounter as expressions of a single, interconnected whole. Moreover, its first installment, with the famous depiction of "the death of the sun," emerged only one month before William Thomson published his description of solar heat death, "On a Universal Tendency in Nature to the Dissipation of Mechanical Energy." Not only would these texts come to stand as two of the most powerful visions of solar collapse penned in the nineteenth century, they both, in different ways, suggested a relationship between distant cosmic events and the earthbound workings of an emergent industrial order. Although Dickens could have had no knowledge of Thomson's lecture while he was writing *Bleak House*, the shared imagery speaks to a set of ideas shared by scientist and novelist alike. The use and waste of resources, the relationship between individual units and system-wide conditions, the conceptual isomorphism between capital and energy, the appropriation of the natural world through the use of industrial technology – all of these issues were of deep interest to Dickens and his thermodynamic contemporaries alike. As Kuhn, Mirowski, and Underwood have demonstrated, the energy concept traces its roots to both Romantic discourse and metaphorical complexes borrowed from nineteenth-century political economy; the entropy concept, meanwhile, as we have argued, was adumbrated in discussions of urban sanitary reform, and in representations of city systems as machines that consumed energy resources in an unsustainable fashion. In other words, even if he wasn't poring over engineering diagrams in his spare time, Dickens had plenty of access to the kind of discourses that formed the conceptual armature of the thermodynamic research project.

Bleak House, then, might be usefully understood as a thermodynamic text. But if, to understand it this way, we must necessarily expand the definition of what counts as "thermodynamic," we must also look at what the novel does differently, how its own commitments, interests, and generic requirements provide us with a representation of energy that both echoes and challenges the way it was represented in Victorian scientific discourse. If we accept the premise that Thomson and Dickens share common interests, that both are preoccupied with work, waste, efficiency, and systematicity as those things that helped define the shape of an emergent industrial culture, we should also attend to the differences in the ways in which those various preoccupations are staged. In what follows, I want to consider this shared and contested ground in order to consider how *Bleak House* functions as an *alternative thermodynamic narrative*, one that puts the environment and the appropriation of nature at the center of the representation of energy forms.

Resources and costs

Above all else, perhaps, Dickens represents the Court of Chancery as a resource-intensive system. It exacts a toll in time and money, of course, but it also exacts a toll in material things: ink, paper, candles, rubber, tape, wax, wood, oil, grease, gas.[8] Dickens insists on their sticky, mildewed, jumbled, flickering, scattered, messy presence in almost all of his descriptions of the Court and its environment. But he is also interested in laying bare the networks of resource extraction, and tracking the pathways that supply Chancery specifically, and the city more generally, with materials. Take, for example, this description of the network of resource extraction that feeds the Court:

> From the verdant undulations and the spreading oaks of the Dedlock property, Mr. Tulkinghorn transfers himself to the stale heat and dust of London. His manner of coming and going between the two places, is one

of his impenetrabilities. He walks into Chesney Wold as if it were next door to his chambers, and returns to his chambers as if he had never been out of Lincoln's Inn Fields ... Like a dingy London bird among the birds at roost in these pleasant fields, where the sheep are all made into parchment, the goats into wigs, and the pasture into chaff, the lawyer smoke-dried and faded ... comes sauntering home.[9]

There are multiple agents of transformation in this passage. First, there is Chancery, which separates the sheep from the goats only to turn them into different forms of waste. Second, there is Dickens's own prose, which registers the casual brutality of these transformations. The language reminds us of where Chancery's materials come from, but also plainly skips over the violent process by which sheep are turned into parchment, pasture into chaff. Dickens's language both exposes and, in a sense, performs the hidden ruthlessness of these transformations. In the meantime, we realize an even more extensive transformation is taking place: a natural space has been transformed into urban space, a quarry for the city.

Indeed, Tulkinghorn's seeming ability to teleport himself between disparate locales mirrors these sudden, wholesale transformations, and suggests the way surface distances only serve to hide the deeper and more intimate passages through which these various zones are fused into a single system. The effortlessness of the lawyer's locomotion is surprising in a novel in which the process of moving from one place to another is often described in great detail, and often exacts a heavy toll – think of Jo's "moving on," or Esther's exhausting pursuit of her mother through the streets of London near the conclusion. Indeed, to "move," or to "make a motion," is always a costly proposition where Chancery lawyers are concerned. Dickens's language here – "as if it were next door to his chambers" – forces the reader to picture Tulkinghorn materializing and dematerializing at will at the very moment she is being reminded that such a power is only a trick of language, a kind of fiction. For if Tulkinghorn appears to violate the laws of physics, it is only because there is, somewhere else, a corresponding cost in resources that allows such an effect to be produced – a carriage must be hired, a horse must be fed. His fiction of power is sustained not simply by his clients' bank accounts, but by the sheep and goats, the wigs and parchment that represent the Court's – and, by extension, his – power. Natural resources, in a sense, are converted into semiotic resources that allow men like Tulkinghorn to create their own aura of disembodied mastery over the environment.

If this scene gives us a sense of the larger grid of resource expenditure, in other places *Bleak House* maps smaller circuits of the network. We are shown how Mr. Turveydrop's deportment is only possible by exhausting the very bodies of his family; how Mr. Chadband's rhetorical flights are always connected to oil, grease, and the consumption of other people's food; how Skimpole's airy fictions come at the expense of Coavinses and his children. Every effect produced – and especially those that seem the most disembodied – always has a cost from another point in the system. The omniscient narrator works by tracing this network from above, while Esther physically walks its pathways to their terminals: to the Brickmaker's, to Coavinses's apartment, to the interiors of the Jellyby house. In different ways, we are put in touch with the hidden places that both sustain and bear the brunt of the culture's various fictions of frictionlessness. And we are made aware of the way in which the transformative "power" of language or of storytelling works to disguise the resources it secretly depends upon.

As we saw in Chapter 2, the narratives articulated by the first generation of thermodynamic scientists – whether the grand-scale accounts of the future history of the universe, or the more close-focus depictions of energy's flow through isolated systems – paid little attention to the kinds of intermediate zones, the social systems and human-built environments, that provide the setting for realist narrative. For Dickens, energy appears not as a quantifiable abstraction, but as a complex field of environmental effects and transformations, in which buildings, persons, things, institutions, city streets, industrial by-products, and natural formations are interconnected and mutually defining. Entropy is not a leftover quantity in diagrams of heat flow, but a thick medium of contamination. *Bleak House*, moreover, grounds its representation of energy in the networks of industrial extraction and dispersal that shape the environment and the human body in estranging and unprecedented ways. The "Megalosaurus, forty feet long or so, waddling like an elephantine lizard up Holborn-hill"[10] is a vision of a dislocating ecological breakdown that suggests, more specifically, something of the curious temporal collapse at work in fossil-fuel consumption. Coal is solar energy stored and compressed through millions of years of subterranean pressure, so the sprawling growth of Victorian London is quite literally emerging from the sunlight of the Mesozoic. Whereas, as we have seen, the natural-theological narratives out of which thermodynamics arose would treat England's coal consumption as both a sign of, and turning point in, a linear, Providential model of historical development, for Dickens, such consumption appears as temporal disorganization, the overwhelming of an environment's carrying capacity through an "unnatural" pace of energy release. Dickens's megalosaurus, in other words, doesn't just stand for primeval muck and confusion, it represents the spectral imprint of that earlier era, an almost Gothic return of the earth's stored energy, released through a wilderness of London chimneys. The blackened windows, the soot, even the undifferentiated muck through which the passersby slip – all of these things testify to the destabilizing effects of an energy-intensive economy, one that draws its power from a base of finite resources, and must dump the spent remains of those resources *somewhere*.

The notion that fossil-fuel energy connects otherwise distinct geological epochs is something Dickens signals more explicitly elsewhere in the novel:

> The blazing fires of faggot and coal – Dedlock timber and ante-diluvian forest – that blaze upon the broad wide hearths, and wink in the twilight on the frowning woods, sullen to see how the trees are sacrificed, do not exclude the enemy. The hot-water pipes that trail themselves all over the house, the cushioned doors and windows, and the screens and curtains, fail to supply the fires' deficiencies, and to satisfy Sir Leicester's need.[11]

Although the representation of Chancery is clearly the novel's most resonant depiction of energy waste, this quieter passage is also significant. The mixed coal and wood fires at Chesney Wold are, in essence, burning two forests at once, the prehistoric and the living. In this description, Dickens not only follows heat energy back to its origins in a specific resource base (coal and timber), he traces the formation of that resource base backwards through time. What emerges is a concern with energy as it moves both spatially and temporally: through natural and into human history, through organic ecosystems, into human-built environments (drawn there by an unsatisfiable human "need") and out through the drafty walls of the empty Dedlock homestead. The Dedlock house is waste-producing like Chancery, just less obviously, and Sir Leicester is as unaware of the part he plays, or of the forces flowing through his world, as the pollution-blind passersby who slip through the muck of London streets "adding new deposits to the crust upon crust of mud."[12] Chesney Wold, like Chancery, is an energy system, and the systemic connection between these two very different locations suggests a universalizing gesture, a sense that energy waste defines city street and country estate, noon and night, middle-class bustle and aristocratic emptiness.

Energy always comes at some personal or environmental expense, and at various points in the novel we reach not only the places where those hidden sources are revealed, but moments where the limits of energy finally put an end to representational games. Take the death of Gridley, who dies, Dickens emphasizes, by being "worn out."[13] Inspector Bucket treats his energy-exhaustion as a mere function of language: "I am surprised to hear a man of your energy talk of giving in," he tells him, "you mustn't do that."[14] The referent is obscure: mustn't do what? Give in or talk of giving in? The obscurity is, in a sense, the point – we are in a world in which verbal and material resources are not clearly distinguished. Bucket tells Gridley: "What do you say to coming along with me, upon this warrant, and having a good angry argument before the Magistrates? It'll do you good; it'll freshen you up, and get you into training for another turn at the Chancellor."[15] Here, he seems to believe the *expression* of energy is the same as the *possession* of energy, when in fact something like the opposite is the case. He also seems to believe a pep talk can restore Gridley to place in the collective fantasy of perpetual motion, to transform him back into the character known as "The Man From Shopshire." Bucket, a character known for his unlimited verbal "resources," finds how little they mean in the face of the limits of material resources. In a parallel deathbed scene a few hundred pages later, Snagsby compulsively donates "magic" half-crowns to a dying Jo.[16] Jo's breath is compared to dragging a heavy cart, and signifies the kind of tremendous energy burden he can no longer sustain. Snagsby's response, like Bucket's, is equal parts comic and pathetic. It exposes the absurdity of repeatedly applying a remedy that has, in a sense, been the cause of the problem. Indeed, of all the various representational fictions this novel shows us, the one that perhaps most thoroughly disguises the true costs of resource use is the language Snagsby speaks – the language of capital. If *Bleak House* and nineteenth-century energy science have much in common – an interest in the processes of transformation, in the behavior of complex systems, in the movement of energy between natural and industrial systems – where they part company, broadly speaking, is in Dickens's deep suspicion that the language of capital is at the root of his culture's persistent misrepresentation of natural resources.

As economic historian Philip Mirowski has argued, nineteenth-century physics developed the energy concept by relying on certain assumptions about nature structured by economic discourse. Revising Kuhn's model of the "simultaneous discovery" of energy conservation, Mirowski writes:

> What is required is an historically grounded understanding of how physicists came to settle upon the construction of events, the prohibitions and the enthusiasms, the pluses and minuses that they finally reified in the

conservation of energy … In other words, there had to be a common context of evaluation, or, if we may be venal about it, a system of accounts for keeping track of completed or useful action. Where did the gaggle of far-flung natural philosophers get their common set of accounts from? Not to indulge in too much periphrasis, they all got it from something shared in their social context; more specifically, they all derived it from their economic milieu.[17]

According to Mirowski, energy and capital were treated as isomorphic, and physics and economics trafficked in a busy exchange of metaphors and conceits. Energy, like capital, was imagined to be a storable, exchangeable "thing" that could serve as a measure of work; it could be tracked and strictly accounted for no matter how many transactions it underwent. Capital, meanwhile, as Catherine Gallagher and others have discussed, was often indexed to value in the form of the laboring power, or energy, that had gone into its creation.[18] The isomorphism between capital and energy was not only of key theoretical significance in the development of the energy concept, it was the linchpin of the comparisons between the social and natural worlds so often found in thermodynamic texts. Stewart and Lockyer can claim, as we saw in the previous chapter, that "energy in the social world is well understood" because they assume that the behavior of capital, and, by extension, the social structure that governs it, are legible and orderly.[19] Stewart writes:

> It is, in fact, the fate of all kinds of energy of position to be ultimately converted into energy of motion. The former may be compared to money in a bank, or capital, the latter to money which we are in the act of spending and just as, when we have money in the bank, we can draw it out whenever we want it, so, in the case of energy of position, we can make use of it whenever we please.[20]

Energy is "fated" to be converted into motion: expenditure is an automatic, agentless, natural process. The representation of energy as a kind of capital in the bank also works to domesticate the natural world, painting a picture of the easy command of nature through the various instruments of social and institutional life.

But if capital and energy can be usefully compared, there is also a crucial difference between them. Capital is just a device to describe value; it is fungible in ways that physical things like energy resources are not. The comparison between capital and energy may have been scientifically useful, perhaps even necessary, but it also becomes misleading when its metaphorical status is forgotten. If energy is defined as capital and vice versa, it's a short step to imagining that money can generate power, that resources are infinitely exchangeable, and that the only limits on the economy are human-made.

Dickens too aligns the vocabulary of energy and capital in *Bleak House*, but does so in order better to show these places of misalignment and ensure we cannot miss the fictive status of the connection. "It's about nothing but Costs, now," Jarndyce says of the suit, "We are always appearing, and disappearing, and swearing, and interrogating, and filing, and cross-filing, and arguing, and sealing, and motioning, and referring, and reporting, and revolving about the Lord Chancellor and all his satellites and equitably waltzing ourselves off to dusty death, about Costs."[21] Jarndyce here is ostensibly discussing the monetary costs of the Chancery system: the fact that the lawyers and all of the various processes are expensive. But clearly the language here is so physical, so invested in embodied activities, that the merely financial gives way to a more encompassing kind of physical depletion, as we *feel* how impossible it would be for a body to keep up all this endless movement. The language in this passage is simultaneously vivid and monotonous, active and stagnant, and it makes palpable the difference between the generation of language and the generation of energy, between all of the motions Jarndyce's descriptions conjure, and the fact that those different motions sum only to exhaustion. If "goats into wigs" suggests the way language can too easily conceal all the messy, complicated steps in the transformation of the physical world, this string of words suggests something like the opposite: the way in which language can be generated far in excess of the narrowed reality it helps bring into being. But both suggest a profound mismatch between resources and the way they are represented.

The force of "Costs," then, inheres in both the assertion and the subversion of the link between the energetic and the economic. As the second law of thermodynamics made clear, every exchange involves some loss of usable energy, and this fact becomes absolutely crucial in a fossil-fuel economy. Thus, I would argue, it is actually not the famous "death of the sun" in the opening, but the metaphor that comes a few sentences later – waste accumulating at "compound interest" – that brings us deeper into the intellectual and cultural ground both shared and divided by *Bleak House* and thermodynamics. Energy does not make more energy; its sources and its sinks are grounded in physical limits that, in the end, resist representational games and fictions of unlimited economic growth. The relationship between energy and capital is not stable and linear, as popular scientific accounts of energy often had it, but divergent, and asymptotic. If capital was frequently subject to all kinds of funhouse-mirror games, such fictions were exposed in visible, material ways in the environment: hence Dickens's emphasis in the opening passage in terms like "deposits" and "compound," which join the financial and the elemental in puns, showcasing the trick of language that would make a financial fiction appear to be natural law, and redrawing the connection between such fictions and their actual physical issue. For Dickens, energy in the social world is not at all "well understood," and it does not help us make sense of material energy forms. Instead, the social world and its fictions of capital work to mystify physical realities, even as its streets and skies display everywhere the consequences of such mystification.

By anchoring his vision of entropy in material environments, including all the challenges to perception those environments pose, Dickens not only emphasizes the route energy travels from sources to waste sinks, he opens up the kinds of questions about human constructions of nature that often went unacknowledged in Victorian discussions of energy. Thomson confidently articulated a new cosmology that turned industrial practices into models for universal processes, thereby obscuring some of the ecological implications of the entropy principle; for him, the universe was not just *like* an engine, it actually *was* one. Dickens, in contrast, stages his "universal" visions in specific, degraded locations, and in self-consciously provisional and equivocal ways. Provisionality only comes into play in Thomson's work at those junctures where thermodynamics might otherwise trespass too boldly on God's law: the universe is wasteful *to us*, energy is running out *as far as we are concerned.* Such qualifications, found everywhere in his work, speak to a sense of investigative modesty before the operations of the divine order. But Thomson *would* draw a clear and direct connection between energy waste in engine technology and the waste of the entire natural world – recall the title of his lecture "On a Universal Tendency *in Nature* to the Dissipation of Mechanical Energy." Dickens, in contrast, gathers a great deal of his rhetorical and imagistic power by suggesting that all of nature might be just as disordered and degraded as Chancery, but *also* by suggesting that to think so might itself be the problem. Chancery, like the pollution it generates, reveals and conceals simultaneously. The Court is to be treated with suspicion not just because it obviously produces so much disorder, but because it can operate only by making itself seem a normal, even inevitable, part of the processes of the world. As Garrett Stewart puts it in his discussion of the layered "reciprocal troping" found in *Bleak House's* opening: "this is the very work of ideology, unraveled only momentarily here by being made brazen and overexplicit."[22] It is precisely this brazen naturalizing gesture that Dickens takes pains to highlight.[23]

If thermodynamics represented a universe of flux and transformation – describing the way in which heat became mechanical motion, for example, or chemical bonds could be converted into electricity – Dickens's startling metaphorical imagination pushes this sense of transformativity into unexpected but revealing places, uncovering a world both vibrating with life and warped by the stress of human need. His use of short, almost brutally clipped descriptions of change, along with his more extended, elaborate, sometimes almost baroque metamorphic conceits – "that blaze upon the broad wide hearths, and wink in the twilight on the frowning woods, sullen to see how the trees are sacrificed" – not only opens up unexpected connections between seemingly disparate phenomena, it also calls attention to the very imposition of language itself as an anthropomorphizing pressure. Transformation is usually neither neutral nor quiet in Dickens; it always showcases itself as both intuitively apposite and startlingly factitious. This stands in stark contrast to the way such figures of speech were employed in Victorian thermodynamic discourse. In both cases, we get anthropomorphized pictures of the cosmos – recall Stewart's description of the sun as "man whose expenditure exceeds his income" in the previous chapter. But where thermodynamics would offer such anthropomorphism, at least ostensibly, as a heuristic to help make sense of the sun's expiring energy, Dickens demands it be recognized as an epistemological problem.

Unsustainable narratives

The fact that the fictions of capital have come decoupled from their material environments is made clear in many places besides Chancery. Smallweed's tremendous financial power, for example, is incongruously housed in an entirely enervated body. Skimpole's self-justifying patter, meanwhile, is a hash of economic casuistry and threadbare natural theology. He turns the energy wasted upon Chancery into a sign of deeper harmony:

> He said, Well, it was really very pleasant to see how things lazily adapted themselves to purposes. Here was this Mr. Gridley, a man of robust will and surprising energy – intellectually speaking, a sort of inharmonious blacksmith – and he could easily imagine that there Gridley was, years ago, wandering about in life for something to expend his superfluous combativeness upon.[24]

This automatic congruence is immediately applied to his own debt: "all that time, he had been giving employment to a most deserving man; that he had been a benefactor to Coavinses; that he had actually been enabling Coavinses to bring up these charming children in this agreeable way."[25] But the energy Coavinses expends chasing Skimpole – like the energy Gridley expends seeking justice – is not replenished, and thus these elaborate fictions have their half-hidden issue in the physical wreckage of his family's dwelling and in his own bodily infirmity. What Skimpole represents as a perfectly self-sustaining system is in fact unidirectional, concealed by euphemisms like "adapted," "purposes," and "employment."

But *barely* concealed. In the transparent absurdity of Skimpole's logic lies one of Dickens's most significant ecological insights. The point is not simply that self-justifying fictions can disguise unpleasant material facts; it is that these fictions can be so obviously nonsensical, and yet can remain so intractably *real* in their psychological grip and material effects. Part of the genius of *Bleak House* resides in the way Dickens takes what is essentially a joke – Skimpole at first seems a recognizably benign Dickensian cartoon – and tracks its metastasization into the operant condition for both ecological disaster and personal tragedy. For it is Skimpole's protégé, Richard Carstone, who splices these ludicrous conceits into his own life-narrative, one that tethers his fate not only to the Jarndyce suit, but to the dynamics of London's ongoing eco-catastrophe. Richard's accounting tricks arise from the Skimpolian school of economics, and at first seem only comic, and mildly troubling:

> I saved five pounds out of the brickmaker's affair; so, if I have a good rat-tle down to London and back in a post-chaise, and put that down at four pounds, I shall have saved one ... And then he showed me, proved by elaborate calculations in his pocket-book, that supposing he had contracted, say two hundred pounds of debt in six months, out of the army; and that he contracted no debt at all within a corresponding period, in the army – as to which he had quite made up his mind; this step must involve a saving of four hundred pounds in a year, or two thousand pounds in five years – which was a considerable sum.[26]

The language of "saving" can refer either to not spending, or to actual capital accumulation; Richard, shuttling freely between these definitions, shows he has internalized the logic by which representation itself seems to generate wealth, irrespective of any material foundations. We have here one of the novel's central preoccupations: the relationship between repetition and dissipation. Gridley's repeated arguments, Snagsby's repeated donations, Richard's repeated justifications; in each case, a process that someone would reduplicate endlessly is put in direct conflict with an exhaustible base of resources. Each of these repeated activities begins as a kind of joke, a bit of comic absurdity; and indeed, vibrant, repetitious expenditure is a staple of Dickensian comedy. But in this novel, that comic expenditure grimly wears down, until it is put into uncomfortably close alignment with the kind of blind expenditure that appears as such a threat to the environment in the opening pages. Indeed, Richard's somewhat cartoonish thinking may seem an exaggeration on Dickens's part, except we have already seen on the streets of London the mismatch between fantasies of limitless growth and the pressing limits of the actual environment.

Richard's accounting is part of an *unsustainable fiction*; that is, the story he tells himself (and Esther) undermines the very conditions that story requires in order to continue being told. The story of his hopeful prospects provides the grounds for these various flights into financial make-believe, which, in turn, make his prospects that much less hopeful, prompting a further descent into fantasy. As the problems mount, the stakes get higher, and so does the commitment to the narrative – in the two passages I quoted above, we can see the contours of a spiral into both greater debt and greater optimism simultaneously. This narrative may keep Richard's spirits temporarily afloat, but it is not itself sustainable, because one cannot subsist on trick bookkeeping, just as the Coavinses family cannot live on "employment." And just as Skimpole's various mystifications have a physical cost in the decomposition of the Coavinses' household, so Richard's narratives begin to wreak havoc on his own material existence. Esther says of his accounting methods: "The number of little acts of thoughtless expenditure which Richard justified by the recovery of his ten pounds, and the number of times he talked to me as if he had saved or realised that amount, would form a sum in simple addition."[27] "Expenditure" is the key word here, since, as Mirowski's work makes clear, it aligns the financial with the physical, and thus suggests the way in which Richard's fictions drain his wallet and his body simultaneously. Dickens emphasizes that (unlike Jo) Richard dies "of no direct bodily illness",[28] an important detail that suggests his end is more about the metaphorics of "Costs" than the metonymics of disease transmission. Just as Krook's spontaneous combustion results from his own manifestly unsustainable commercial practices (his shop was a place where "Everything seemed to be bought, and nothing to be sold"[29]), so do Richard's decline and death suggest a fatally imbalanced economy. His wasting body stands as a kind of microcosm for the systemic exhaustion taking place on the level of the environment itself, and for the way in which elaborate fictions of capital work both to disguise and to accelerate the problem. As Vholes tells him, "Excuse me if I recommend you not to chafe so much, not to be so impetuous, not to wear yourself out so. You should have more patience. You should sustain yourself better."[30]

We might linger on the word "sustain," for it suggests the way in which the ecological and the legal are intimately tied together in Richard's story and in the novel more generally. I have been discussing Richard's narrative in terms of its sustainability – its ability to keep functioning despite the damage it inflicts upon the very world upon which it depends. This of course arises from the modern definition of "sustainable," which the *Oxford English Dictionary* (hereafter *OED*) first locates in 1965, and defines as "capable of being maintained at a certain rate or level."[31] What marks this definition from earlier meanings is the introduction of temporality. The question is not about the viability of a certain activity in the present moment, but about the way in which that activity, if pursued indefinitely, will eventually reach an environmental limit beyond which it cannot continue. The Victorians did not use the term sustainable in quite this way, although the *concept* reaches at least as far back as Malthus, who writes about population growth in these terms: "this is a rate of increase, which in the nature of things cannot be permanent."[32] As we have seen, W. S. Jevons's *The Coal Question* puts a similar pressure on the idea of the rate of fossil-fuel consumption; both writers are interested not simply in the linear relationship between population and resources, but in the way in which growth *itself* grows, and the crisis that then occurs when the forces of exponential increase press upon the limits of the environment.

The word "sustainable" for the Victorians does not involve the conflict between environmental conditions and rates of growth, and it does not involve the same kinds of temporal horizons. Instead, it refers to the ability of an argument to withstand scrutiny: "capable of being upheld or defended," according to the *OED*. The issue is not whether the argument can be repeated indefinitely, but whether it can be maintained *right now*, under current procedural and evidentiary conditions. Here are two examples from the *OED*:

> 1845 T. DE QUINCEY *W. Hazlitt* in *Tait's Mag.* Dec. 758/1 From the verdict of a jury no candid and temperate man will allow himself to believe any appeal sustainable.
> 1884 *Law Rep. Chancery Div.* 27 69 The Defendant has taken several technical objections to the order, none of which … are sustainable.[33]

Although, in the nineteenth century, the word is not found exclusively in the world of jurisprudence, it is deeply tied to it. Indeed, it is still a part of contemporary legal discourse: in the way, for example, objections are either overruled or "sustained" in depositions and trials. As the second example above suggests, the word occurred frequently in the proceedings of Chancery. The word "unsustainable," too, was a part of nineteenth-century legal language. Sustainability and unsustainability in Victorian legal discourse thus refer to structures of argument, logic, and precedent, rather than to the dynamic relationship between a form of activity and the capacity of an environment to support that activity. They suggest a transparent and straightforward process of ratiocination, through which "sustainability" is a quality that inheres in the argument itself. But we can also see, at times, the latter, modern understanding of the word lurking around the edges of the discussion. To take one rather Dickensian example from the annals of Chancery: "They were not appointed the guardians of the infant, nor indeed was any other person appointed her guardian, and, if this bill is sustainable, any person whatever who had expended money for the infant, or the governess, on the ground that she had received an inadequate salary, might file a similar bill."[34] To declare the bill in question "sustainable" is to open the door for untold other claims to be filed against the defendant. Bills beget bills, claims beget claims, and one case suddenly creates a ramifying network of additional plaintiffs, paperwork, lawyers' fees, and other demands made on the defendant's finite resources. The connections to the case itself, and connections *between* the case and other similar cases, suddenly begin to seem frighteningly illimitable. This is the problem Dickens seizes on and amplifies in *Bleak House*: the way in which the world of abstract reasoning cannot seal itself from the world of material processes and demands. We have already seen how Dickens's use of words like "Costs," bridges the divide between the language of the legal process and the world of physical bodies in motion and under duress. Dickens plumbs these words for the materiality that fictions of disembodied, rational adjudication would ignore or deny. That materiality, in turn, is connected to the waste generation and resource loss exacting a toll on the city environment beyond the Court's walls.

Richard's financial fictions are clearly "unsustainable" in the nineteenth-century sense – they cannot withstand the slightest bit of scrutiny. But this kind of unsustainability means little to him: Richard continues operating in his reckless way despite the unmistakable gaps in his reasoning. What enable him to maintain these fictions, at least temporarily, are his own future prospects (which allow him to incur debt) as well as

his own bodily resources (which he expends in pursuit of those prospects). That is, both temporality and materiality are added to the equation, and we thus see dramatized the process by which "unsustainable"
in the logical sense becomes "unsustainable" in the environmental sense.
Richard's increasingly wasted body becomes a metaphor for the degraded
urban landscapes that are also "in Chancery," and thus subject to the
endlessly deferred, hopelessly proliferating arguments that always come
at a material cost. And this structure is what distinguishes Richard's plot
in *Bleak House* from most other mid-Victorian narratives of self-delusion
and comeuppance. In *Middlemarch*, for example, Fred Vincy also falls
into debt and eschews productive labor based on the strength of his supposed expectations. But Eliot is more interested in the conflict between
an individual's design and the contingent pressures of (for lack of a better term) reality. There is nothing *inherently* unworkable in Fred's plan –
with a different person on call, Featherstone might well have been able to
burn that second will. In contrast, Richard's narrative is essentially *self-
consuming*. The more he tells it, the worse his conditions get, the more he
has recourse to it. This scene takes place in his dingy London quarters,
near the end of the novel:

> "We are doing very well," pursued Richard. "Vholes will tell you so. We
> are really spinning along. Ask Vholes. We are giving them no rest. Vholes
> knows all their windings and turnings, and we are upon them everywhere.
> We have astonished them already. We shall rouse up that nest of sleepers,
> mark my words!"
> His hopefulness had long been more painful to me than his despond-
> ency; it was so unlike hopefulness, had something so fierce in its deter-
> mination to be it, was so hungry and eager, and yet so conscious of being
> forced and *unsustainable*, that it had long touched me to the heart. (492,
> my emphasis)

Richard's language is full of abstract motions – spinning, winding, turning – that return us to the operations of Chancery, "motioning, and referring, and reporting, and revolving."[35] But while Richard's labor produces
no useful effect, it *does* have a Cost: "I noticed how sunken and how large
his eyes appeared, how dry his lips were, and how his finger-nails were all
bitten away".[36] His hopeful narrative, Esther says, is "hungry," suggesting
both the emotional need that generates it, and the reckless consumption it
licenses. In this context, the term "unsustainable" unites all of these levels
of discourse – the judicial, the emotional, and the ecological – suggesting
the way in which arguments born out of personal and collective fantasy
have cascading environmental consequences that push one further into

fantasy. Through Richard's logic, the future is mortgaged with itself as collateral.

But the fact that Richard's story functions as a central metaphor for the workings of Chancery also reveals the limits of Dickens's eco-critique. If extrapolating from microcosm to macrocosm – from his story to Chancery to the entire English economic order – allows us to imagine the unsustainable logic of industrial modernity, moving from macrocosm to microcosm – from system to person – brings these questions within limited and legible moral boundaries. Unsustainability appears as the function of a certain problematic mindset and set of behaviors, rather than the unavoidable consequence of participation in a wasteful, resource-intensive economic order. But it is precisely the problem of *de*personalized, collective complicity that makes resource depletion and environmental damage so resistant to solution and moralization. In *The Comedy of Survival,* Joseph Meeker puts it this way:

> Environmental disasters can never be tragic, for they cannot be conceived as the moral error of an individual. Oedipus caused the pollution of Thebes by his sinful murder and marriage, but who causes the pollution of New York? What was rotten in Denmark could be remedied by Hamlet, but who will take responsibility for what is rotten in Chicago? No hero will suffer transcendently for the extermination of hundreds of animal species, or for the degradation of the oceans. Environmental guilt is collective, distributed unevenly among the people now living, and those who have lived before. Without a personality to focus upon, ecological crisis presents merely a spectacle of catastrophe with none of the redemptive prospects of genuine tragic experience.[37]

Richard is not, like Oedipus, the cause of the pollution of his world, but he nevertheless functions as an agent of its expiation. His death coincides with the folding up of the Jarndyce case, which is consumed in "Costs," and thus no longer the same signifier of systemic collapse. Not to say that the ecological threat has passed altogether, but its edges have been dulled by being pressed into the mold of an individual, tragic narrative. Energy and waste are no longer frighteningly indistinguishable, as they were in the opening chapters; instead, waste has been clearly identified through its expression in certain definable character traits, and endowed with narrative significance. Just as Esther can stop the spread of disease in the novel by containing it within her own body, Richard ends the energy waste by being offered up as its sacrificial victim. Richard's narrative may be unsustainable, but *Bleak House* finds a way to put it to work. Through Richard, the novel can organize a problem of disorganization, and personalize a problem of systemic, transpersonal expenditure.

Entropic systems, narrative systems

For the Victorians, as for us, the possibility that the social and economic order is unsustainable means facing not only an environmental disaster, but the collapse of some deeply cherished beliefs. To imagine that consumption practices could result in a despoiled earth; in depleted farmlands, rivers, and forests; in discarded lives, both human and animal, means facing some unpleasant existential questions about the place of human beings in the natural order, and maybe even the fate and purpose of the species itself. Broadly speaking, there's a choice: a culture can change the way it consumes resources, or it can change the story it tells itself to keep the consequences out of view. Just as Richard keeps modifying his story to sustain an increasingly unsustainable state of affairs, so did many Victorians admit that natural resources were being recklessly consumed, only to double down immediately on the idea of a reassuring teleological narrative. In an article on resource exhaustion published in *The Examiner* a few years after *Bleak House*, an anonymous writer says, "We do not believe, however, that the calamity we are imagining will ever come to pass, because we have faith in science and invention."[38] Coal and timber supplies will probably give out, the writer admits, but if they do, surely some other form of energy will be found to take their place. If, in the meantime, the environment has become thoroughly polluted, surely something will be invented that can clean it up, put the waste to use, or bury it elsewhere. As we have seen in Chapter 1, faith in Providence smoothly grades into faith in technology; indeed, the development of the latter was often imagined as a means to fulfilling the divine design of the former. This is Richard's logic: the endless deferral of a solution into an imaginary future, while the present is shadowed by the damaged future already coming into being. As England's economic and cultural life came not simply to use but to *depend upon* energy-intensive practices, and as those practices came to seem increasingly unsustainable, the Providential narrative became, like Richard's, simultaneously more precarious and more necessary.

The most surprising part of *The Examiner*'s expression of "faith" in invention is the reference to Dickens that immediately follows: "As Mr. Micawber was wont to say, 'Something will turn up.'"[39] That the writer would invoke fiction's most notorious spendthrift as a model for national resource husbandry shows how confused this question was, and how unthinkingly the rhetoric of faith and belief could be transferred from Providence to technology. At first glance, it also seems to be a misreading of Dickens. Except that, however much we are encouraged to look askance at Richard Carstone, or Skimpole, or Micawber for their belief that things will "turn up," things do, in fact, "turn up" in his fictions. While Dickens clearly mocks those who would use Providential narratives in order to shirk responsibility, or indulge profligate tendencies, he *does* seem to believe that those who work honestly, and who put their faith in Providence to support and, yes, *sustain* them, do eventually find that faith rewarded. Although *Bleak House* is about forms of waste and dissipation we here also recall the observation, made so often about this novel, that it is organized in such a way that even the smallest characters, incidents, and events are never wasted.[40] This is one of the versions of the "energy" of Dickens's fictions I discussed at the opening – the idea that even the most seemingly insignificant detail in this novel seems charged with potential value, or capable of doing significant thematic, narrative, or symbolic "work." As Dorothy Van Ghent puts it, in Dickens's worlds, "No thing must be lost, as it is doubtless essential to the mysterious organization of the system."[41] If Jo the crossing sweep is easily discarded by the urban system in which he barely scrapes out an existence, he is indispensable to the narrative system of *Bleak House*. His significance to the world of the novel, in other words, looms in inverse proportion to his insignificance to the world at large, as Dickens reclaims as valuable a life that would otherwise be obliterated. Despite the claustrophobia-inducing grip, and despite the sense of helplessness and revulsion at the waste in which the world seems to be drowning, the narrative logic of Dickens's novel nevertheless seems to imply that nothing is ever *really* wasted. Where Chancery scatters, dissipates, and degrades, the novel structures, organizes, and builds; what the legal system would forget, lose, or deem irrelevant, the narrative system rescues, reclaims, and infuses with significance.

It is here, I think, that we can see how Dickens's fictions and Victorian thermodynamics, despite their ecological and ideological differences, begin once again to find a kind of common ground in the notion that even waste can be fully accounted for in some representational schema, and thus *translated* into something else. We might return to Mirowski's account of the conceptual roots of thermodynamics for a moment and his argument that, for energy scientists to be able to keep track of energy as it moved through all its various transformations, "there had to be a common context of evaluation, or, if we may be venal about it, a system of accounts for keeping track of completed or useful action." But we could modify this a bit, and say that, in the entropy principle, thermodynamics also devised a system for keeping track of *non*-useful actions, of dissipated energy. For, as we have seen, entropy didn't come into being as merely a descriptive term for disorder or waste; it was, instead, a theoretically definable quantity that could be tallied on energetic balance sheets just like the useful energy that had been harnessed to create some productive effect. For Thomson and his cohort, the energy principle served to reinforce a religious ideal that there was no action so small or inconsequential that it would fall through the cracks of the universal record-keeping. Even if it was wasted, in practical terms, to the world at large, it still "counted" somewhere. Not to say that they weren't concerned about energy waste – they were, as evidenced by their tireless work on improving engine efficiency – but they were also fortified by a faith that what was lost to the material world was not really lost. In their discussion of dissipated energy in *The Unseen Universe*, Stewart and Tait make these assumptions explicit, stressing the interconnected totality of all activity through the matrix of energy relations, and tracing thermodynamic thought back to its roots in early-nineteenth-century natural theology:

> For every thought we think is accompanied by a displacement and motion of the particles of the brain, and we may imagine that somehow ... these motions are propagated throughout the universe. Views of this nature were long ago entertained by Babbage, and they have since commended themselves to several men of science, and amongst others to Jevons. "Mr. Babbage," says this author, "has pointed out that if we had power to follow and detect the minutest effects of any disturbance, each particle of existing matter must be a register of all that has happened."[42]

The passage from Babbage they mention, from his *Ninth Bridgewater Treatise* of 1837, is even more explicit in its proscription of waste from the order of things:

> No motion impressed by natural causes, or by human agency, is ever obliterated ... Interrogate every wave which breaks unimpeded on ten thousand desolate shores, and it will give evidence of the last gurgle of the waters which closed over the head of his dying victim: confront the murderer with every corporeal atom of his immolated slave, and in its still quivering movements he will read the prophet's denunciation of the prophet king.[43]

Although Stewart and Tait do not make their moral case as vividly as Babbage does, this idea of a world fully watched, tracked, and measured helps them build their own argument for a natural theology grounded in the energy relations of a moral universe. What I want to note here is how closely "wasted" motion and thought are brought into alignment by both Babbage and the physicists who followed him. Individual experiences, even those seemingly consigned to oblivion, are in this view preserved as part of the material record and recognized by the perceiving mind – or, as it is tellingly framed in Babbage, by the "reader." In this way, the world of thought, underwritten by faith, is both rescued by, and promoted beyond, the world of matter. We might recall Thomson's remark in "A Universal Tendency" that I discussed in Chapter 2: "as it is most certain that Creative Power alone can either call into existence or annihilate mechanical energy, the 'waste' referred to cannot be annihilation, but must be some transformation of energy."[44] While this is, on one level, an assertion of the complete compatibility of the conservation and dissipation of energy (energy may dissipate, but it can never be destroyed) the religious overtones are unmistakable. Thomson employs a classic natural theological move, suggesting that waste and loss are only appearances that will be transformed when viewed from the right perspective.

Just as thermodynamics used the very inescapability of energy dissipation as a way to argue – implicitly and explicitly – for the existence of another "system" of tabulation that keeps things ordered, so does Dickens make Chancery the force that drives the novel's own movement towards fashioning a greater narrative economy of order.[45] It is no accident that the novel of his most invested in describing a systemic disorganizing principle is the one most deeply invested in tracing astonishing concatenations and networks of buried significance, affording us something akin to the contextualizing, transformative perspective Thomson adopts. While Chancery is "closing in," as the title to Chapter 48 has it; as it, indeed, comes to seem more and more like a "closed system" from which there is no earthly escape, the Providential narrative organization itself becomes the way out. In fact, the two systems – legal and narrative – develop in tandem, as the progressive revelation of coincidences and hidden connections between characters seems to reinforce Chancery's closing walls (for who, it turns out, is not somehow a party in the suit?) while they simultaneously lend the novel a sense of governing structuration and supervision. The novel thus comes to seem its own kind of rival "closed system," one in which expended action is not wasted, but retained and transformed into patterns of signification, a complex symbolic order, and a legible narrative whole. As Tina Young Choi has brilliantly demonstrated, the emphasis on closure and Providential patterning in Victorian narrative often meant that seemingly wasted energy forms were symbolically and rhetorically recuperated within the narrator's "encompassing vision."[46] She writes: "The necessity for moral action, through which all potential loss might be recuperated, is here sublimated into narratorial agency – energy is in fact conserved, both by thermodynamic principles and narratorial ones, which contain and control energy's distribution within."[47] *Bleak House* seems both to mimic Chancery's systemic constriction and to provide an alternative to it in which energy is not expended in vain. By implicitly offering "narratorial agency" as a possible means to reorganizing seemingly dissipated energy, Dickens's novel can be aligned with the work of Thomson, Stewart, and Maxwell, and their various attempts to posit the mind as a means of transcending the waste of the material world.

I would take this point further, and suggest that, as the walls close in, and the sense of an ordered design becomes more apparent, the narrative's treatment of sustainability undergoes a corresponding transformation. The opening of the novel, where passersby contribute to waste build-up under a dead sun, is frightening because it depicts the teeming city population as both excessive and anonymous. There is in this image a quasi-Malthusian nightmare, in which the environment groans under the strain of so many people dissipating energy and adding to the build-up of pollution by walking and moving – by simply *existing*. This emphasis on the impact of the anonymous passersby and the pollution of the city suggests not merely a concern with the environment, but a disquieting and even radical challenge to the reader. As Ken Hiltner has persuasively argued, a major difficulty involved in writing about environmental contamination and resource waste is that responsibility is collective: everyone generates waste and everyone burns fossil fuels, so everyone is to blame for their own environmental misery. Hiltner asks: "how exactly does one portray a problem that no one wishes to acknowledge because everyone is in fact its cause?"[48] Too often, he argues, writers tended to sidestep this difficulty by laying the blame wholly at the doorstep of industry, or specific individuals or interests. *Bleak House* initially refuses this kind of easy circumscription of blame, or the localized identification of responsible parties. The generation of waste is so disquieting in the opening precisely because it *doesn't matter* what the intentions and purposes of those passersby are – the environment is degraded, resources are taxed, the sun shines obscurely on the virtuous and wicked alike. The energy crisis subverts the underpinnings of humanist narrative, because it suggests that all action, any action, involves the expenditure of finite resources. Ordinary life, in its teeming numbers, is unavoidably bound up with environmental degradation in a resource-intensive culture. The view in the opening of *Bleak House* matches the view from Mayhew's balloon in *The Criminal Prisons of London* we discussed in the opening chapter, where the expenditure of energy, decoupled from narrative reference points, becomes impossible to distinguish from the generation of waste. Chancery, it is suggested, cannot be differentiated in any precise way from the motions of the city, and the cultural logic of resource exploitation. Once again, the lack of clear differentiation in the opening – between epochs, between natural and industrial processes, between individuals, between inside and outside the Court – is simultaneously a form of obfuscation and revelation. The diffusion of pollution throughout the urban environment suggests the diffusion of responsibility, the lack of perceptual clarity expressing a profound environmental insight.

But one by one, *Bleak House* pulls individual narratives out of this anonymous mass, and, in doing so, bestows shape upon the city's seemingly haphazard expenditure. In the process, the energy expended by the characters is also separated into wasteful and non-wasteful varieties: Skimpole, Richard, Vholes, Smallweed come to represent, in different ways and for different reasons, vectors of energy waste; meanwhile Esther, John Jarndyce, Woodcourt, and Bucket, in similarly various ways, represent careful husbandry, repair, organization, and the "good" use of energy. Energy expenditure, in other words, becomes morally valenced, attached to characters' actions, intentions, and moral orientation. This kind of schema – where villains are wasteful and heroes are not – is such a common feature of Dickens's worlds that we may not notice how it neutralizes the more radical ecological vision that opened the novel. *Bleak House* thus also works effectively to shrink the population, so what initially looked like an overwhelming sea of people turns out to be defined by a limited network of individual stories. That is to say: the sense of inescapable, involuntary anonymity that was so threatening at the outset is replaced, by the end, by a well-managed, fully personalized systematicity, in which human relations and narratives are restored to significance. As George Levine has argued, narrative interconnectedness carries an ecological valence, a clear affinity with Darwin's metaphor of the "entangled bank":

> To discuss the life and nature of any organism requires discussion of the many others with whom it struggles, on whom it depends, in seemingly endless chains of connection. Victorian realist narratives equally entail complex and intricately inwoven stories of many figures so that it is often difficult to determine which characters are the true protagonists, which the subordinate ones.[49]

Yet by the end of *Bleak House*, this is much less difficult to determine. We may not be able to draw a stark dividing line between "true" protagonist and subordinate character, but we have a better relative sense, I think, of who is more significant, who less so. More importantly, in the very act of tracing out the chains of connections, those chains no longer seem "endless," since Dickens so carefully ties up loose ends.[50] This bears on the ecology of the novel because it has the effect of implicitly de-pressurizing the population question. What initially looked like an overwhelming sea of people turns out to be a large, but manageable, network; indeed, the very fact that there are always such a great many characters to keep track of, but that we *can*, ultimately, keep track of them, slowly turns an overwhelming excess into a reassuringly circumscribed plentitude.

The shift in the representation of energy in the novel illustrates Hiltner's argument about the difficulties representing collective environmental responsibility. He argues that, from the point of view of ordinary citizens who are "desperately maintaining a life grip on the very practices [fossil-fuel consumption] threatening life, it might be difficult to confront, let alone explain, such actions." To overcome such difficulties, "one solution would be to suggest, though obviously counter to the facts, that consumers themselves are not the cause of the problem. Instead, it could be argued that other individuals, through selfish and insensitive acts, are bringing it about."[51] Ultimately, the novel's depiction of energy waste is structured in such a way as to undermine some of the more radical possibilities implied in the opening. Where earlier we saw the drafty Dedlock household working as an unwitting agent of energy dissipation, in the penultimate chapter, the novel seals up the leak: "A little more, in truth, and it will all be extinguished for Sir Leicester; and the damp door of the mausoleum which shuts so tight, and looks so obdurate, will have opened and relieved him."[52] Dickens still employs the language of heat and energy in reference to Chesney Wold – a few pages after hearing that Sir Leicester and his line will soon be "extinguished" we learn there will be "no rows of lights sparkling by night" in the house, and no visitors to the "cold shapes of rooms"[53] – but now that language is put to a slightly different purpose. Whereas the earlier description of the house's energy consumption implicitly linked Chesney Wold to Chancery and to a ubiquitous system of resource extraction and waste, here that vocabulary is used not to suggest deep connections, but to enforce final containment. Chesney Wold's energy dissipation is no longer a metonymic link in a wider complex of social and environmental waste, but a metaphorical device used to conjure a sense of the moral decline of a specific family and mode of social organization. It is the energy of Sir Leicester himself – his own personal and lineal life-force – that is now in danger of expiring. What's more, this is felt to be a fitting, if melancholy, conclusion – the punishment meted out to a short-sighted and outmoded way of life. Dickens backs away from the more radical vision of widespread waste that is such a key part of the novel's opening movements by corralling energy as a moral signifier, rather than as a limited natural resource. In this way, energy as a *problem* is symbolically contained – as well as contained as a symbol – and snuffed out.

Moving from perceptual confusion to perceptual clarity, from a welter of undifferentiated city dwellers to a large but circumscribed cast of characters, from the diffusion of responsibility to the location of moral failure in specific modes of behavior and forms of class blindness, the narrative logic is consistently moving away from the opening vision of universal complicity, and towards a more reassuring, and less searching, kind of environmental awareness. At the end of the novel, the new Bleak House itself is now immune to fears about energy dissipation. The language of heat and cold, expenditure and waste, the imagery of guttering candles and dying fires, all of which figured so heavily in descriptions of place throughout the novel, and connected disparate locales, are now no longer to be found. Esther, sitting on the porch, burns no coals: the temperature outside is, one imagines, roughly the same as it is in. The self-sufficient, functional, middle-class family is finally marked off from these other zones – London, Chesney Wold, even the old Bleak House – where energy dissipation, we now see, signified moral and spiritual corruption, rather than a structural problem with the consumption patterns of an entire cultural order.

In a sense, we return to where we started, to the question of language and energy: whether these symbolic forms of meaning can somehow rescue all the waste we've seen, turn it to some kind of account, transform it. Or, whether the narrative devices that help bring the novel to a close and gather all this stray energy are meant to seem patently artificial. The elaborate and implausible coincidences, the preternatural powers of detection Bucket uses to tie up loose ends. All these things contribute to its final sense of an ordered narrative economy, but are they meant to reflect a reassuring Providential economy? Or, on the other hand, are they meant to *feel* like the conventions they are: more fictions through which unpleasant truths are managed or kept at bay? These questions are irresolvable, I think, because they testify to the clash of incompatible narrative patterns – Providential and ecological – that were (and perhaps still are) competing to structure the culture's conceptualization of energy resources.

CHAPTER 4

The renewable energies of Our Mutual Friend

The near-simultaneous emergence of Dickens's *Bleak House* and William Thomson's "On a Universal Tendency in Nature to the Dissipation of Mechanical Energy" represents, as I have argued, a striking publishing coincidence – a moment where scientist and novelist articulate similar, if distinct, visions of system-wide energy exhaustion and collapse. *Our Mutual Friend*, in contrast, appears some ten years later, when the conservation and dissipation of energy, the death of the sun, and other components of the thermodynamic research project have all been firmly ensconced in the public imagination. The years between these two novels featured the publication of, among other works, John Tyndall's popular lectures on energy conservation, *Heat: A Mode of Motion*; William Thomson's essays introducing popular audiences to the laws of thermodynamics; and Herbert Spencer's *First Principles*, which attempted to fashion an entire philosophical system out of the laws of energy and evolution.[1] The gathering interest is reflected in *Household Words* and *All the Year Round*, which in the late 1850s and early 1860s featured articles on Tyndall's lectures ("Is Heat Motion?" and "Heat and Work"), on the popular work of W. R. Grove and Alfred Smee on energy conservation ("Physical Force"), on the energy of organic life ("Vital Heat"), and on the question of solar death and universal energy loss ("Small-Beer Chronicles," "Earth," "Respecting the Sun").[2] As with any emergent discourse, terms fluctuated ("force" was still often used as a synonym for "energy," for example), but overall the movement was towards the increased visibility of thermodynamic concepts and a growing acceptance of "energy" as the preferred term to describe a quantity of motive power. Along with the interest in the scientific discourse of energy, there was rising concern about the demands put upon the country's natural resource base. As we have already seen, W. S. Jevons's *The Coal Question* (1865) was the most rigorous articulation of these concerns, but interest was stirring beforehand. William Armstrong, the President of the British Association for the Advancement of Science, made coal exhaustion the subject of his

1863 address, and popular journals like *The Living Age* and Dickens's own *All the Year Round* featured extended discussions of the topic.[3]

The laws of energy, as they were popularized at this moment, conjured two very different, almost incompatible, ideas about transformation. On the one hand, since absolutely everything, at bottom, was just a different form of energy, the cosmos was fashioned as a zone of, as Tyndall puts it, "incessant transference and conversion."[4] An astonishing range of technological developments in fields as diverse as engine technology and agricultural chemistry suggested that humans were learning to command these transformations. But the laws of thermodynamics also set strict quantitative limits on the malleability of energy forms, and thus punctured fantasies of endless transformability. As we have seen, the second law described the production of unusable heat as inevitable: every energetic transaction generated a wasteful remainder that could not be transformed again. As we have also seen, the second law described the irreversible direction of a fossil-fuel-based economy, in which certain resources can never be replenished and pollution does not "naturally" return to stable cycles of decay and renewal.

In what follows, I discuss the way in which the imaginative world of *Our Mutual Friend* resides on the very fault line of these conflicting notions of energy transformation. For Dickens, language is an agency of transformation: it can turn water into fire, make the inert vital, and return the dead to life. The verbal imagination, indeed, can be said to have a certain vivifying "energy" in all of Dickens's works, but it is nowhere more expressly and complexly thematized than in this, his last finished novel.[5] The power of language to create order out of chaos and life out of death becomes a crucial "resource" for those who would attempt to build local pockets of meaning in a world crumbling into fragments.[6] At the same time, many of the characters in *Our Mutual Friend*, unlike those in *Bleak House*, are intensely self-conscious about the newly articulated thermodynamic worldview in which every energetic outlay can, theoretically, be measured, tracked, and defined on an abstract balance sheet of work and waste. Dickens's last finished novel focuses not just on the personal and collective warping effects of a resource-exploiting cultural order, but on the various attempts of characters to reflect upon the place of human life in such an order, and to find meaning in a world defined by an inescapable economy of energy relations.

Energy in the 1860s

As historian of science Graeme Gooday has shown, the thermodynamic definition of "energy" – a measurable quantity of motive power, or work – was in wide circulation in the British periodical press by the 1860s.[7] Despite this, the quantitative definition was nevertheless still in competition with the longstanding, non-technical use of the word, which could signify a personal *quality* of autonomy, diligence, or activity. "Energy is a force of character – inward power," wrote the Methodist minister Daniel Wise in 1860, to take one typical example.[8] In a notable article from 1862 entitled "Energy," published in the journal *Good Words*, William Thomson and Peter Guthrie Tait begin by squarely confronting this semantic tension:

> The non-scientific reader who may take up this article in the expectation of finding an exhortation to manly sports or a life of continual activity, with corresponding censure of every form of sloth and sensual indulgence, will probably be inclined to throw it down when he finds that it is devoted to a question of physical science. But let him not judge too hastily.[9]

The tone may be facetious, but it shows Thomson and Tait aware of the task they face in trying to appropriate for science a word already in wide popular circulation. They reassure their readers that what seems like an esoteric definition corresponds to everyday experience and "admits of being made, at all events in its elements, thoroughly popular."[10] Indeed, this is a key part of their agenda – to make their quantitative definition of "energy" popular, and further consolidate the term's meaning in scientific and amateur domains alike. Others took a more aggressive approach. The astronomer J. P. Nichol, for example, opens his entry on "Energy" in his *Cyclopaedia of the Physical Sciences* (1860) by declaring the primacy of the physicists' definition and introducing his readers to the term, he says, "in its larger and only true sense."[11] And Balfour Stewart argues for a thorough redefinition of the term: "we must learn to regard energy not as a quality, but rather as a *thing*."[12]

This kind of definitional rigor was difficult to attain, though, because the cultural associations that attended both definitions of the word overlapped significantly. For one thing, both uses of "energy" mingled freely in discussions of national strength, productivity, and identity. Quantitatively speaking, it was widely recognized that England's position as a global power was predicated upon its energy resources. At the same time, it seemed to many observers that there was some quality in the national character that made the English better managers of those resources, and thus uniquely deserving of that power. This sense of merit was, as we have seen, sometimes religiously tinged, and sometimes represented in more secular terms. In both cases, energy-as-quality and energy-as-quantity were mutually reinforcing concepts. The sanitary reformer Edwin Chadwick boasts that: "two English labourers or artisans are proved to be equal in productive power to three Danes, or three Norwegians, or three Swedes, or three Norman labourers, or three Germans," and then goes on to note that, "if two capitals or two labourers are equal to three, two populations, speaking roundly, are economically equal to three, and it may be confidently asserted that the twenty-seven million of population in Britain are from this very cause, in economical force at least, equal to the thirty-seven millions of the population of France."[13] Chadwick is discussing energy as a quantifiable resource, but he frames it as an expression of national quality, as an index to something peculiarly "energetic" about the English character.

Moreover, it was (many believed) the engineers, the statesmen, the leaders – the "men of energy" – who made the exploitation of those resources possible. A writer in *All the Year Round*, touring the National Portrait Gallery in 1863, muses on the quality that unites all of the personages depicted: "if you were asked what was the leading characteristic, the pervading peculiarity, of the countenances of all the most notable and distinguished men portrayed, probably your reply would be ENERGY." The writer then explicitly unites the worlds of national character and national industry when he discusses one of the values of the gallery for the contemporary world: "the blackened engineers who drop into these rooms for an hour from the works hard by, and the other intelligent mechanics who find their way here on Saturday afternoons, are probably stimulated by the sight of the self-made men who have risen to the distinction of having their portraits hung in a National Portrait Gallery."[14] In a mutually reinforcing logic, energy-the-time-tested-personal-characteristic helps unlock energy-the-physical-principle; the enormous power produced by industry, in turn, becomes a further sign of the quality of the English people. Just as it does in thermodynamic discourse, "energy" serves here as the underlying principle of unity beneath the diversity of surface expressions. If magnetism, heat, light, and motion are, at bottom, all forms of the physical principle energy, so the statesmen, military heroes, thinkers, and scientists in the gallery all represent expressions of the same characteristic British energy.

But while "energy" thus functioned as a complex, multi-faceted signifier for British national power, the qualitative and quantitative valences also existed in an unresolved tension. If the idea of "energy" found on the walls in the National Portrait Gallery aggrandized individual effort, the scientific-industrial definition treated individual human effort as merely one unit in the total energy budget. Thomson and Tait write:

> in a bayonet charge, then, the soldier's rations are the potential energy of war; in a cavalry charge, we have in addition that of the forage supplied to the horses; and when artillery or small arms are used, the potential energy of a mixture of nitre, sulphur and charcoal is the tranquil antecedent of the terrible kinetic effects of noise and destruction.

When they go on to say that, in addition to rations, an army's resources include "the forage supplied to the horses" as well as "the potential energy of a mixture of nitre, sulphur and charcoal" in gunpowder, they define the soldier as simply another unit in the "energy of war." [15] Notice too, in the passage from Chadwick, how quickly he moves from a discussion of the force of "two English labourers" to that of "twenty-seven million." Once energy could be described as a quantity, it became a routine gesture to frame the individual as a part of a vast, aggregated energy regime.

Whereas in the early nineteenth century, as Underwood notes, energy as a personal characteristic "covertly aggrandizes the individual's subjectivity," the new sense of the word threatens to undermine subjectivity by treating the individual as another measurable, fungible unit within a larger system of motive power. [16] "Energy" increasingly meant "resources," but since it was already used to describe a quality of personhood, it opened up a darker connotation: people defined as fuel within a system of production. Catherine Gallagher has usefully termed this relationship between the individual body and the national system of resource transformation "bioeconomics," and Jules Law describes this period as featuring a "contested shift" from a conception of bodily resources as personal and individual, to one in which those resources were seen in "collective, rationalized, even technocratic" terms. [17] While Law is interested in the representation of bodily fluids – blood, milk, and water – the shift he describes from personal to collective tracks the change in the conception of energy as well. For energy itself was (and is) represented as a kind of fluid. [18] Energy could also be said to "flow" in a slightly different sense: in the eyes of sanitarian reformers like Liebig, Chadwick, Hawksley, and others, energy resources were flowing through human bodies and out of the city in the form of sewage and other waste products that still retained fertilizing "vitality."

Law's work on fluids, then, can be usefully applied to the discussion of this metaphorical fluid, energy, and the way its flow connected the individual to a wider, transpersonal matrix of energy use, conservation, and dissipation. As Law argues, "the discourse of sanitarianism (with its over-riding mission of regulating the social circulation of biomaterials) provided a model for thinking about the individual body as a social resource, as a model that was infinitely manipulable for ideological purposes – reassuring at one moment, horrifying the next."[19] Indeed, the discourse of energy conservation in the 1860s was caught between these poles of reassurance and horror. On the one hand, the ability to quantify all activity – mechanical, animal, natural – as a form of energy meant that every component of national life could be conceptualized as a part of a single system of expenditure, providing the underpinnings for the rational management of resources. On the other hand, the fact that any function of existence could be submitted to this totalizing logic seemed alarmingly reductive. Thinking about one's energy in national or even global terms was a significant first step in articulating an ethic of energy conservation – sanitarians like Chadwick were some of the first to call for the implementation of sustainable energy practices. But thinking about resources in these technocratic terms also meant thinking of oneself as a unit of expenditure, and submitting one's own conception of personhood to a dehumanizing logic. If any individual expression of work achieved its significance through its participation in a larger system of productivity, it was always in danger of being emptied of significance by means of that very participation.

The idea that human labor could be understood this way, as another form of energy among many, was key to Marx's philosophy of history and his concept of alienation. As Anson Rabinbach makes clear, Marx's work in the 1850s increasingly shows the influence of thermodynamic thought; his mature theory "is largely indifferent to the qualitative distinction between human labor power and any other inorganic productive force in nature or in technology."[20] But for Marx, the reduction of life to labor power, and the idea of the unity of all forces – natural, industrial, animal – was a necessary step towards emancipation. If human labor and machine labor can both be conceived of as expressions of the same fundamental principle, then society can look forward to the day when the former will be fully replaced by the latter; the "true realm of freedom," he writes, "can flourish only upon that realm of necessity as its basis."[21] As many commentators have pointed out, Marx's Communist future depends upon the technological infrastructure brought into being by capitalism. But the waste of resources, the exploitation of labor power, and the "stultification" of human life into mere "material force" are imagined as products of the social relations of capitalism, "the limited bourgeois form" that will disappear in a post-revolutionary society.[22] The energy concept and the actual material exploitation of energy are key components to capitalist domination of man and nature, but they also hold the promise of future material abundance in the next stage of history.

"Energy" had thus become, by the 1860s, an unstable mediator between the qualitative, moral order of individual autonomy, and the quantitative, systematized complex of aggregated national and historical motive power. The quantitative definition meant that *any* action, no matter how small, could be conceptualized as a vector of energy expenditure; the thermodynamic discourse of energy conservation and dissipation could thus be extended into all domains of human activity. This extension, in turn, raised troubling questions about the relationship between work and identity. Edwin Chadwick's address to the British Association for the Advancement of Science in 1862, for example, discusses the traffic between mental and bodily energy:

> The most correct adjustment of human force for the most productive application, as an investment, would require considerable observation of varied sanitary and other conditions over long periods of time. Amongst the means of sustaining that force, would be what may be termed the metaphysical means; – pleasurable mental excitement accompanying the work, or in the results. On physical means alone, as food, clothing, housing, however good the work after a time often goes on heavily, wearily, slowly, and it requires mental stimuli to sustain the bodily energy.[23]

For Chadwick, the human being is a store of "productive force," which becomes depleted not only by disease and malnutrition, but by dissolute leisure activities, stress, boredom, and lack of self-respect. Over the course of the address the word "force," which Chadwick mainly uses to signify a physical laboring power, gradually gives way to the word "energy," with which he indicates something more capacious and mixed – a power seemingly drawn from physical and mental sources alike. The extension of the energy laws into all corners of human experience provided a unifying paradigm through which, for Chadwick, the problems of modernity could be addressed.

But such an emphasis on maximizing energy threatens to evacuate meaning from the productive process, and from the forms of work that provided stable grounds for individual identity. This point was made by *Punch* a few years after Chadwick's address in a letter to the editor entitled "Hard-Labour in Store." The letter can be read as a cagey deconstruction of Chadwick's report, and of the subjection of all facets of human life to a quantifying logic of energy conservation. It opens with a brief discussion of the conservation of energy and argues that since "scientific men cannot at present conceive what we shall possibly do for force when all our coals will have been used up … we ought to economise force as much as we can, and not throw away any force which we could anyhow save." Concluding that prisoners represent a gigantic waste of energy, both in terms of the food they consume and the issueless "hard-labour" they perform, the writer suggests a system "to store up the force which many of our convicts in working a mere handle, or treading a bare plank, unconnected with any useful mechanism, are now only wasting on the prison air." [24] This directly echoes Chadwick, who expresses concern over prisoners "kept unproduct-ively, generally, at double the expense of maintaining a pauper," but takes it a step further. The logic of efficiency leads in short order to a vision of slave labor, of harvesting energy from those whose lives have been deemed "unproductive." It's almost hard to tell that this is meant as a joke, so close in spirit is it to the preoccupations and contradictions of the era. Indeed, the only giveaway that the letter is meant as satire is its conclusion: "P.S. I am trying to invent some means of effecting the conservation of that force which is vainly expended, and as I say, squandered, in dancing."[25] If dancing squanders energy, then *life itself* looks like a waste of resources. "Hard-Labour in Store" moves from a literal imprisonment (harvesting the energy of actual convicts) to a more figurative kind of entrapment, one defined by a morbid self-awareness of the energy loss involved in any activity. "We live in a world of work," writes Stewart in a popular essay on energy, "from which we cannot possibly escape."[26]

The extension of this logic could lead to some frightening conclusions. In an article entitled "Up-Hill Work" published in *All the Year Round* in 1865, the author discusses the energy waste involved in, of all things, medi-ocre poetry:

> Far better that [a bad poet] should sit in a shady corner of the highway for the great ones' chariots to pass over, than lose time and strength and the substance of his hand in enacting the part of old Sisyphus in Hades. Whatever our sorrow and sympathy for him individually, the eternal laws of failure remain the same, and the fact that wasted strength is so much loss to the world of man … will not be modified even for the bitter heart-pain of an inglorious Milton mistaking his vocation, and rolling stones up Parnassus to end in failure and a shower of dust and mud.[27]

Activity is measured not only in terms of the loss of the individual's "time and strength," but in terms of the loss or gain "to the world of man." An individual's energy in some sense *belongs* to the energy of the entire national system. It's far better, the writer says, to do *nothing* – "to sit in a shady corner of the highway" – than to expend the nation's energies in hopeless pursuits. And yet, we might wonder, what is the value of *successful* poetry in such a context? Is poetry itself a productive use of resources? If not, what is? Once the pleasure of an activity is eliminated from consideration, and the activity judged solely in terms of energy conservation and dissipation, we find ourselves caught up in a nihilistic logic of production for its own sake. Without a coherent narrative by which to understand the purpose of activity, the emphasis on productivity creates, paradoxically, a vision of universal waste.

This, then, is where the discourse of energy departs from Law's discussion of the circulation of fluids. Energy, understood as a resource, is both something that circulates and something that gradually *stops* circulating. Understanding the human body as a channel through which energy flows threatens to make the boundaries of the self seem porous and unstable; but understanding the human body as a channel through which energy is *lost* makes the dust, smoke, and soot seem not simply a by-product of activity, but its chief production. While the discourse of energy conservation often fashioned a contrast between human life and waste – insofar as life was a way to channel and harness energy for production – it also implicitly set up an uncomfortable identification between them. "We can make no movement which is not accounted for by the contemporaneous extinction of some other movement," wrote an anonymous contributor to *All the Year Round* in 1865.[28] Although such a formulation suggests a stable model of equivalent action and reaction, the word "extinction"– especially post-*Origin of Species* – plainly suggests irreversible loss. All movement must be understood within this system of energy expenditure; in a system dependent on finite resources, all movement drives it towards extinction. This, then, is what is so disturbing about the representation of human activity in terms of fossil-fuel energy: it makes life itself a form of pollution.

"Idiots talk of energy"

As George Levine notes, in *Our Mutual Friend*, "the crisis of modern capitalism ... takes the form of the impossibility of finding a vocation that is not compromised and corrupted."[29] The terms "compromised and corrupted" are very precisely connected to the question of energy: work is "corrupted" because all forms of it are unavoidably connected to the larger inhuman production complex; it is "compromised" because characters cannot help but *be aware* that their actions are embedded in this complex. At times, Dickens uses this awareness to comic effect, as

when Silas Wegg first sizes up Mr. Boffin: "are you in independent circumstances, or is it wasting the motions of a bow on you?," and later
remarks to himself, "a bow gone!"[30] Wegg's interest in conservation is
especially absurd because his own behavior is so obviously characterized
by excess – sudden eruptions of poetry, extravagant locutions, endless
machinations and imaginings that get him nowhere. There is a sense
of overspilling comic plentitude about Wegg that stands in contrast to
his own miserly, self-conservative calculations. His individuality exceeds
such quantifying frameworks almost in spite of itself. But in this way, he
perfectly encapsulates Dickens's own ambivalence about the very logic
of conservation. We *like* Wegg for his unproductive extravagance, and
yet we *don't like* him for his entirely self-interested (and thus socially
irresponsible) ethic.

Indeed, this depiction of Wegg suggests a tension between Dickens's own
fictional practices and the emergent culture of energy conservation. While,
as we discussed in the previous chapter, his novels are structures that "conserve" energy – recycling characters, turning seemingly wasted actions into
patterns of order and symbolic meaning – they are also deeply invested in
the pleasures of dispersal, pointlessness, and prodigality. Orwell described
the hallmark of Dickens's style as the use of the "unnecessary detail," the
imaginative surplus that imbues his fictional worlds with its peculiar viv-
idness.[31] There is a tension, then, between the larger, retentive structures
of his fiction – in which everything seems strictly accounted for – and the
moments of dispersive, imaginative lavishness that give pleasure precisely
because they *don't* seem so strictly tabulated. But, as we have seen, the concept of energy frames such a tension – as it framed all activity – in a vocabulary of work and waste. On some level, to waste energy is to *live*, while
jealously to conserve it is to die; and yet, in the context of an environment
straining under a pall of pollution, such a spirit is also ecologically dangerous. Wegg (the storyteller) embodies this tension, jealously managing his
own energetic economy while throwing off sparks of pointless, pleasurable
nonsense.

Wegg's comic imaginings both reinforce and leaven the darker sense of
enforced participation within a social energy regime explored elsewhere in
the novel. Like Wegg, Eugene Wrayburn is aware of his place within a system of conservation and expenditure. And unlike his precursor, Richard
Carstone, whose fog-blind assimilation of Chancery's logic strands him
in a spiritual no-man's land, Wrayburn's paralysis seems to arise out of an
overly acute awareness of his condition. For Richard there are viable alternatives to pursuing his interests in the Jarndyce suit; honest work is an

option he continually forgoes. For Wrayburn, the world of work has been drained of significance and the problem has to do with energy:

> "Then idiots talk," said Eugene, leaning back, folding his arms, smoking with his eyes shut, and speaking slightly through his nose, "of Energy. If there is a word in the dictionary under any letter from A to Z that I abominate, it is energy. It is such a conventional superstition, such parrot gabble! What the deuce! Am I to rush out into the street, collar the first man of a wealthy appearance that I meet, shake him and say, 'Go to law upon the spot, you dog, and retain me, or I'll be the death of you'? Yet that would be energy."[32]

Indeed, Wrayburn's is essentially a critical commentary on the energy dynamics of the legal world we saw in *Bleak House*, in which the elaborate choreography of Chancery – "motioning, and referring, and reporting and revolving"[33] – had its physical issue in exhausted and disordered environments. To respond to the social imperative that he become a man of "energy" – a man of character – Wrayburn gestures both to his profession and to the city streets, zones in which the traditional characteristics of energy – autonomy, initiative, activity – have been reduced to a wasteful pantomime. Energy-the-quality becomes energy-as-mere-expenditure. There is no Chancery in *Our Mutual Friend*, no single hated institution or profession that embodies and concentrates the problem of energy waste; instead, Wrayburn's caricature of energy serves as a more far-reaching indictment of the value of work itself.

Dickens underscores this in what follows, as Lightwood commiserates, "show me something really worth being energetic about, and I'll show you energy."[34] Through the attention they pay to the word itself, both characters suggest a gulf between an individual's idea of his own work, and the actual system within which it must take form. The narrator then pans out from this conversation to give us a glimpse of that encompassing system: "And it is likely enough that ten thousand other young men, within the limits of the London Post-office town-delivery made the same hopeful remark in the course of the same evening."[35] The novel moves here from the qualitative to the quantitative, from the question of how two individuals should "energetically" conduct themselves to the fact that "ten thousand" are stuck in the same dilemma. Even their protest is indistinguishable from other protests; they are drawn into an anonymous aggregate through their very rejection of it. Thus what was for Chadwick a liberating self-awareness about the universality of energy relations and the role individuals played in the productive life of the nation becomes in *Our Mutual Friend* a paralyzing vision of activity emptied, quantified, and divorced

from legible human ends. As Law argues, "In *Our Mutual Friend* ... public spaces – and particularly the river – raise directly the question of the
borders between self and other, body and environment, possession and
self possession."[36] Wrayburn and Lightwood seek to maintain the borders
of self by refusing to participate in the world beyond the confines of the
cab in which they are traveling – it's telling that Wrayburn shuts his eyes –
but participation in the energy regime is not a matter of choice. Dickens
stages the conversation in a moving carriage, so that the lawyers' spirited
rejection of the word "energy" takes place *within* the urban transportation
network that seemed to some observers to give London its very spirit of
dynamism and unity.[37] There is no work – and thus no identity – that
does not, in some way, participate in, or depend upon, the wider matrix
of energy relations. All expressions of energy are, at bottom, represented
as different forms of dust-generation: "The grating wind sawed rather than
blew; and as it sawed, the sawdust whirled about the sawpit. Every street
was a sawpit, and there were no top-sawyers; every passenger was an under-
sawyer, with the sawdust blinding him and choking him."[38] As with the
tension within the words "energy" and "resource," the contrast between
"top-sawyer" and "under-sawyer" inscribes a dynamic in which individual
quality is subsumed in a vision of aggregated expenditure. A "top-sawyer" is
literally the person who works the upper handle of a pit-saw, but the term
also once signified a man of quality, a distinguished person. Here, that distinction is swallowed, obscured materially in the waste-whirling action of
the under-sawyers, and obscured metaphorically in the decoupling of those
forces from legible ends.

Fantasies of perfect recycling

The only possible avenue of escape from wasted energy in this novel is
recycling, which, as many have noted, defines the work of numerous
characters. In *The Body Economic*, Catherine Gallagher describes the way
in which the "sanitary imagination" – the vision of urban recycling propounded by Chadwick and other reformers – informed Dickens's representation of the transformation of waste products back into life in *Our
Mutual Friend*. Gallagher shows how Dickens and Ruskin, despite their
hostility to political economists like Malthus and Ricardo, nevertheless
replicated their arguments about the abstract quantity of "life" that, paradoxically, is most easily recognized and valorized when suspended in
non-living substances.[39] Gallagher's "bioecomomics" offers us a glimpse
into the way in which the reification of vitality allowed the functions of

life itself to be commodified and introduced into a circulatory economy.[40] These seemingly lifeless materials could become productive again, and Chadwick and other recycling advocates argued that carelessly disposing of city waste was tantamount to flushing energy away.

But "energy" differs from "vitality" in that, after 1860, the former is indissociably tied to the emergence of a fossil-fuel-driven economic order. In such an economy, commodities do not embody the "vitality" of the laboring time it takes to create them; instead, the production of some kind of local order like a commodity *necessarily* entails greater disorder (energy loss and waste) in the wider environment. As we have seen, the by-products of fossil-fuel expenditure – soot, smoke, and dust – do not return to a vital condition through "natural" cycles of decay and renewal. Sanitarians like Chadwick were, at heart, productivists who believed that the circulation of energy had simply become interrupted by inadequate waste management plans; the consumption of fossil fuels, however, doesn't merely disrupt this circulation, it operates according to an entirely different pattern. The change is now historical, unidirectional. To focus on the circulation of energy through agriculture, bodies, and sewage, as the sanitarians did, is to miss the irreversible dynamics of a new kind of energy economy.

Thus while Gallagher is certainly right to point out all the strange forms of suspended vitality in the novel, as well as Dickens's debt to the discourse of urban recycling developed by Chadwick, F. C. Krepp, and others, I would argue that *Our Mutual Friend* also stages a conflict between this older model of cyclical decay and regeneration and a modern, entropy-centered economy in which waste represents not unused potential, but the end of transformation itself. When Gaffer tells Lizzie: "the very fire that warmed you when you were a baby was picked out of the river alongside the coal barges,"[41] his vivid synecdoche suggests a magical process of transformation – "fire" arising directly from water, warmth from cold. Gaffer wants an ungrateful Lizzie to consider the river, despite its noxious qualities, as the source of sustenance: "As if it wasn't your living! As if it wasn't meat and drink to you ... How can you be so thankless Lizzie?"[42] As Gallagher argues, by calling the river "meat and drink" Gaffer collapses the larger network of exchanges that convert the river's waste into money and then into sustenance. Such a self-construction is essentially defensive, because it skips over the dubious intermediate steps (fishing out dead bodies, rifling through pockets) and implies a more direct transformative power. Waste becomes value, water becomes fire, cold becomes heat: the states are sharply distinguished. Both metaphorically (the river *is* Gaffer) and metonymically (the river provides him with valuable things), this vision obscures the problem of entropy, and the potential identification of Gaffer's own person with the waste of the river. It wards off the troubling connection between life and pollution by imagining a magical transformative capacity that can redeem what seems irretrievably lost.

But if Gaffer imagines transformation and distinctness, the river itself, as both the medium and metaphor of circulation, offers a vision of intermixture and termination:

> Not a lumbering black barge, with its cracked and blistered side impending over them, but seemed to suck at the river with a thirst for sucking them under. And everything so vaunted the spoiling influences of water – discoloured copper, rotten wood, honey-combed stone, green dank deposit – that the after-consequences of being crushed, sucked under, and drawn down, looked as ugly to the imagination as the main event.[43]

Gaffer's metamorphic description of coal is made possible by this transportation network, which itself depends upon the dynamics of mass consumption, and produces an undifferentiated mingling of organic and inorganic forms, the loss of both order and energy. Fire does not come from water; it is filched from a corroded infrastructure. While Dickens is interested in the ways in which seemingly spent forms of energy can be "restored to life," he is just as interested, I would argue, in the ways in which fictions of a fully recyclable, cyclical economy have been awkwardly grafted upon a system of non-renewable resource exploitation. In this, Dickens distances himself from the discourse of urban sanitary reform, and the kind of metamorphic language it often employed. Dr. Andrew Wynter's "The Use of Refuse" seems to dwell in the same imaginative landscape as Dickens's novel: not only does it feature London's dust mounds and describe the process of extracting value from them, it represents waste and inorganic materials as if they are animated with a strange, transformative life-force of their own:

> what diverse forms of new life await the old bone as the rag-picker recovers it from the ash-heap! Its substance, in the form of handles of knives, chessmen, paper-knives, &c., mingles with the everyday concerns of life – its hard work and its enjoyments and intellectual amusements; whilst in its fluid and manorial products yet more astonishing changes attend it the moment it falls into the hands of the manufacturer.[44]

For Wynter, science opens up a window into a "land of wonders," in which disordered materials can be easily sorted – or can automatically sort themselves – and the energetic potential of seemingly inert matter, discards, and by-products is fully reclaimed. The scientific investigation of waste materials, even "the most offensive refuse," will reveal funds of untapped energy: "in this way our stores are replenished, and it often happens that dearth, by the energy it gives to human research, is turned into plenty."[45] We have seen this move before – the haziness of the word "energy" allows Wynter not only to imply that science *itself* is a source of energy, but that it produces the most when actual resources are most scarce.

Not all sanitary reformers were quite as blithe about the transformability of urban waste as Wynter; many discussed the profound engineering difficulties involved. Nevertheless, as Nicholas Goddard points out, the discourse was characterized by "extreme optimism," and although proponents of urban recycling were admirably calling attention to the need for a more careful husbanding of energy resources, they also often engaged in a mystifying discourse that represented energy as fully renewable, and waste as a temporary problem. Recall F. C. Krepp's comment, quoted in the introduction, that "[b]y a judicious use of the immense resources placed at our disposal by modern science ... a peaceful, moral, and social revolution will be effected such as the world has hardly seen before!" (above, 11). Seen correctly, waste is actually an immense *supply* of energy, one that simply awaits transformation. But Krepp's vision of "boundless plenty" is made possible through energy inputs he mentions but fails to count – "pneumatic force, steam-power, and agricultural chemistry."[46] That is, the very process of recycling depends upon a tremendous amount of additional energy, an expenditure that will result in additional waste, and additional consumption of resources, and so on. *This*, then, is the geometric figure at issue – a spiral, not a circle. And this is the besetting problem with urban recycling programs as they confront the restrictions described by the laws of thermodynamics: although they promise to address energy scarcity and dissipation – sometimes with the conservation law an explicit part of their conceptual armature – there is often an undisclosed, or uncounted, input of energy that makes the scheme possible in the first place. Douglas Galton writes that sewage was "like gold in the sands of the Rhine, its aggregate value must be immense, but no one has succeeded in raising the treasure."[47] But this is not a negligible problem – the energy needed to "raise" the treasure is not an incidental question when the very question is the economization of energy.

Dickens's heaps do not automatically "reascend" the scale of value; they require massive additional inputs of energy:

> The train of carts and horses came and went all day from dawn to nightfall, making little or no daily impression on the heaps of ashes, though, as

the days passed on, the heap was seen to be slowly melting. My lords and gentlemen, when you in the course of your dust-shoveling and cinder-raking have piled up a mountain of pretentious failure, you must off with your honorable coats for the removal of it, and fall to the work with the power of all the queen's horses and all the queen's men, or it will come rushing down and bury us alive.[48]

Whereas sanitary reformers went out of their way to insist that waste forms represent untapped energy – arguing, in essence, that the very size of the problem revealed the power of the solution – Dickens reveals the way in which wasted energy forms drain even *more* energy. Dust in the novel is possessed of no transformative properties itself; instead, the language of transformation – "was seen to be slowly melting" – turns out to be only a trick of perspective, a function of distanced representation that overlooks the tremendous amounts of physical labor required. *Our Mutual Friend* insists, likewise, on the bodily experience of scavenging. In the above passage, Dickens facetiously imagines the lords and gentlemen rolling up their sleeves, but in the novel itself he focuses on the additional energy extracted from the bodies of the lower classes. If *Bleak House* seemed to feature a guttering candle in every room, *Our Mutual Friend* is filled with people leaking heat, rubbing hands together, struggling to stay warm. After a night out on the river, Gaffer says to Lizzie, "I ain't of a glow, that's certain. And my hands seemed nailed through to the sculls. See how dead they are."[49] Gaffer's numb hands, the Inspector later notes, play a role in his death. He may be able to describe fire as something plucked directly from the river, but verbal resources do nothing to warm his extremities. Throughout the novel, the river is a zone not only of waste disposal, but of heat loss, as if the imaginary locus of metamorphic recycling and urban circulation is, in reality, an energy drain:

> Cold on the shore, in the raw cold of that leaden crisis in the four-and-twenty hours when the vital force of all the noblest and prettiest things that live is at its lowest ... Perhaps fire, like the higher animal and vegetable life it helps to sustain, has its greatest tendency towards death, when the night is dying and the day is not yet born.[50]

This discourse of bodily warmth works as a counterpoint to fictions of energetic cyclicality. For Wynter, scavenging and recycling are part of the same process – "there is not one particle in the heap the scavenger removes from our houses that is not again, and that speedily, put into circulation and profitably employed" – and the scavenger appears as nothing more than a disembodied adjunct to the circulatory process.[51] In *Our Mutual*

Friend, for the dust heaps and the river to produce any kind of energy, more work must be done, and more life must be expended. The recycling in *Our Mutual Friend* is either extremely limited, as in the living the Hexams eke out on the tides of river waste, or else it is illusory, a kind of fiction, as in the seeming animation of the body towed by Gaffer or the factitious "rebirth" of Harmon.

As Nancy Metz has argued, *Our Mutual Friend* features the "artistic reclamation of waste" – an emphasis on individual acts of imagination that confer order upon the manifest disorder of Victorian London: "the idea that everything is of potential value, that nothing is so trivial, vulgar, or superficially unlovely that the imagination cannot reanimate it and make it new."[52] But the distinction between a healthy "artistic reclamation" of waste, and obfuscating fantasies about the transformativity and malleability of the environment, has become entirely untenable. The metamorphic imaginary of the sanitarians – so close to Dickens's own – fails to maintain a firm distinction between the levels of verbal and material transformation: through imaginative linguistic flights, waste becomes raw potential and material abundance, and a destructive system of production looks imminently – and eminently – sustainable. In the hands of urban sanitary reformers, the conversion of waste into value suggested possibilities for ecological transformation, but, more often than not, this was effected through the transformative power of language to disguise the depths of the problem. The discourse of energy transformation and productivism may seem to be able to vivify the inert and "reclaim" waste, but such collective fantasy disguises the stubborn, unregenerate materiality of pollution. Environmental concern thus shifts towards industrial *apologia*. *Our Mutual Friend*, in contrast, showcases both the power the imagination possesses and the threat that power poses to a clear-eyed reckoning of the contours of the problem.

Energy and endings

As the novel moves towards its conclusion, the emphasis shifts from concerns about pollution and resources to an interest in the language of energy as a marker of class difference. This shift cuts two ways, ecologically speaking. On the one hand, Dickens rightly critiques the way in which the discourse of energy conservation was used by the ruling classes to depict workers as a kind of motive power. Recall Chadwick's objection to unproductive leisure activities, which was aimed solely at the laboring classes, whose "waste is chiefly in the misapplication of the hours of his days, commonly to the extent of one-half the productive power."[53] On the other hand, class also helps Dickens alter the terms of the debate, to turn his attention from questions about how an individual can act and work meaningfully in a world defined by energy waste, to a critique of the misappropriation of the *vocabulary* of energy by a specific class.

As we have seen, Wrayburn complains about the use of the word "energy" in the opening pages, and despite his aloofness, he remains part of the larger system. But as the novel develops, this more intractable, global problem of energy and irreversibility becomes a class-inflected conflict between Wrayburn and Headstone. The latter is consistently described in a vocabulary of magnetism, heat, and force. He tells Lizzie Hexam, "I am under the influence of some tremendous attraction which I have resisted in vain and which overmasters me. You could draw me to fire, you could draw me to water … you could draw me to any good – every good – with equal force";[54] the narrator says he has a "wild energy"[55] about him, and his seething emotions are compared to a furnace.[56] He is a kind of energy – raw, formless, volatile – that must go *somewhere*. Lizzie could channel him into good, perhaps, but Wrayburn, instead, channels him into that zone of dissipation, the city streets. He tells Lightwood: "One night I go east, another night north, in a few nights I go all round the compass. Sometimes, I walk; sometimes, I proceed in cabs, draining the pocket of the schoolmaster, who then follows in cabs."[57] If Wraybrun's quarrel is with "energy" at the beginning of the novel, it is with a particular embodiment of energy – Headstone – by the end.

The city streets have been depicted as a zone of wasted motion throughout the novel, and this is precisely the side of the city Wrayburn uses to wear the schoolmaster out: "looking like the hunted, and not the hunter, baffled, worn, with the exhaustion of deferred hope and consuming hate and anger in his face, white-lipped, draggled-haired."[58] Headstone later erupts in vengeance when he ambushes Wrayburn, who sees "flames shot jaggedly across the air" and feels as if he has been struck by lightning.[59] Dickens maintains this language of energy after the attack, as Headstone sits contemplating his fate: "Rigid before the fire, as if it were a charmed flame that was turning him old, he sat, with the dark lines deepening in his face, its stare becoming more and more haggard, its surface turning whiter and whiter as if it were being overspread with ashes."[60] Headstone is energy that has been channeled into futile purposes, released violently, and lost altogether. The futile purposes, it should be added, include not only his pursuit of Wrayburn, but his own pointless work. Headstone's teaching, Dickens makes clear, participates in a kind of closed system of endless recycling, where the purpose of education seems to be nothing more than "mechanical stowage"[61] and the manufacture of more teachers.

Dickens's interest in Headstone's thwarted and misdirected energy helps establish the terms by which the middle class can be valorized and set apart from the world of waste and damage. Like Veneering, Headstone offers a nightmare version of middle-class energy, a raw upward striving that is closely aligned with the blind forces of mechanization and commerce. Dickens defines Headstone by the improper regulation of energy – the mechanical channeling of his forces into work that leads to frustration:

> Suppression of so much to make room for so much, had given him a constrained manner over and above. Yet there was enough of … what was fiery (though smouldering) still visible in him, to suggest that if young Bradley Headstone, when a pauper lad, had chanced to be told off for the sea, he would not have been the last man in a ship's crew. Regarding that origin of his, he was proud, moody, and sullen, desiring it to be forgotten.[62]

But this is where Dickens makes a key distinction. Headstone, in fact, only *looks* like he's a member of the middle class; his origins have been obscured in his upward march. His "smouldering" suggests not just a fiery emotional life, but a kind of ambition fueled by class resentment. In this way, the grounds are being prepared for a healthy and genuine version of middle-class energy to emerge.

The shift he makes through the character of Headstone – the valorization of middle-class marriage as a proper channel for energy – is reinforced at the very end of the novel, in an explicit discussion of energy conservation and marriage by members of the Veneering set. "The Contractor," speaking to Lady Tippins, describes Lizzie's future and her relationship with Eugene in terms of a Chadwickean energy calculus:

> Lady Tippins next canvasses the Contractor, of five hundred thousand power. It appears to this potentate, that what the man in question should have done, would have been, to buy the young woman a boat and a small annuity, and set her up for herself. These things are a question of beefsteaks and porter. You buy the young woman a boat. Very good. You buy her, at the same time, a small annuity. You speak of that annuity in pounds sterling, but it is in reality so many pounds of beefsteaks and so many pints of porter. On the one hand, the young woman has the boat. On the other hand, she consumes so many pounds of beefsteaks and so many pints of porter. Those beefsteaks and that porter are the fuel to that young woman's engine. She derives therefrom a certain amount of power to row the boat; that power will produce so much money; you add that to the small

annuity; and thus you get at the young woman's income. That (it seems to the Contractor) is the way of looking at it.[63]

Lady Tippins and "the Contractor" represent Lizzie's life in terms of its energy content, and the joke, like the one contained in the *Punch* article, hinges on the absurdity of reducing human activity to a function of fuel. But it also showcases the casualness with which the lives of the lower classes could be framed as units of motive power. Lady Tippins and the Contractor seem entirely unaware of the irony of their applying the strictures of "sustainable" energy practices while mingling in the patently unproductive, wasteful world of the Veneerings, Podsnaps, and Lammles. They are clearly taken aback by Wrayburn's marriage to a "factory girl,"[64] and the Contractor's response suggests not only an inability to fathom such a match, but a desire to cut her back down to size, to reduce her life to nothing more than an economy of energy calling for strict management.

But Lizzie will simply not be reduced in this way. For one thing, she is already married to Wrayburn, a fact that makes the Contractor's elaborate plans seem not simply obtuse, but beside the point. More importantly, this marriage has lifted her out of the lower classes, and thus out of the sphere that was most often manhandled by such a calculus. If Wrayburn is no longer concerned with the opinions of the Veneering set, Lizzie is no longer subject to their representational practices. This discussion between Lady Tippins and the Contractor, while it seems to echo concerns about energy raised earlier in the novel, also renders such concerns in starker and more narrowly satirical terms, framing them as comically misapplied artifacts of class antagonism. The discourse of energy, which, in the early stages of the novel, seemed inescapable, is here lodged in the mouths of patently ridiculous and ineffectual characters, and thereby cordoned off, made less threatening. When Wrayburn complains at the beginning of the novel that "idiots talk ... of Energy," his remark leads us into complex territory, raising questions about the viability of individual activity within an energy regime governed by laws of dissipation and conservation. Here, by the end, it is merely an idiot talking of energy.

By rejecting the Veneering set, Wrayburn leaves behind his (half-hearted) interest in this status-seeking world as well as its empty discursive practices; likewise, by leaving her factory employment and marrying him, Lizzie escapes the world of empty mechanical labor. They have met in the middle, in a sense, where marriage both solidifies their status as members of the middle class, and rescues them from both the reduction of life into the terms of energy, and the actual deployment of energy in industrial toil. The resolution, fittingly, is framed using this vocabulary:

> "Well. If I live, you'll find me out."
> "I shall find out that my husband has a mine of purpose and energy, and will turn it to the best accounts?"
> "I hope so, dearest Lizzie," said Eugene wistfully, and yet somewhat whimsically. "I hope so. But I can't summon the vanity to think so. How can I think so, looking back on such a trifling, wasted youth as mine! I humbly hope it, but I daren't believe it."[65]

Again, the language of energy and waste is usefully flexible, and here it helps bend the novel towards its conclusion. If the recycling of wasted material energy forms is elsewhere represented by Dickens as a grotesque fantasy, it is reclaimed here, through its translation into metaphors for the emotional life and character, into an achievable personal goal. Wrayburn's "wasted" youth can be transformed by means of a narrative of redemption, in which the past is not changed but recontextualized. His dispersal of Headstone's energy, and his participation in the waste of the London streets, only lend the final conversion more metaphorical power. Notice that the phrase "mine of purpose and energy" bridges the question of material energy resources, with which the novel has been concerned, and the idea of the resources of the heart, on which it ends. The word "mine," indeed, is subtly transformed in this passage, from a source of industrial power to something one owns, a part of one's personal story – "such a trifling, wasted youth as *mine*!" The former can be exhausted; the latter is a narrative one can change. And through these various narrative and linguistic conversions, the word "energy" itself is returned to its earlier semantic condition – its definition as a quality.

The fluid movement the novel allows between the world of industrial production and the world of the emotional life, mediated through the vocabulary of energy, suggests a retreat from the ecological catastrophe into a private sphere of inexhaustible and unwasteful energy, signified by a reappropriation of terms the world of production and waste had commandeered. On the other hand, the continuity of terms offers a solution to that catastrophe through the activation of the energy of the emotional life; it implies there are still untapped "sources" of energy available. As we have seen in this chapter and throughout this book, the latter has been a much-used strategy in this period, as fears of unsustainable energy consumption were often quelled by an appeal to the "energy" generated by other, non-material sources: science, the English character, the spiritual life, the heart. Wrayburn has been returned to pure potentiality; his character has become a kind of untapped resource awaiting expression. He is "renewable." But this returns him precisely to the problem the novel set out to solve: what actual use of energy does not participate in the system of production in which everyone is embedded? Here I think we see the dynamic described by Gallagher, wherein life can only be valued in its suspended form, where the only pure energy is still-unused energy. Dickens may attempt to restore the word to its original condition, but language, like energy, is itself irreversibly transformed by the way it is used.

For Mary Poovey, the end of *Our Mutual Friend* is about "converting the abstraction of commodification into a metaphorics of worth." Dickens attempts to do this with the commodified "energy." In doing so, however, in rejecting the idea of human energy as simply one more commodity within a larger world of commodified energy relations, he forgoes the chance to think about energy as an ecological signifier, about how the individual can come to terms with his or her own energy use within a system of waste generation. Instead, we are returned to a mysterious idea of energy – one that, through linguistic continuity, seems to address the problems raised, but actually simply refers us, in Poovey's phrase, to "forces beyond men's control."[66]

In pointing to the way the endings of both *Bleak House* and *Our Mutual Friend* sidestep some of the more disturbing implications of energy waste, I don't mean to be too critical of Dickens. In both novels he grapples with questions about the way individuals participate in transpersonal systems of expenditure and waste that are deeply resistant to easy solution, and to representation. Chadwick's interest in efficient energy husbanding is easy to mock, and we can see why Dickens mocks it – it seems inhuman to reduce the activities of human life to aggregated units. And yet Chadwick's thinking – blinkered as it is – also represents the stirrings of some kind of environmental consciousness, the understanding that one's own actions contribute in their small way to the larger system in which everyone has to live. In order to imagine that connection, and to have it influence one's own behaviors, one must, on some level, necessarily imagine oneself as a resource-consuming, pollution-producing unit. Counter-intuitive as it might sound, environmental consciousness *is*, in some ways, a quantitative consciousness. This is what is behind the slogan "think globally, act locally" – a sense that one's individual consumption must be understood in reference to the conditions of a larger order of resource use and waste. To reject the quantification of human life, as Dickens clearly does in *Our Mutual Friend*, is to resist the subordination of one's identity to the logic of a wasteful and destructive system, but it is also to deny the reality of one's own position as a consumer – the fact that, as long as Eugene and Lizzie continue living in London, burning coal, buying commodities, working in occupations supported by resources imported from elsewhere, they *are* participants in this system, and part of this regime. This is why Dickens can only represent their future as having a "mine of purpose and energy" – that is, as pure disembodied potential – because any actual activity involves contributing to the eco-catastrophe still unfolding in the streets, skies, and waterways of England. Indeed, what kind of life does not? Dickens asks this question in the beginning of the novel and it remains unanswered by the end. One can take a stand against the reduction of human life, but one cannot, simply by taking that stand, escape from the very real ways in which life has already been reduced. By shifting to an allegorical mode by the end of the novel, by presenting us with the unsatisfying idea that middle-class marriage makes possible some kind of clean, untapped, uncompromised energy source, Dickens suggests what kinds of responses are no longer available when one rejects quantifying logic out of hand.

CHAPTER 5

John Ruskin's alternative energy

John Ruskin has long been regarded as a crucial figure in the environmental tradition in English literature. Along with that of Blake, Wordsworth, and John Clare, Ruskin's work has been seen as pivotal in beginning, as Timothy Clark puts it, "a green political movement whose importance few would now question."[1] Jonathan Bate places Ruskin squarely in the tradition of "Romantic ecology," focusing on his interest in ecological holism and conservation, and on his critique of dehumanizing working conditions that severed the vital connection between laborers and the environment.[2] Ruskin's influence as an environmental thinker extends into the late nineteenth century, in the work of William Morris and Patrick Geddes, and into the twentieth, in the work of J. A. Hobson, Lewis Mumford, and Gregory Bateson, among many others. In recent years, he has also become something of a touchstone for the emergent field of ecological economics, which seeks to reorient the discussion of growth by emphasizing the ways in which economic activity alters – and is altered by – the complex dynamics of both local and global ecosystems. This influence can be traced through Frederick Soddy and E. F. Schumacher in the early twentieth century, and through contemporary thinkers like former World Bank Economist Herman Daly, and economic historian Juan Martinez-Alier. Ruskin is valued by these writers both for his insistence on the purposes and ends of productivity as a necessary metric for judging economic activity, and for his interest in energy as the biophysical nexus between human and natural systems.[3] Indeed, as I hope to show in the following pages, Ruskin's work is the most profound meditation on an emergent energy-intensive culture the Victorian period produced.

Ruskin's discussion of energy is deeply idiosyncratic and yet, as we will see, it also shadows – and sometimes explicitly engages with – contemporary developments in thermodynamic science. Like Dickens, like Thomson and his fellow physicists, Ruskin is interested in energy as a property of *system*, but what separates him from his contemporaries is his interest in representing the all-inclusiveness of this system, the way that energy serves as a mediator between environmental, aesthetic, and economic domains. Ruskin's vision of energy is comprehensively ecological, since it involves not simply a consideration of natural systems, but the manifold, shifting, strange, unbounded zones of interchange among natural formations, cultural productions, working conditions, modes of economic organization, transportation networks, and human-constructed environments. In its comprehensive reach, this vision allows Ruskin to offer a powerful, multi-leveled critique of Victorian energy consumption, and locate the roots of the ecological crisis not in a specific class or industry or mode of thinking, but in a ramified, reinforcing dynamic between aesthetic standards and environmental conditions. Using "energy" as a capacious signifier, Ruskin focuses on the transformational junctures that unite seemingly disparate phenomena and modes of human behavior. The energy that powers the natural world powers the body, which channels that energy into cultural productions, which shape the environment, which shapes working conditions and aesthetic standards, which transform body and mind, and so on. Ruskin's critical writings on art, on economics, and on the natural environment are all attempts to intervene at various points in this cycle, always with an eye to defining an alternative to contemporary patterns of energy-intensive consumption. But the capaciousness of this vision, which had once been a sign of its critical power, ultimately comes to create a sense of total enclosure, of rapidly foreclosing possibilities and an encircling nimbus of contamination. If Ruskin, like Dickens, tells alternative thermodynamic stories by following the movement of energy through seemingly disparate but nevertheless interconnected zones, he also ultimately follows it to a terminal point of breakdown and disorganization. By the time he writes his famous *Storm Cloud* lecture near the end of his career, the entire atmosphere seems to have become urbanized, its very character irreversibly altered by the energy-wasting processes that define the values and the economic life of the dominant order. Thus what appears at first as a network of relations comes, in his late writings, to look more like a feedback loop or spiral into irreversible climate chaos: degraded environments producing degraded tastes producing degraded consumer choices producing a degraded world. This is, of course, a very different kind of feedback loop from those that modern scientists have identified fueling climate change – in which mounting carbon dioxide levels produce environmental effects that release more CO_2 – but Ruskin follows its logic to a decidedly unscientific but nevertheless powerful narrative of anthropogenic global ecocide.

Energy and architecture

In the late 1840s, when Ruskin famously shifts his attention from painting to architecture in works like *The Seven Lamps of Architecture* and *The Stones of Venice*, the move is underwritten by a crucial change in his use of the word "energy." In the early volumes of *Modern Painters*, Ruskin used the term to argue for a deeper unity among seemingly disconnected levels of experience, and to combine the moral categories of his evangelical upbringing with a decidedly Romantic holism. He writes in Volume II: "There is certainly a sense of purity or impurity in the most compound and neutral colours, as well as in the simplest; a quality difficult to define, and which the reader will probably be surprised by my calling the type of Energy, with which it has certainly little traceable connection in the mind."[4] Here, Ruskin plays upon the Aristotelian definition of *energeia*, which, in both the *Metaphysics* and *Rhetoric*, signified the active movement of an object.[5] Aristotle's use of it in the latter text, as Ted Underwood notes, gave rise to an interesting confusion in his later interpreters: "Aristotle advises speakers to describe activity, or to describe things as if they were active, in order to create a vivid effect. But Aristotle's medieval interpreters blurred the distinction between the activity described and the vivid effect produced."[6] Ruskin seems to be after a similar blurring in *Modern Painters*; by making "energy" the metric of evaluation, Ruskin attempts not only to elide the distinction between the aesthetic object and the perceiving mind, but also between represented object and its representation. "Energy" thus merges material, moral, and aesthetic registers: "I think the original notion of this quality," he says of purity/energy, "is altogether material."[7] But despite its capaciousness, the term sometimes introduces unresolved tension in these early writings. At times, the identification of energy with purity creates a moral dualism that sits uneasily with his interest in holism and unity.

> And so in all cases I suppose that pureness is made to us desirable, because expressive of that constant presence and energizing of the Deity by which all things live and move, and have their being; and that foulness is painful as the accompaniment of disorder and decay, and always indicative of the withdrawal of Divine support ... with the idea of purity comes that of spirituality; for the essential characteristic of matter is its inertia, whence, by adding to its purity of energy, we may in some measure spiritualize even matter itself.[8]

If energy is defined as an active principle, then decay and putrefaction are kinds of energy transformation just as health, growth, and development are – recall Carlyle's description of the dead leaf in *Heroes and Hero*

Worship, where even rotting is an expression of force (see above, 45). For Ruskin, however, the moral categories he wants to enforce at times wind up dividing the world between that which is inspirited with divine energy, and that which isn't.

When the discussion shifts to architecture, the meaning of energy changes. Unlike painting, architecture requires the use of energy as a *resource*; paintings may represent the "divine energy" of the natural world, but architectural production depends upon the physical energy of labor. When Ruskin writes in *The Two Paths* that "all art worthy of the name is the energy – neither of the human body alone, nor of the human soul alone, but of both united, one guiding the other: good craftsmanship and work of the fingers joined with good emotion and work of the heart,"[9] the word signifies not just aesthetic quality or physical expenditure, but the way in which both phenomena have become mutually defining in an architectural structure. *The Seven Lamps of Architecture* was published in 1849, *The Stones of Venice* in 1851–1853: significantly, these were the years in which James Joule and Hermann von Helmholtz were themselves drawing on their own Romantic presuppositions about the unity and interchangeability of all natural forces, to formulate the mechanical equivalent of heat, and energy as a quantifiable measure of *work*. The shift we see in Ruskin's discussion of energy is mirrored by contemporary developments in the physical sciences.[10]

The turn towards architecture, and towards an understanding of energy as a measure of work, fuses questions of bodily resources and aesthetic value, and thus makes indissociable the zones of production and consumption. For Ruskin, the Gothic succeeds because it allows room for the expression of the individual within a larger system of production: the "love of variety," he says, coalesces in the "culminating energy" of the structure as a whole.[11] The opposite of this is any architecture that, in privileging uniformity, demands precision and regularity from workers, processing their energy as machines process fuel:

> If you will have that precision out of them, and make their fingers measure degrees like cog-wheels, and their arms strike curves like compasses, you must unhumanize them. All the energy of their spirits must be given to make cogs and compasses of themselves. All their attention and strength must go to the accomplishment of the mean act. The eye of the soul must be bent upon the finger-point, and the soul's force must fill all the invisible nerves that guide it, ten hours a day, that it may not err from its steely precision, and so soul and sight be worn away, and the whole human being be lost at last.[12]

Since "energy" can mean both the effort expended in work *and* the expression of that effort, the term unites the act of commodity production with the act of commodity consumption. For Ruskin, the Gothic does not simply allow for the healthy exercise of human energy, it embodies it structurally, and shapes the viewer's experience. Notice his vocabulary of energy in this passage comparing the Gothic to other forms of architecture:

> [I]n the Gothic vaults and traceries there is a stiffness analogous to that of the bones of a limb, or fibres of a tree; an elastic tension and communication of force from part to part, and also a studious expression of this throughout every visible line of the building. And, in like manner, the Greek and Egyptian ornament is either mere surface engraving, as if the face of the wall had been stamped with a seal, or its lines are flowing, lithe, and luxuriant; in either case, there is no expression of energy in the framework of the ornament itself. But the Gothic ornament stands out in prickly independence, and frosty fortitude, jutting into crockets and freezing into pinnacles; here starting up into a monster, there germinating into a blossom, anon knitting itself into a branch, alternately thorny, bossy, and bristly, or writhed into every form of nervous entanglement; but, even when most graceful, never for an instant languid, always quickset.[13]

Not only in phrases like "communication of force" and "elastic tension," but through his reliance on participial verb forms like "flowing," "jutting," and "germinating," Ruskin's Gothic is a system pulsing with activity. The Gothic is both self-performing and uniquely captivating because it is both fixed in place and yet impossible to fix; thus it presents the consumer with an inexhaustible, because ever-shifting, source of interest. He writes:

> The vital principle is not the love of *Knowledge*, but the love of *Change*. It is that strange *disquietude* of the Gothic spirit that is its greatness; that restlessness of the dreaming mind, that wanders hither and thither among the niches, and flickers feverishly around the pinnacles, and frets and fades in labyrinthine knots and shadows along wall and roof, and yet is not satisfied, nor shall be satisfied.[14]

Although the passage is ostensibly about the spirit of Gothic creation, clearly enough the entity that "wanders hither and thither among the niches" is also Ruskin himself, or anyone willing to follow in his steps. The energy involved in the production lives on in the structure itself, as well as in the "vital principle" of the attentive critic.

The very capaciousness of the term "energy" introduces a tactically useful vagueness here, because it allows Ruskin to finesse what is, at times, a circular argument. The aesthetic worth of the Gothic can be gauged by the health of the laborers who made it. But how do we know the laborers were healthy? The aesthetics tell us that. Through its ability to conjure both material and qualitative domains simultaneously, "energy" helps him elide the issue, making it seem that aesthetic worth and bodily health are united in a common metric *already*. Nevertheless, despite the slipperiness, the broadening of terms is significant. Aesthetics and energy are now aligned in such a way that artistic production can be directly compared to any other kind of commodity production, as the use and expression of the resources of the nation and the labor power of the individual worker. If this move shrouds the actual facts of Gothic production in a haze of misplaced nostalgia, it also works to indict the needlessly wasteful expenditure of energy involved in modern production, and links that wastefulness to a degraded consumer aesthetic. The Gothic "can shrink into a turret, expand into a hall, coil into a staircase, or spring into a spire, with undegraded grace and unexhausted energy";[15] in this way it stands in direct contrast to a Victorian commodity culture that was, for Ruskin, premised on novelty and dependent upon resource-intensive production practices. Thomas Richards argues that in passages where Ruskin extols the Gothic spirit that "is not satisfied, nor shall be satisfied," and is capable of "perpetual novelty," he unconsciously replicates the values of the culture he seeks to indict.[16] But I would argue that Ruskin deliberately invites this parallel in order to draw the terms of art and commodity culture into the same discursive field, and thus compare them as competing vectors of expenditure. By emphasizing the "unexhausted energy" of the Gothic, Ruskin attempts to locate a form of aesthetic production that responds to the "insatiability of human wants," to borrow Regenia Gagnier's phrase, without visiting that insatiability on the natural environment or the body of the worker.[17] The key driver of industrial production and the human pressures behind it are not ignored, but reconfigured into the building blocks of an alternative system of organization. This is a key element in Ruskin's argumentative strategy throughout his career: begin by accepting the terms of the opposition but show how they can be differently arranged. As he says of businessmen in *Unto This Last*: "they neither know who keeps the bank of the gambling-house, nor what other games may be played with the same cards, nor what other losses and gains, far away among the dark streets, are essentially, though invisibly, dependent on theirs in the lighted rooms."[18] Indeed, we might think of the word "energy" itself as one of those cards – a signifier increasingly tied to the world of industry and technology that he would put to moral and aesthetic ends.

For Ruskin, the key to building an alternative energy system is the development of a healthy consumer ethic. This means both cultivating a more demanding aesthetic in the general public – one that will shun cheap, wasteful pleasures – and also developing an ethical awareness of the physical sources of commodities, and refusing to purchase anything built on the back of human misery or environmental destruction. In *The Stones of Venice*, Ruskin's interest in returning our attention to the physical sources of commodities is consistently communicated through a discourse of energy – not just in the actual terms like "energy," "force," and "motive power," but through an entire metaphorical complex of flux, conversion, process, and transformation, by which he emphasizes the identity of phenomena beneath dynamic changes in form or appearance. It is his interest in tracking these changes – an interest very much in line with the incipient thermodynamic worldview – that allows him to stage his own sustained exposure of what Marx would theorize as commodity fetishism. He writes:

> And now, reader, look round this English room of yours, about which you have been proud so often, because the work of it was so good and strong, and the ornaments of it so finished. Examine again all those accurate mouldings, and perfect polishings, and unerring adjustments of the seasoned wood and tempered steel. Many a time you have exulted over them, and thought how great England was, because her slightest work was done so thoroughly. Alas! if read rightly, these perfectnesses are signs of a slavery in our England a thousand times more bitter and more degrading than that of the scourged African, or helot Greek. Men may be beaten, chained, tormented, yoked like cattle, slaughtered like summer flies, and yet remain in one sense, and the best sense, free. But to smother their souls with them, to blight and hew into rotting pollards the suckling branches of their human intelligence, to make the flesh and skin which, after the worm's work on it, is to see God, into leathern thongs to yoke machinery with, – this is to be slave-masters indeed; and there might be more freedom in England, though her feudal lords' lightest words were worth men's lives, and though the blood of the vexed husbandman dropped in the furrows of her fields, than there is while the animation of her multitudes is sent like fuel to feed the factory smoke, and the strength of them is given daily to be wasted into the fineness of a web, or racked into the exactness of a line.[19]

It is an extraordinary passage, in part because of the way Ruskin begins with seemingly static objects, and reads in them the living world of energy transformation from which they arose. Notice how the passage moves from organic metamorphosis (skin transformed into leather) to the world of industrial energy exchange, where human lives are converted directly into pollution. If the creative energy of the Gothic worker lives on in the structure he helps build, the toilsome energy of the English worker lies wasted in the commodities he produces, and in the fashionable drawing room that would forget his existence. In both cases, Ruskin's task is to lay bare the hidden world of disordered energy behind "finished" artifacts. Indeed, one might say the point of this passage is to bring that disorder back into the comfortable zones that depend upon suppressing it – "Gothic" in a slightly different sense. Ruskin's outlook here is thoroughly, even radically, thermodynamic. The creation of intricate, delicate structures of order – the "exactness of a line" or "fineness of a web" – requires the expenditure of energy, and every expenditure has a cost, and thus involves an increase in disorder, or entropy, elsewhere. Though we are accustomed to thinking that manufactured goods represent a higher level of order and energy than raw materials, and that industrial processes augment standards of efficiency, the situation, in thermodynamic terms, is exactly the opposite. Where Victorian thermodynamic writers describe how an engine dissipates energy in order to produce some kind of local order (useful work, or a commodity), Ruskin in this passage imagines English culture itself as a giant engine, creating pockets of order in the commodities it produces while spreading disorder in the larger environment and among the "multitudes" it uses as fuel. Indeed, that latter construction –"the animation of her multitudes is sent like fuel to feed the factory smoke" – is particularly striking, since it suggests that the end of production is not the creation of value, but smoke. Ruskin means this quite seriously: the ornaments, luxuries, fine webs, and exact lines become essentially worthless when one tallies the cost in both natural resources and human energy required to produce them.

We might note how different Ruskin's reading of the drawing room is from Dickens's in *Our Mutual Friend*. The Veneerings' highly finished room seems to be spun out of nothing – indeed the present tense of the prose suggests the spontaneous generation of *arriviste* "newness" before our eyes: "The great looking-glass above the sideboard reflects the table and the company. Reflects the new Veneering crest, in gold and eke in silver, frosted and also thawed, a camel of all work."[20] And yet, as critics have long pointed out, Dickens is intent on connecting this shiny world with the entropic underside of London that it would conceal or ignore: the scavengers on the river, the dust mounds, the chaotic streets. But Dickens's satire, wonderful and effective as it is, also distances the reader from the Veneering set. The looking-glass in which the assembled guests all appear is a figure for the reader – a silent, all-seeing witness to the proceedings that judges the obliviousness of those present.[21] For Ruskin, in contrast, the passage *itself* functions as a mirror, reflecting to the reader the objects filling his or her own drawing room, and the grotesque depths behind the surfaces of line, edge, and polish. Where Dickens disrupts this world with the narrative of "The Man from Somewhere," Ruskin would disrupt it by a reminder of a frighteningly illimitable and irretrievable number of narratives that have been deliberately submerged in darkness. Recall the line from *Unto This Last*, quoted above, about the "other losses and gains, far away among the dark streets ... essentially, though invisibly, dependent on theirs in the lighted rooms," suggesting a complex network of relationships spreading out beyond any locally circumscribed center of order. In short, Ruskin's own stories of energy often contain an anti-narrative impulse, showcasing the breakdown of traditional modes of plotting and organization.

Ruskin's work is radically thermodynamic because while his emphasis is on the flow of energy resources, he refuses to consider energy solely in reference to a given machine or energetic reaction. Instead, the thermodynamic vocabulary of waste, efficiency, and productivity is redefined through an attempt to grasp the total environment in which energy is transformed and utilized. The engine in question is not a particular motor or rifle, but the entire economic organization of the nation, just as the energy stock in question is not a lump of coal or handful of gunpowder, but the sum total of natural resources and human labor that drives production. In his writings on political economy, to which we are about to turn our attention, Ruskin consistently imagines energy as a national aggregate with which only so much can be done, but upon which everyone depends. If, for Liebig, "civilization is the economy of power," for Ruskin, culture is the economy of energy.[22] Everything that is produced depends upon a common stock of resources, but exactly *what* is produced – food, furniture, stained-glass windows, or explosives – depends upon aesthetic ideals, cultural demands, and habits of consumption. He attempts to maintain a stable field of aesthetic reference against which all acts of production should be judged. Like Marx, Ruskin sees culture as an expression of the material conditions of production; unlike Marx, however, he believes culture has the potential to exert a powerful shaping influence over those conditions.

Energy and the critique of political economy

In his 1884 work *John Ruskin, Economist*, the Scottish biologist Patrick Geddes, precursor to the twentieth-century school of "ecological economics," makes the case that the thermodynamic conception of energy – the ability to do work – structures Ruskin's critique of modern political economy, and that, furthermore, this emphasis on energy is the foundation of its originality and argumentative strength. Geddes writes of the political economists: "nothing more effectually demonstrates the extraordinary slenderness of their scientific pretensions than that their physical discussions are heedless of the very existence of the modern doctrine of energy (if indeed they do not involve some contradiction of its fundamental law)."[23] This attention to energy, Geddes argues, is precisely what makes Ruskin's economic writings in *Unto This Last* and *Munera Pulveris* so valuable. Geddes is on to something here, but the repeated references to "economists" as a monolithic block tends to muddy the waters where the question of energy is concerned. It's hard to blame him for this, since Ruskin, like Carlyle, is often fond of lumping economists together as "them" just before sweeping their arguments aside. But one of the most crucial aspects to Ruskin's status as an economic thinker is the way he positions himself between different schools of thought and approaches to the economic calculus. On the one hand, he is in a dialogue with the classical tradition of Smith, Malthus, and Ricardo, and on the other, with the neoclassical "marginalist" school of W. S. Jevons, which was just ascending to prominence during his lifetime. It is his unusual position between these two camps that makes his energy-based critique legible.

In *Unto This Last* and *Munera Pulveris* we can see an even more thorough embrace of the thermodynamic conception of energy that we tracked in *The Stones of Venice*. In *Munera Pulveris*, energy is often coded as "intrinsic value," which he uses to attack what he considered the overreliance on "exchange value" in mainstream economic thinking. He writes:

> Intrinsic value is the absolute power of anything to support life. A sheaf of wheat of given quantity and weight has in it a measurable power of sustaining the substance of the body; a cubic foot of pure air, a fixed power of sustaining its warmth; and a cluster of flowers of given beauty a fixed power of enlivening or animating the senses and heart.[24]

The connection with the thermodynamic definition of energy is evident in the emphasis he places on the quantification and measurability of power, the idea that the energetic content of a commodity can be defined and "fixed" in mathematical terms. (We will return to the "cluster of flowers" in a moment.) For Ruskin, value is defined not by price, or by market mechanisms of supply and demand, but through an understanding of what "avail[s] towards life," by which he means, in part, the ability of a given commodity to compensate for the energy expended during its production.[25] A silo of wheat is intrinsically more valuable than a diamond ring, even if (say) both can fetch the exact same price on the open market. J. A. Hobson puts it this way: "in considering Mr. Ruskin's doctrine of 'intrinsic value,' attention has already been called to the just, scientific instinct which leads him to resolve both 'cost' and 'utility' into their physical equivalents," which is "the idea of a physical replacement of energy given out in work."[26]

But, as Catherine Gallagher has demonstrated, the classical political economists actually do not ignore the energy of the physical body, nor do they fail to observe the distinction between exchange value and use value.[27] Geddes claims that "economists" ignore or even contradict the modern doctrine of energy, but this is precisely what writers like Malthus and Ricardo *do not* do. Indeed, they put energy at the very center of their work, if we define energy as Ruskin does: "the absolute power of anything to support life." Malthus's law of population and Ricardo's theory of rent are in fact premised on the productivity of the soil, and the ability of a given quantity of land to support a population (Malthus) or yield a profitable return for the work put in (Ricardo). There were, to be sure, internal disputes among these writers about the way to account for the role energy played in economic life – Malthus's critique of Ricardo's labor theory of value, for example, held that it did not take sufficient account of the energetic differences between commodities – but overall the classical political economists cannot be accused of ignoring the significance of energy.

In fact, it might be argued that classical political economists were *too* focused on energy, since their interest in maximizing productivity could appear to reduce human beings to units of laboring power. This is the kind of economic thinking that, as we have seen, Dickens satirizes relentlessly in *Our Mutual Friend* and elsewhere in his fiction. Indeed, Geddes himself makes this argument:

> Thus machines, men, women, and children alike are to be worked to the full: "Wages are what maintain the labourer," says Mr. Ricardo, for once no metaphysician, but a physicist – since they are all mechanisms alike, no fuel is to be wasted upon them. To maximise production we need simply "Bastilles for Labour built by Capital," and of course freedom of contract, so that the worker may be free to contract between work there and starvation anywhere else.[28]

Ricardo is now *too much* of a physicist for Geddes, since he is too intently focused on a bottom line defined by efficient fuel expenditure and productivity. Ruskin takes up this line of critique against classical political economists himself, arguing against the notion that the greatest amount of work will be produced if wages are determined by the operations of the labor market:

> That, however, is not so. It would be so if the servant were an engine of which the motive power was steam, magnetism, gravitation, or any other agent of calculable force. But he being, on the contrary, an engine whose motive power is a Soul, the force of this very peculiar agent, as an unknown quantity, enters into all the political economist's equations, without his knowledge, and falsifies every one of their results. The largest quantity of work will not be done by this curious engine for pay, or under pressure, or by help of any kind of fuel which may be supplied by the chaldron. It will be done only when the motive force, that is to say, the will or spirit of the creature, is brought into its greatest strength by its own proper fuel: namely, by the affections.[29]

This is a familiar strategy of Ruskin's: not only is the opponent morally blinkered, he is not even succeeding on his own terms. In this case, in the quest to obtain maximum productivity, political economists treat the laborer as a mere piece of machinery, an engine; despite this, they still do not attain the kind of productivity they value. Here, Ruskin's use of terms like "force" and "fuel" does not seem physically rigorous at all, and he clearly plays loosely with the link between "motive power" and human "motivation" to expand the definition of what can be counted as energy. Although he claims that treating the affections as a motive power will produce the largest quantity of work, this must be understood in the context of his ethical approach to economic matters. As he spells out explicitly in *Munera Pulveris*, Ruskin defines "work" not in terms of raw productive power, but as a creative, even joyous experience, which he calls *opera*. The opposite of opera is labour, which he defines as "the quantity of 'Lapse,' loss or failure of human life, caused by any effort. It is usually confused with effort itself, or the application of power (opera) … labour is the suffering in effort. It is the negative quantity or quantity of de-feat, which has to be counted against every Feat."[30] Ruskin wants to count the cost of production in terms of an ethically admirable but empirically vague metric of human suffering. Thus when he makes claims about obtaining "the largest quantity of work" we have to keep in mind that quantity for Ruskin is always also a measure of quality.[31]

As James Clark Sherburne has argued, the clash between Ruskin and the classical political economists arises out of a fundamental difference in their frame of reference. For the older generation of economic thinkers, the besetting problem facing any society was natural scarcity, from which it followed that maximizing productive output was the single most important goal. For Ruskin, in contrast, the frame of reference is plenty, which leads him, in turn, to emphasize distribution and consumption.[32] In *A Joy Forever* he writes:

> The world is so regulated by the laws of Providence, that a man's labour, well applied, is always amply sufficient to provide him during his life with all things needful to him, and not only with those, but with many pleasant objects of luxury; and yet farther, to procure him large intervals of healthful rest and serviceable leisure. And a nation's labour, well-applied, is, in like manner, amply sufficient to provide its whole population with good food and comfortable habitation; and not with those only, but with good education besides, and objects of luxury, art treasures, such as these you have around you now ... Wherever you see want, or misery, or degradation in this world about you, there, be sure, either industry has been wanting, or industry has been in error. It is not accident, it is not Heaven-commanded calamity, it is not the original and inevitable evil of man's nature, which fill your streets with lamentation, and your graves with prey. It is only that, when there should have been providence, there has been waste; when there should have been labour, there has been lasciviousness; and wilfulness, when there should have been subordination.[33]

The inversion of the terms of popular *laissez-faire* arguments couldn't be clearer: scarcity is not a condition to be explained by reference to a market operating in accordance with divinely mandated laws; instead, it is the sign of the grotesque squandering of a divinely bestowed abundance. The switch from the upper- to lower-case initial for "providence" at the end puts the onus squarely back on the role of human management in the economic process. On these same grounds, Ruskin absolutely denies the Malthusian pressures of overpopulation: "there is not yet, nor will yet for ages be, any real over-population in the world; but a local over-population, or, more accurately, a degree of population locally unmanageable under existing circumstances."[34] The question thus shifts from how to produce enough to what should be produced, under what conditions, and how it should be distributed: "I believe the sudden and extensive inequalities of demand, which necessarily arise in the mercantile operations of an active nation, constitute the only essential difficulty which has to be overcome in a just organization of labour."[35]

In such a context, freed from the problem of resource scarcity, Ruskin questions what seems like a fixation on productivity for its own sake. Discussing a list of key terms from the political economy lexicon, he comments: "But the last, Produce, which one might have thought the clearest of all, is, in use, the most ambiguous."[36] John Stuart Mill, he (unfairly) argues, in his single-minded pursuit of increasing productive labor, fails to see that such a concept cannot be considered a good in itself without regard to the social uses of production:

> [A] steel fork might appear a more substantial production than a silver one: we may grant also that knives, no less than forks, are good produce; and scythes and ploughshares serviceable articles. But, how of bayonets? ... Or if, instead of bayonets, he supply bombs, will not the absolute and final "enjoyment" of even these energetically productive articles (each of which costs ten pounds) be dependent on a proper choice of time and place for their *enfantement*; choice, that is to say, depending on their philosophical considerations with which political economy has nothing to do?[37]

Thus, to return to an earlier passage, we can see that Ruskin's interest in comparing the "fixed power" of a cluster of flowers to the energy contained in a bushel of wheat is meant as something of a provocation, designed to open up the definition of energy past its meaning as raw productive power, in order to consider the variety of uses to which resources can be committed once the bare necessities are taken care of. This is, in some ways then, simply an extension of his work in *The Stones of Venice*, of bringing terms from seemingly disparate disciplines or modes of evaluation into alignment. The wider definition of energy arises from, and argues for, an awareness of the wider array of choices about the ends and purposes to which it can be put. Thus at the end of *Unto This Last* he writes, "consumption is the crown of production; and the wealth of a nation is only to be estimated by what it consumes."[38] The key then, to a healthy economy, is a consumer ethic that can rightly judge what not to consume.

So what to make of Geddes's claims about Ruskin's physics? If anything, it seems this capacious definition of energy would put Ruskin at odds with contemporary trends in the physical sciences, which increasingly restricted its definition to the ability to do work. But Geddes's argument makes a great deal more sense if we consider Ruskin's emphasis on energy in the context of the neoclassical or "marginalist" school that came to dominate economic thinking in the latter decades of the nineteenth century. Like Ruskin's, their economic model privileged consumption over production, and linked energy with pleasure or "utility." We might hear echoes of Ruskin's interest in the motive power of flowers in comments like this one by the Victorian economist Francis Edgeworth: "pleasure is the concomitant of Energy. *Energy* may be regarded as the central idea of Mathematical Physics."[39] Indeed, critics like Sherburne and William

Henderson see Ruskin's emphasis on consumer desire, his rejection of the labor theory of value, and his emphasis on what economists would call "negative utility" as anticipating the so-called "marginalist revolution" that took place in the seventies and eighties.[40]

But despite surface commonalities with the new generation of economists, there are even deeper fissures. If the problem with the classical framework is that it suggests there are simply not enough resources to go around (and hence implicitly justifies the existence of poverty), the problem with the neoclassical framework is that it suggests that value is *merely* a function of subjective desire, and thus the qualitative differences between resources matter only insofar as they respond to those desires. "Value depends entirely upon utility," argued W. S. Jevons.[41] Regenia Gagnier tracks this historical shift:

> The culture that had not seen beyond the horizon of scarcity and struggle in the face of nature dissolved toward the end of the nineteenth century, as Western society saw surplus and excess. It became possible to contemplate abundance and the capacity of human industry to control nature. Although economics was still called the "science of scarcity," scarcity was no longer a material obstacle but a recognition of society's ability to create unlimited new needs and desires as its productive capacity and leisure time increased.[42]

Scarcity is still an essential term, but it has taken on a completely different significance because it no longer describes a natural limit. There is no such thing as natural scarcity in this new paradigm, only scarcity of demand, or of capital. The problem with such reasoning is that it reduces natural resources to the status of all other commodities when they are, in fact, the *basis* of all other commodities. The neoclassical framework was premised upon a world of unlimited fossil-fuel resources because only in such a world could one imagine that productive capacity only increases, that commodities are endlessly substitutable, and that economic growth can continue indefinitely. As Philip Mirowski has shown, the neoclassical research program, despite its attempts to ground itself in contemporary thermodynamics, completely ignored the second law of thermodynamics and the idea of irreversibility – the fact that resources, once used, are gone forever.[43]

For Geddes, then, Ruskin's insistence on the importance of energy in economic equations helped to set him apart from growing trends in economic thinking that imagined natural resources as simply another fungible commodity. Ruskin was an inspiration to Frederick Soddy, another heterodox economist, whom many credit as one of the founders of the ecological economics. Soddy, echoing Geddes, takes Ruskin's engagement with thermodynamic concepts seriously. He writes:

> Ruskin, in solitary and picturesque protest against the hallucinations of his age, pleaded in vain for an economics founded on life. Hostile in spirit to science, or rather to the chrematistic pursuit of science which desecrated the countryside and doomed the workers to bestial conditions of existence, and a great champion of the cause of the higher spiritual and aesthetic values against the onrush of a sordid materialism, yet it is to materialistic science we must turn if we require the theory and justification of his philosophy.[44]

Despite Ruskin's insistence on irreversible processes and energy sources; the criticism of wasteful, reckless expenditure; and the importance of his economic texts for later environmental thinkers like Geddes and Soddy; he is not, in *Munera Pulveris* and *Unto This Last*, primarily leveling an environmental critique, or articulating what ecological economists would later refer to as a "limits to growth" argument. Concern for the environment is implicit in these works, but his primary interest is the irreversibility of human life. Workers "sent like fuel to feed the factory smoke" are experiencing the economic process as an entropic one-way street, with their bodies used up like batteries in a system of mechanical production. At this stage he is chiefly concerned with pollution as a sign of moral decay and misplaced values, rather than as a sign of a threat to the integrity of the natural world and of the materially unsustainable direction of capitalist development.

Instructive here is Ruskin's discussion of John Stuart Mill's chapter "Of the Stationary State" from *Principles of Political Economy*. Mill's text has itself become something of a touchstone for modern ecological economics, because it argues that while industrial development has enabled tremendous economic growth, the finite quality of land and resources means that such growth cannot continue forever. It is a significant text in the theorization of the modern concept of sustainability. As Mill notes, the inevitability of the "stationary state" – where population and resources reach an equilibrium point, and economic development stops – was something the preceding generation of economic thinkers understood well. But where Malthus and Adam Smith saw the end of progressive economic development as leading to (in Mill's words) a "pinched and stinted" condition for the mass of humankind, Mill argues that it should be viewed as a potentially beneficial situation.[45] Raw economic growth means little, he argues, since continued population expansion and grotesque inequalities of wealth keep a large portion of humankind mired in subsistence poverty anyway. The onset of a stationary state would force humanity to concentrate on the careful management of population and a more equitable distribution of resources. It is, in essence, a Malthusian argument that makes due allowance for the productive powers developed by industry, and ends happily. The stationary state would not mean the end of "progress"; in fact, it would be an important next step in the moral and cultural improvement of human civilization:

> It is scarcely necessary to remark that a stationary condition of capital and population implies no stationary state of human improvement. There would be as much scope as ever for all kinds of mental culture, and moral and social progress; as much room for improving the Art of Living, and much more likelihood of its being improved, when minds ceased to be engrossed by the art of getting on. Even the industrial arts might be as earnestly and as successfully cultivated, with this sole difference, that instead of serving no purpose but the increase of wealth, industrial improvements would produce their legitimate effect, that of abridging labour. Hitherto it is questionable if all the mechanical inventions yet made have lightened the day's toil of any human being. They have enabled a greater population to live the same life of drudgery and imprisonment, and an increased number of manufacturers and others to make fortunes. They have increased the comforts of the middle classes. But they have not yet begun to effect those great changes in human destiny, which it is in their nature and in their futurity to accomplish. Only when, in addition to just institutions, the increase of mankind shall be under the deliberate guidance of judicious foresight, can the conquests made from the powers of nature by the intellect and energy of scientific discoverers become the common property of the species, and the means of improving and elevating the universal lot.[46]

The critique of "getting-on," the deep suspicion of the supposed benefits of mechanical production, the evident sympathy for working-class suffering, the idea that the point of economic development should be the cultivation of the "Art of Living," the need for superintending institutional guidance and foresight: if this were written at a higher rhetorical temperature, it could almost pass for Ruskin himself. And yet, strangely, it is this passage with which Ruskin wants to quarrel in the final pages of *Unto This Last*. Stranger still is the specific argument of Mill's that he singles out for critique. Mill writes:

> Nor is there much satisfaction in contemplating the world with nothing left to the spontaneous activity of nature; with every rood of land brought into cultivation, which is capable of growing food for human beings; every flowery waste or natural pasture ploughed up, all quadrupeds or birds which are not domesticated for man's use exterminated as his rivals for food, every hedgerow or superfluous tree rooted out, and scarcely a place left where a

wild shrub or flower could grow without being eradicated as a weed in the name of improved agriculture.[47]

This too sounds like a Ruskinian argument, but the man himself disagrees:

> [W]e may spare our anxieties on this head. Men can neither drink steam, nor eat stone. The maximum of population on a given space of land implies also the relative maximum of edible vegetable ... All England may, if it so chooses, become one manufacturing town; and Englishmen, sacrificing themselves to the good of general humanity, may live diminished lives in the midst of noise, of darkness, and of deadly exhalation. But the world cannot become a factory nor a mine. No amount of ingenuity will ever make iron digestible by the million, nor substitute hydrogen for wine ... so long as men live by bread, the far away valleys must laugh as they were covered with the gold of God, and the shouts of His happy multitudes ring round the winepress and the well.[48]

Again we find a critique of the idea of substitutability: market valuations notwithstanding, commodities do not all possess the same capacity to provide sustenance. Ruskin here frames the economy as a world system, one that depends upon the influx of energy from *somewhere* in order to keep itself running. This, of course, is Mill's point too. Ruskin's suggestions notwithstanding, Mill is not arguing that the world might someday be turned into one giant city, but, rather, that the energy needs of an urbanized civilization might be so great that there would be no scrap of land left unexploited. Both Mill and Ruskin base their argument on the apprehension of natural limits, on the fact that human energy consumption exacts a toll on the environment and must, at some point, confront boundaries past which life as currently organized can no longer be sustained.

There are, I think, a number of things motivating this rather puzzling critique of "Of the Stationary State." On the most basic level, Ruskin simply seemed to have an irrational animus towards Mill. His tendency to fulminate against his own fun-house distortions of Mill's humane and nuanced arguments is well known.[49] Further, Ruskin scorned mainstream economic reasoning *itself*, and thus seems to have been unwilling to entertain the idea that a valid conclusion might be achieved through what he considered a worthless methodology. Although Ruskin does not make this claim himself, I also suspect he objects to the role Mill assigns to culture in his vision of the stationary state. Where Mill here seems to imagine economic development eventually producing a humane economy where cultural development can be given the attention it deserves, Ruskin always insists on the primacy of culture in economic matters. For him, the need to reform culture comes first; only higher standards of morality and taste will bring a humane economy into being.

Ruskin, though, doesn't make this argument, which suggests there is something else behind his critique. I would submit that, on a more substantive level, Ruskin is uncomfortable with Mill's argument in "Of the Stationary State" because it highlights an unresolved contradiction in his own theorization of the role of energy in economic life. Like Ruskin, Mill is attempting to reckon with the relationship between productive economic abundance and a limited biosphere. Unlike Ruskin, however, Mill accepts the fact that industrial technology, and its ability to utilize energy resources, has made this abundance possible in the first place. Recall Mill's vision of the stationary state: "Even the industrial arts might be as earnestly and as successfully cultivated, with this sole difference, that instead of serving no purpose but the increase of wealth, industrial improvements would produce their legitimate effect, that of abridging labour."[50] This is precisely what Ruskin cannot accept. His suspicion of mechanism and industry in all forms causes him to deny that it can have *any* beneficial effect. We have previously encountered his willingness to play "different games" with the "same cards," but that willingness ceases when he confronts the machine. He asks in *Fors clavigera*: "Have the Arkwrights and Stephensons, then, done nothing but harm?," then answers himself: "Nothing."[51] But despite the confidence, this is a deeper problem for Ruskin than he will admit. On the one hand, he wants to assume a world of abundance, both to undermine Malthusian arguments that would frame poverty as a result of natural scarcity, and to justify the commitment of resources to aesthetic pursuits. After all, it's easier to argue for the value of "non-productive" activities in the context of a surplus. On the other hand, he wants to deny the fact that industrial development has had anything to do in making that abundance possible; here he echoes the classical political economists and physiocrats in denying the productivity of industry.

This accounts for the odd note on which the passage quoted above ends: "so long as men live by bread, the far away valleys must laugh as they were covered with the gold of God, and the shouts of His happy multitudes ring round the winepress and the well." Where Mill premises his healthy stationary state, in part, on an abundance created through industrial energy (a naïve position, perhaps, in its own right), Ruskin roots his idea of energetic abundance in an idealized, almost magical vision of agricultural plentitude that has seemingly freed humans from toil. There is, to be sure, a healthy ecological insight to be found in the notion that agricultural, rather than industrial, energy provides bodily sustenance unobtainable elsewhere (a point not lost on Mill), but it is thoroughly undermined by the mystification of agriculture and the denial of the contributions of industry to abundance. When Mill comments that machinery has not yet lessened the toil of a single worker, he acknowledges the fact that it *could*.

Elsewhere, Ruskin takes a different, and more disturbing, approach to this question. In *Time and Tide* he argues that "a great number of quite necessary employments are, in the accuratest sense, 'Servile'; that is, they sink a man to the condition of a serf, or unthinking worker, the proper state of an animal but more or less unworthy of men."[52] These "necessary" employments, he says, include the dirty work of fossil-fuel extraction, processing, and production: mining, stoking, and forging. Because these jobs cannot be dispensed with, he argues that, unfortunately, it may be necessary to determine which children are hopelessly lost, in order to "supply candidates enough for degradation to common mechanical business."[53] In other words, in the name of defending workers from degradation, Ruskin comes perilously close to advocating for a system whereby some people are condemned to slave labor. In *Munera Pulveris* he shifts this position by arguing that "necessary" manufacturing work should be done by criminals and "those who, for the time, are fit for nothing better."[54] This is scarcely more reassuring. We can see almost in slow motion how Ruskin's peculiar form of liberal guilt leads him into the most grotesque forms of illiberal thought.[55]

In short, Ruskin struggles with the unseemly underside of modern production: not simply the fact that it degrades the worker, but the even more troubling, because far more intractable, idea that this degradation is *unavoidable*. The world of abundance that Ruskin requires to stage his arguments against the exploitation of the working poor, and establish his utopian vision of plenty, is itself dependent on the exploitation of *some* kind of surplus energy. It is a contradiction that troubles him, but one he fails to face squarely. Either he attempts to imagine a class of people who, by nature, somehow *deserve* to be degraded, or, more typically, he retreats into nostalgia for a pre-industrial social organization, where the class on the bottom of the hierarchy is not degraded by virtue of its position there. Of course, neither solution is tenable: the first is unacceptable because of the obviously monstrous moral choices it entails, and the second because of both the haze of idealism it casts over the history of worker exploitation, and its obvious disconnection from modern working conditions. At these moments of contortion and contradiction we can clearly see the superiority of Marx's theory of surplus value.

But I think it's important to refrain from either valorizing Ruskin for his moments of prescience or condemning him for his blindness. More instructive, I think, is to recognize that we have in him a writer attempting to think his way through the contradictions and compromises involved in an emergent machine-driven and resource-intensive civilization. As we have seen, he wields the term "energy," expands it, and transforms it in a lifelong attempt to come to some kind of understanding of the complex relationship between energy and culture. In the last section, I want to turn to the way in which his understanding of energy informed his environmental vision.

Energy and the environment

As I mentioned above, Ruskin's critique of political economy as laid out in *Unto This Last* and *Munera Pulveris* is mainly focused on energy insofar as it bears upon the expenditure of labor power and the health of the laborer. He expands his understanding of energy to include things like flowers and works of art in order to counter what he considered the prevailing tendency to treat the laborer as merely a source of motive power, and the creative or spiritual or emotional life as an ancillary concern; on the other hand, he also insists upon energy as a material quantity in order to question the worth of commodities that direct resources away from the biological necessities of life.

But though he does not stress it in these works, he is equally concerned with the impact of energy use on the natural world. This may seem a rather obvious point, since anyone with even a passing familiarity with Ruskin's social critique knows of his vivid fulminations against the soot-covered skies, rivers, and streets of Victorian England. But Ruskin's environmental critique is shaped in specific and significant ways by his understanding of the function of energy in economic life, and the ability of economic action to inflict irreversible transformations upon natural environments. It is his interest in energy as an aggregated quantity that informs this critique, and leads him, finally, to a vision of human-made global ecocide.

Ruskin's perception begins with the aggregated energy needs of the modern city. He shares with sanitary reformers like Chadwick and Hawksley an interest in the city as a kind of engine that imports energy supplies from the countryside and produces enormous amounts of waste, even if he does not share their interest in technocratic questions about waste management and recycling. For one thing, as we have seen, his definition of "waste" encompasses far more than the conventional forms – sewage, coal dust, smoke – and includes the kinds of frivolous, ill-made consumer goods that others might consider valuable commodities. He envisions the city as a giant consumer producing almost nothing but waste: "the whole smoking mass of it one vast dead-marine storeshop."[56] He discusses energy flow in these terms:

> Hence over the whole country the sky is blackened and the air made pestilent, to supply London and other such towns with their iron railings, vulgar upholstery, jewels, toys, liveries, lace, and other means of dissipation and dishonour of life. Gradually the country people cannot even supply food to the voracity of the vicious centre; and it is necessary to import food from other countries, giving in exchange any kind of commodity we can attract their itching desires for, and produce by machinery. The tendency of the entire national energy is therefore to approximate more and more to the state of a squirrel in a cage, or a turnspit in a wheel, fed by foreign masters with nuts and dog's meat. And indeed, when we rightly conceive the relation of London to the country, the sight of it becomes more fantastic and wonderful than any dream.[57]

Unmasking commodity fetishism reveals an unsustainable system in which available resources cannot keep up with the desire for frivolous commodities. Again we see the connection Ruskin wants to draw between aesthetic standards and energy use, and his focus on the way basic biological needs are mystified by contemporary productive practices. More importantly, the perception of this unsustainable situation allows for a key analogical comparison: the relationship between city and country becomes the dynamic between the whole of England and the zones of agricultural productivity still viable elsewhere. England's desire for a supply of cheap manufactured goods has enslaved it to other countries that provide it with the food it can no longer produce itself. As we shall see in Chapter 7, this does not in any way describe the relationship between the industrial powers and the regions that supplied them with resources. For now, I want to note that Ruskin imagines this dynamic as confined to England, because "the world cannot become a factory nor a mine." Insatiable demand does, at some point, collide with the carrying capacity of the natural world.

If in *Unto This Last* the need for energy ensures that, somewhere at least, there will still be fertile valleys "covered with the gold of God," elsewhere he imagines the way capitalist development will destroy the very sources of energy on which it depends. That is to say, he imagines a system that will consume itself through its own irrational, embedded contradictions. Unlike Marx's account of this eventuality, however, Ruskin's is informed by the fear that the ecological damage being done is so great that there will be little left. We catch a glimpse of this fear in *The Two Paths*:

How would you like the world, if all your meadows, instead of grass, grew nothing but iron wire – if all your arable ground, instead of being made of sand and clay, were suddenly turned into flat surfaces of steel – if the whole earth, instead of its green and glowing sphere, rich with forest and flower, showed nothing but the image of the vast furnace of a ghastly engine – a globe of black, lifeless, excoriated metal?[58]

Ruskin suggests that this would be the endpoint of capitalist development were it not for nature's ceaseless restorative work: "assuredly it would be, were it not that all the substance of which it is made sucks and breathes the brilliancy of the atmosphere; and, as it breathes, softening from its merciless hardness, it falls into fruitful and beneficent dust; gathering itself again into the earths from which we feed, and the stones with which we build."[59] The argument here – and in this entire chapter of *The Two Paths* – is that iron is "natural," and that, despite appearances to the contrary, it participates in natural cycles of decay and renewal. Note how far Ruskin has come from *Modern Painters*, where processes of decomposition were signs of the withdrawal of divine energy. In this essay, in contrast, rust becomes *necessary* to the energy cycle. But we also see the persistence of the classic natural-theological arguments in this passage. The natural economy seems designed to absorb and repair whatever depredations human beings inflict upon it: iron, that quintessential element of industrial production, is reclaimed by, and on behalf of, nature.

In this argument we can see how difficult it is for Ruskin to imagine fully what his imagery seems everywhere to suggest: that the *entire* earth might someday be rendered unfit for the habitation of human life. In all of the passages we've looked at describing the future prospects of a recklessly industrializing world, there is always *some* kind of location promising restoration, a refuge from total ecological breakdown. In *Unto This Last*, it is the vision of a magically unspoiled golden valley; in *Time and Tide*, the appeal to a restorative Providential nature; in *Fors Clavigera* it is the "foreign zones" that maintain their own energy and environments at the expense of England's. This "elsewhere," this place that can be kept apart from the depletion and spoliation of the entire globe, is continually shifting and vaguely imagined; the continual reimagining of this elsewhere suggests both its insufficiency as a solution to the unfolding ecological catastrophe, and the need to keep believing in one.

But as Ruskin ages, he increasingly shuns the consolations of natural theology, and the idea of an elsewhere; instead, he comes to embrace a totalizing vision of pollution. This culminates in his late work *The Storm*

Cloud of the Nineteenth Century, in which his imagining of global environmental breakdown dominates his vision of energy, nature, and economic life. The text is toweringly apocalyptic, with its roots in Ruskin's Presbyterian upbringing. And yet, I also would argue, it also has roots in a thoroughly secular understanding of the use and mystification of energy in economic life, and the heedless consumption of the resources of the natural world.

The *Storm Cloud* text is divided into two main sections. The first is the often-anthologized lecture given to the London Institution on February 4, 1884; the second is a more obscure sequence of explanatory notes Ruskin later gathered and dubbed a second "lecture." The first section is organized around Ruskin's diary, entries from which are reproduced verbatim and used as "evidence" in making his case that the past four decades have witnessed unprecedented changes in England's weather patterns. Both the diary entries and the notes contained in the second lecture function as a means of endowing the *Storm Cloud* text with a patina of scientific rigor. The former offers an account of weather patterns based on years of patient observation and meticulous record-keeping: "I am able, by my own constant and close observation, to certify you that in the forty following years (1831 to 1871 approximately – for the phenomena in question came on gradually) – no such clouds as these are, and are now often for months without intermission, were ever seen in the skies of England, France or Italy."[60] The entries that follow are part of this "certification," building a case through the accumulation of data. Ruskin says in the preface that there is not "a single fact stated in the following pages which I have not verified with a chemist's analysis, and a geometer's precision,"[61] and the notes of the "second lecture," which contain numerous references to some of the most prominent scientific texts of his day, seem intended to provide us not just with verification, but with verification of that verification.

Such gestures are not so much signs of respect for contemporary scientific discourse as they are attempts to bring the fight into the enemy's camp. Ruskin's strategy here, as elsewhere, is to out-science the scientists, to play their own game better than they do; once that is done, he can bring to bear the kind of aesthetic, sympathetic, and moral vision they lack. While he begins the first lecture modestly enough, proposing simply "to bring to your notice a series of cloud phenomena, which, so far as I can weigh existing evidence, are peculiar to our own times; yet which have not hitherto received any special notice or description from meteorologists,"[62] he grows increasingly caustic and dismissive of scientific conceptualizations of natural processes: "the scientific men are busy as ants, examining the sun and the moon, and the seven stars, and can tell me all about *them*, I believe, by this time; and how they move and what they are made of. And I do not care, for my part, two copper spangles how they move, nor what they are made of."[63] What he wants to know about, instead, is the storm cloud

> where this bitter wind comes from, and what *it* is made of … It looks partly as if it were made of poisonous smoke; very possibly it may be: there are at least two hundred furnace chimneys in a square of two miles on every side of me. But mere smoke would not blow to and fro in that wild way. It looks more to me as if it were made of dead men's souls.[64]

Thus the lecture's movement – from modest data collection to scathing moral denunciation – employs scientific discourse to showcase both his mastery of it, and its inherent epistemological limitations. The *Storm Cloud* lecture is thus deeply performative, staging Ruskin the investigator stepping across disciplinary boundaries and rhetorical registers with total indifference.[65]

Such strategies are informed by a keen sense of professional rivalry, since, as Greg Myers notes, "sages" like Carlyle and Ruskin increasingly found themselves having "to compete for authority as readers of … signs with scientists, first geologists, then biologists and physicists, who claimed a professional monopoly on the interpretation of nature."[66] But I want to stress here that the quarrel in *The Storm Cloud of the Nineteenth Century* is specifically a quarrel with physics – and even more specifically with thermodynamics. We hear the opening strains of this in the preface, where he boasts that he enjoys as much command of his imagination "as a physicist's of his telescope."[67] During the first lecture, Ruskin's fixation on the composition of the "storm cloud" or "plague-wind" is really a fixation on energy forms as redefined by scientific discourse; as we discussed, thermodynamics conceptualizes industrial and natural processes as indistinguishable insofar as they both can be defined as transformations of energy. As Ruskin describes it, the storm cloud is an unstable amalgam of industrial pollutants and chaotic weather patterns, and thus an instantiation of this breakdown of meaningful distinction between industrial and natural. In one journal entry, he describes a cloud formation as a "dense manufacturing mist."[68] and in another, a storm front rumbles "like railway luggage trains, quite ghastly in its mockery of them – the air one loathsome mass of sultry and foul fog, like smoke."[69] We may be reminded of the soot "as big as full-grown snow-flakes" falling upon Dickens's London.[70] Ruskin soon dispenses with measured similes in favor of more unstable syntactical mixtures:

> Three times light and three times dark since last I wrote, and the darkness seeming each time as it settles more loathsome, at last stopping my reading in mere blindness. One lurid gleam of white cumulus in upper lead-blue sky, seen for half a minute through the sulphurous chimney-pot vomit of blackguardly cloud beneath, where its rags were thinnest.[71]

The terms of the comparison are no longer obvious here – it's not clear whether the "sulphurous chimney-pot vomit of blackguardedly cloud beneath" is smoke that looks like a cloud, or a cloud that looks like smoke. This seems to be the point: for Ruskin, the industrial and the natural have become syntactically, categorically, and materially indistinguishable. Industrial energy has so thoroughly infiltrated the natural atmosphere that it has created its own patterns of both weather and thought. Thomas Richards remarks that the imagery Ruskin deploys in the *Storm Cloud* lecture is strikingly thermodynamic, and argues that he "assembles an inventory of metaphors of heat and wind without ever realizing that what he faces, and most fears, is entropy."[72] But if Ruskin does not quite realize that he fears entropy, he does seem aware that his text represents an extended quarrel with Victorian thermodynamics, and with the changes it was visiting upon the understanding of the natural order. This quarrel, implicit in the imagery of the first lecture, becomes explicit in the second, when Ruskin calls out Tyndall, Stewart, and Thomson by name.[73]

Although Ruskin comes at these scientists from all angles – including the occasional *ad hominem* jabs he used to direct at Mill – the main thrust of his attack on thermodynamics involves an objection to the breakdown of categorical distinctions. He complains in the beginning of the notes that, while he speaks of "beautiful things as 'natural' and of ugly ones as 'unnatural,'" science would deny any such boundaries can be drawn: "In the conception of recent philosophy, the world is one Kosmos in which diphtheria is held to be as natural as song, and cholera as digestion."[74] The need expressed in this remark, to wall off "the natural" as a stable, comprehensible phenomenon and object of inquiry, is precisely what is at stake, what the storm cloud threatens, and what the text itself will undermine. While he does not single out thermodynamics at this moment, behind Ruskin's objection is a concern over the assertion of identity between the organic and inorganic realms represented in the energy concept. Later he makes this clear, first taking issue with Tyndall's conception of energy, and then turning to Stewart's:

> Mr. Balfour Stewart begins a treatise on *The Conservation of Energy*, – which is to conclude, as we shall see presently, with the prophecy of its [energy's] total extinction as far as the present world is concerned, – by clothing in a "properly scientific garb" our innocent impression that there is some difference between the blow of a rifle stock and a rifle ball.[75]

Ruskin argues that Stewart fails to respect the distinction between living and non-living agencies:

> Now, had Mr. Stewart been a better scholar, he would have felt, even if he had not known, that the Greek word "energy" could only be applied to the living – and of living, with perfect propriety only to the *mental* –, action of animals, and that it could no more be applied as a "scientific garb," to the flight of a rifle ball, than to the fall of a dead body.[76]

But here there is some equivocation on Ruskin's part: is he objecting, as a lexical prescriptivist, to the appropriation of the word "energy" by thermodynamic discourse? Or is he objecting to the entire picture of the unitary natural world offered by energy science? The latter, the more wholesale critique, seems to be what he wishes to level – Ruskin's target, after all, is the bankruptcy of the modern worldview – but sensing, perhaps, that he is not on stable scientific footing, he shifts his arguments onto the firmer ground of classical philology.

There is, then, throughout the text, uneasiness with thermodynamic discourse, a desire to confront it on its own terms, but an unwillingness to commit fully to such a line of attack. Ruskin was right to hesitate, since his attempts to re-fortify the distinctions broken down by thermodynamics are full of mystification: it's hard to credit his implication that diphtheria is not "natural," for example, or the argument that "there is no more quality of Energy … in the swiftly penetrating shot, or crushing ball, than in the deliberately contemplative and administrative puncture by a gnat's proboscis, or a sempstress' needle."[77] Not only would such distinctions collapse under scrutiny, they seem to resurrect the kind of dualistic thinking that we saw in Volume II of *Modern Painters*. That kind of dualism now sits uneasily with the decades of later writing that are the record of a lifelong attempt to locate, in Sherburne's word, "interdependence, continuity, and unity" in seemingly disparate phenomena.[78]

This quarrel with thermodynamics and the retreat into fine philological distinctions or discarded metaphysical dichotomies might seem odd given all we have discussed about Ruskin's own attempts to use a capacious understanding of energy in order to break down distinctions between different spheres of existence. We have seen how Ruskin's own interest in the thermodynamic idea of energy as a measurable quantity only grew as his career progressed and he sought material grounds from which to launch his attack on the waste of modern consumer culture. But by the time we reach *The Storm Cloud*, the effort to appropriate the vocabulary of energy for aesthetic judgment has completely broken down. It has become clear that Ruskin wants to expand the definition of energy only insofar as that means bringing the various possible expressions of energy under moral and aesthetic direction. To Ruskin, the thermodynamic version of energy does the exact opposite: it brings all expressions of energy under the sign of industrial motive power.

In light of his quarrels with thermodynamic scientists in the second lecture, we can understand Ruskin's use of solar "heat death" imagery at the end of the first as an implicit critique. He writes:

> Blanched Sun, – blighted grass, – blinded man. – If, in conclusion, you ask me for any conceivable cause or meaning of those things – I can tell you none, according to your modern beliefs; but I can tell you what meaning it would have borne to men of old time. Remember, for the last twenty years, England, and all foreign nations, either tempting her, or following her, have blasphemed the name of God deliberately and openly; and have done iniquity by proclamation, every man doing as much injustice to his brother as it is in his power to do. Of states in such moral gloom every seer of old predicted the physical gloom, saying, "The light shall be darkened in the heavens thereof, and the stars shall withdraw their shining."[79]

Ruskin attempts here to reclaim the dying sun imagery from thermodynamics and "modern beliefs." He does so by returning it to its status as an apocalyptic and intensely moral symbol. The dying sun has no "conceivable cause or meaning" from the scientists' point of view; it is only through the prophet's interpretive vision, grounded in scripture, that such a sign even becomes legible. He concludes that "the Empire of England, on which formerly the sun never set, has become one on which he never rises,"[80] thus connecting the obscurities of London weather with the overreach and enervation of worldwide empire.

We can see, then, on almost every level of the *Storm Cloud* text, both the desire to draw bright diving lines and the continual frustration of that desire. This dynamic takes place on the level of scientific argument, where Ruskin tries to make untenable distinctions between natural and unnatural, living and unliving; it takes place on the level of imagery, where he struggles to reappropriate a shared network of cultural symbols and metaphors; it takes place on the level of public credibility, where he seeks to differentiate his own position in the public eye from those who also speak with authority about nature; finally, it takes place on the level of the material environment, where the atmospheric disturbances he tracks indicate a growing and irreversible interpenetration of nature and industry, to the point where one can no longer be distinguished from the other. This final, and most disturbing, level of boundary breakdown is a result of the others: a thermodynamic universe simultaneously brought into being by, and interpreted through, the technoscientific appropriation of nature.

Curious, then, is Ruskin's own unwillingness to abide any distinctions when it comes to his own rhetorical posture and mode of argument. By moving through and among various personas over the course of the first lecture – modest observer, amateur artist, expert philologist, Romantic visionary, biblical scourge – he attempts to address the storm-cloud threat in all its different guises: natural phenomenon, aesthetic blight, moral catastrophe, apocalyptic sign. It is a strategy that can be read as both cagey and desperate. On the one hand, as I've noted, Ruskin dramatizes his own freedom from the kind of disciplinary boundaries that, he suggests, prevent scientists from understanding the phenomena they would explain. Regarding what he considers an overly rigid scientific taxonomy of cloud formations, he says, "thanks to the sagacity of scientific men, we have got no general name for the bottom cloud … Under *their* line, drawn for the day and for the hour, the clouds will not stoop, and above *theirs*, the mists will not rise."[81] This critique of scientific line-drawing becomes a refrain throughout the essay, and a metaphor for the way science cordons off certain realms of experience and modes of knowing. On the other hand, however, Ruskin's eclectic holism also seems scattershot, like he is coming at his adversaries from a variety of postures and angles of approach without fully committing to one, lending the text a curious mixture of hesitancy and bombast. We may read the instability of Ruskin's narrative voice as a dramatization of the various genres of response – scientific, moral, spiritual, aesthetic – that such a crisis requires, but we may also read it as the inability to locate the stable ground from which he can launch his critique. Is he attacking Thomson and friends as bad scientists, sloppy writers, poor scriptural exegetes, shallow materialists? When, by the end of the first lecture, he is in full prophetic mode, reading nature as a semiotic system of apocalyptic omens, the move seems both aggressive and defensive, the charged rhetoric concealing a retreat from the naturalist's domain. Just as we saw Ruskin seeming to back away from a full-fledged scientific critique of the energy concept by making it a question of scholarly terminology, we see him at the end of the first lecture once again moving from world to book, from questions about how nature behaves to questions about how signs are to be read and interpreted.

Ruskin's seeming inability to locate stable ground or a coherent set of first principles with which to attack the scientists has come about because "nature," as he has known it, will no longer underwrite his arguments. It has become a shifting, contested, polluted thing, a domain that industry has redefined both materially and conceptually. This confusion brought about by the alteration of nature is what muddies his argument, but what also lends it its considerable ecological power. He writes: "This wind is the plague-wind of the eighth decade of years in the nineteenth century; a period which will assuredly be recognized in future meteorological history as one of phenomena hitherto unrecorded in the course of nature."[82] Here is the key to the entire lecture: not only does Ruskin imagine nature as having a history; he accepts that human action, in the form of pollution, is altering that history. We have come untethered from the kinds of natural balances and limits to which he previously had recourse: this storm cloud is not part of a cycle, or an entry on the balance sheets of the natural "economy," but a new and unprecedented formation, the product of a headlong trajectory driven by heedless expenditure.

This is, indeed, a thermodynamic universe, one defined by irreversible change, the interpenetration of nature and industry, and the generation of waste. And yet, it is a very different picture from what Thomson and other Victorian physicists were painting. For them, nature was remade in the image of industry under the auspices of the energy concept – its wastefulness was a sign that the ever-running engines of the natural world simply needed to be channeled, wherever possible, into human purposes. For Ruskin, nature had become chaotic and wasteful through the deranging effects of industrial energy use and heedless resource consumption, and the question of what counted as legitimate human purposes was still very much an open one. For Thomson and his circle, waste was inevitable; for Ruskin, it had become so only because a vast, nature-changing capitalist system was premised upon its generation. We can see, I think, how close their areas of concern really were, and yet how crucially different both their assumptions and conclusions.

To get at the significance of Ruskin's use of storm imagery, we might take, as a point of contrast, the astronomer Richard Proctor's use of it in his popular book on astronomy. For Proctor, as for Ruskin, storms are an expression of natural energy:

Storms are roused which blow with vehemence for a while, and then sink into rest without having accomplished any purpose necessary to the wants of terrestrial races. Here at once we see a large amount of energy not fully utilized. I do not indeed say that this apparently useless expenditure of force has no purpose in the economy of nature. Doubtless every natural event has its end and object. What I would dwell upon is, that if the energy which thus seems wasted could be made available to subserve human wants, it might be used without any fear that the economy of nature would suffer from such an application of her energies.[83]

Proctor is concerned about the waste of resources through industrial production, and thus he argues here for developing a means of exploiting the untapped power of storms. In its way, it is an early call for "green" energy technologies to replace an overreliance on fossil fuels. But despite his concerns about environmental damage, Proctor still fashions nature as something that exists to serve human desires; "Doubtless every natural event has its end and object" suggests both a vague awareness of a non-human-centered conception of nature, and a lack of interest in that conception. For Proctor, the more important point is that even the most seemingly "useless" natural events can be brought to heel and converted into fuel. Nature is still, as it was in earlier works of natural theology, an "economy" – a bookkeeping system requiring tabulation and management, rather than a material ecosystem operating without reference to human needs, economic practices, or structures of meaning. By the end of the century, the physicist William Crookes was openly speculating about not only harnessing storm energy, but achieving "control of the weather."[84]

Ruskin's storm cloud, on the other hand, suggests precisely this ecosystemic awareness: it is not a source of energy awaiting its use at human hands, it is itself the ripple effect arising from the human appetite for resources. Proctor implies that it is possible for the entire economy of nature to "suffer" through human energy exploitation but his aim is to argue for the complete technological management of nature. His implication is significant, though, since it allows for the possibility that human activity *could* alter the face of nature; Ruskin seizes on such a possibility and makes it central. For him, the storm cloud is a vision not just of local contamination, but of irreversible changes visited upon the atmosphere itself.[85]

But one of the crucial difficulties of Ruskin's position has to do with tensions we have seen elsewhere, between the conceptual armature of thermodynamics and the uses to which the laws were often put. That is, the laws of thermodynamics are, and have been, invaluable ecological tools, because they can puncture cultural fantasies about unlimited energy generation, waste-free production, and models of economic growth that deny or obscure environmental limits. The laws, indeed, have been used powerfully in the twentieth century by Soddy, Georgescu-Roegen, Herman Daly, and countless others to describe the impossibility of endless economic expansion. But this, as we have seen, was *not* how they were used by the first generation of thermodynamic thinkers. And herein lies Ruskin's problem. He wants to make essentially thermodynamic arguments about the limits to resource consumption and the problem of entropy generation, but he finds thermodynamic discourse itself already employed by those he takes to be his ideological opponents. This is why his emphasis on the role of material energy forms in the economic process has to be recuperated by Geddes, who sees Ruskin as a physicist; Geddes recognizes, if Ruskin does not, that his insights are deeply consonant with thermodynamic theory, even if they don't square with the positions and preoccupations of its initial exponents. The lecture's tendency both to deploy and to renounce scientific argument speaks, in part, to its uneasy position between an ecological commitment to the material world, and a rejection of the *way* in which materialist claims about energy were articulated in Victorian scientific discourse.

But the most significant contribution of *The Storm Cloud of the Nineteenth Century* resides less in its quasi-scientific foundations than in its imaginative scope. In it, Ruskin conjures a vision of irreversible global eco-catastrophe arising as the result of humankind's unlimited appetite for energy – what we today call climate change. Although, on some level, it is indulging in anachronism to apply such a term to Ruskin's Victorian text, Gillen Wood has brilliantly demonstrated the ways in which the early nineteenth century saw the first stirrings of concern about a causal, non-theological dialectic between human action and weather formation. By 1820, he argues, "natural philosophers had begun to recognize that that relation was not simply formal and timeless, but dynamic and historically specific, dependent on human activity."[86] Alan Bewell has similarly argued that, in nineteenth-century America, "climate change was one of the most talked about subjects during the early life of the republic," and used to argue for imperial expansion.[87] The argument, made by Luke Howard, the comte de Buffon, Thomas Jefferson, and others was that human settlement had the effect of *improving* the climate. Our contemporary understanding of climate change posits something like the inverse relationship, of course, but the point is that *some* kind of relationship had become imaginable in the first place. Imagining a causal, historical relationship challenged both the natural theological and biblically apocalyptic "readings" of atmospheric formations, since it denied both the eternal stability of the natural world, and the interpretation of weather patterns as signs of divine favor or displeasure. Ruskin, typically, mixes these discourses in the *Storm Cloud* lecture. As we have seen, he draws upon the biblical language of apocalypse, but he applies it to what is clearly a human-made problem. Indeed, one of the ironies he mines in the lecture is the fact that a godless world is itself creating the kinds of catastrophic consequences warned about in scripture.

As is often the case with Ruskin, the profundity of his insights is to be found in the force of his images, and the power of his imaginative extension, rather than in the strict logical coherence of his arguments. The problem becomes thinkable only through a rational understanding of the material limits to the "transformation of matter and energy" combined with the ability – and willingness – to imagine how those limits interact with actual social practices, patterns of consumption, and human desires. While aspects of Ruskin's argument are certainly far from logical, his wide-ranging and unruly approach; his combination of rational analysis and imaginative extension; his interest in energy as a material, social, and aesthetic signifier show this "new phenomenon" – the conceptualization of a worldwide ecological crisis – in its earliest stages. This is why he is a touchstone for Soddy, Geddes, and a whole host of twentieth- and twenty-first-century ecological economists who seek to put thermodynamic concepts, aesthetic health, and environmental concerns at the center of economic and social analysis.

CHAPTER 6

Personal fantasy, natural limits: Robert Louis Stevenson's Dr. Jekyll and Mr. Hyde

Since its inception, thermodynamics has had at its center the question of the reversibility of physical transformations. After the second law of thermodynamics introduced the problem of the universal dissipation of energy, irreversibility became an increasingly central theoretical question in physics, especially during the 1860s and 1870s. In 1867 James Clerk Maxwell proposed his famous "sorting demon," which could, in theory, conquer the otherwise irreversible build-up of entropy. William Thomson delivered a lecture later dubbed "On the Reversibility of Motion" in 1874 to the Royal Society of Edinburgh, and Joseph Loschmidt, responding to the work of Maxwell and Ludwig Boltzmann, first articulated his famous "reversibility paradox" in 1876. The question of irreversibility represents the point of most profound disjunction between classical Newtonian mechanics and thermodynamics, between a universe defined by balance and order and one defined by unidirectional flow and probability. The work done by Maxwell, Boltzmann, Loschmidt, and others during this period is thus not simply indicative of a paradigm shift; it is in many ways a conscious struggle to understand this shift and reconcile seemingly incompatible modes of scientific reasoning. The interest in the unidirectionality of energetic processes was also, as we have seen, key to understanding the fossil-fuel economy and the culture that had been built upon the consumption of cheap, available energy. Irreversibility thus had both a cosmological and an ecological valence, even if the relationship between those two domains was sometimes obscured in popular thermodynamic writing. In what follows, I discuss the ways in which Robert Louis Stevenson's *Dr. Jekyll and Mr. Hyde* works as both a mythical elaboration of contemporary thermodynamic tropes and an eco-fable about the irreversible depletion of resources. The plot is not only about the transformations undergone by its main character, it is explicitly imagined by Stevenson as a kind of engine, a device governed according to the logic of irreversibility. More than that, I argue, it is an unsustainable narrative, one in which the conditions required to maintain the fiction are consumed by the very investment in that fiction. The novel dramatizes the shift in the scientific conceptualization of nature, but it embeds this drama in the resource-dependent environment of late-Victorian London. It uses thermodynamic concepts to structure its magical premise, and, in doing so, implicitly critiques the "magical thinking" that often structured the conceptualization of energy in both scientific and popular domains.

The thermodynamic world of Jekyll and Hyde

Thermodynamic principles were in wide circulation by the 1880s, when *Dr. Jekyll and Mr. Hyde* was written, but they have special value in interpreting a writer like Stevenson, who came from a family of engineers, was himself trained as an engineer, and whose earliest published work includes a paper presented to the Royal Society of Edinburgh, "On the Thermal Influence of Forests," in 1873.[1] That paper discusses heat dissipating from forest canopies, "towards the stars and the cold interstellar spaces," and evinces a young mind interested not just in precise measurement, but in the energy differentials that define the relationship between different parts of an ecosystem – in this case, the forest and the atmosphere.[2] Edinburgh in Stevenson's day was at the very center of the development of energy science. Maxwell trained at the University of Edinburgh, as did the thermodynamic physicist William Macquorn Rankine. During their time there, both men were profoundly influenced by J. D. Forbes, Chair of Natural Philosophy, who emphasized the industrial application of scientific inquiry and whose own experimental work centered on the propagation of radiant heat.[3] Hailing from Glasgow, William Thomson and his brother, the industrial engineer James Thomson, were also close with Forbes.[4] As we discussed in Chapter 2, William presented his landmark paper on the second law of thermodynamics, "On a Universal Tendency in Nature to the Dissipation of Mechanical Energy," to the Royal Society of Edinburgh. As the work of the brothers Thomson illustrates, the close connection between practical engineering and natural philosophy was critical to the development of the laws of thermodynamics and characteristic of nineteenth-century Scottish intellectual culture. In contrast to the prevailing norms of a Cambridge education, Crosbie Smith and Norton Wise argue, the Scottish approach exemplified by Forbes, with its roots in the "Common Sense" school of Thomas Reid and John Robison, stressed "the unity of science and art, conceived in terms of the relation of mind to the material world."[5] The unity of abstraction and application, mind and matter, will be critical to our reading of Stevenson's novel.

In Stevenson's day, the University of Edinburgh was a thriving center of engineering and scientific research, and Stevenson attended the lectures of two notable members of the faculty. Fleeming Jenkin, Chair of Engineering, was William Thomson's collaborator in his work on undersea telegraph lines and a particularly important figure for the young Stevenson. In later years, he would write an admiring biography of his teacher and friend, *Memoir of Fleeming Jenkin*, just after completing *Dr. Jekyll and Mr. Hyde*.[6] The successor to Forbes in the Chair of Natural Philosophy was Peter Guthrie Tait, whom we have already encountered as a key popularizer of thermodynamic concepts, and a collaborator of Thomson's and Stewart's. Tait was also one of Stevenson's instructors at the University, and his *Lectures on Some Recent Advances in Physical Science* (1876), which was dedicated to Stevenson's father, is likely what the younger Stevenson would have heard in his class as an undergraduate.[7] Its descriptions of thermodynamic processes will therefore serve as an invaluable gloss on the tropes of energy transformation found in his fiction.

Dr. Jekyll and Mr. Hyde is a novel acutely concerned with questions central to the thermodynamic research program: the transformation of physical form, the continuity of identity through transformations, the expenditure of resources, and the phenomenon of irreversible change. Jekyll's is, at heart, an experiment in human engineering, one that unlocks Hyde's "energy of life"; the novel's opening describes the misdeeds of Utterson's associates as the "high pressure of spirits," and prepares us for a work that will draw upon the principles of engineering to structure not only the course of the physical metamorphosis but the shape of the plot.[8] The irreversibility of physical transformations represents one of the most critical points of disjunction between "classical" and modern science, and it informs Stevenson's modern rewriting of Ovidean metamorphic tropes and structures of allegorical representation.[9]

That the fictional metamorphosis is akin to a thermodynamic transformation is signaled by the way Stevenson differentiates the two alter egos as distinct forms of energy. Jekyll describes Hyde's "raging energies of life,"[10] as well as his "spirits more tensely elastic."[11] Jekyll, on the other hand, becomes "languidly weak both in body and mind"[12] and "wanting in the strength to keep to it,"[13] "it" being the path of self-restraint. That last comment is critical, because it suggests one way of thinking about the relationship between energy and identity in this novel.

The social world in which Jekyll moves, and the integrated persona he has developed in order to navigate it successfully, require an unceasing expenditure of energy. Jekyll accounts for Hyde's younger and less developed appearance by arguing that while his has been "nine tenths a life of effort, virtue and control," Hyde "had been much less exercised and much less exhausted."[14] Just being Jekyll is tiring; indeed, even enjoyment in this world is imagined as a kind of energy drain. "The expense and strain of gaiety,"[15] echoing "the high pressure of spirits" from the opening, describes the tense joviality of a gathering of Jekyll's well-heeled associates. The description of Jekyll "trimming the midnight lamp" after his return from one of Hyde's adventures may be a minor detail, but it nicely suggests his confidence in the easy manipulability of energy forms.[16] *Dr. Jekyll and Mr. Hyde* is a story of metamorphosis updated for the industrial age, for a world in which great transformative capacity was at the command of engineers; industrialists; and, increasingly, ordinary people.

The success of Jekyll's project depends entirely upon this command, and upon the complete reversibility of the transformation; Jekyll can indulge himself in Hyde, but Hyde must also be able to become Jekyll in order to realize the dream of the full "separation of these elements."[17] The plan seems to work at first, and Jekyll describes his initial mastery of the change:

> Let me but escape into my laboratory door, give me but a second or two to mix and swallow the draught that I had always standing ready; and whatever he had done, Edward Hyde would pass away like the stain of breath upon a mirror; and there in his stead, quietly at home, trimming the midnight lamp in his study, a man who could afford to laugh at suspicion, would be Henry Jekyll.[18]

Such a system of total reversibility, imperfectly carried out though it may be, represents a departure from conventions of metamorphic writing. As Marina Warner argues, transformation in Ovid and in other mythic literature is usually a singular event, signifying a being's attainment of appropriate and eternal form. The ability to transform oneself repeatedly and at will is a power reserved for the gods, but that is precisely what Jekyll's experiment in double living requires.[19] As we have seen throughout this study, metamorphic myths were habitually invoked in popular discussions of energy science. Tait, along with co-writer Balfour Stewart, invokes the god Proteus to illustrate the difference between matter and energy: "The one is like the eternal, unchangeable Fate or *Necessitas* of the ancients; the other is Proteus himself in the variety and rapidity of its transformations."[20]

And science was working to harness this god-like Protean transformability, a point made explicitly by Stewart and Lockyer:

> There are several varieties of energy in the universe, and, Proteus-like, it is always changing its form. Had it not been for this habit we should have understood it long since, but it was only when its endeavours to escape from the grasp of the experimentalist were of no avail, that it ceased its struggles and told us the truth.[21]

If myth helps structure scientific understanding, science, in turn, shapes myth; Warner writes, "it is characteristic of metamorphic writing to appear in transitional places and at the confluence of traditions and civilizations ... magic may be natural, not supernatural, and the languages of science consequently profoundly affect visions of metamorphic change."[22] Half novel and half allegory, half prose and half poetry (according to Nabokov), *Dr. Jekyll and Mr. Hyde* draws upon both the possibilities and the pressures of physical "realism" to restructure mythic conventions for the age of energy. At the same time, Stevenson draws upon the reader's awareness of those conventions, and Jekyll's violation of them, to challenge the fantasies of command often embedded in both popular and specialist discussions of energy.

Energy forms can indeed be turned one into the other, but never without cost. Because of its genesis in industrial engineering and considerations of work and waste as they relate to profit and loss, thermodynamic discourse, as we have seen, has always been suffused with metaphors from the world of political economy. Tait uses specifically economic terms to describe energy use: the "expenditure" of work and the "refund" of output for a given input, for example.[23] And if energy could be understood as a kind of capital, capital in turn was often defined in terms of the energy it represents – T. H. Huxley's essay on political economy, "Capital: The Mother of Labour," published four years after *Dr. Jekyll and Mr. Hyde* (and which we will look at in more detail in the next chapter), is a prime example. The first consequence of Jekyll's transformation is leveled in a cost of the most literal variety, that is to say, the monetary. Hyde's apprehenders decide to "make capital"[24] out of an incident: 100 pounds for the family of the child he has trampled in the street. At this point money is enough to reverse *some* of the damage done. Hyde can purchase back the liberty and safety his actions might otherwise have forfeited and Jekyll can "*afford* to laugh at suspicion" (my emphasis).[25] But it's important to note, as we have seen throughout this study, that while capital might be used to represent energy, it is not itself energy. Money cannot reverse all the consequences of Hyde's behavior. Most significantly, his anonymity has been punctured in a way that will prove very "costly" later.

In his "Full Statement of the Case," Jekyll further glosses incidents like this one, explaining that he "would even make haste, where it was possible, to undo the evil done by Hyde. And thus his conscience slumbered."[26] The combination of those two sentiments – "where it was possible" and "his conscience slumbered" – gives us, in a nutshell, the entire shape of the predicament. From the start, there is a problem "undoing" what has been done. Hyde's actions can be rolled back only partially, provisionally. And yet, in the early going, they can be rolled back just enough – through financial restitution – that he can convince himself that his experiment is both effective and harmless.

As the novel progresses the transformations exact a mounting psychic, social, and physical toll upon Jekyll and Hyde themselves. Jekyll keeps a ledger detailing the increasing amount of chemical formula needed to effect a restoration of his identity: "Here and there a brief remark was appended to a date, usually no more than a single word: 'double' occurring perhaps six times in a total of several hundred entries."[27] The movement of the plot is structured around the mounting difficulty of reversing the transformation, as Jekyll finds it becomes increasingly difficult to restore his identity to its original conditions. Jekyll begins to revert spontaneously to Hyde, and "only by a great effort as of gymnastics, and only under the immediate stimulation of the drug" is he "able to wear the countenance of Jekyll."[28] The finitude of this resource becomes a major concern: "Expense is no consideration," Jekyll writes to the chemist, hoping to procure the agent of transformation.[29] The chemical, however, is nowhere to be found; money no longer avails. Chemical resources and strenuous effort – both in increasing amounts – become the cost of simply restoring Jekyll to his original bodily condition. Tait writes:

> [E]very time that a transformation takes place, there is always a tendency to pass, at least in part, from a higher or more easily transformable to a lower or less easily transformable form ... Thus the energy of the universe is, on the whole, constantly passing from higher to lower forms, and therefore the possibility of transformation is becoming smaller and smaller.[30]

The moral valence of words like "higher" and "lower" will be discussed shortly, but for now, it is essential to see that Jekyll has discovered for himself what Thomson, Tait, and other thermodynamic scientists had taken such pains to explain: the energy of a system undergoing transformations simply cannot be restored without an input of external energy. The "perfect thermo-dynamic engine," one that could be run backwards to restore itself to its initial state, cannot be built; additional labor or fuel must be added to effect a full reversal. And that additional input always represents more energy than the work done. So while an engine can work to "produce" motive power, it can only do so at the cost of further draining the energy of the surrounding environment. Although, as we have seen, popular thermodynamic accounts often did not stress the ecological dimension of energy use, it was implicit in their descriptions of the relationship between energetic systems and the environments in which they are embedded. More on this in a moment.

The recognition that animal life is subject to the laws of energy science arises from the powerful influence chemistry and physics had upon biology in the nineteenth century. Historian of science Everett Mendelsohn writes that the nineteenth century saw "the steady invasion of the fields of functional biology by men oriented, through training, to the sciences of the inorganic realm."[31] Mediated through the metaphor of the steam engine, living systems could be understood as energy systems, as Tait argues:

> It was a grand step in science which showed that just as the consumption of fuel is necessary to the working of a steam-engine, or to the steady light of a candle, so the living engine requires food to supply its expenditure in the forms of muscular work and animal heat … it may be startling to some of you, especially if you have not particularly considered the matter, to hear it surmised that possibly we may, by the help of physical principles, especially that of the Dissipation of Energy, some time attain to a notion of what constitutes Life – mere Vitality, I repeat, nothing higher.[32]

What Tait, following the work of Hermann von Helmholtz and Julius Robert Mayer, makes clear throughout his lectures is that the concepts of energy conservation and dissipation obliterate the strict dividing line between organic and inorganic spheres of being.[33] Of course, what Stevenson makes clear is that many remained who would retain such a line; Jekyll himself deploys these terms in an attempt to wall himself off from his alter ego: "he thought of Hyde, for all his energy of life, as of something not only hellish but inorganic."[34] As this sentence is rhetorically structured, "inorganic" trumps even "hellish," suggesting Jekyll's need to find grounds of distinction beyond the moral categories that have already failed to mark his separateness. The attempt to use "inorganic" as the final redoubt of differentiation signals that Jekyll's "transcendental medicine"[35] is another name for the kind of discredited vitalism that Tait and others derided; this is one indicator that Jekyll's assumptions belong to an outmoded brand of scientific thinking. The other, of course, is a belief in perfect reversibility.

Jekyll and Hyde together represent two poles. Jekyll is the highly structured resources, figured in both the plentiful financial capital that funds Hyde's nocturnal adventures and the social capital that provides cover, an alibi, a veneer of respectability for his supposed protégé. Jekyll's is the world of work, and even his social circle comprises only other professional men. The long line of acronyms trailing his name, "M.D., D.C.L., L.L.D., F.R.S."[36] punctuates the point. Hyde, on the other hand, described as "on fire with sombre excitement,"[37] is indeed the fire to Jekyll's fuel – the one who, Enfield says, "brought out the sweat on me like running";[38] who burns documents, cheque books, and letters; who erupts "in a great flame of anger"[39] before killing Carew; who consumes money, the chemical salts, and the good name Jekyll has "laboured, in the eye of day"[40] to construct. It is a simple matter to turn work into heat, Tait argues, but another thing entirely to turn dissipated heat back into work. Jekyll's world is painstakingly put together, but it is quickly consumed.

To dream of perfect reversibility is to dream of a world in which events don't matter and marks on a reputation dissolve, "like the stain of breath upon a mirror."[41] Of course, events in the world do have real consequences, and Stevenson's emphasis on the physicality of the transformation ties the metamorphosis to a world in which energy is finite and acts cannot be undone. In fact, Jekyll's experiment in reversibility is not just about sidestepping the consequences for specific acts; it is also about reversing that other irreversible human problem, the aging process. Stevenson's interest in this theme is understated, and as a result not much commented upon, but it shows itself at key junctures in the novel. When Hyde visits Lanyon still wearing Jekyll's clothes, he cuts a ridiculous figure, the picture of a child playing in a father's wardrobe:

> dressed in a fashion that would have made an ordinary person laughable: his clothes, that is to say, although they were of rich and sober fabric, were enormously too large for him in every measurement – the trousers hanging on his legs and rolled up to keep them from the ground, the waist of the coat below his haunches, and the collar sprawling wide upon his shoulders.[42]

This is a comic introduction to the more serious theme developed in Jekyll's narrative: the fear of getting old.[43] He says of his need to find an outlet for his pleasures: "I was not only well known and highly considered, but growing towards the elderly man,"[44] echoing an earlier remark by Lanyon regarding his own old age. Jekyll describes his first turn in

Hyde's body as an experience of youthful vigor: "There was something strange in my sensations, something indescribably new and, from its very novelty, incredibly sweet. I felt younger, lighter, happier in body ... I stretched out my hands, exulting in the freshness of these sensations."[45] Hyde, Jekyll thinks, represents untapped energy, a "new power,"[46] and his wish to move reversibly between bodies, between the financial and social power of age and the energy of youth, is a wish to escape the irreversible direction of time's flow in his life. It is here perhaps that we see most clearly the deep connection to Oscar Wilde's novel *The Picture of Dorian Gray*, published just a few years later. While Stevenson's work is more interested in questions of physical energy and is, in many ways, less moralistic than Wilde's, both have their magic flights structured according to a strict economy that proscribes the cost-free access to youth. As the saying goes, "the light that burns twice as bright burns half as long," and Hyde has burned very brightly; at least, he has expended his energy heedlessly. But he does not represent a reservoir of additional energy, nor the reversal of time; instead, his nocturnal excesses speed up the process of their joint demise, destroying the resources and the very structure of the world upon which the existence of both depends. Despite his youthful vigor, he is imprinted with "deformity and decay."[47] Hyde is not a fountain of youth, but a constituent part of an existing economy.

It is worth noting that Stevenson himself, in ailing health for most of his life, struggled continually with a feeling of bodily inanition. In letters written to Frances Sitwell and to his mother, written in the early 1880s, he described his lack of energy.[48] At the age of thirty-seven he signed a letter to a friend "An OLD, OLD man,"[49] and at twenty-three he wrote Sitwell: "If you knew how old I felt! I am sure this is what age brings with it – this carelessness, this disenchantment, this continual bodily weariness. I am a man of seventy: O Medea, kill me, or make me young again!"[50] Notice how, in the last example, Stevenson's loss of bodily vigor prompts an appeal to myth. Such a move reveals both the desire for transformation into a state of increased energy, and the acknowledgment that this desire is futile. Transformation backwards exists only in fantasy.

The irreversible depletion of resources, and the steam engine metaphor that focuses it, provides one set of terms through which to understand the imprint of thermodynamics on tropes of transformation in *Dr. Jekyll and Mr. Hyde*. The second, related, set of terms is the gradual but inevitable transition from order, which requires energy for its maintenance, to disorder, the increase of which represents a loss of usable energy. As scientists like Maxwell and Ludwig Boltzmann began to discuss the relationship between micro and macro states, between the motion of particles on the molecular level and the overall direction or organization of a system, the steam engine was supplemented with other heuristic devices for imagining the flow of energy and the problem of irreversibility. When discussing the behavior of gases, Maxwell often posited two chambers: one hot, with fast-moving molecules, the other cold, with slow-moving ones. Such a set of circumstances is highly ordered, as it is extremely unlikely that all the molecules of one speed would randomly collect in one place. Maxwell and others are still, of course, discussing energy – heat, velocity, the difference between states that can be turned into work – but now explicitly couched in the language of organization, probability, and order.

This is crucial for Jekyll and Hyde, who are described not merely in terms of their respective expressions of energy, but also as separable identity compartments; indeed this is explicitly Jekyll's project, to effect a complete division of his "elements." With the discussion of separable chambers in physics experiments in mind, the description of unmodified human nature as an "incongruous compound"[51] takes on added significance. Thus it is not simply that Jekyll represents ordered energy and Hyde dissipation and increasing disorder – though that is suggested too – but the separation *itself* represents a particular vision of order that maintains a division between disparate states of existence. Peter Garrett describes the experiment as "a process of chemical purification," and here it may be helpful to follow Jekyll's lead and for the moment imagine the idea of "purity" simply as an ideal, unmixed concentration – that is, Hyde as "pure evil"[52] In an 1870 address, Maxwell explains the science behind separation on the molecular level:

> One of the most remarkable results of the progress of molecular science is the light it has thrown on the nature of irreversible processes – processes, that is, which always tend towards and never away from a certain limiting state. Thus, if two gases be put into the same vessel, they become mixed, and the mixture tends continually to become more uniform … In the case of the two gases, a separation may be effected by chemical means.[53]

Although the strictness of the division between Jekyll and Hyde is troubled from the very first transformation – there is, for instance, immediate confusion over pronoun attribution – the breakdown, the growing uniformity of their states, is also progressive: "when I slept, or when the virtue of the medicine wore off, I would leap almost without transition (for the pangs of transformation grew daily less marked) into the possession of a fancy brimming with images of terror."[54] The reason for the growing ease of transition is that the Jekyll and Hyde identities, united by the fear of death, grow towards each other and seep through whatever barriers – physiological, linguistic, social, moral – would keep them separate. Jekyll develops "a certain callousness of soul"[55] and becomes an accessory to murder, while Hyde, exposed and hunted, learns how to navigate the conventions and institutions of the social world: "Yet the creature was astute; mastered his fury with a great effort of the will; composed his two important letters, one to Lanyon and one to Poole; and that he might receive actual evidence of their being posted, sent them out with directions that they should be registered."[56] Thus while of course we never believe any "purity" of state was attained even briefly, whatever differences of concentration obtain between the two men clearly grow less stark as the novel progresses. The process is one of gradual intermingling, but not in the direction of cohesion. Rather, the amalgamation of Jekyll and Hyde represents a growing disorganization of identity, something the Beckettian struggle with pronouns – "He, I say – I cannot say, I"[57] – highlights, as it exposes the artificial demarcations of the language of selfhood. When Lanyon and Poole break down the door to Jekyll's chamber, the final barrier between himself and everything not himself, it externalizes and finalizes a process that had been occurring gradually and internally.

The plot is thus itself a kind of irreversible force in the novel. The directionality of narrative is explicitly discussed in the first chapter, when Enfield tells Utterson why he has not looked further into the strange case of Mr. Hyde:

> I feel very strongly about putting questions; it partakes too much of the style of the day of judgment. You start a question, and it's like starting a stone. You sit quietly on the top of a hill; and away the stone goes, starting others; and presently some bland old bird (the last you would have thought of) is knocked on the head in his own back garden and the family have to change their name.[58]

No doubt the kernel for this comparison came from a novel Stevenson knew well, Sir Walter Scott's *Waverley*:

> But before entering upon a subject of proverbial delay, I must remind my reader of the progress of a stone rolled down hill by an idle truant boy (a pastime at which I was myself expert in my more juvenile years): it moves at first slowly, avoiding by inflection every obstacle of the least importance; but when it has attained its full impulse, and draws near the conclusion of its career, it smokes and thunders down, taking a rood at every spring, clearing hedge and ditch like a Yorkshire huntsman, and becoming most furiously rapid in its course when it is nearest to being consigned to rest for ever.[59]

In both texts, the path of the stone is irreversible, but Stevenson emphasizes this by tying its descent not only to public exposure and injury (however comically depicted) but also to Judgment Day and the end of time.
In his hands, the comparison no longer describes the variable speeds of a
well-told tale and a narrator in command of his material, but exactly the
opposite: narrative as loss of control. This is a fitting description of the
plot of *Dr. Jekyll and Mr. Hyde,* which employs a series of narrators and
storytellers, each of whom unwittingly plays a part in bringing about the
plot's violent conclusion. The novel's asymmetrical structure – the third-
person omniscient narrator gives way to Lanyon's letter and then Jekyll's
"Full Statement," and does not return to close the "frame" – only emphasizes the feeling that nothing in this world returns to its initial conditions. As Jekyll ruefully notes, "The movement was thus wholly toward
the worse."[60]

The downhill metaphor was also, it is worth noting, one often used in
physics to describe the relationship between energy of position (potential
energy) and energy of motion (kinetic energy). It was an especially critical
concept for engineers designing waterwheels to harvest energy from the
downhill flow of rivers. Tait writes:

> When you are converting energy from the high form into the low, you can
> carry out the process in its entirety, but when it comes to be a question of
> the reversal – going up-hill, as it were – then … [it is] only a small fraction
> of the lower kind of energy which can be raised up again into the higher
> form. All the rest sinks down still lower in the process.[61]

Stevenson frequently compared the methods and representational practices of science and literature, which is perhaps not surprising for a person who abandoned one discipline to pursue the other. He writes in his
Records of a Family of Engineers: "engineering looks one way, and literature
another," but the grounds on which that work posits the difference in perspective is illuminating.[62] Engineering and literature may look in different
directions but they do so, Janus-like – or Jekyll-and-Hyde-like – from a
shared vantage point, animated by a similar set of concerns and impera-
tives. Both depend for their success on careful attention to the contours
of the external world, using that attention to shape and manage material according to their different mandates. Stevenson writes in "A Humble
Remonstrance" on the need for judicious abstraction: "Man's one method,
whether he reasons or creates, is to half-shut his eyes against the dazzle
and confusion of reality."[63] In *Records* he affectionately criticizes his grandfather's engineering diary, not because he thought Robert Stevenson's

interests insufficiently interesting, but because he thought them handled with insufficient art:

> So far as the science can be reduced to formulas and diagrams, the book is to the point; so far as the art depends upon the intimate study of the ways of nature, the author's words will too often be found vapid ... Of such are his repeated and heroic descriptions of reefs; monuments of misdirected literary energy, which leave upon the mind of the reader no effect but that of a multiplicity of words and the suggested vignette of a lusty old gentleman scrambling among tangle.[64]

The phrase "misdirected literary energy" unites the worlds of literature and engineering by noting how his grandfather, dazzled and confused, has sundered them in his prose. What Stevenson admires most about the practice of engineering is precisely what he finds missing in his grandfather's writings about it: the careful, necessary arrangements that channel energy and minimize waste. He writes:

> The duty of the engineer is twofold – to design the work and to see the work done ... Perfection (with a capital P and violently under-scored) was his design. A crack for a penknife, the waste of "six-and-thirty-shillings," "the loss of a day or a tide," in each of these he saw and was revolted by the finger of the sloven.[65]

We can see in Stevenson's portrait of his grandfather something of the tension that shapes his depiction of Jekyll: the engineer/scientist strives towards capital-"P" perfection in his designs, while his actual interaction with his environment is one of scrambling, lost energy, and entanglement in the material realities of the surrounding environment.

In its perfectly honed and gem-like sentences, in the almost clinical precision with which the plot orders its interlocking voices, Stevenson's novel is a work of marvelous engineering, of masterfully directed literary energy.[66] The craftsmanship is evident in the care he takes with the textured details of his world; for example, in the pause he inserts between Utterson's request to Hyde to show his face and the latter's accession to it: "Mr. Hyde appeared to hesitate, and then, as if upon some sudden reflection, fronted about with an air of defiance."[67] It is a tiny moment, but in it we see Stevenson's minute attention to psychological detail in the characters' interaction with their own physical beings. Confronted by someone who knows Jekyll's appearance so intimately, the fear of detection momentarily seizes Hyde; with characteristic hubris, he then declares his absolute belief in the efficacy of his experiment by throwing his transfigured face directly under the gaze of an old friend. The physical world exerts a real pressure in this novel, and if the fantastic change manages a small triumph over it in this early scene, the terms of the struggle are nevertheless set. For Stevenson, the more fantastic the story, the stronger the imperative to retain a sense of fidelity to the contours and strictures of physical reality. Robert Kiely, writing on Stevenson's adventure tales, notes: "Stevenson refuses to leave even the trace of a possibility that dream, magic, or obscure powers of the will may have been at work in shaping the weird worlds into which his heroes wander. There is only one way to distort dull reality, and that is by faking."[68] Jekyll isn't faking the transformation, of course, but over the course of the novel, "dull reality" reasserts its inviolability and refuses to be sidestepped or altered by his obscure powers. At the outset of his experiment, Jekyll believes, "the situation was apart from ordinary laws,"[69] but physical law cannot be evaded by even the most ingenious engineering or fantasy; his attempt to do so brings it back upon him with a "more unfamiliar and more awful pressure."[70]

The moral dynamics of *Jekyll and Hyde*

Thus far the discussion of the transformation between Jekyll and Hyde has been limited to imagining it as a purely physical phenomenon, a problem of dissipation and loss of structured differentiation. But of course those features of the novel are tied intimately to the story of a person's loss of internal moral bearings. Jekyll cannot endlessly return himself to his original state, not simply because transformation by nature degrades energy and irreversibly homogenizes differentials, but because after so many iterations, and so much moral confusion, he begins to lose a sense of what that original state *was*. Who is Jekyll if he enjoys Hyde's experiences vicariously (or viscerally), covers up his crimes, allows him the license to indulge what he otherwise thinks he condemns? Is he anything more than a name, a social position, a set of clothes? The novel stages a complex interplay between the physical-scientific and internal-moral domains that will become more clear in the light of Stevenson's poetics of abstraction.

Stevenson's essay "A Humble Remonstrance" was written to object, politely, to the kind of journalistic realism championed by the novelist and historian Walter Besant in his essay "The Art of Fiction." Stevenson bases his argument for abstraction on the symmetries he finds between literature and science:

> The arts, like arithmetic and geometry, turn away their eyes from the gross, coloured and mobile nature at our feet, and regard instead a certain figmentary abstraction. Geometry will tell us of a circle, a thing never seen in

nature; asked about a green circle or an iron circle, it lays its hand upon its
mouth. So with the arts. Painting, ruefully comparing sunshine and flake-
white, gives up truth of colour, as it had already given up relief and movement; and instead of vying with nature, arranges a scheme of harmonious
tints. Literature, above all in its most typical mood, the mood of narrative,
similarly flees the direct challenge and pursues instead an independent and
creative aim.[71]

If *Dr. Jekyll and Mr. Hyde* has this abstract quality it is, curiously, to be
found in its description of moral action. The novel refrains from speci-
fying not only the nature of most of Hyde's sins but also that of Jekyll's,
Utterson's, and Enfield's as well. Thus we get moral life couched in these
terms:

> Many a man would have even blazoned such irregularities as I was guilty
> of; but from the high views that I had set before me, I regarded and hid
> them with an almost morbid sense of shame. It was thus rather the exacting
> nature of my aspirations than any particular degradation in my faults, that
> made me what I was and, with even a deeper trench than in the majority of
> men, severed in me those provinces of good and ill which divide and com-
> pound man's dual nature.[72]

It is precisely because of this essentially abstract moral discourse and the
omission of specific facts about both transgressive and virtuous behavior
that we can see how the physical-scientific and moral forms of transformation are essentially coextensive in this novel, and why it is important
that they are so. The kind of rhetoric quoted here, found throughout the
novel, structures its moral world in terms of a play of forces rather than in
terms of the details of observable and therefore appraisable action. What
is emphasized is the power of certain states of mind rather than their particular moral contents.[73] Because of this, particular emphasis is placed on
Jekyll's *assessment* of his transgressions, rather than his direct description of
them, and his assessment is often contradictory and incoherent. He tells
us that, "my pleasures were (to say the least) undignified,"[74] and then, two
pages later, that "the pleasures which I made haste to seek in my disguise
were, as I have said, undignified; I would scarce use a harder term."[75] In
the first instance, "undignified" is a euphemism for his actions ("to say
the least"), whereas in the second, he tells us "undignified" is just about
the hardest term he would apply to them. On one level, this inconsistency is surely a product of Jekyll's loss of moral bearings; it illustrates his
inability to judge the relative moral weight of his actions from moment to
moment. But it also signals the novel's own interest in the constructedness
of the moral life, and the way that moral being is created and sustained

only by keeping hold of stable definitions and conventions. "Undignified" is a loaded word in this context, since it frames moral action in terms of how it appears in a social context, and suggests that Jekyll's deepest investment is in the construction of a moral persona rather than in the articulation of absolute standards of right and wrong.

If, as almost all critics have noted, the novel upsets any simple allegorical attempts to index moral nature to the appearance of a body or a face, it nevertheless does track a relationship between inner and outer states. This is perhaps nowhere more clearly seen than when Jekyll, sunning himself on a park bench, indulges in a reverie of self-congratulation and then immediately finds himself changed into Hyde. Here, there is a direct avenue of influence between moral life and physical expression. At other moments, however, the physical world retains a life of its own, a pressure and a reality not immediately traceable to any particular moral trigger. When Jekyll begins to change into Hyde whenever he falls asleep, for instance, there is no specific act or thought that catalyzes the transformation. But if the moral and the physical worlds are at times immediately linked, and at other times only distantly so, in all instances they track each other in general direction: the more irreversible the transgressive acts that mar their collective conscience (from physical assault to murder), the greater the moral confusion and the greater the physical instability. The way in which the moral life, however vaguely or provisionally defined in the characters' own minds, undergoes a process of irreversible change and expresses itself in physical terms suggests that the material world of the novel is not defined according to a stable system of moral reference, as in traditional allegory, but, instead, by the principles of energy. The energy forms underwrite moral allegory by mapping the deterioration of physical states to the deterioration of moral being, where the natural tendency is always towards "lower," "dissipated," or "degraded" forms; but the discourse of energy also subverts allegory insofar as it always describes a continuum, one in which the singularity of states and the stark dividing lines that maintain them – good/evil, high/low, organic/inorganic – are broken down in a universe tending towards both homogenization and dispersal.

That moral transformation is structured in rough accord with the laws of energy physics does not make Stevenson a thoroughgoing materialist. The point is not that a person's moral nature is nothing more than an energy system that inevitably and invariably degenerates over time; rather, it is that maintaining any *sense* of a moral self requires constant effort, and when the effort ceases, the moral self does not hold together naturally. We can easily imagine the moral world of the novel structured quite

differently: the transformation into *both* states could have become easier over time. In that case, the novel would have suggested how readily a
person can reconcile himself to a two-faced existence. By structuring the
moral life in terms of a one-way energy system, Stevenson insists upon
how palpable and undeniably real are its requirements. It *costs* something
to preserve one's sense of identity as a moral being.

The imaginative way in which these domains are inter-braided in the
person of Dr. Jekyll and Mr. Hyde may bear the imprint of Stevenson's
peculiar genius, but the relationship between morality and energy science has an extensive history in scientific and popular writing. Stevenson
could structure the moral world of his novel according to physical laws
because those physical laws had already been thoroughly moralized. Most
of the key terms used in thermodynamic science carry with them moral
implications: the inflection of words like "higher" and "lower" as descrip-
tors of energy in Tait's lectures is subtle, while terms like "squandered"
or "wasted" are more overt, and "dissipated" or "degraded" unavoidably
loaded. As we have seen, the fact that there were also neutral descriptions
in circulation – "unavailable" or "unusable" energy as a working definition
of entropy, for example – means that the use of a word like "dissipated"
even more clearly highlights not simply the presence of moral valences
but also the desire for them to be embedded in scientific discourse. As
Norton Wise and Crosbie Smith have shown, energy science, free-market
economics, and religion are discourses involved in a complex interchange
of values, metaphors, and assumptions: for example, all three disciplines
treat as axiomatic the evil of waste, as in "the finger of the sloven" that
Stevenson's grandfather sees at work in the loss of form, time, and money
alike. Similarly, as we have already seen, accounting metaphors were used
to describe capital, energetic, and moral transactions, as ledgers mundane
and transcendent could make sense of a welter of chaotic events by organizing them into columns of energy and entropy, profit and loss, good and
evil: as in, "Hyde is gone to his account."[76] The moralizing of energy is
thus not confined to phenomena like dissipation, but includes conservation and notions of universal record keeping. For example, Ruskin
discusses the conservation of value and energy interchangeably and in
explicitly moral terms in *Munera Pulveris*:

> The world looks to them as if they could cozen it out of some ways and
> means of life. But they cannot cozen IT: they can only cozen their neigh-
> bours. The world is not to be cheated of a grain; not so much of a breath
> of its air can be drawn surreptitiously. For every piece of wise work done,
> so much life is granted; for every piece of foolish work, nothing; for every
> piece of wicked work, so much death is allotted.[77]

In the human realm, one can profit through fraud, but the physical universe is more exacting: the laws that proscribe creation and annihilation of matter and energy ensure that even the smallest transaction is being "watched" and accounted for. Energy conservation, in this sense, becomes a surrogate for the divine.

In a recent work on "The Moral Economy of the Ocean Steamship," Crosbie Smith and his co-authors describe the moralization of engineering science in a particular nineteenth-century commercial enterprise. The divide between Unitarian and evangelical perspectives on efficient steamship design is stark: while both equate waste and sin, Unitarian optimism contrasts with evangelical beliefs about the inescapability of both. For evangelicals, the systemic degradation of energy is tied to a notion of the innate moral depravity of human beings and the imperfections that mar their creations. Just as the divine economy is a system in which few are saved and most are consigned to damnation, the inherent wastefulness of nature ensures that human intervention in its processes will never provide an escape from the laws of the system.[78] For the evangelical William Thomson, any escape from the second law of thermodynamics could come from divine intervention alone; such a notion is in perfect consonance with a notion of grace bestowed upon an unworthy individual sinner, who can do nothing himself to win salvation.

Along this dividing line, we can see how, on one level, Stevenson's own tale of moral engineering falls squarely on the side of evangelical assumptions. The experiment in self-division is badly engineered, but it couldn't have been well-engineered. Stevenson makes clear that this rapidly unraveling existence of Jekyll and Hyde is only an extreme, externalized, and accelerated vision of the inner lives of the other characters in the novel. Hyde's depredations flash through Utterson's mind like "a scroll of lighted pictures":[79]

> The figure in these two phases haunted the lawyer all night; and if at any time he dozed over, it was but to see it glide more stealthily through sleeping houses, or move the more swiftly and still the more swiftly, even to dizziness, through wider labyrinths of lamplighted city, and at every street corner crush a child and leave her screaming.[80]

The nightmare is not that Hyde could be anywhere, it is that he already *is* everywhere. The experiment, as Jekyll notes himself, reveals what was already there: "I have been made to learn that the doom and burthen of our life is bound forever on man's shoulders, and when the attempt is made to cast it off, it but returns upon us with more unfamiliar and more awful pressure."[81]

The relationship between energy and moral allegory, then, is tangled. On the one hand, in its broad outlines, the novel seems to index irreversible decline to the indulgence of evil behavior. It is as if the moral universe has its own power, is imbued with the pressure and reality of physical law. On the other hand, the novel's emphasis on the effort required to maintain definition, order, and consistency, means that, on another level, the downward thermodynamic movement does not track states of good and evil, but order and disorder. Morality, it is suggested, might simply be another element of identity construction; in that case, the problem with indulging in evil is not that it will be punished by the universe, but that it makes it too difficult to maintain the fiction of an ordered, coherent self.

Apocalypse and ecology

As we have seen, the "flaw" in individual energy transactions led scientists directly to visions of the eventual "heat death" of the universe. In similar fashion, the narrative of Jekyll's transformation at times seems to function as a synecdoche for a larger calamity in the world beyond. In one evocative passage, Stevenson describes the city in these terms:

> The fog still slept on the wing above the drowned city, where the lamps glimmered like carbuncles; and through the muffle and smother of these fallen clouds, the procession of the town's life was still rolling in through the great arteries with a sound as of a mighty wind. But the room was gay with firelight. In the bottle the acids were long ago resolved; the imperial dye had softened with time, as the colour grows richer in stained windows; and the glow of hot autumn afternoons on hillside vineyards, was ready to be set free and to disperse the fogs of London. Insensibly the lawyer melted.[82]

The reference to the apocalypse as described in the book of Revelation is impossible to miss ("The stars of heaven fell unto the earth, even as a fig tree casteth her untimely figs, when she is shaken of a mighty wind" [7.12–13]), but just as evident in this passage is the interest in energy forms and chemical processes. The passage itself works by blending opposites: the word "carbuncles" yokes value and disease, fixity and decay, while the onrushing of life sounds phantasmal and vacant, the heedless and issueless expenditure of motion. The acids have inexorably merged into homogeneity, and opening the bottle will effect yet another dispersal, but one that will not, genie-like, fill the room and sweep aside the fog that is already everywhere. The stored-up heat of autumn might give a warm rush and banish the gloom inside Utterson's head, but, as with Jekyll's tincture, the supply is limited and the effect only temporary.

The passage thus brings into relation the small physical processes taking place in the room, the fate of the larger world beyond, and the language of Christian eschatology. Indeed, as the novel moves towards its conclusion, it increasingly draws upon scriptural references as a way to make sense of Jekyll's demise; he comments on one alarming, spontaneous reversion to Hyde: "This inexplicable incident, this reversal of my previous experience, seemed, like the Babylonian finger on the wall, to be spelling out the letters of my judgment."[83] Notice how "reversal" here has become something very clearly outside his control, forced upon him by the logic of external circumstances, and thus a counterpoint to the "reversibility" that had earlier made his double life possible. By connecting his own downward transformation with the signs of divine judgment and doomsday, the novel echoes the apocalypticism that, as we have already seen, shaped scientific accounts of the second law and helped reinforce a theistic cosmology. Thomson's descriptions of heat death in particular were often inflected with scriptural rhythms and references. Stevenson's passage, then, not only describes the irreversible merging of seemingly separate material entities, it also blends the religious and the scientific, ancient and modern forecasts of doom, just as many Victorian thermodynamic texts had. Jekyll notes:

> Strange as my circumstances were, the terms of this debate are as old and commonplace as man; much the same inducements and alarms cast the die for any tempted and trembling sinner; and it fell out with me, as it falls with so vast a majority of my fellows, that I chose the better part and was found wanting in the strength to keep to it.[84]

Jekyll, like Thomson, Tait, Stewart, Maxwell, and other religious-minded scientists, comes to realize that the laws of energy only work to reinforce a picture of the purposeful, divinely ordered universe revealed by scripture.

And yet *Dr. Jekyll and Mr. Hyde* also departs in significant ways from the work of Tait and Thomson, especially from their tendency to frame energy exhaustion as a function of the natural order. In Stevenson's world, there does seem to be a "universal tendency" for things to run downhill, but he takes pains to depict this decline as a social and cultural malady, rather than simply a natural inevitability. The crucial element here is the tremendous emphasis he places on the material resources that Jekyll uses to effect his transformation. For one thing, Jekyll's need for the chemical to return to his "original" identity severely complicates any straightforward reading of the story as an allegory of the internal struggle between good and evil. If Hyde represents his evil nature, how is it that consuming a potion could make him "good" again? The chemical formula helps embed Jekyll and Hyde's actions in a wider material environment, so that the different personae are not simply indexed to internal conditions, but are bound up from the beginning in a larger social world and an economy of resources. Indeed, it is Jekyll's naïve belief that the chemicals can furnish an escape from the strictures of this world that leads him into trouble to begin with. Reality dawns on Jekyll (and the reader) only gradually: the secret formula used to effect the transformation changes over the course of the novel from a frothing beaker, a kind of prop, to a very specific substance drawn from the inventories of chemical retailers. Jekyll simply has it in his possession at the beginning; he has "London ransacked"[85] to try to acquire it by the end. The movement of the plot is thus from seemingly self-contained internal spaces to the resource networks of the surrounding environment. If Stevenson's vision for *Dr. Jekyll and Mr. Hyde* "came out of a deep mine," the particular salt needed for the transformation does not.[86] The shift in the novel's interest in the material fact of the compound marks a growing awareness of finitude, both in Jekyll's own internal world and in the external world that is becoming an increasing problem for him. The London streets, filled with vendors "laying out the surplus of their grains"[87] in the novel's opening, are desolate by its end. The urban setting serves as a continual reminder that this is a human-made desolation.

The novel's emphasis on resource exhaustion is echoed in other works of Stevenson's, which often critique heedless behavior and fantastical thinking by insisting on the limited availability of some essential material item. The plot of *Treasure Island*, for example, hinges on the pirates' blind consumption of precious resources:

> They had lit a fire fit to roast an ox; and it was now grown so hot that they could only approach it from the windward, and even there not without precaution. In the same wasteful spirit, they had cooked, I suppose, three times more than we could eat; and one of them, with an empty laugh, threw what was left into the fire, which blazed and roared again over this unusual fuel. I never in my life saw men so careless of the morrow; hand to mouth is the only word that can describe their way of doing; and what with wasted food and sleeping sentries, though they were bold enough for a brush and be done with it, I could see their entire unfitness for anything like a prolonged campaign.[88]

This exorbitant expenditure draws a dividing line between the two mini-societies – Long John Silver's brigands on the one hand, and Jim

Hawkins, Dr. Livesey, Squire Trelawney, and the "civilized" men on the other – marking the pirates as "unfit" and suggesting their downfall will be, in part, self-inflicted. Although *Treasure Island* is in many ways a morally complicated novel, this moment firmly links vice and virtue to waste and economy: the conventional social world, embodied by Jim Hawkins, Dr. Livesey, and the other "non-pirates" has its success made possible by its virtue, and its virtue confirmed by its success. Both are functions of careful economization. *Dr. Jekyll and Mr. Hyde*, on the other hand, while also playing with such dichotomies, features a much darker and more searching consideration of resource depletion. Jekyll's impossible quest for youth and energy, his geometrically progressing consumption (recall his ledger: "Here and there a brief remark was appended to a date, usually no more than a single word: 'double' occurring perhaps six times in a total of several hundred entries"[89]), and his decision to have London ransacked to supply his need – all of these elements may suggest (as they have to many critics) the logic of alcoholism or opium addiction.[90] But we might also read such dynamics in the context of *The Coal Question*, and other neo-Malthusian works on resource depletion, as signs of a more general cultural problem of upward-spiraling consumption patterns. Those patterns, the novel makes clear, are rooted in personal fantasy, in the belief that all of one's desires can be indulged without consequence, and that youthful energy can be commodified. Jekyll's fantasy is premised not just on complete reversibility, but on the idea that there are unlimited supplies of what he needs. The escape into Hyde is, as we have seen, an attempted flight into greater energy; it is thus also an attempted escape from natural limits and a desire to indulge the delusion that there is such a thing as *cost-free* energy expenditure.

We might recall Malthus's critique of Godwin in the *Essay on the Principle of Population*. For Malthus, Godwin's arguments for the "power of the mind over the body" were dangerous because they ignored bodily limits and the effects of real energy loss. Stimulants that increase mental "energy" only served to disguise the demands and weaknesses of the body, with disastrous results: "could such stimulants be continually applied, instead of tending to immortalize, they would tend very rapidly to destroy the human frame."[91] It's worth noting that Malthus had recourse to folktale to illustrate his point:

> [A]ll these efforts are like the vain exertions of the hare in the fable. The slowly moving tortoise, the body, never fails to overtake the mind, however widely and extensively it might have ranged, and the brightest and most energetic intellects, unwillingly as they may attend to the first or second

summons, must ultimately yield the empire of the brain to the calls of hunger, or sink with the exhausted body in sleep.[92]

In similar fashion does Stevenson slyly refashion myth and fairytale to provide a counterweight to cultural fantasies of unlimited resources, and secret, internal wellsprings of energy.

Like the pirates in *Treasure Island*, Jekyll/Hyde is punished for his extravagances, and marked as a social outcast for his reckless disregard of the limits others seem to respect. In this way, there is a sense that, like Long John Silver, he is to be viewed as an example of the refractory, antisocial forces that the ordinary social world properly and efficiently manages. But Stevenson also makes clear that Hyde serves as a convenient scapegoat for a culture that does not want to admit that it has, in fact, produced him. When Jekyll says, "my devil had been long caged, he came out roaring,"[93] he points to a dynamic in which repression exists in inverse proportion to the force of eventual release. The hedonist's squandering is only the inevitable underside of the respectable man's attempts to assert control. The pressurized world of reputation-making; professional success; respectability; social and financial capital-accumulation; and all of the other elements that characterize the lives of Utterson, Jekyll, and their circle, comes at an unacknowledged cost, embodied in the dissipations of Hyde. Indeed, Jekyll's futile attempts to draw a bright dividing line between his "good" and "evil" selves is recapitulated in the other characters as a more widespread refusal – fortified by the terms they apply to him, like "abnormal" and "misbegotten" – to acknowledge their basic kinship with Hyde, and his appearance among them as an outgrowth of their own cultural logic.[94] As Stephen Arata argues, "The novel continually turns the question of Hyde back on his interlocutors so that their interpretive procedures become the object of our attention."[95]

The novel thus dramatizes a key narrative that we have been tracking throughout the study: the dream of unbounded energy that will provide an escape from an enclosing, limited environment. Just as critics of Malthus saw in industrial and agricultural energy the solution to his population "trap"; just as Dickens located in untainted, middle-class energy a way out of the restrictive logic and waste of capitalist production; just as Ruskin attempted to locate in great works of art a bottomless form of energy that would provide an alternative to industrial, utilitarian values and the environmental havoc he thought they were wreaking; so does Jekyll look to Hyde as a form of energy that will allow him to make his own escape. Indeed, his own account is filled with this rhetoric: recall his description of the transformation when it is working: "Let me but escape into my laboratory door ... and whatever he had done, Edward Hyde would pass away like the stain of breath upon a mirror."[96] At first, Hyde does indeed represent an escape from Jekyll's stolid, respectable life, as well as from the aging process. But as the novel moves on, Jekyll himself comes to function as an escape from the *consequences* of his own previous escape attempts. That is, the dream of Hyde's unlimited energy itself creates a problem that requires even more energy to solve. In this way, the novel dramatizes a crucial ecological narrative: the fictions of escape from a constricting environment themselves produce further constrictions through the toll they take on that very environment.

Although Dr. Lanyon dismisses Jekyll's research as "unscientific balderdash"[97] it is, in fact, uniquely expressive of the contradictions that often troubled the discussion of energy in the period. Those contradictions are encapsulated in a remark of Jekyll's, part of which we have already discussed:

> For two good reasons, I will not enter deeply into this scientific branch of my confession. First, because I have been made to learn that the doom and burthen of our life is bound forever on man's shoulders, and when the attempt is made to cast it off, it but returns upon us with more unfamiliar and more awful pressure. Second, because as my narrative will make alas! too evident, my discoveries were incomplete.[98]

There is perhaps no better example of the cognitive dissonance that troubled the discussion of energy in many thermodynamic texts during the period. On the one hand, Jekyll's discovery of irreversibility has led him to the conclusion that there is no escape from the strict laws that govern the universe. Those laws are described here, as they were in many thermodynamic texts, as scientific expressions of longstanding religious truths about both the deficiencies and the constraints of material existence. But in the next breath, and seemingly without noticing the contradiction, Jekyll comes to the exact opposite conclusion: the problem, he says, was *not* that his dream of reversibility was fundamentally incompatible with material limits, but that his scientific research had just not developed enough to allow him to overcome those limits. This, as we have seen at many junctures in this study, was a problem with the way energy was often conceptualized. Even as writers like Tait, Stewart, and Thomson were framing the science of thermodynamics as a set of laws that would chasten fantasies of unlimited energy production (like the perpetual motion machine), and even as they seemed to indicate that waste and disorder were *inescapable* by-products of energy-intensive industrial practices, they also imagined that the development of finer and finer industrial technologies held the answer to the problem of pollution and waste. Recall Stewart and Lockyer's "machine of infinite delicacy of construction," which would produce a "stupendous result ... through the agency of a very small amount of energy bestowed," and which the writers deem "not inconceivable."[99] Such speculations lead quite naturally to Maxwell's famous "sorting demon," a thought experiment that suggests how entropy might indeed be overcome through the power of "infinite delicacy." Just as the problems caused by Jekyll's experiment somehow prompt him to believe that further experimenting will provide the solution, the same industrial technologies that had turned entropy, waste, and resource exhaustion into pressing social and environmental problems were imagined as the solution to those very problems. Thus scientific reason, taken to an extreme, begins to breed monsters that that reason is then tasked with fighting. Logic and language in this novel both ultimately become self-creating and self-unraveling. Take, for example, Lanyon's remark about Jekyll's experiments; he says they "had led (like too many of Jekyll's investigations) to no end of practical usefulness."[100] While Lanyon is ostensibly trying to say that Jekyll's experiments have no practical purposes, "no end of practical usefulness" can also be read as meaning the exact opposite: that his experiments have *limitless* potential. While Lanyon would deny Jekyll a place among the annals of respectable scientists, the alternative reading of his remark, and Jekyll's simultaneous respect and disregard for limits, suggest he might embody the attitudes and procedures of mainstream science more fully than many would care to admit. The novel always simultaneously encodes both the material rigor of scientific laws, and the hidden fantasies that are concealed within, or subtly expressed by, that very sense of rigor. "Doubleness" thus functions not merely as a question of personal identity construction, but as a trope for conceptualizing the discursive contradictions in the culture's attitude towards materiality and ecological limits.[101]

In this context, we might usefully recall a remark of T. H. Huxley's, discussed in the second chapter: "Fragile reed as he may be, man, as Pascal says, is a thinking reed: there lies within him a fund of energy, operating intelligently and so far akin to that which pervades the universe, that it is competent to influence and modify the cosmic process. In virtue of his intelligence, the dwarf bends the Titan to his will."[102] Such a sentiment speaks to the sense that human intelligence is somehow exempt from the scientific laws that seem to govern all other material processes. Jekyll's is a fantasy of exemption, a dream that there is a hidden "fund" of special energy within the self that the ingenious thinker can somehow extract and

manipulate. But the pressure of resource scarcity and energy loss effectively revises the metaphor in Huxley's last sentence: it is the dwarf Hyde
who bends the intellectual Titan, Jekyll, to his will. If Huxley's metaphor
encodes a self-serving picture of humanity asserting its special place in the
cosmos, Stevenson's novella tells a more subversive story of human self-
aggrandizement thwarted by its own dreams of exemption.

   In similar fashion, the novel subverts the connection between energy
waste and class found in the degenerationist imaginary. As we will discuss
in Chapter 8, the discourse of degeneration often functioned as a conduit
for middle-class fears and desires, framing the underclass as a form of
waste within economic and evolutionary energy systems, and the aristocracy as energy-less beings who could contribute nothing to the productive
force of the nation or to the evolutionary future of the race. Middle-class
industry, discipline, and virtue could thus be constructed in biological
terms, as forms of energy powering the species towards higher levels of
development, conceived of in technological, moral, and economic terms.
Thus the subversive power of Stevenson's novel: while the atavistic, "trog-
lodytic" Hyde bears many of the familiar marks of the degenerate, the
novel insists he is a distinct production of the pressures and hypocrisies
of middle-class respectability. As Arata argues, Stevenson goes out of his
way to represent degeneracy as a function "not of lower-class depravity
or aristocratic dissipation but of middle-class 'virtue.'"[103] The problem of
energy waste is not located in the upper and lower classes, but in the
self-serving fictions of the middle class, including the discourse of degeneration itself. It is the middle-class professionals in the novel who cloak
their secret "dissipations" under cover of professional reputation and
social position, and who seem to represent, in their bachelor solidarity, a
reproductive dead-end.

   The discourse of degeneration biologized class difference, dividing
production from contamination; middle-class energy from underclass
entropy; and healthy evolutionary growth from malignancy, atavism, and
evolutionary retrogression. Such divisions obscured the fact that industrial production necessarily involves pollution, that middle-class "energy"
depends upon working-class impoverishment, that the conditions of progress are tied to the dynamics of contamination and waste. *Dr. Jekyll and
Mr. Hyde* works everywhere to disrupt such neatly compartmentalizing fictions, revealing the intimate passages between seemingly divided entities.
The ultimate collapse of the Jekyll–Hyde binary thus has a critical ecological significance: the degenerate figure, the very embodiment of wasted
energy, is shown to be a scapegoat born of middle-class fear, delusion, and

desire. Jekyll constructs Hyde in order to exploit energy without having to face the consequences; his compatriots, meanwhile, construct him as "inhuman" and "other" in order to avoid accepting his origins in their own social and professional sphere.

Jekyll's story, then, is not simply an irreversible fiction, but an unsustainable one. It is unsustainable because it attempts to yoke the desire for an unbounded life to a bounded world, to imagine that endless transformations can be produced by a finite supply of resources. To keep itself going, Jekyll's plot depends upon certain conditions – including, and especially, the availability of the chemical – that the movement of the plot ruthlessly undermines. The novel reveals the way in which the processes of fiction making function as attempts to sustain a certain understanding of reality that those very processes are, simultaneously, making untenable. The salient division the book dramatizes is not between good and evil, but between what one wants to believe about oneself (or one's class or species) and all the messy, troubling, disconfirming evidence one has to ignore to continue to do so. The assorted professionals have their own fictions of respectability challenged by the very presence of Hyde in their midst. Jekyll, for his part, harbors fictions of mastery over the transformation of energy that are undone by his very attempts to exert it.

Stevenson's novel, then, is one of the most vividly and complexly imagined representations of the relationship between personal fantasy and resource consumption the Victorian period produced. It dramatizes the conflict between the infinite vistas of an individual's inner life and the enclosing limits imposed by biophysical law and a finite material environment. It makes clear the personal and environmental recklessness of dreams of endless supplies of energy, and of the belief that such supplies are available for the realization of every individual desire. And it looks forward to a century where such dreams and beliefs would become deeply embedded in the cultural and commercial imaginary. As the philosopher Allan Stoekl has argued, the symbolic power of certain energy-intensive technologies such as the automobile resides not in their functional utility, but in the way they allow the consumer to "liv[e] out the multiple fantasies of what one would (sequentially) like to be."[104] *Dr. Jekyll and Mr. Hyde* not only dramatizes the multiple selves contained within each individual, it makes the material instantiation of those selves dependent upon the particular conditions of an emergent modernity. The anonymity of the city, the stark division of public and private spheres under industrial capitalism, the constructedness and contingency of identity and moral being: this quintessential Victorian text looks ahead to the next century by bringing to the surface the fissures and unresolved contradictions of its own era. This is nowhere more true, I submit, than in the representation of energy resources, its depiction of the way an individual's access to extra-human stores of energy gives rise to unsustainable fantasies of boundless self-creation and extension.

CHAPTER 7

Joseph Conrad: energy, entropy, and the fictions of empire

In an 1897 letter, Joseph Conrad describes to R. B. Cunninghame Graham the power of the character Singleton in *The Nigger of the "Narcissus"*: "Nothing can touch him but the curse of decay – the eternal decree that will extinguish the sun, the stars one by one, and in another instant shall spread a frozen darkness over the whole universe."[1] Explicit reference to the sun's extinction crops up in several other letters, as well as in Conrad's essay on Henry James, while descriptions of the sun as a waning or dying ember occur in *Heart of Darkness*, *The Secret Agent*, and elsewhere in his fiction. In other works, however, the sun appears at the opposite extreme, as an agent of undiminished, even oppressive, power. The extreme difference in these representations of the sun's energy, this chapter argues, corresponds roughly to a distinction between the tropics and the imperial "center," between nature's power as it is experienced, and nature as it is harnessed, channeled, and utilized by industrial civilization. Energy raw versus energy cooked. The "Author's Note" to *The Secret Agent* plays upon this contrast by describing that novel, Conrad's first (and only) novel set entirely in London, as a departure from its immediate predecessors, *Nostromo* and *The Mirror of the Sea*, and casting the difference in terms of energy:

> One fell to musing before the phenomenon – even of the past: of South America, a continent of crude sunshine and brutal revolutions, of the sea, the vast expanse of salt waters, the mirror of heaven's frowns and smiles, the reflector of the world's light. Then the vision of an enormous town presented itself, of a monstrous town more populous than some continents and in its man-made might as if indifferent to heaven's frowns and smiles; a cruel devourer of the world's light.[2]

This description prepares us to read *The Secret Agent*'s imagery of light and darkness not simply as moral signifiers, but more particularly, and more materially, as components in the representation of a global economy of energy forms. The sunlight in the tropics is in a "crude" state; it is part of a matrix of bottomless consumer desire in the imperial center. Indeed, the sun is colored in the novel in the muted shades of metal: copper, gold, and rust. While critics have called attention to the centrality of energy and entropy to the political and moral world described in *The Secret Agent*, Conrad himself suggests in this note that a full accounting of the significance of such tropes depends upon contextualizing them within his oeuvre and in terms of the geographic and economic spaces it covers: the imperial "periphery," the sea, and the "the very centre of Empire,"[3] the city of London. Taken within the wider, intercontinental perspective Conrad provides, the word "devourer" suggests an essentially metabolic vision: the city as a consumer within – indeed, a parasite upon – the greater natural-economic world system. If we read *The Secret Agent* alongside *Heart of Darkness*, *Nostromo*, *The Mirror of the Sea*, and other works of Conrad's major period, we can see this system of dependency extending far beyond the bounds of London and other western capitals, and Conrad plotting the coordinates of an exploitative, directional, global economy imagined in the thermodynamic vocabulary of energy flow, efficiency, and waste.

Early Victorian thermodynamic writing, especially in its popular guises, often came loaded with military metaphors and imperial undertones: "the fact is well known to artillerymen, for a ball with double velocity will penetrate much more than twice as far into an obstacle opposing its progress."[4] Such comparisons not only drew a direct connection between knowledge and power, they suggested that knowledge *justified* power and vice versa. The increasingly efficient use of energy was a clear sign of material progress, and that progress was instantiated and ratified by national superiority and imperial control. Stewart and Lockyer write:

> Suppose, for instance, a gun loaded with powder and ball, and very delicately poised, then by the expenditure of a very small amount of energy upon the trigger a stupendous mechanical result may be achieved, which may be greatly varied; touch the trigger, and the gun is discharged, driving out the ball with great velocity. The direction of its path will, however, depend upon the pointing of the gun; if well pointed, it may explode a magazine, – nay, even win an empire.[5]

Imperial growth is founded not on brute force, but delicacy, on the intelligent, efficient use of energy that expresses itself as a form of physical power. That sense of controlled efficiency was key to broader distinctions drawn between Europe and Africa: the former knew how to manage its resources, while the latter did not. Words like "efficiency," "energy," and "waste" became rhetorical touchstones within the subgenre of imperial apologetics. In his *Social Evolution* (1894), Benjamin Kidd writes:

> Even now all that is required to ensure its success is a clearly defined conception of moral necessity. This, it would seem, must come under the conditions referred to, when the energetic races of the world, having completed the colonization of the temperate regions, are met with the spectacle of the earth still running largely to waste under inefficient management.[6]

The terms of comparison in this excerpt are those of the book as a whole: the West is efficient and full of energy, the tropical regions are inefficient and wasteful. Such rhetoric was necessary, for as even Kidd himself acknowledges, immense resources, including energy resources, were flowing from the imperial holdings to the European centers, and industrial civilization was becoming increasingly dependent upon them. Kidd writes in *The Control of the Tropics* (1898):

> If we turn at the present time to the import lists of the world and regard them carefully, it will become apparent to what a large extent our civilization already draws its supplies from the tropics ... it is curious to reflect to what a large extent our complex, highly organized modern life rests on the work and production of a region of the world to which our relations are either indefinite or entirely casual.[7]

Africans living in King Leopold's Congo, or in British Rhodesia, had reason to question the extent to which the word "casual" accurately described European involvement in the region. In any event, Kidd's account nicely gets at the way in which British dependency could be acknowledged and then, in the next breath, euphemized in such a way as to obscure the well-planned systematization of exploitation and the rapacity with which it was carried out. Sociologist Stephen Bunker writes: "Modern systems are themselves highly energy-intensive and can only emerge in regions where industrial modes of production derive large amounts of energy and matter from subordinate modes of extraction."[8] Describing a colony as a "dependency" is thus, in an important sense, putting things exactly backwards. Kidd's rhetoric of the efficient, energetic European served to suggest equitable, even altruistic, terms of exchange concealing the one-way extractive flow of resources. The citizens of the tropics suffered from a "lack of energy," by which Kidd of course means something like "lack of initiative," that could only be rectified by an influx of energized Europeans.[9] It is precisely the elasticity of the term "energy" that allows Kidd to proffer a balance sheet that is in fact the inverse of the actual energy relations obtaining between Europe and its imperial interests.

A similar dynamic appears in the astronomer Richard Proctor's discussion of resource waste. Concerned about the diminishing stocks of coal and other resources in England, Proctor both troubles and fortifies the distinction between Europeans and "savages":

> Precisely as the superiority of civilised races over barbarous tribes is shown in nothing more clearly than in the fact that the former are not content, as the latter are, merely to supply the wants of the moment, or of a few days, but seek to make provision, not only for future years, but for the wants of their immediate descendants, so it behoves the leaders of the great movement which during the last few years has so greatly changed the aspect of the human race, to show the superiority of the new order of things by a careful provision for, and anticipation of, the wants of the races which will inhabit the Earth thousands of years hence.[10]

While the explicit concern is the impact waste will have on future generations, the implicit concern is its impact on a present generation of Europeans, and their ability to maintain their putative superiority over "barbarous tribes." What's perhaps most interesting about this passage is that Proctor's emphasis is not exactly on developing new sources of energy, but on showing that they will be developed. The *image* of European civilization is as much at stake as its actual resources, and the passage can be read as a call to maintain the correct framing device. He writes: "What must be done, then, is *to show* that by the progress of that very course of events which results in the rapid use of those stores, the means will spring into existence for obtaining fresh and inexhaustible supplies."[11] The logic is faith-based: proving what is already believed. And the article of faith is that the patently inefficient use of resources today is simply the means of achieving efficiency and abundance tomorrow. This must be the case because if not (the implicit reasoning goes) we would be no better than the inefficient barbarians. "What saves us is efficiency – the devotion to efficiency," Marlow tells his listeners on the *Nellie*, pinpointing, he believes, the quality definitively separating modern, civilized man from his Roman forebears and, it is implied, the "savages" of the Congo.[12] But Conrad suggests here the distinction is merely rhetorical, and it is buttressed by faith in this empty signifier. Europe's devotion is not to efficiency, but to "efficiency."

The idea that guano deposits, copper ore, ivory tusks, or rubber trees are "running to waste," as Kidd puts it, because they aren't being harvested and hauled away by Europeans is an absurd conceit, the prejudice of a kind of utilitarian techno-fetishism, rationalized by such distortions of language and by the prevailing metaphors of economic discourse. Kidd's argument draws upon the rhetoric of thermodynamic dissipation to describe unrealized profits, but it is, in fact, very much at odds with the laws of thermodynamics themselves. Cultural anthropologist Alf Hornborg writes about the discrepancy in efficiency that characterizes the difference between industrial and non-industrial economies:

> Industry's demand for profit is not, as Marx saw it, a specifically "capitalist" problem which can be neutralized by altering the system of ownership and distribution, but a symptom of the thermodynamic *inefficiency* of industrial as compared to biological production. Whereas hunter-gatherers, even in areas such as the Kalahari Desert, may retrieve 9.6 times the energy they spend on hunting and gathering, industrial agriculture often yields only a fraction of the total, human-orchestrated energy input.[13]

In Hornborg's thermodynamic account, which is indebted to the work of Georgescu-Roegen, "productive" industry does not produce anything; in fact, in global energy terms, it is monumentally wasteful. The irretrievable energetic expenditure involved in the industrial system of production was not, as we have seen with Ruskin and others, a phenomenon for the twentieth century to discover. John Herschel noted in a letter in 1866: "we are using up our resources and expending our national life at an enormous and increasing rate and thus a very ugly day of reckoning is impending sooner or later."[14] He blames "the populations calling themselves civilized but in reality luxurious and selfish" for the "enormous and outrageously wasteful consumption of every other article that the earth produces."[15]

The recipient of Herschel's letter was the economist W. S. Jevons, a person who, as we have already seen, stands at the very fault line of the shifting terrain on which ideas of energy uneasily rested in the latter half of the century. We have discussed the ways in which *The Coal Question* was a crucial early document in the development of a discourse of "sustainability." But its argument was, at bottom, profoundly nationalistic: his warning about the exhaustion of natural resources is often framed in reference to the prospects for England's continued global supremacy, rather than out of concern for environmental integrity or humankind conceived more broadly. Thus, the dynamics of imperial power are never far from his calculations. In the concluding pages of that work, he explicitly links the exploitation of energy with empire building, arguing that it is the use of coal that has enabled England to extend its civilizing influence over the face of the globe. Although Jevons predicts the contraction of the British Empire, his language rings with an ominous imperial logic: "When our great spring is here run down, our fires half burnt out, may we not look for an increasing flame of civilization elsewhere? Ours are not the only stores of fuel."[16] Thomas Richards writes: "The conclusion forced on Jevons is that the reserves of energy will soon be exhausted and that new reserves of energy must be found elsewhere in the world. He ends his book with a new kind of call to empire, a call that has since become a war cry: an ecological call for the seizure of new resources, a call based on the dwindling resources of the home economy."[17] The "flame of civilization" was thus, in the hands of writers like Jevons and Kidd, not simply part of a light/dark moral rhetoric, but a reference to the material energy flows and funds at the heart of the imperial project.

Jevons's focus on the value of coal leads him to ignore a crucial fact that critics had long been pointing out: the industrial system in Britain was *already* dependent upon the energy resources of its imperial holdings. As Foster and other ecological historians have shown, "The Great Guano Rush" of the mid nineteenth century occurred because of widespread fears about the exhaustion of European and American soil vitality.[18] In 1858 American economist Henry Charles Carey, discussing the proceedings of the Geographical Society of New York, notes that:

> as the whole energies of the country are given to the enlargement of the trader's power, it is no matter of surprise that its people are everywhere seen employed in "robbing the earth of its capital stock." Let the existing system be continued, and "the hour is surely fixed" when, to use the words of the author of the passage given above, "America, Greece and Rome will stand together among the ruins of the past."[19]

The exhaustion of soil vitality in the industrialized West (and the shrinking profit margins it entailed) meant that for capitalist agriculture to continue to grow, an influx of natural resources and fertilizing agents from other regions became a necessity. The chemist Justus von Liebig, who, as we have seen, criticized the waste of fertilizing agents through inefficient urban disposal methods, explicitly criticized British imperialism in energy terms: "Great Britain robs all countries of the conditions of their fertility."[20] Following Liebig, Marx saw in the imperial project a structural analogy to the city's depletion of the soil of the countryside. In his work on Marxist ecology, Foster argues: "For Marx, the metabolic rift associated at the social level with the antagonistic division between town and country was also evident on a more global level: whole colonies saw their land, resources *and soil* robbed to support the industrialization of the colonizing countries."[21] Though Carey was explicitly concerned with the rift between city and countryside, and the growing distance between markets and the centers of agricultural production within the United States, the terms in which he levels his critique make it equally applicable to the logic of the emerging imperialist system described by Liebig and Marx: "Trade tends … to increase the necessity for resorting to the great central cities of the world. Every stage of its progress towards power is, therefore, attended by … a diminution in the power of man with constantly increasing exhaustion of the soil, requiring resort to new lands, to be in their turn exhausted" – a state of affairs that is, in Carey's opinion, "the road to centralization, slavery, and moral and physical death."[22]

Although Jevons argued in *The Coal Question* for the primacy of energy in political and economic spheres ("Coal in truth stands not beside but entirely above all other commodities"[23]), his next major work, *The Theory of Political Economy* (1871), a founding text for neoclassical economics, would, oddly enough, work to obscure the importance of the laws of thermodynamics in the economic process. His conception of "utility," the exchange value of a commodity determined by market preferences, renders entirely irrelevant any reckoning of its "use value," its ability to do work or sustain the conditions for work. Economist Juan Martinez-Alier asks why Jevons would neglect in one book what he had taken such pains to explore in another, previous work, and Mirowski provides something of an answer.[24] Mirowski argues that in his interest in drawing connections between physics and economics, Jevons wrongly equated energy with utility, and thus no doubt believed his equations did justice to a science it was in fact casting aside. Thus it was that just as the energy conservation and dissipation were becoming more firmly entrenched as principles with which to model the transformations of the physical world, economic discourse was abstracting out the pressures, restrictions, and limitations such principles described, while still freely borrowing the terminology.[25] This led to paradoxical, if not outright Orwellian, linguistic issues. Terms like "waste," "efficiency," "productivity," and "energy" are troubled by contradictions because they are shared by these two occasionally analogous but distinct discursive fields: thermodynamics, or the economy of energy, on the one hand, and mainstream economics, the economy of commodities, on the other.

The source of much of the confusion in fact comes from the misleading isomorphism between capital and energy, which we have encountered in previous chapters. There is perhaps no better example of the ideological use of this seeming conceptual symmetry than T. H. Huxley's 1890 essay "Capital: The Mother of Labour." In this work, one can actually observe the rhetoric of thermodynamics changing into that of capitalist economics. Huxley begins by discussing the principles of energy science in order to demystify the labor theory of value as described in Henry

George's *Progress and Poverty*. Huxley notes that, strictly speaking, labor is not "productive" since it can only transform the energy made available to it through nature. The plant is the only truly productive laborer, he says, and the sun "the primordial capitalist."[26] Huxley, in short, asks us to picture energy as a kind of natural capital through which all activities are "funded." But Huxley is not giving a discourse on ecological economics; rather, he is trying to shore up the legitimacy of current economic arrangements by arguing for the productivity of capital. He threads this needle by quietly inverting his terms over the course of the essay: energy is like capital at the outset, but capital *is* energy by the end. The turn leads to some startling conclusions:

> The savage, like the child, borrows the capital he needs, and, at any rate, intentionally does nothing towards repayment; it would plainly be an improper use of the word "produce" to say that his labour in hunting for the roots, or the fruits, or the eggs, or the grubs and snakes, which he finds and eats, "produces" or contributes to "produce" them. The same thing is true of more advanced tribes, who are still merely hunters, such as the Esquimaux. They may expend more labour and skill; but it is spent in destruction.[27]

"Destruction" here is a person's consuming naturally found energy in order to live his or her life; because it is the life of a savage who builds nothing, "produces" nothing, it seems to Huxley a kind of waste. He also argues that soil is not even "one of the essentials of economic production," a remarkable conclusion given the primacy of place he had earlier afforded agriculture. This position comes to seem more comprehensible, if no less illogical, when we consider that the goal of his essay is to define capital as the only absolutely essential component of economic activity, and that, towards that end, he has to devalue the other two elements of the economic triptych, labor and land.[28] When capital is mistaken for energy in this way, manufacturing comes to seem a "repayment" of invested energy rather than what it is in thermodynamic terms: the *further* use, or, to follow Huxley, the further "destruction," of resources.

The fluidity of the energy concept and the mystification of capital thus directly feed the rhetoric of imperial superiority. In *Nostromo*, the incoherence is foregrounded for comic effect, as capital understood as motive power meets physical limits in the construction of a railroad designed to abet the extraction of silver from the Sulaco mine:

> Afterwards, late at night, pacing to and fro outside, he had a long talk with his chief engineer. He knew him well of old. This was not the first undertaking in which their gifts, as elementally different as fire and water, had

worked in conjunction. From the contact of these two personalities, who had not the same vision of the world, there was generated a power for the world's service – a subtle force that could set in motion mighty machines, men's muscles, and awaken also in human breasts an unbounded devotion to the task. Of the young fellows at the table, to whom the survey of the track was like the tracing of the path of life, more than one would be called to meet death before the work was done. But the work would be done: the force would be almost as strong as faith. Not quite however ... the voice of the engineer pronounced distinctly the words: "We can't move mountains!"[29]

Capital is in fact doubly mystified in this passage, with force and motion seeming to arise directly out of the personalities of its human representatives, the railway chairman and his chief engineer. The former, incredibly, has his faith that "[nature's] hostility can always be overcome by the resources of finance"[30] only slightly troubled by the intransigent mountains of Costaguana. The emphasis on the two "elemental" men presents an absurd version of the novel's more serious preoccupation with the "force" of personality in South American political affairs. But it also suggests the ways in which the idea of capital is itself bound up in a belief system that is both required by the imperial project and threatened by contact with the physical realities of that project. The language of the entire passage is patently artificial – from the obtrusive alliteration of "set in motion mighty machines, men's muscles," to the euphemism "called to meet death before the work was done," clumsily concealing the wasteful, exploitative nature of the enterprise. As Conrad puts it in *Lord Jim*, "beyond the end of telegraph cables and mail-boat lines, the haggard utilitarian lies of our civilisation wither and die."[31]

Hornborg argues that the mystifications of capital accumulation can only be recognized by viewing the industrial system within a global framework: "Such a wasteful form of production can only continue so long as it is 'subsidized' by an asymmetric world trade in energy. Only from a *local* perspective can it appear 'productive' or 'efficient.'"[32] It is not simply that the idea of capital as a form of energy founders upon contact with the physical facts of the tropics, but that the very conceit of capital's endlessly expansive productive power actually depends upon the raw materials industry can siphon from such regions.[33] Hornborg's account is an explicitly thermodynamic updating of Rosa Luxemburg and Lenin, who each argue that flaws intrinsic to capitalist production itself make the exploitation of foreign resources, both natural and human, a requirement for the system's survival. Luxemburg writes:

The general result of the struggle between capitalism and simple commodity production is this: after substituting commodity economy for natural economy, capital takes the place of simple commodity economy. Non-capitalist organisations provide a fertile soil for capitalism; more strictly: capitalism feeds on the ruins of such organisations, and although this non-capitalist *milieu* is indispensable for accumulation, the latter proceeds at the cost of this medium nevertheless, by eating it up. Historically, the accumulation of capital is a kind of metabolism between capitalist economy and those pre-capitalist methods of production without which it cannot go on and which, in this light, it corrodes and assimilates ... Only the continuous and progressive disintegration of non-capitalist organisations makes accumulation of capital possible.[34]

Luxemburg's model and the terms she uses to describe it – "ruins," "corrodes," "disintegration," and especially "metabolism" – emphasize the enormous physical and natural cost of the accumulation of capital and the directional "flow" of order and energy from country to city. Such an analysis stands in stark contrast to those proffered by mainstream neoclassical economists in the late nineteenth and early twentieth centuries, whose abstract models of endless exchange bracketed out the natural basis of production, made no qualitative judgments on the intrinsic value or usefulness of the commodities being transferred, and thus could conceive in the interchange between imperial center and colony a system of reciprocal benefit and development.

The difference between city and tropics is drawn starkly in energy terms in *Heart of Darkness*. When Marlow arrives in Africa, it is bright with the "fierce sun," a startling contrast to the London skies, which are proleptically dim with heat death: "without rays and without heat, as if about to go out suddenly."[35] What strikes Marlow even more strongly is the sight of natives who possess "a wild vitality, an intense energy of movement, that was as natural and true as the surf along their coast," suggesting "a world of straightforward facts."[36] Although such exoticization suggests something of the warping effect of Marlow's perspective, his account of healthy, free men stands in stark contrast to the description a few paragraphs later of drained laborers dressed free-indirectly in the rhetoric of imperial euphemism: "Brought from all the recesses of the coast in all the legality of time contracts ... they sickened, became inefficient, and were then allowed to crawl away and rest."[37] The construction "became inefficient" displays, with blackly comic insufficiency, the rhetorical lengths one had to go to maintain the fiction of a supremely efficient European order. A dying, emaciated African man Marlow encounters has a piece of worsted wool tied around his neck, a "bit of white thread from beyond the seas."[38] That accessory is inexplicably unnerving to Marlow, perhaps because it joins the ends of an almost inconceivable world picture. The wool from beyond the seas, along with the "stream of manufactured goods, rubbishy cottons, beads, and brass-wire set into the depths of darkness,"[39] represents not only the meager compensation for so much labor, but also, more horribly, the trivial products into which the very vitality of African lives are being converted. In the eyes of the European invaders, these lives are, like ivory or rubber, just so much "raw matter"[40] required by the system.

Humans beings drained like batteries and used to power an invader's elaborate designs also represent a theme of Conrad and Ford Madox Ford's odd, little-read science-fiction novel *The Inheritors* (1901). The "dimensionists," a race of beings from the fourth dimension, are making their preparations to invade earth: "they were to come as the grey hairs come, to sap the strength of us as the years sap the strength of the muscles."[41] Part of their baroque scheme involves interfering in European imperial interests in Greenland's coal resources. *The Inheritors*, begun while Conrad was busy composing *Heart of Darkness*, can be read as an updating of Bulwer-Lytton's *The Coming Race* (1870), another inverted invasion narrative that imagines energy manipulation as the crucial characteristic defining the difference among civilizations.[42] But, crucially, unlike Bulwer-Lytton, Conrad and Ford posit this difference as inherently and systematically parasitic.

When Marlow returns to Europe, he follows the "trickle of ivory"[43] to its destination, Brussels, also described in metabolic terms as a center of heedless consumption: "I found myself back in the sepulchral city resenting the sight of people hurrying through the streets to filch a little money from each other, to devour their infamous cookery, to gulp their unwholesome beer, to dream their insignificant and silly dreams."[44] The sepulchral hue of the city itself suggests another kind of material and economic conversion: the ivory drained from the Congo instantiated in the very physical structure of Brussels itself. Such a connection is suggested earlier in the novel when "the Accountant," one of Marlow's listeners, sits "toying architecturally" with his box of dominoes, associating the abstractions of capital with the manhandling of ivory and material construction.[45] Indeed, one of the novel's preoccupations – appropriate for a story set on a river – is tracing the direction in which things flow. In the opening, Marlow thinks of London as the source of those sea-going men spreading over the earth, "bearers of a spark from the sacred fire."[46] The image mirrors Jevons's chauvinistic industrial boosterism – "In the ancient mythology, fire was a stolen gift from heaven, but it is our countrymen who have shown the powers of fire, and conferred a second Promethean gift upon the world" – but seems a hopelessly backwards description of the flow of things, morality and energy both, by novel's end.[47]

Like the London of *Heart of Darkness*, the imperial capital in *The Secret Agent* is watched over by a feeble, "bloodshot"[48] sun. Conrad develops this connection between the urban landscape and energy forms through frequent references to the guttering street lamps and the gas jets of the Verloc household. The Assistant Commissioner reflects upon the streets outside his window and the lamps fighting a losing battle with the elements:

> It was a very trying day, choked in raw fog to begin with, and now drowned in cold rain. The flickering, blurred flames of gas-lamps seemed to be dissolving in a watery atmosphere. And the lofty pretensions of a mankind oppressed by the miserable indignities of the weather appeared as a colossal and hopeless vanity deserving of scorn, wonder and compassion.[49]

The heart of empire, the fabled source of the sacred fire spreading over the world, can barely keep its own lights burning. The insomniac Verloc listens at night to the noises rising up to his window: "Down below, in the quiet, narrow street, measured footsteps approached the house, then died away, unhurried and firm, as if the passer-by had started to pace out all eternity, from gas-lamp to gas-lamp in a night without end; and the drowsy ticking of the old clock on the landing became distinctly audible in the bedroom."[50] Those same streets are patrolled by the aptly named Chief Inspector Heat, who stands as the most overt sign of the novel's preoccupation with energy forms. Like "productive" or "efficient," "heat" is a term riven with inconsistency, as Barri Gold notes: "*Heat* is its own opposite; its popular usage suggests usable energy, what scientists and engineers call heat sources, bodies at higher temperatures, from which we can derive warmth or run steam engines. However, *heat* in technical parlance as often evokes the heat sink, 'waste places' that form the repositories of energy that is past its usefulness.[51]

London in *The Secret Agent* is in fact menaced by two forms of destruction by heat – the explosive and the dissipative. The first is featured most prominently in the narrative – in the Professor's detonator, the Greenwich attack, the death of Stevie – but it is the second that ultimately has the more significant impact on the world of the novel. The anarchists are described as "incendiaries"[52] early on, but the adjective, which ostensibly refers to their fuse-lighting ways, comes to seem an even more apt description of their slow burning out. Yundt peers out with "extinguished eyes,"[53] and his, "evil gift clung to him yet, like the smell of a deadly drug in an old vial of poison, emptied now, useless, ready to be thrown away upon the rubbish heap of things that had served their time."[54] Michaelis delivers a speech to his comrades, but "the shortness of breath took all fire, all animation out of his voice."[55] The description of the anarchists as suffused with bodily and spiritual inanition reflects the pointlessness of their plotting; as Vladimir notes, "your friends could set half the Continent on fire without influencing the public opinion here in favour of a universal repressive legislation. They will not look outside their back yard here."[56] The inexorable dissipation of characters' energy is complemented by a preoccupation with all forms of gradual wearing away. The ticking of the clock, the pacing footsteps on the sidewalk outside Verloc's bedroom window – these sounds of dull repetition keep an unceasing beat throughout the novel, becoming audible after the endless talk of revolution and counter-revolution die away. The metronomic monotony is linked explicitly to ebbing life at novel's end, when Winnie mistakes the sound of Verloc's blood dripping on the floor for the sound of the clock.[57] The one explosion that does occur – the Greenwich bomb – has no impact on the life of the city; it is, rather, absorbed by the daily newspapers as a passing curiosity before it is forgotten altogether.

While the principals are all focused on the issue of terrorism and the possibility of explosion, the novel itself is more interested in the burning out and the wasted effort beneath the surface of action. The rhetoric of energy loss occurs nowhere more insistently than during the extended chapter near the novel's end where Winnie realizes that her life's effort has been entirely misspent, and murders her treacherous husband. The emotional states of both are described in terms of blazing up and burning out: Vladimir's imprecations feel to Verloc like "a hot brand which set his internal economy in a blaze";[58] but its ultimate effect is to weigh his "energies to the ground"[59] as "the last particle of his nervous force had been expended."[60] For Winnie, the account of her brother's death is like "a white-hot iron drawn across her eyes; at the same time her heart, hardened and chilled into a lump of ice, kept her body in an inward shudder."[61] The shock she receives is taken in stillness and silence, and likened to an awed reckoning with the death of the sun: "She kept still as the population of half the globe would keep still in astonishment and despair, were the sun suddenly put out in the summer sky by the perfidy of a trusted providence."[62]

That last passage is crucial because it highlights the different uses to which the rhetoric of energy is put in the novel. In a perfect illustration of Verloc's titanic self-absorption, it is his own restricted realm, his "internal economy" of shock and fatigue, that is at issue for him. For Winnie, in contrast, the vision is of an external world that has been stripped of all consolation. Verloc's unending, self-pitying monologue about his own fatigue strikes her as something alien and incomprehensible, and Conrad's pseudo-scientific prose suggests that her illusions have given way to an experience with raw, phenomenal reality: "The waves of air of the proper length, propagated in accordance with correct mathematical formulas, flowed around all the inanimate things in the room, lapped against Mrs. Verloc's head as if it had been a head of stone."[63] Of course, the prose itself is highly artificial, anticipating the other discovery that Winnie is about to make: the systems of thought and behavior ordering her world are inescapable. To her, Stevie's death represents the cancellation of an enormous amount of labor:

> It was a crushing memory, an exhausting vision of countless breakfast-trays carried up and down innumerable stairs, of endless haggling over pence, of the endless drudgery of sweeping, dusting, cleaning, from basement to attics; while the impotent mother, staggering on swollen legs, cooked in a grimy kitchen, and poor Stevie, the unconscious presiding genius of all their toil, blacked the gentlemen's boots in the scullery.[64]

Explosion is thus converted into a vision of life worn away, work expended for years for nothing. Winnie's own sudden death is then similarly converted by the newspaper into trite formulations, described as an inscrutable happening which will "for ever" remain a mystery. Ossipon carries the ten-day-old account in his pocket, now just a piece of detritus that renders the very words "for ever" a blackly comic comment upon the city's ephemeral daily record keeping. In *The Soul of London* (1905), a book Conrad read with much appreciation as he was writing *The Secret Agent*, Ford discusses the forgotten lives embedded in city structures: "To the building up of this railway, of this landscape of roofs, there went so many human lives, so much of human endeavour, so many human hopes … And for me at least it is melancholy to think that hardly one of all these lives, of all these men, will leave any trace in the world."[65] If Ford reflects in general terms upon an accumulation of disappeared lives, Conrad traces a specific gradual disappearance – from married sister, to brotherless widow, to a handful of words in a newspaper already out of date.

The most extended description of the unreal city occurs in the second chapter, during Verloc's walk to Vladimir's office:

> The very pavement under Mr. Verloc's feet had an old-gold tinge in that diffused light, in which neither wall, nor tree, nor beast, nor man cast a shadow. Mr. Verloc was going westward through a town without shadows in an atmosphere of powdered old gold. There were red, coppery gleams on the roofs of houses, on the corners of walls, on the panels of carriages, on the very coats of the horses, and on the broad back of Mr. Verloc's overcoat, where they produced a dull effect of rustiness. But Mr. Verloc was not in the least conscious of having got rusty. He surveyed through the park railings the evidences of the town's opulence and luxury with an approving eye. All these people had to be protected. Protection is the first necessity of opulence and luxury. They had to be protected; and their horses, carriages, houses, servants had to be protected; and the source of their wealth had to be protected in the heart of the city and the heart of the country ... Mr. Verloc would have rubbed his hands with satisfaction had he not been constitutionally averse from every superfluous exertion.[66]

Verloc's work, like Heat's and Vladimir's, is dedicated to protecting the system itself. What ostensibly threatens it is anarchism, explosion; but the threat that Verloc cannot see, the passage tells us, is rust, the natural corruption persisting within the fantastic world of capital accumulation, the shadow thrown across his back in a seemingly shadowless land. Verloc sees himself as a guardian of the "source" of European wealth that "had to be protected in the heart of the city and the heart of the country." "The heart of the country" may mean the center of England to Verloc, but to readers of Conrad's other novels, it also conjures images of the natural world of Africa and South America: the heart of darkness and "the weary heart of the land" towards which civilization is extending its reach in *Nostromo*.[67] Indeed, in the Embassy, Vladimir reminds Verloc that his work is in fact a small part of protecting an entire global system of transnational business interests. And Vladimir would surely know, as Conrad undoubtedly does, the true source of the coppery gleam lighting up everything in Verloc's path to his office, since copper, absolutely foundational to European industrial production, was as much the driving force for British imperial interests in Rhodesia as ivory was for Leopold's in the Congo.

This is how imperialism appears in *The Secret Agent*: a system existing at the very heart of the city's operations yet appearing only on the fringes of perception. Such a shadowy position in the narrative is in keeping with both the limited radii of most of the characters' minds, and also the mystification of imperial relations. The troubling idea of the "source" of wealth is only quietly raised in the above passage, but the term resurfaces briefly as an explicit subject of discussion in Vladimir's office. Walking Verloc through the reasoning behind the plot to bomb the observatory, Vladimir says of the middle classes: "They believe that in some mysterious way science is at the source of their material prosperity."[68] The fruit of this observation is the decision to attack the Greenwich observatory, a locale that stands for science, of course, but that also represents the center of the imperial project: the standardization of time and the establishment of the Prime Meridian. Discussing the observatory in their biography of Lord Kelvin, Norton Wise and Crosbie Smith write: "In the late Victorian and Edwardian eras, Britannia's rule depended less on the military power of earlier empires than on geometrical conventions imposed upon the material world in order to make possible the maritime trade and communication, without which the widely scattered and largely island Empire could scarcely have existed."[69]

As we have seen, thermodynamics uncovered not only the inefficiency at the heart of industrial production, but the waste involved in all energy transactions, undermining any vision of an orderly natural world. Nature "monstrous and free" in Africa appears as "the shackled form of a conquered monster"[70] in urbanized Europe; and yet nature's corrosive and disorderly forces are at work in the corners and interstices of the city: the rust on Verloc's back, the waning sun in the London sky, the guttering lamps and the flagging energies of the city's denizens. The novel is preoccupied with uncovering the unruly and elemental forces that are available to the senses on the open sea and in places not bathed in coppery light, but working more obscurely beneath the surface of networks of power and management. Hugh Epstein notes of the London of *The Secret Agent*, "we become aware of a severe attenuation of energy and a much sourer representation of inertness than in the earlier works. Of course, what offered itself to Conrad's eye was something both more stable and more in decline than that which Dickens and even Ruskin saw."[71] "More stable and more in decline" gets at the tension in Conrad's vision of the city as a place in which the very monumentality of an imposed order raises, inevitably, the specter of its undoing: slow corrosion and energy waste.

Corrosion and waste are also preoccupations of *The Soul of London*. Ford points to the city-dweller's habitual unconsciousness of the unceasing outlay of resources needed simply to maintain the city's physical capital and its "business capacities" against the work of entropy:

> For supposing that Physical Deterioration to exist, we must lose our business capacities; a sound mind going with a healthy body, London must lose her trade ... A very little want of attention to the sewers, the embankments

and the up-river locks would swamp at each tide all the City and all London. The sliding sands would get into motion beneath Saint Paul's; all the hidden streams and rivulets that London has forgotten would swell, burst their bonds, and beneath the ground eat into the foundations of the houses.[72]

The Soul of London insists upon the unceasing, unseen repair work required to ward off collapse and keep the city dry and functioning; in *The Secret Agent*'s decidedly darker view, the city is a place in which all activity is already suffused with its eventual futility; the apocalyptic future vision of London underwater is superimposed upon the present city, just as the "heat death" of the sun, forecast millions of years in the future, casts a pall over human work. In both cases, the city is imagined not as an engine of productive activity, but rather as a precarious arrangement dedicated to self-maintenance. The science that is imagined as an agent of order and a source of wealth describes, in the end, a natural world working ceaselessly to undo that order and dissipate that wealth.

Entropy thus menaces the capitalist order in two ways. On one level, it is the principle of opposition, nature's inescapable law giving the lie to any notion of human rationality progressively or finally subduing the world. Conrad was fond of using the future history of the "heat-death" as a way of puncturing the pretensions of imperial ambition. In as unlikely a place as an essay on Henry James, Conrad writes, "When the last aqueduct shall have crumbled to pieces, the last airship fallen to the ground, the last blade of grass have died upon a dying earth, man, indomitable by his training in resistance to misery and pain, shall set this undiminished light of his eyes against the feeble glow of the sun."[73] From the Roman imperial aqueducts to the present (and future) conquest of the air, the entire trajectory of humanity's "progress" will leave it, in the end, no less vulnerable to the pressures of the natural world and the inexorable dissipation of energy. But – and this is the more trenchant aspect of Conrad's critique – entropy is also the principle at work *within* the logic of industrial capitalism and imperial exploitation, the almost unthinkable amount of work expended to worse than no purpose. It is the spectacle of the French schooner firing blindly into the Continent at the beginning of Marlow's journey or, perhaps more to the point, the pilgrims he encounters unloading their guns into a seemingly immortal hippopotamus: "The pilgrims used to turn out in a body and empty every rifle they could lay hands on at him. Some even had sat up o' nights for him. All this energy was wasted, though."[74] Taken individually, the tendency of human nature is recklessly to expend whatever excess power is afforded it; taken as an aggregate, as a vast system of profit-seekers, the tendency of imperial capitalism is towards monumental forms of waste and inefficiency; the entire operation of managers and accountants, waystations, steamboats, agents, rifles, and rivets is dedicated merely to keeping a "trickle of ivory" flowing out of the Congo.

In similar fashion, *The Secret Agent* combines talk of an imposing, systematic efficiency with a pervasive sense of the absolute futility and waste of characters' actions. The Assistant Commissioner boasts to Sir Ethelred: "the foreign governments cannot complain of the inefficiency of our police ... In less than twelve hours we have established the identity of a man literally blown to shreds, have found the organizer of the attempt, and have had a glimpse of the inciter behind him."[75] Yet while considering his position within the system, he comes to a very different conclusion: "He felt himself dependent on too many subordinates and too many masters ... the rough east winds of the English spring (which agreed with his wife) augmented his general mistrust of men's motives and of the efficiency of their organization. The futility of office work especially appalled him on those days so trying to his sensitive liver."[76] The Assistant Commisioner's private mistrust is well founded. His description of the efficiency of the investigation – in a sense, a description of the unfolding of the novel itself – is undermined by the pointlessness of the entire exercise. The identities of the bomb-plot participants may have been uncovered with great dispatch, but the bomb-plot itself, as we know, even had it been competently carried out, was designed only to strengthen the prevailing system of political and economic relations.

The narrative form of *The Secret Agent* is, in fact, pulled in these two directions at once: on the one hand, the prose is not only corrosively ironic (Irving Howe says it "steadily eats away at the features, the energies, the very vitals of its major characters"[77]), it can also be ostentatiously inefficient:

> But there was also about him an indescribable air which no mechanic could have acquired in the practice of his handicraft, however dishonestly exercised: the air common to men who live on the vices, the follies, or the baser fears of mankind; the air of moral nihilism common to keepers of gambling halls and disorderly houses; to private detectives and inquiry agents; to drink sellers and, I should say, to the sellers of invigorating electric belts and to the inventors of patent medicines. But of that last I am not sure, not having carried my investigations so far into the depths. For all I know, the expression of these last may be perfectly diabolic. I shouldn't be surprised. What I want to affirm is that Mr. Verloc's expression was by no means diabolic.[78]

This is very nearly Conrad parodying Conrad. In *Heart of Darkness* the frequent talk of the "indescribable" is meant to conjure a moral atmosphere that exceeds a shared frame of reference; here, a foray through the "depths" of the city ends in an awkward retreat, and a rather mild, minor stroke of characterization touching up our picture of shallow Verloc. The novel dilates frequently, almost perversely, upon such seemingly insignificant details, keeping the prose in sluggish step with the torpid lives being described.

On the other hand, the narrative itself is ruthlessly efficient in putting together the elements of the chain reaction that unravels the entire Verloc family. Conrad breaks a rather straightforward time sequence in Chapter 8 by circling back to the episode in which Mrs. Verloc's mother moves into an almshouse in the hopes of cementing Stevie's place in the household. The irony, of course, is that it is precisely this protective move that delivers Stevie to Verloc's machinations, and to the demise of both. But because we don't yet know at this point that it is, in fact, Stevie who has been killed in the Greenwich explosion, this chapter's place in the novel's chronology as an active, authorial intervention and reconstruction of Stevie's history is concealed until after we have returned to the primary chronology. Thus, upon first reading, this interpolated section seems to march on with the same, grim, forward monotony that describes the pace of the rest of the novel; only in retrospect does it snap into place as a crucial moment upon which the entire plot hinges. The actions taken by the principal characters in *The Secret Agent* thus have an insidiously double character: on the one hand, they contribute, like the working of a diabolically efficient mechanism, to hasten the downward spiral and dissolution of the Verloc household; and on the other, they move with a kind of meandering irrelevance, having absolutely no lasting effect on anything else.

As Stephen Bunker notes, "While [dominant] groups, using and directing the energies generated or transformed by subordinate groups, may transform their physical and social environments, they themselves become dependent on the social and material organization they have created. Humans become the prisoner of their own transformation of nature and society."[79] Verloc's "constitutional" inanition, his fatigue, inefficiency, and even his girth, have reference points within nineteenth-century imperialist discourse. The argument that the indolent condition of urban dwellers was a direct result of their dependence upon imperial exploitation was a topic taken up by many end-of-the-century commentators. J. A. Hobson notes that in becoming a manufacturing and commercial center England was no longer "breeding in rural life the bone, muscle and brain which have made the empire, but depending for its force in the future on colonial lives."[80] With three-quarters of the population living in cities, Hobson asks, how can England "preserve intact the vigour of physique and character which is essential to the progress of a nation"?[81] Dwindling energy levels in the form of exhaustion and torpor characterize exploiter and exploited respectively. Hobson applies this analysis to both urban dwellers in Europe and the colonies:

> Even in the parts of South Africa where whites thrive best, the life they lead, when clearly analysed, is seen to be parasitic. The white farmer, Dutch or British, does little work, manual or mental, and tends everywhere to become lazy and "unprogressive"; the trading, professional or official classes of the towns show clear signs of the same laxity and torpor, the brief spasmodic flares of energy evoked by dazzling prospects among small classes of speculators and business men in mushroom cities like Johannesburg serving but to dazzle our eyes and hide the deep essential character of the life.[82]

Hobson, like Conrad, subverts the myth of the "energetic" European flogged by apologists like Kidd. At opposite ends of the world, the city inhabitants of *The Secret Agent* represent the flip side of the African laborers drained of energy and left to die in *Heart of Darkness*. They are not wasted bodily from too much labor, but grown fat and spiritually exhausted from sloth, dependency, and purposeless effort. Hobson here is also attacking the eugenics program of Karl Pearson, which was often framed in energy terms. As we will see in the next chapter, concern about managing the evolutionary energy of the race fed the discourses of degeneration and eugenics.

Of course, physical and spiritual energy loss are, strictly speaking, only metaphorically related. And yet, in another sense, they are intimately tied together, since they are both grounded in the idea of the value of work. As Georgescu-Roegen notes, the entropy law is, at heart, an unavoidably anthropomorphic concept: "A non-anthropomorphic mind could not possibly understand the concept of order-entropy which, as we have seen, cannot be divorced from the intuitive grasping of human purposes."[83] Without consideration of these purposes, the economic process can seem merely a vast system dedicated to degrading energy, in which the human participants serve the needs of the system, rather than the other way around. This, indeed, was how it appeared to Conrad, for whom the value of work and the value of life were mutually defining. Uniting the many tropes of energy loss, the death of Stevie, and the vision of the city as an imperturbable, inescapable system, is an anxiety running throughout *The Secret Agent* about the waste of human work. "Activity – activity" is what Vladimir demands from Verloc, and this imperative is followed a few pages later by the sight of a fly buzzing against the windowpane, an image that could serve as the central symbol for the entire novel: "The useless fussing of that tiny, energetic organism affected unpleasantly this big man, threatened in his indolence."[84] The novel is replete with descriptions of the uselessness of action: Mrs. Verloc's mother has a "mania for locomotion,"[85] for example, and Heat reflects that criminals and police are "products of the same machine, one classed as useful, the other as noxious," and that "they take the machine for granted in different ways, but with a seriousness essentially the same."[86] "Useful" work is thus imagined as a convention, and "Heat" just part of the functioning of the machinery. The invisible medium against which the fly buzzes, cast into human terms, is the system of entrenched, interlocked power relations in London, within which a tiny particle can work only to wear itself out.

In a grim 1898 letter to Graham, Conrad explicitly links the "heat death" of the sun to the ends of human activity:

> The fate of a humanity condemned ultimately to perish from cold is not worth troubling about. If you take it to heart it becomes an unendurable tragedy. If you believe in improvement you must weep, for the attained perfection must end in cold, darkness, and silence. In a dispassionate view the ardour for reform, improvement for virtue, for knowledge and even for beauty is only a vain sticking up for appearances as though one were anxious about the cut of one's clothes in a community of blind men.[87]

The city only intensifies this dismal feeling. Verloc's "unbelief in the effectiveness of every human effort,"[88] a position that is only lent credence by the novel, suggests one reason *The Secret Agent* seems such an anomalous work in Conrad's oeuvre: its very locale inverts many of the relationships that readers of his sea fiction are accustomed to finding. Marlow says, "I don't like work – no man does – but I like what is in the work, – the chance to find yourself. Your own reality – for yourself, not for others – what no other man can ever know."[89] Valuable work, as Marlow describes it, and Conrad frequently imagines it, is a direct struggle against the forces of natural chaos and a refusal to be reduced despite the palpable smallness of one's position. Paradoxically, the magnitude of the forces confronting his characters on the open seas works to aggrandize the value of life. Although the human struggle against disorder is ultimately a lost cause anywhere, as Conrad pointed out to Graham, the moment-by-moment demands made by the ocean retract the horizon of danger from the heat death of everything to the threat of a broken mast or flooded deck. Such hazards infuse work with an immediate, palpable worth, and provide a forum in which efficacy, valor, self-sacrifice, solidarity, and other human traits are valued for the tenacity with which they are upheld. Conrad writes in *The Mirror of the Sea*:

> As men of scrupulous honor set up a high standard of public conscience above the dead-level of an honest community, so men of that skill which passes into art by ceaseless striving raise the dead-level of correct practice in the crafts of land and sea. The conditions fostering the growth of that supreme, alive excellence, as well in work as in play, ought to be preserved with a most careful regard lest the industry or the game should perish of an insidious and inward decay.[90]

Conrad's essay on Henry James makes this point as well, albeit with different emphasis. There, the remaining humans on earth, looking up at a dying sun and stripped of the protective illusions of Western civilization, return to the kind of inward defiance that Conrad associates with the work of the artist:

> The artistic faculty, of which each of us has a minute grain, may find its voice in some individual of that last group, gifted with a power of expression and courageous enough to interpret the ultimate experience of mankind in terms of his temperament, in terms of art ... It is safe to affirm that, if anybody, it will be the imaginative man who would be moved to speak on the eve of that day without tomorrow – whether in austere exhortation or in a phrase of sardonic comment, who can guess?[91]

Conrad's praise for James is couched in the language of energy throughout the essay – he describes the "inextinguishable youth" and "perennial spring" of his imagination, the "force" of his body of work, and the renunciation of the world that is, for Conrad, the ultimate wellspring of great art:

> All adventure, all love, every success is resumed in the supreme energy of an act of renunciation. It is the uttermost limit of our power; it is the most potent and effective force at our disposal on which rest the labours of a solitary man in his study, the rock on which have been built commonwealths whose might casts a dwarfing shadow upon two oceans.[92]

The constructive, retentive energy of art is thus set against both the entropy of the world and the profligate dissipations of imperial society. Conrad means for the juxtaposition to be taken quite seriously:

> Action in its essence, the creative art of a writer of fiction may be compared to rescue work carried out in darkness against cross-gusts of wind swaying the action of a great multitude. It is rescue work, this snatching of vanishing phases of turbulence, disguised in fair words, out of the native

obscurity into a light where the struggling forms may be seen, seized upon, endowed with the only possible form of permanence in this world of relative values – the permanence of memory.[93]

Such a paradox – permanence in impermanence – refuses the false order trumpeted by apostles of progress, as the essay as a whole locates abiding energy and meaningful work wholly within the inner sphere of perception, in memory, art, and the defiance of implacable circumstances.

When in *The Mirror of the Sea* Conrad describes the metabolism of a steamship, driven by an engine that "beats and throbs like a pulsating heart" and "sickens and dies on the waves" when it exhausts its energy, he is talking about thermodynamic flow and the decay that is part of the processes of machine technology.[94] But he is also comparing modern seamanship with an earlier mode of exploration, dominated not by global business concerns and systems of imperial management but by intrepid individuals who navigated uncharted regions and faced directly the capricious, destructive power of the open ocean. Thus the seamen setting out from London, "bearers of a spark from the sacred fire" in *Heart of Darkness*, suggest not merely an ironic comment on European hubris, but the expression of a much more complex consideration of the past and present of seafaring. The contrast is between explorers like "Sir Francis Drake" and "Sir John Franklin … Hunters for gold or pursuers of fame,"[95] and their modern descendants, the gallery of mediocre functionaries Marlow encounters on his journey, and the established networks of trade and commercial machinery they unthinkingly serve. At times, Conrad has something resembling nostalgia for the former, and seems to regret the decline in valor and self-sufficiency that has accompanied the systematization of the entire globe and modern man's dependence upon institutional structures and the labor of others.

This nostalgia is not unmixed, however, and Conrad is well aware that the earlier era of exploration was driven by a ruthless pursuit of resources. In *Lord Jim*, Marlow says of seventeenth-century traders:

Where wouldn't they go for pepper! For a bag of pepper they would cut each other's throats without hesitation, and would forswear their souls, of which they were so careful otherwise: the bizarre obstinacy of that desire made them defy death in a thousand shapes … it made them heroic; and it made them pathetic, too, in their craving for trade.[96]

And villainous figures like Chester and Gentleman Brown function ambiguously in this context: on the one hand, since they work on the margins and in the interstices of the globalized economy, they seem dark throwbacks to that earlier era of seafaring. For Chester, there are still unexplored regions of the map, flush with riches and untapped resources; for Brown the pirate, there are still kingdoms to conquer, and a life that can still be fashioned beyond the bounds of international management networks. But these men also seem to function only as ironic alternatives to such networks; while they appear to work the boundaries and unmapped areas of global commerce, they nevertheless embody the presiding spirit and prevailing logic of modern imperial practices. Chester's interest in an untapped guano island is framed in the familiar language of exploitation and waste, and imagined as a potential node in the global energy economy: "It was awful to think of all that lovely stuff lying waste under the sun – stuff that would send the sugar-cane shooting sky-high."[97] Meanwhile, Brown's titanic appetites, his desire to "squeeze everything dry," suggest an insatiable, world-consuming rapacity; he seems, that is, not so much an alternative to modern imperial practice, but the personification of it.[98] In other words, the complicated way in which these figures both do and do not seem to mark a difference between modern and bygone modes speaks to Conrad's own ambivalence about history. The modern, bureaucratized system of steam transport and routinized extraction seems to embody a new, "flabby, pretending, weak-eyed" spirit,[99] and a compromised relationship to the natural world. But it also seems a global-scaled instantiation of appetites that have always been with us. Conrad's critique of the ideology of progress is, in this way, double-sided: in the ways in which things are not monstrously worse, they are just as bad as they have ever been.

Conrad's nostalgia, then, is always partial, ironized, provisional. In this way, sea-faring life allows not so much for a fully committed belief in human nobility and heroism, but only for the willing suspension of disbelief. *Lord Jim* itself is a narrative constructed around the search for a place in the world where such a suspension of disbelief can be practiced without interruption. The European dependence on energy and other resources, the bureaucratic infrastructure designed to manage the flow of those resources, and the mechanized transportation grid designed to systematize their extraction make it increasingly difficult to maintain this suspension, to commit oneself to a life organized around the moral ideals of heroism, sacrifice, and solidarity. It is no accident that Conrad's early story of disillusionment, *Youth*, centers upon a ship transporting coal: the exuberant idealism of the youthful Marlow is counterpointed with the gradual disintegration of the ship, the spontaneous combustion of its cargo, and the captain's absurd obsession with salvaging parts of the ship "for the underwriters."[100] The youthful Marlow appears fazed neither by the routinized mundanity of the ship's original mandate, nor by the increasingly farcical conditions into which the situation descends. But we feel – and the older, narrating Marlow confirms – how untenable these youthful ideals are becoming, how many shocks from sordid reality they must absorb, and how intimately they are bound to structures – physical, economic, psychological – that are entirely inimical to them. Continued belief in them can no longer speak to a kind of quixotic nobility; it can only represent a form of madness or blindness. The process of disillusionment that is represented in *Youth* in ironic-elegiac terms appears in *The Secret Agent* almost exclusively in tones of caustic cynicism. What appears in the former – and in *Lord Jim* – as a suspension of disbelief that can endow action with provisional significance appears in the latter as merely a collective illusion maintained in the name of comfort and security.

As with Dickens and Ruskin, Conrad's use of the rhetoric of energy dissipation blends elements of both reactionary and left-wing critiques of modernity. On the one hand, he uses it to expose the contradictions of capitalist hegemony and the rhetoric of energy and efficiency. The city as devourer stands for a global economy in which world capitalism fosters not the development of Third World economies, the spread of wealth, and the efficient use of resources, as was often maintained in imperialist tracts, but a relationship of dependency characterized by rapacity and exhaustion. On the other hand, Conrad exposes as fallacious the Marxist-anarchist dreams of "a self-regenerated universe," which Michaelis "pathetically" tries to embrace in Verloc's living room as "the coals in the grate settled down with a slight crash."[101] Michaelis's vain faith that the forces of historical materialism will inexorably drive society towards a just distribution of wealth and a classless society is bookended with pointed irony by a description of heat escaping on one end, and an acid remark about the fate of the universe on the other. Conrad's reactionary tendencies, as we have seen, are not limited to denials of the utopian socialist project, but also extend, at times, to a desire to valorize the heroism and diligence of a way of life passing out of existence. *The Secret Agent* imagines what will take its place: "the poor expedients devised by a mediocre mankind for preserving an imperfect society from the dangers of moral and physical corruption, both secret, too, of their kind."[102] The interest in forms of secret corruption suggests that perhaps it is not just Verloc who is the novel's "secret agent," but entropy itself, the secret denied by the rhetoric of imperial civilization, but working everywhere to undermine its pretensions to advancing order, progress, and prosperity.

CHAPTER 8

Evolutionary energy and the future: Henry Maudsley and H. G. Wells

In his address to the Association for the Promotion of Social Science in 1865, Dr. John Edward Morgan discussed the depletion of energy resources in English cities and the threat it posed to the future of the nation. Although his address appeared the same year *The Coal Question* was published, and, like that more well-known work, focused on the sustainability of contemporary social and economic practices, Morgan was not discussing the supplies of fossil-fuel resources, nor was he writing about guano, agricultural fertility, the second law of thermodynamics, or any of the other narratives of exhaustion we have thus far been discussing. His interest, instead, was the energy of the "race," which seemed to him to be threatened by urban growth and the possibility of "degeneration," a process of evolutionary backsliding that could return humans to a more primitive biological condition. For Morgan, as for many writers on degeneration, the problem was life in the modern city. Urban centers were permeated by a "dismal list of noxious gases" produced variously by coal combustion and unsanitary sewage disposal, which contaminated the streets, water, and atmosphere.[1] His patients among the urban poor, he notes, lack stamina, have weak hearts and musculature, and seem incapable of "arduous or sustained labour."[2] Morgan translates these enervated bodies into national and historical terms, arguing that, through them, one can diagnose the coming decay of England itself: "May not nations, like individuals, curtail their day of power in the world's history, by overtaxing the physical and mental energies at their disposal, thus prematurely consuming that national life-blood on which permanent greatness mainly depends?"[3]

What troubles Morgan is not simply that city-dwellers are wasting away under a canopy of smoke and filth, but that, as the city continues to expand, it subjects an increasing percentage of the population to such conditions. The country, which breeds healthy, "energetic" bodies, surrenders an ever-increasing number of them to the insatiable city: "The country is robbed of a large portion of its productive population; men and women in the prime of their strength, when their chances of life are the most promising, emigrate to the towns, and then a comparison is instituted between the places they have deserted and those to which they have removed."[4] Just as Jevons and Liebig warn about how the expansion of urban areas could tax the resources of the nation beyond its capacities, so Morgan warns that current patterns of growth and consumption are unsustainable. The difference is that Morgan is not talking about coal deposits or fertilizing agents, but human "resources," which are in danger of becoming less productive over time through degeneration. For Morgan, the working-class body was a kind of engine – a "human motor" in Anson Rabinbach's phrase – that required maintenance and a steady supply of resources. But it was also *itself* a resource, a kind of energy that fueled the national economic engine and shaped the course of history. As Daniel Pick writes: "The body, it seemed, could not be left to itself, since it was a crucial racial patrimony."[5] These resources were breaking down because they were undernourished; housed in badly ventilated, diseased-filled quarters; and stunted by pollution. When a writer on degeneration in *The Lancet* describes the working poor as "devoid of the tension on which the easy and harmonious working of the whole system so mainly depends," the word "system" seems to refer simultaneously to the nervous systems of the individual bodies under consideration, and the larger social and economic system that depends upon them.[6] The discourse of degeneration thus united physics and biology by representing the body as a nexus of production. Morgan uses the words "energy," "power," "life-blood," and "vitality" interchangeably throughout the essay, referring to the aggregated physico-biological material threatened with exhaustion.

Degeneration fashioned the body as a source not only of productive power, but of *re*productive power. City life didn't just sap the energy of the laboring bodies of the present-day workers, it affected the vitality of their offspring. Morgan sees an emergency brewing because of the alarming demographic trends – an increasing percentage of the population moving to the city in search of work – but also because of a process of evolutionary retrogression: "that lowered standard of the public health which I have spoken of under the ominous title of threatened deterioration of race ... handed down as an abiding legacy to the offspring."[7] This is the key to the discourse of degeneration: the anxiety that unsanitary modern conditions did not just stunt the bodies of the current generation, but had a permanent effect on the "energy" of the nation. In this way, health *itself* was turned into a kind of resource in danger of depletion. Degeneracy could be defined as anything that departed from the productive norm – not just the sick, the debilitated, and the mentally ill, but criminals, decadents, and, for some writers, socialists and homosexuals. This discourse lumped these disparate groups together by fashioning them as etiolated, enervated, and listless, and therefore threats to the nation's productivity. Indeed, we might imagine the "generation" in "degeneration" to refer simultaneously to the biological generation of offspring and the generation of energy.

Thus while degeneration was primarily an evolutionary discourse, it was also an industrial discourse, one that used as a metric of assessing "fitness" the ability to contribute laboring power. In this chapter I want to trace some of the implications of the way degeneration combined evolutionary theory with a concern about the use and waste of energy resources in the city. I follow Gareth Stedman Jones in his understanding of degeneration as a myth that tapped into middle-class fears, and served to segregate the working classes (and, less commonly, the aristocracy) as biological "others," and thus to obscure some of the real economic and political grievances that informed working-class unrest.[8] But my focus here is on the ecological valence of this discourse, the way in which the class divisions reified by the discourse of degeneration worked to biologize pollution, waste, and resource-depletion, and thus shift responsibility away from the environmentally destructive industrial system from which they arose. The result of such a shift in emphasis was to represent the poor as the *source* of the contamination, rather than the victims of a degraded environment. Although I draw on a number of theorists of degeneration, I focus primarily on the English psychiatrist Henry Maudsley, whose influential work on mental pathology employs a vivid vocabulary of energy, waste, and pollution. In the second half, I turn my attention to a novel that both deployed and critiqued tropes of energy depletion found in much degenerationist discourse: H. G. Wells's *The Time Machine*. The novel's conclusion, I argue, draws crucial distinctions between evolutionary and thermodynamic discourses too often muddied in discussions of "race energy" that featured prominently in the work of degenerationist writers.

Degeneration and the environment

The discourse of degeneration first arose in England in *The Lancet* in the 1860s, which called attention to the serious, long-term public health issues arising as a consequence of industrial production, improper waste disposal, and overcrowding. Early degenerationist writers insisted on the plight of the urban poor, as well as the susceptibility of all city-dwellers to a host of environmental contaminants. As a writer in *The Lancet* asks: "Are not the aristocracy and the careworn denizens of the city … breathing all day long pestilential exhalations, subject to them too? And how can the unhealthy semen of such produce healthy offspring?"[9] The working-class body was the canary in the coal-mine, so to speak, and by imagining it as both a kind of synecdoche for the national body and a glimpse into the enervated future the entire species might face, degeneration suggested that the fate of the working class was the fate of *everyone*. The degraded environments in which the poor lived were the conditions out of which the evolutionary history of the nation emerged: "If the consequences, then, of this social agglomeration be, on the one hand, increase of political power, of wealth, of commercial and social prosperity, and successful competition with other nations, they are, on the other, an overtaxing of the physical and mental energies at our disposal, and a premature consumption of national life-blood."[10] As we can see here, the discourse of degeneration was initially grounded in an adversarial position towards the effects of industrial modernity. But the emphasis placed on "national life-blood" and the fusion of the discourses of biology and physics would help turn degeneration, in the hands of later writers, towards a kind of industrial apologetics.

By the 1880s the discourse of degeneration had become ubiquitous, and it helped transform the way in which urban poverty was conceptualized. Jones writes: "The theory of 'degeneration' … prepared the middle-class public to see chronic poverty as an endemic condition of large masses of the population, rather than as the product of exceptional misfortune or improvidence on the part of isolated individuals."[11] The poor were environmental victims, bearing in their bodies, and in their genetic materials, the scars and deformations wrought by a contaminated world. At the same time, however, the degenerationist appeal was usually made not to the reader's sympathies or sense of responsibility, but rather to concerns that these degenerated bodies might have slipped irretrievably down the evolutionary ladder. Therefore, they threatened to spread the damage both through reproduction, and through contact with the non-degenerated. It was, in Jones's formulation, "not guilt but fear" that fueled the interest in the poor and the environments in which they lived.[12] Concern about urban conditions stemmed, in part, from fear of mass political unrest and the loss of the traditional boundaries among and between different segments of the lower classes – between, for example, artisans and casual laborers, or the working poor and criminals. For a variety of reasons – the riots in London in 1886, the rise of the Social Democratic Federation and other radical organizations, mixed housing conditions in lower-class

neighborhoods – the traditional division between the "respectable" working poor and the "disreputable" underclass – the so-called "residuum" –
threatened to give way.[13] The fear was that the residuum might contaminate
the class immediately above it, and drag the working class in its entir-
ety into an atavistic swamp. In the parliamentary debates over the 1867
Reform Act, John Bright argued:

> there is a small class which it would be much better for themselves if they
> were not enfranchised, because they have no independence whatsoever,
> and it would be much better for the Constitution also that they should be
> excluded; and there is no class so much interested in having that small class
> excluded as the intelligent and honest working men. I call this class the
> *residuum*, which there is in almost every constituency of almost hopeless
> poverty and dependence.[14]

As Bright's argument suggests, the discourse of degeneration could stiffen
the line of demarcation between the working classes and the "degenerate"
underclass. At the same time, degeneration was also used to argue that
the potential breakdown of that line was a biological, rather than a political, issue. Fear of working-class political organization could be converted
into concern about evolutionary processes, and the fate of the species.
Meanwhile, the language of ecological damage was used to turn pollution
into a function of class difference.

If the term "residuum" obviously dehumanized the very poor by
converting them into a kind of undifferentiated waste product, it also
suggested the flip-side: the commodification of the "respectable" working classes into energy resources for use in a vast system of production.
Concern for the urban poor and their surroundings was thus structured,
in degenerationist discourse, primarily through reference to the imperative for unceasing economic growth. As we have seen, Morgan's interest
in working-class bodies is premised on their reification as raw materials,
and this language remained a part of the discourse through the end of the
century. As F. W. Headley would argue, seemingly without irony, in his
early-twentieth-century text on evolution and degeneration: "There is still
a very considerable fund of potential strength in our poorer classes which
remains to be thus exploited."[15]

Thus while the discourse of degeneration could be used to argue, as
Morgan does, for the need to improve the environments in which the
poor lived, it could also be used to argue for the need to quarantine some
of them – conceptually and otherwise – as irretrievably "other." What
began as a cry for better sanitation and living conditions for the urban
poor became, in some hands, a way of reifying them as a different species

through the mechanism of heredity. The urban poor troubled the degener-ationist imagination as vectors of disease that could threaten anyone who came into contract with them, *and* as carriers of blighted genetic material that threatened the gene pool, turning whole segments of the poor from victims of urban pollution to forms of pollution themselves. The philan-thropist Samuel Smith writes, "while the flower of our population emi-grate … the residuum remains behind, corrupting and being corrupted, like the sewage of the metropolis which remained floating in the mouth of the Thames last summer because there was not scour sufficient to propel it into the sea."[16] In *The Physiology and Pathology of Mind*, Maudsley describes the mentally ill specifically, and the poor more generally, as waste prod-ucts: "[I]t is no marvel, it appears indeed inevitable, that those who, either from inherited weakness or some other debilitating causes, have been ren-dered unequal to the struggle of life should be ruthlessly crushed out as abortive beings in nature. They are the waste thrown up by the silent but strong current of progress."[17] Although Maudsley elsewhere discusses the "insanitary" living conditions as the cause of disease and deterioration, we can see in the above passage the way in which the poor are themselves turned into walking biohazards. Maudsley's image of the "silent but strong current" as an evolutionary metaphor lends both a temporal and a spatial dimension to the phenomenon of bio-waste, which, in turn, hints at an unresolved tension in his work. On the one hand, imagined temporally, the forward-flowing current suggests an irresistible historical trajectory that leaves the weak and debilitated behind. "Waste," in this case, means something like "that which is not needed." And, indeed, at this moment Maudsley believed, following the French psychiatrist Bénédict Morel, that degenerate forms would eventually become sterile, and thus were mere evolutionary discards that posed no lasting threat to the future develop-ment of humanity. On the other hand, however, imagined spatially, the metaphor of waste being "thrown up" along the banks of a current sug-gests a process of environmental contamination. This is waste defined not as the "not needed," but as pollution. This is, as we shall see in a moment, the direction in which Maudsley's later thinking will go, as he becomes increasingly concerned that "degenerates" will not die out and fall safely into history's rearview mirror, but might become an intransigent problem that could permanently debilitate the species.[18] The shift in Maudsley's thinking – from *The Physiology and Pathology of the Mind*, published in 1874, to *Body and Will*, published in 1884 – corresponds to a deepening sense of crisis in the culture about the city environment and the biological intractability of poverty.[19]

The tension embedded in the image of the current speaks to tensions in the discourse of degeneration as a whole, which fashioned the degenerate as something both merely discardable and deeply threatening to the health of the species. Because degeneration was imagined as a phenomenon that was on display in the bodies of the working classes, but also, possibly, represented a threat to the bodies of *everyone*, the poor could be all too readily fashioned into the ghoulish "others" stalking the sanctuaries and future prosperity of middle-class life. Kinship was thus both affirmed and denied: the degenerationist taxonomy asserted enough of a link to stoke anxieties of contamination, while simultaneously suggesting that such links had been permanently forfeited through an estranging biological transformation. But it also meant that the environmental problems of the industrial world could be personified, and thus, perhaps, marked as divisible from the dominant order. Waste and pollution were not inevitable by-products of industrial production and organization; they were confined to certain types and groups, which could, hypothetically, be weeded out.

Energy, entropy, and evolution

Degenerationist discourse was deeply invested in the language of energy because it helped to consolidate a normative standard of evolutionary progress against which deviations could be measured. The evolutionary *telos* was the same as the industrial: increased productivity and increased energy. Notice how, in Maudsley's description of evolutionary development, the progress of the organism is defined by increasingly sophisticated methods of storing energy:

> Power which has been laboriously acquired and stored up as statical in one generation manifestly in such case becomes the inborn faculty of the next; and the development takes place in accordance with that law of increasing specialty and complexity of adaptation to external nature which is traceable through the animal kingdom ... simpler and more general forces are gathered up and concentrated in a more special and complex mode of energy; so again a further specialization takes place in the development of the nervous system.[20]

This is essentially a biologizing of the thermodynamic program we saw defined by Stewart and Lockyer, where increasing technological sophistication might lead, they imagine, to "a device of infinite delicacy of construction" that could command massive amounts of energy with a mere flicker of the will.[21] In both cases, complexity is linked to the ability to harness energy more effectively. Maudsley imagines the development of the nervous system as the consolidation of force, the harnessing of "motions," and the concentration of energy. He imagines "degenerates," conversely, as defined by an uncontrolled expenditure of energy: "they are examples of decaying reason thrown off by vigorous mental growth, the energy of which they testify."[22] The complex operations of human reason, like the complex operations of technology, are uniquely able to gather, channel, and direct energy; without such controls, the energy will be expended in wasteful and haphazard fashion. Morgan fears the depletion of national energy through degeneracy; Maudsley's concern about "vigorous mental growth" seems to suggest the opposite, the fear of *too much* energy. But the ideas are both rooted in the concern that energy will be mismanaged, squandered. Morgan fashions degeneracy in terms of sickness and physical debility, while Maudsley emphasizes mental illness and criminality, but both see the degenerate condition as one that threatens the national resource base and the controlled, "productive" use of energy.[23]

If Morgan and Headley imagined the poor as energy resources fueling the industrial economy, degenerates were imagined as forms of entropy, as spent fuel or agents of waste and disorder. Like entropy, they could be cordoned off and managed through increased efficiency and the march of progress; on the other hand, just as entropy threatened "to bring the present system to an end," in the words of Stewart and Tait, degeneracy was imagined as a threat to progress and national productivity.[24] The combination of belief in progress with apocalyptic forecasts of the way progress was undone from "within" unites the thermodynamic and degeneratonist imaginaries.[25]

Defining degeneracy in terms of energy was key to constructing the degenerate as the bogeyman of the middle classes. As Ted Underwood has argued, in the late eighteenth and early nineteenth centuries the word "energy" connected the middle-class work ethic with the industrial energy forms propelling England's imperial rise.[26] This association continued through the century; as we have seen, it was often suggested that England's industrial supremacy flowed from the "energy" of its national character, rather than from its supplies of resources. Francis Galton uses this very confusion to describe his standards for eugenic selection:

> Energy is the capacity for labour. It is consistent with all the robust virtues, and makes a large practice of them possible. It is the measure of fulness of life; the more energy the more abundance of it; no energy at all is death; idiots are feeble and listless ... Energy is an attribute of the higher races, being favoured beyond all other qualities by natural selection.[27]

The first definition of energy he uses, "the capacity for labour," is informed by the thermodynamic conception of energy-as-work. We can see, however, how Galton easily slides from that definition towards energy defined as a moral quality. His focus is often the upper classes, rather than the urban poor, since he sees hereditary privilege as an obstacle to the management of genetic inheritance, [28] but his work shares with other writers on degeneration an interest in classifying races according to a vocabulary of energy, efficiency, and waste. Imagining two hypothetical castes of people, he divides them into the talented and the "refuse"; the latter is what eugenics seeks to eliminate altogether in favor of the production of morally and physically energetic individuals.[29]

Although the discourse of degeneration may have had at its roots concerns about the degraded environments created by industrial production, its moralization of energy and reification of different classes into forms of energy and pollution obscured both the dependence upon fossil-fuel resources and the ecological costs of energy-intensive production. Waste and disorder could seem like something one could attach to "them," and thus problems that were potentially separable from the course of technological development and industrial growth. The industrialists and the middle classes could be cleansed and refashioned as the embodiment of pure potential energy. The middle classes represented the "capacity for labour," and the "concentrated," "stored up," "specialized" force, in which the future potential of the race was located. The urban residuum and the effete aristocracy, meanwhile, were imagined as embodiments of used-up energy. The aristocracy was spent historically, while the very poorest members of society were merged with the contaminants in their environment. In this way, waste was fashioned not as an intrinsic part of the system but as something that, through better engineering, could be entirely separable from it. By concentrating the decay and entropy of modern industrial civilization primarily in the bodies of the poorest of the poor, degeneration produced a wide array of schemes designed to divide the country from its "waste" once and for all. Eugenics proposed to accomplish this through reproductive engineering, but other plans floated more immediate geographical solutions. As Jones argues, social theorists like Samuel Barnett, Charles Booth, and Alfred Marshall argued for the forced relocation of the hopeless urban underclass either to industrial labor camps outside the cities, or to the colonies.[30] In such environments, under a strict disciplinary regime, perhaps they could be redeemed; at the very least, they would be removed from those locations where they threatened national health. Thus, not only were the poor described as waste products, the solution of the problem of urban poverty took a similar shape to the solution of the problem of urban pollution – ship the "contaminants" elsewhere. In both cases, the belief in engineering as a panacea was a mix of utopian thinking and the desire simply to remove the problem from view.

The consequences of industrial production were further obscured by the way in which evolution was often discussed as a kind of generator of energy, or a force unto itself. Headley, for instance, discusses the way the "machinery" of evolution produces something he calls "race energy" or "race vigour."[31] "Energy is born of conflict," he argues, and softening the edges of that conflict means that there will be no weeding out of "the weak and unenergetic."[32] Similarly, following the German biologist August Weismann, Headley discusses the counter-principle of "panmixis," which he defines as "the cessation of selection" – a condition of ease that, he believes, has increasingly come to characterize modern civilization.[33] Without the invigorating action of natural selection, the machine breaks down and the tendency is towards degeneration and disintegration: "Panmixis compared with Natural Selection may be a clumsy manipulator, but it has more material at its disposal. Total or great defect in individuals followed by loss of stability in the group or species may clearly produce great results. It is easier to pull down than to build."[34] The terms could hardly be clearer: natural selection is a principle of energy, panmixis is a principle of entropy. He elaborates the architectural metaphor implicit in the word "build" to describe the process of degeneration: "panmixis, by merely allowing disintegration, can bring about loss of whole structures, the masterpieces of organic architecture, imitating in the work of undoing the cumulative action of Natural Selection in building."[35] For Headley, anything that interferes with the action of struggle and competition, including modern comforts, charity, and socialism, allows the force of panmixis to undo the complex forms created and sustained by natural selection. Ease and equality threaten the energy of the race:

> Were it possible, through a great increase in the national wealth, to make life equally easy for all children, to give them all a good start in life, feed them with the best of food, clothe them and house them well and give them all a splendid education, then, no doubt, among the myriads of competitors thus brought into the field, many first-rate men would be found. But for the sake of this brilliant outburst we should have done much to exhaust our great reserve or potential vigour, the hardy lower stratum of society, from which alone the upper stratum that is perpetually tending to become used up and effete, can be regenerated.[36]

Like Morgan, Headley imagines the lower classes as a stock of energy; unlike Morgan, he worries that they are becoming *too comfortable*, that they are not being pruned vigorously enough by natural selection.

English civilization, then, is in grave danger because of its comforts, and its improved standards of living for increasing numbers of people: "By means of good food, warmth, comfort, [the English] are making the most of the existing generation, but at the cost of much race-vigour. This involves a great danger."[37] Notice that this is a twisted cousin of the proto-sustainability arguments made by Jevons, Mill, Ruskin, and others. Headley focuses on the resource depletion involved in the escalating demands made by increasing numbers of people, but his concern is not with the toll these demands take on the natural environment, but with the toll they take on the energy embodied in the blood of the race. Nature is conceived here not as a material environment with a limited capacity to sustain growth, but as a mythical reification of the process of natural selection. And unfettered capitalism, allowing natural selection to work in the social world, is a generator of energy; state-planning and socialism, meanwhile, threaten to drain the supply.

We have seen how, in Victorian thermodynamic discourse, nature was often represented as a profound squanderer of energy, and industrial development a means of capturing some of this otherwise wasted motive power. Although Headley and others argued for allowing "nature" to work untrammeled in human society by letting natural selection take its course, the process of selection is continually imagined in technological or indus-trial terms. The selection "mechanism," like industrial technology, was imagined as a gatherer, or even a generator, of energy; panmixis, on the other hand, could be cast as the careless, wasteful principle of nature, as entropy had been. That is to say, although it seems as though Headley wants to allow "nature" to take its course through the operations of nat-ural selection, he has aligned that selection process with the work of indus-trial production. Industrialism, then, can be seen as a full participant in the processes of nature – as it had in an earlier generation of productivist writing – while other kinds of human interventions, including any kind of state-sponsored charity, appeared as a divergence from, or an obstruc-tion of, those processes.

Maudsley also discusses evolution and degeneration using a vocabulary of waste, force, and energy, and, like Headley, plays upon the implications about the natural world encoded in Victorian thermodynamic discourse. In *Body and Will* he describes with alarm the "waning of the evolutional or generative force in nature," as well as the loss of "evolutionary energy" in the human race.[38] In this formulation, criminals, the mentally ill, the disabled, and other members of the residuum appear as the expressions of some universal principle of dissolution at work, unraveling the gains made by civilization. Although he doesn't use the word "panmixis," Maudsley employs a similar binary: "Are we to look forward to a continued becoming or to an ultimate unbecoming of things?"[39] "Becoming" and "unbecoming" give Maudsley's discussion of evolutionary energy a metaphysical cast, framing "degenerates" as manifestations of a dark, cosmic principle set in conflict with the world of order. This works to dehumanize these various groups, of course, but it also turns them into agents in a doomsday scenario that Maudsley increasingly believed was inevitable. He not only draws on a thermodynamic vocabulary, he borrows its most well-known symbol for energy dissipation and collapse – the death of the sun – to fashion human degeneration as a process with apocalyptic implications for the entire cosmos: "the extinction of evolutional energy that must follow the gradual extinction of solar energy will involve in its consequences the extinction of the upward-trending ideal and mankind will go on contentedly with a downward-tending ideal."[40] Society's "degenerates" – the poor, the mentally ill, the disabled – are not humans as much as they are forms, representations of an unfolding evolutionary drama of the struggle of order with chaos, energy with entropy, light with darkness.

Wells's *The Time Machine*: chronologies of degeneration

Like *Body and Will*, Wells's *The Time Machine* ends by suggesting continuity between the decline of the species and the end of the cosmos. The novel's vision of the "heat death" of the sun occurs just after the Time Traveller has left behind the degenerate Morlock and Eloi species of the year 802701, and seems to serve as a kind of apocalyptic coda to the narrative of biological and cultural decline that occupies the majority of the novel. By punctuating a narrative of degeneration with a vision of heat death, Wells's novel seems to make the same kind of imaginative leap as *Body and Will*, suggesting a connection between a downward evolutionary trajectory and an entropic principle at work in the cosmos. In a recent critical study of the English novel, Elizabeth Ermarth calls attention to this connection, arguing that the Morlock–Eloi plot is an illustration of "heat death of civilization," and that the novel works out the implications of this connection in an incoherent fashion. Reading the scene of solar collapse as an extension of the social allegory, she asks: "Would a little less softness to the poor, one wonders, have prevented the heat death of the sun?"[41] As we have seen, these issues – entropy, natural selection, social engineering, and charity – mingled freely in the degenerationist imaginary. And Wells's novel, I would argue, *is* somewhat incoherent along the lines Ermath suggests, but this stems from his attempt to work out the relationship between evolution and thermodynamics, and his own relationship to the discourse of degeneration, through the structure of the narrative. There is an unresolved tension at the heart of the novel, an ambivalence about the idea of degeneration that appears in the mismatched generic chronologies of social allegory and scientific realism.[42]

The story of the Morlocks and Eloi, which makes up the bulk of *The Time Machine*'s plot, is stocked with all the objects of degenerationist anxiety. The Morlocks, a race of brutish, machine-tending creatures, are the descendants of lower-class Londoners, exhibiting all the qualities featured in alarmist rhetoric about the consolidation of the working classes into a separate species. Their harsh working environment (it is suggested) has caused them to evolve into some kind of cross between a monkey and a spider; they live in unfathomable numbers underground, emerging at night to prey upon the effete, upper-world Eloi. The Eloi, meanwhile, represent the other focal point of degenerationist concern: the aristocracy, members of the leisure classes, and "decadent" groups whose plush life has so insulated them that they have lost their mental and bodily vigor: "This has ever been the fate of energy in security; it takes to art and to eroticism, and then come languor and decay."[43] Degeneration, again, is framed as a kind of evolutionary energy loss, made possible by the easing of the pressures of natural selection. The Eloi have surrendered their ability to compete in the struggle for survival: the Time Traveller soon learns they are little more than the Morlocks' livestock. This surprising reversal of the usual power dynamics between upper and lower classes is also an elaboration of conventional anxieties about the swelling, overpopulated ranks of the working classes in English cities. *The Time Machine* seems to borrow a page straight from degenerationist literature, not only in the shape of the evolutionary future it imagines, but through the kinds of fears it plays upon.

Despite the alien features of the new world, and despite the pains the Time Traveller takes to describe the extensive, astonishing topographical transformations and sheer chronological duration separating present from future, we are never far from the social dynamics of Victorian England. The degenerationist imaginary was so apocalyptically metamorphic to begin with, so fully furnished with human apes, human swine, human rats, and other Gothic monstrosities, that Wells's future world seems a ready elaboration of contemporary political and cultural tropes, rather than a radical departure into a distant future. This, of course, is part of the point: the allegorical connections are not only clear, they are insisted upon, discussed at length by the Time Traveller himself, and framed as the salient issue by the narrator at novel's end. But the polemical thrust, conveyed, as it is, largely through the Swiftean social allegory, introduces a tension between the novel's generic paradigms. By so clearly superimposing Victorian class issues and contemporary concerns about degeneration, the novel's allegory collapses the vast stretches of time the machine traverses in its journey. If we are meant to believe that, almost a million years into the future, the human race is still sorting out the effects of the English class system, then the sheer duration of a million years is somewhat blunted. The Morlock–Eloi world represents both an imaginative leap ahead, carried by the speculative, secular resources of fictional narrative, and an anchor, chained by the static correspondences of allegory that ground the novel in the present.[44] Wells remarks on this paradoxical temporal movement, "there is something specially and incurably topical about all these prophetic books; the more you go ahead, the more you seem to get entangled with the burning questions of your own time. And all the while events are overtaking you."[45]

The sun, too, is turned into a signifier in this social allegory, fashioned by the Time Traveller into a correlative to the waning energy of human civilization. He remarks: "It seemed to me that I had happened upon humanity upon the wane. The ruddy sunset set me thinking of the sunset of mankind."[46] The title of the chapter – "The Sunset of Mankind" – ensures we don't miss the point. This sunset is not yet the final "death" of the sun, of course, but it anticipates that concluding apocalyptic vision; indeed, the chapter prepares us to read that ending in anthropocentric terms, as the culmination of the narrative of evolutionary degeneration and cultural decay. This is the basis of Ermarth's critique. As we have seen in previous chapters, such connections between the state of civilization and the state of the cosmos were common in Victorian discussions of the sun's energy, and often worked to merge incommensurable timescales. Recall Stewart's admonition: "we have been content very much to remain spectators of the process, apparently forgetful that we are at all concerned in the issue. But the conflict is not one which admits of on-lookers – it is a universal conflict in which we must all take our share."[47] Dickens and Ruskin used the image of catastrophic solar decay for different purposes – to condemn the waste and chaos of industrial civilization – but their imagery also worked to squeeze cosmic chronology into the procrustean parameters of human history. Indeed, the opening of *Bleak House* is itself a kind of time-travel narrative, collapsing both prehistoric beginnings – "it would not be wonderful to meet a Megalosaurus, forty feet long or so, waddling like an elephantine lizard up Holborn Hill" – and the apocalyptic ending of a universal winter upon the present moment. In both *Bleak House* and *The Time Machine*, the city in effect functions as time-travel

device, its estranging, fantastical conditions (*Bleak House*) or its patho-
logical topography of class division and segregation (*The Time Machine*)
making the future's threatening contours available to present experience.
Bleak House's vision of the dying sun occurs at the opening, a sign of the
ecological devastation and widespread energy waste from which the narrative will attempt to find paths of escape. *The Time Machine's* vision of
heat death, conversely, occurs at the very end, a sign of the concealed conditions the narrative has had to work to uncover. These are two different
Londons and two different sets of problems, but the dying sun functions
in both cases by lending contemporary social concerns apocalyptic power.

But, like *Bleak House*, *The Time Machine* also raises questions about
the trust we can put in this allegory-making. After discussing his ideas of
what happened to cause the degeneration of the Morlocks and Eloi, the
Time Traveller reflects self-consciously on the generic uncertainty of his
narrative: "This, I must warn you, was my theory at the time. I had no
convenient cicerone in the pattern of the Utopian books. My explanation
may be absolutely wrong. I still think it is the most plausible one."[48] It's
a significant moment because it moves the text in two competing directions simultaneously. On the one hand, the Time Traveller's admission
that he might be wrong actually helps make the social allegory seem even
sturdier, since, over the course of his narrative, we watch him construct
and test it according to a procedure resembling the scientific method. He
floats a hypothesis, measures it against further observations, and revises it
based on the new information. This dialectical movement produces the
allegory: we watch as the shape of the Eloi–Morlock relationship is more
sharply defined, and, through that process of definition, the symbolic divide between upper and working classes in Victorian England emerges even
more clearly. On the other hand, however, this very sense of constructedness also makes the allegory seem a somewhat unstable framework, and
it puts the Time Traveller, and not Wells himself, in the role of allegory-
maker. This dynamic movement of interpretation also moves the novel's
chronology in two directions at once. It brings present (Victorian) and
future (Eloi–Morlock) England into more direct alignment, as the latter
comes to seem an increasingly clear representation of the former. But it
also moves present and future further apart, since it dramatizes the way
in which the process of drawing correspondences between the two time
periods is *itself* subject to the movement of time, and, moreover, the needs
of an imagination immersed in the concerns of its own present.

It is important to note, too, that while the vocabulary of energy and the
references to the "sunset of mankind" seem to reinforce the connection

between degeneration and heat death, Wells elsewhere takes pains to point out that the sun of the future has, in fact, grown even hotter:

> I think I have said how much hotter than our own was the weather of this Golden Age ... It is usual to assume that the sun will go on cooling steadily in the future. But people unfamiliar with such speculations as those of the younger Darwin, forget that the planets must ultimately fall back one by one into the parent body. As these catastrophes occur, the sun will blaze with renewed energy.[49]

The Time Traveller is referring to Charles Darwin's son George, who argued in his paper "On the Precession of a Viscous Spheroid" (1879) that orbital friction would eventually cause the moon to fall back into the earth.[50] If the sun is burning *more* brightly in the future world, this introduces a certain tension in the Time Traveller's representation. Although he would attempt to fashion the sun into a symbol of waning cultural energy, his scientific background leads him to acknowledge the ways in which its condition cannot actually be indexed in any clear allegorical manner to the condition of humanity.

It is when the Time Traveller journeys into the even more distant future that the tension between the symbolic appropriation and the scientific investigation of nature surfaces, and the novel's generic commitments shift decisively away from allegory. If the Eloi–Morlock world is saturated with commentary upon the Victorian present, the final scenes of the novel, in contrast, are thoroughly purged of any trace of it. Pushing "thousands of millions"[51] of days beyond the world of 802701, the Time Traveller stops his machine on a beach populated by "a huge white butterfly" and dozens of monstrous crabs. We sense in these two species another dyad of the delicate and the brutish, the high and the low – that is, the structural differences that defined the Eloi–Morlock split. There is a suggestion that we have come upon the descendants of the Eloi and Morlocks in a state of even more radical degeneration, a connection reinforced by the fact that the Time Traveller's encounter with these creatures follows the same narrative pattern as earlier encounters: he first notices the harmless half of the dyad (butterfly/Eloi), then notices the menacing half (crab/Morlock), realizes the latter is a threat to him, then flees from them into the future. It is a recapitulation of his earlier adventure, the rapidity with which the second episode unfolds suggesting the accelerating chronology of the machine's headlong plunge into the future.

Despite the structural similarities, however, it is just as strongly implied that these new organisms actually have nothing to do with the Morlocks and Eloi, because they have absolutely nothing human about them: "Can you imagine a crab as large as yonder table, with its many legs moving slowly and uncertainly, its big claws swaying, its long antennae, like carters' whips, waving and feeling, and its stalked eyes gleaming at you on either side of its metallic front?"[52] The comparison with familiar human objects serves only to emphasize the awkward thing-ness of the creature. While we may be invited to discern certain abstract commonalities between the Eloi–Morlock, Butterfly–Crab pairings (high/low, delicate/brutal, oblivious/scrutinizing), and recognize, perhaps, the persistence of certain broad traits through the various degenerated shapes, we are also now so far from the human form that such connections also seem contrived. Whereas the main surprise of the Eloi–Morlock world hinged upon recognizing that the conventional associations between "highness" and "lowness" had been inverted – the underground Morlocks having become evolutionarily "ascendant" – the butterfly and crab have no discernible relationship to each other besides their positions in an analogy. The imagery of this scene is such a grotesque elaboration of the degenerationist plasticity that the usual drama of disavowal and recognition so often provoked by an encounter with the degenerated body is turned into a disordered reverberation. In this way, the novel stages something of a reversal of its earlier procedures. If the Time Traveller's journey among the Eloi and Morlocks was about recognizing the familiar and human in that which first appeared to be alien, the journey beyond that world shows how the desire to make such connections is undermined by the inability to find any solid purchase on the future. If the novel has taught us to read it by decoding the future in familiar terms, it presents here a scene that both invites and blocks that process. It is a shift in genre, dramatizing the collapse of the allegory it had earlier worked to build. The un-building of the human world that takes place within the story itself is simultaneously happening on the level of narrative form.

Whereas, in previous sections, the movement forwards in time had provided further information about the Morlock–Eloi dichotomy and had thus deepened and elaborated the future's symbolic connection to the present, here the movement forwards in time only works to strip the world of anything that would lend itself to a sense of identification. After the butterfly–crab world, The Time Traveller journeys forwards to witness the death of the sun:

> At last, more than thirty million years hence, the huge red-hot dome of the sun had come to obscure nearly a tenth part of the darkling heavens. Then I stopped once more, for the crawling multitude of crabs had disappeared,

and the red beach, save for its livid green liverworts and lichens, seemed lifeless. And now it was flecked with white. A bitter cold assailed me. Rare white flakes ever and again came eddying down. To the north-eastward, the glare of snow lay under the starlight of the sable sky, and I could see an undulating crest of hillocks pinkish-white. There were fringes of ice along the sea margin with drifting masses further out; but the main expanse of that salt ocean, all bloody under the eternal sunset, was still unfrozen.[53]

Whereas, in the earlier sections, the allegorical correspondences undermined the sense of temporal extension, now the brute duration of time breaks down the network of linkages that had once connected future and present. We still look for points of significance and identification, since that is how the novel has taught us to read it, but the external world resists such gestures almost completely. Here, the only remaining holdouts against the creeping tide of universal energy exhaustion seem to be forms of blind, inorganic motion: the eddying flakes, the drifting ice masses, the "still unfrozen" ocean, and the "undulating" hills. The motion of the undulating hills, of course, is not really motion at all – it is merely a function of perception and language, bestowed upon an unmoving landscape by a human mind still, at this late hour, trying to impose its own idea of order upon the external world. Whereas earlier we were confronted with the anthropocentric imagery of the "sunset of mankind," and the implication that cosmic happenings provided some kind of commentary on the fate of civilization, here, as the sun *actually* wanes, the future has been thoroughly and systematically dehumanized. By revealing a future that has scraped off the last traces of the human, Wells not only leaves the world of social allegory behind, he makes us feel its lack of traction. What takes its place is a kind of scientific realism, informed by the laws of thermodynamics, which propels the narrative forwards into a vision of a future structured not by the human, but by predictions derived through following the logic of scientific law. Time is no longer collapsed, it is radically extended, and the sun becomes something more than a mere symbol for the state of human development.

In this way, Wells's novel departs in significant ways from most other nineteenth-century representations of the heat death of the sun. Take, for example, Maudsley's version:

> If the force at the back of all becoming on earth is that which the sun has steadily supplied to it through countless ages, and still steadily supplies, it is plain that when it fails, as fail it one day must, there will be a steadily declining development and a rapidly increasing degeneration of things, an undoing by regressive decompositions of what has been done by progressive

combinations through the succession of the ages ... The nations that have risen high in complexity of development will degenerate and be broken up, to have their places taken by less complex associations of inferior individuals; they in turn will yield place to simpler and feebler unions of still more degraded beings.[54]

It's a grim prospect, but reading the passage alongside Wells's highlights the covert anthropocentrism at work in the former. Maudsley imagines that when the sun starts to die out millions of years in the future, there will still be human beings standing around to watch it happen. Not only is the sun transformed into a symbol for the decline of civilization, the earth, by extension, is implicitly fashioned into a stable, permanent home for humanity until the bitter end. For Maudsley, the second law of thermodynamics holds for microcosm and macrocosm alike, so that the individual, the nation, the species, the cosmos, all develop and decay according to the same trajectory: "the common law of life is slow acquisition, equilibration, decay, and finally death. It is a law which governs the growth, decline, and fall of nations as well as of individuals."[55] Such analogizing, as it plays out in Maudsley's descriptions of heat death, allows him to imagine civilizational and cosmic decay as reciprocal, vaguely coterminous, phenomena; it allows him to "read" degenerates as a form of entropy. His concept of "evolutional energy" binds human evolution to this thermodynamic trajectory, turning species degeneration into a signifier for cosmic dissolution.[56] Historical, evolutionary, and cosmic narratives are bound together on a structural level, suggesting that the death of human civilization *is* the death of the universe, and vice versa.[57]

In contrast, *The Time Machine*'s relentless temporal extension, the work it does systematically to purge the future world of familiar features, its interest in the wholesale transformation of the earth's ecosystem – all of these things help remove the implicit anthropocentrism in the vision of solar death. If Wells's target in the Eloi–Morlock section is the kind of social complacency that would allow class division to harden into protoplasmic fact, his target in the ending pages is the kind of epistemological complacency that would install human life at the very center of the universe. Indeed, we can see in many of the non-fiction pieces he published while composing *The Time Machine* a determined rejection of the notion that human life is a cosmically significant phenomenon, or a necessary fixture on the planet: "it is part of the excessive egotism of the human animal that the bare idea of its extinction seems incredible to it. 'A world without us!,' it says, as a heady young Cephalapsis might have said it in the old Silurian sea ... Surely it is not so unreasonable to ask why man should be an exception to that rule. From the scientific standpoint at least any reason for such an exception is hard to find."[58] One of the aims of *The Time Machine* is to question this sense of human exceptionalism by making the "incredible" idea of extinction fully believable and imaginable. It does so by decoupling the cosmic and civilizational narratives and undoing the symbolic linkage found in many accounts of degeneration. It is a vision of a dialectical (rather than analogical) relationship between thermodynamics and evolutionary pressures, one that borrows a page from Wells's mentor, T. H. Huxley. In "The Struggle for Existence in Human Society" (1888) Huxley argues that evolution would be affected by entropic heat death not because the processes are structurally analogous, but because evolution is an adaptive process that responds to significant environmental change.[59] This is very different from Maudsley's heat-death story, in which the creeping cold of an expiring sun leaves only:

> a few scattered families of degraded human beings living perhaps in sno-whuts near the equator, very much as the Esquimaux live now near the pole, [who] represent the last wave of the receding tide of human existence before its final extinction; until at last a frozen earth incapable of cultivation is left without energy to produce a living particle of any sort and so death itself is dead.[60]

For Maudsley, "life" means human life.

While Wells and Huxley shared with Maudsley and other degenerationists the belief that evolution did not necessarily unfold in the direction of greater progress and complexity, they did not ascribe degenerative change to some kind of fixed and universal process of entropic decline or the depletion of a fixed stock of "evolutionary energy." For one thing, to believe that all civilizations decay in some thermodynamically predictable path is to leave little room for reform or political intervention. The grim inevitability of solar death, if fashioned into a metaphor for all human processes, was at best a recipe for quietism and at worst a means of ratifying the status quo. As Thomas Richards argues: "entropy, like evolution, would seem to place history outside the domain of human activity. Because it transfers agency from human beings to physical principles, it ostensibly represents a pessimistic relinquishing of all the possibilities of social control."[61] For Huxley, as for Wells, natural processes were not assumed to be the processes by which all systems worked; instead, nature is what human social institutions need to manage. Huxley writes:

> Social progress means a checking of the cosmic process at every step and the substitution for it of another, which may be called the ethical process;

the end of which is not the survival of those who may happen to be the fittest, in respect of the whole of the conditions which obtain, but of those who are ethically the best.[62]

We can see in this point of view a strain of thinking that informs Huxley's thoughts on coal in "On the Formation of Coal," which we discussed in the first chapter. Coal energy is imagined in that essay as a means of allowing humans to transcend the limitations and pressures of natural processes through increasing technological sophistication and material abundance.

The Time Machine, then, stages a complex interplay between the theory of evolutionary degeneration and the second law of thermodynamics. Since, as we have seen, degeneration was commonly framed in apocalyptic terms, as a form of energy loss that unfolded according to the downward trajectory described by the second law, the death of the sun at the end of the novel on some level feels like a fitting, almost logically necessary, coda to the Eloi–Morlock decline narrative. By ending the novel in this way, Wells seems to reinforce the symbolic connection between degeneration, entropy, and the death of the sun that was often made by Maudsley, Nordau, and other writers. It is for this reason that Ermath notes the seeming continuity between the social questions the book raises and the cosmic eventualities that seem to result from them, and reads this as incoherence. On the other hand, however, when we look more closely at the novel's representation of heat death and note the ways in which Wells's version of this event differs from the conventional representations of it, we can see how *The Time Machine* also rejects the anthropocentric view that would index cosmic events to human narratives, and turn the distant future into just another version of the present.

While Wells's revision of the heat-death trope works to puncture myths of human exceptionalism and confront a future stripped of human significance, it also works, on another level, to aggrandize the power of human consciousness. If the social allegory of the Eloi–Morlock section makes the future into a funhouse version of England *circa* 1895, the scientific realism of the end does something like the opposite: it allows the mind to travel, imaginatively, beyond the limits of its own biological, historical, and temporal confines. The astronomer Richard Proctor, in an article on past and future time, argues that, "the notion is inconceivable to us that absolutely endless series of changes may take place in the future and have taken place in the past."[63] *The Time Machine* confronts both the anthropocentrism and the limits to human imagination implicit in this idea of "inconceivability." Informed by scientific prediction, the novel provides a glimpse of a future that cannot be experienced, but is *not* entirely unknowable or

impossible to conceive. Indeed, on some level, Wells's very ability to conjure such a scene represents a triumph for both the scientific imagination
and the spirit of fearless, rational inquiry. It is a testament to the power
of the human mind that it can put itself in a position to imagine its own
extinction and peer into a vista impossible to see. We may be reminded
of Tyndall's comment in *Heat Considered as a Mode of Motion*, that, by
means of the laws of thermodynamics, "it is our privilege to rise above
these standards, and to regard the sun himself as a speck in infinite extension."[64] The point of view and tone are very different from Wells's, yet
there is a similar aggrandizement of the mind powered by science. Unlike
Tyndall, however, Wells makes the very power of this imaginative faculty
the source of the novel's sense of tragedy, since, in the end, that faculty too
must succumb to the indifferent natural forces it has labored to reveal.

Thus far I have been discussing a kind of tension in *The Time Machine*
among different generic paradigms and epistemologies. That tension is
embodied in the last few pages of the novel by the conflict of perspectives
between two characters: the Time Traveller and the "frame" narrator who
has been telling us the story. In the final chapter, that narrator explains the
difference between them:

> I, for my own part, cannot think that these latter days of weak experi-
> ment, fragmentary theory, and mutual discord are indeed man's culminat-
> ing time! I say, for my own part. He, I know – for the question had been
> discussed among us long before the Time Machine was made – thought
> but cheerlessly of the Advancement of Mankind, and saw in the growing
> pile of civilization only a foolish heaping that must inevitably fall back
> upon and destroy its makers in the end. If that is so, it remains for us to
> live as though it were not so. But to me the future is still black and blank –
> is a vast ignorance, lit at a few casual places by the memory of his story.
> And I have by me, for my comfort, two strange white flowers – shrivelled
> now, and brown and flat and brittle – to witness that even when mind and
> strength had gone, gratitude and a mutual tenderness still lived on in the
> heart of man.[65]

This raises significant questions. On the one hand, the deliberate forgetting the narrator seems to counsel – "to live as though it were not so" –
smacks of denial. His response to the tale is to push whatever seems grim
and uncomfortable out of mind in order to go on living. In a strange
way, fiction and reality seem to trade places here, as the story of the Time
Traveller's journey embodies scientific facts too dispiriting to accept, making existence possible only by pretending these things are not the case.
In other words, *ordinary life* requires the willing suspension of disbelief.

The frame narrator suddenly seems more unreliable than the man who has just told us about his travels through time, and his optimism seems almost absurdly sentimental. He fixes upon one detail – the flowers the Time Traveller received from his Eloi consort, Weena – and decides to invest it with more significance than the bifurcation and devolution of the entire human race and the final heat death of the world, all for the sake of his "comfort." This is fiction-making framed as avoidance mechanism, a "casual" process of selecting only the agreeable details. The Time Traveller plays a kind of Cassandra here, and we are left to contemplate the possibility that the fact that his vision is too difficult to bear is precisely what will ensure it comes to pass.

But if this passage is viewed in terms of Wells's own development as a fiction writer and social thinker, we can see that the narrator's decision to imagine a "black and blank" future – a light waiting to be lit, a canvas waiting to be filled – is also productive. Productive of further speculative fictions that will populate that blankness, and productive of alternative conceptions of the ways in which evolutionary and thermodynamic pressures might be effectively managed by human institutions. The strain of utopian political thinking that emerges in Wells's writing in the decades following the publication of *The Time Machine* is not attained by a mere denial of the grim inevitabilities that structure the Time Traveller's vision, but by activation of some of the other work the novel does to reveal the immensity of the unwritten blankness, the enormity of the intervening time. The future is a "vast ignorance" for the narrator, a formulation that may conjure his denial and willed unknowing, but that also reminds us of the sheer chronological extension the novel has, at times, taken pains to represent. While the cosmic indifference and decentering of human chronology in the final future vision may produce some existential anxiety, they also, on a different level, effectively remove entropic heat death from any practical concerns with which human civilization need trouble itself.

Such a move, I would add, was crucial to the development of science fiction. While Victorian thermodynamics offered a scientific, secularized description of the future, that secularization was, as we have seen, really only skin deep. The laws of energy may have helped open the future to scientific representation, but, as I argued in the first two chapters, that future was still being imagined by the first generation of thermodynamic writers within strictly defined theological parameters. Thermodynamics simply provided another window into God's apocalyptic master narrative – in *The Unseen Universe* it is elaborated in explicit detail as a drama of (energy) loss and redemption. Although, as many critics have noted, apocalyptic traditions were formative influences upon the science fiction imaginary, they also presented serious impediments to the ability to imagine an "unwritten" future. In 1834, the French writer Félix Bodin argued that the problem with both utopias and apocalypses was that the futures they projected were essentially static – everything in the narratives tended towards establishing either a fixed utopian community, or conditions culminating in the climactic end of human time. Such works were thus at odds with the development of secular narratives where human action and development mattered more than the unveiling of a divine plan. In his view, both utopian and apocalyptic traditions needed to be overhauled if the novel of the future was to be realized.[66] *The Time Machine* represents such an overhaul, thoroughly secularizing thermodynamic prophecy of solar decline and a static, lifeless future, in order to make room for the intervening time. The Time Traveller's vision may present us with the foreclosure of possibility on the grand scale – the cosmos is not centered around human beings, and not, ultimately, to be redeemed in any way – but it affords, perhaps, an abundance of time on the human scale with which to fashion all manner of futures.

In contrast, the Time Traveller gives us a version of the implacable degenerationist logic when he imagines that civilization is "only a foolish heaping that must inevitably fall back upon and destroy its makers in the end." Linked to this sweeping judgment, the novel's image of inevitable heat death becomes a sign of the inevitability of all kinds of collapse, just as it does in Maudsley. Indeed, the Time Traveller's expression of pessimism is an uncanny echo of a passage from *Body and Will*: "where then the organism – biological, social, or national – has reached a certain state of complex evolution it inevitably breeds changes in itself which disintegrate and in the end destroy it."[67] Whether Wells is deliberately referencing Maudsley or not, his novel has clearly worked elsewhere to decouple the cosmic and human timescales that Maudsley would merge, to suggest that while the heat death of the sun may be inevitable, all systems do not necessarily obey, on a local level, the same trajectory of internal disorganization and collapse. As we have seen, entropy is not the Eloi and Morlocks' undoing, and degeneration is not the product of some kind of "evolutionary energy" running out. *The Time Machine* ends in grim fashion, but taken as a whole it challenges the idea that all stories can be reduced to microcosmic versions of the same master thermodynamic narrative. By insisting upon the disconnection between distant cosmic events and specific trajectories of human development, Wells is, in effect, "de-Victorianizing" the heat-death imagery. The willing suspension of disbelief counseled by the narrator involves a deliberate forgetting of the sun's extinction, and, in turn, a willingness to subscribe to local fictions of order, and alternative future speculations.

This is a tenuous solution, pivoting uneasily between the extreme positions of these characters. As is so often the case with Wells, the question is one of freedom and entrapment.[68] The Time Traveller, accepting the grim inevitability of his future vision, embraces a purely personal freedom, and uses his time machine to range as he pleases over the centuries: "He may even now – if I may use the phrase – be wandering on some plesiosaurus-haunted Oolitic coral reef."[69] As Robert Philmus notes, he "vanishes into the world of his vision," remaining sealed forever within the structuring device (the time machine and *The Time Machine*).[70] The narrator, meanwhile, by denying the Time Traveller's vision and by asserting a connection with a world beyond the text ("it remains *for us* to live as though it were not so") suggests a route of escape from the novel's confines and the future it describes. Yet, in doing so, he seems simply to adopt another kind of fiction, the "as though it were not" gesture that can only make the real world "real" through a leap of imagination and forgetting. Each figure is free from one kind of fiction, and trapped within another. In presenting these rival responses, Wells describes the contours of the epistemological trap into which his scientific interests have taken him. To accept that human life is the mere plaything of evolutionary pressures and doomed to extinction in a dying solar system is a recipe for a retreat into merely personal forms of meaning, and political quietism. On the other hand, to ignore or deny such scientific principles is perhaps to retreat into a different kind of complacency and quietism. This is the paradox: for productive social reform to happen, the implications of modern scientific thought must be confronted without illusion. But confronting them in all their grim inexorability corrodes the very impetus to reform.

For Wells, the answer to the stalemate lies in energy. The escape from natural processes that seemed impossible at the end of *The Time Machine* is imagined as a real possibility in the aptly titled utopian work *The World Set Free* (1915). In it, he imagines a future of plentitude unleashed by the discovery of radium and subsequent development of nuclear technology:

> This – this is the dawn of a new day in human living. At the climax of that civilization which had its beginning in the hammered flint and the fire-stick of the savage, just when it is becoming apparent that our ever-

increasing needs cannot be borne indefinitely by our present sources of energy, we discover suddenly the possibility of an entirely new civilization. The energy we need for our very existence, and with which Nature supplies us still so grudgingly, is in reality locked up in inconceivable quantities all about us.[71]

The metaphor of the human "day," which had been so ruthlessly exploded by the temporal extension of *The Time Machine*, is here restored. The atomic revolution is framed as part of a coherent, cosmic evolutionary narrative, complete with climax and dramatic rescue. Just as coal energy functioned for an earlier generation as an escape from the Malthusian trap, so does nuclear energy function as an escape from the neo-Malthusian concerns articulated by Jevons. Moreover, energy liberates humankind from Darwinian pressures, revealed as a function of energy resources: "that perpetual struggle for existence, that perpetual struggle to live on the bare surplus of Nature's energies will cease to be the lot of Man. Man will step from the pinnacle of this civilization to the next."[72] Evolution has been effectively decoupled from natural selection, and Wells's Darwinism becomes Darwinisticism (to use Morse Peckham's useful distinction) – a shift from a scientifically rigorous to a metaphysical evolutionism.[73] As he did in *The Time Machine*, Wells details the dialectical, rather than the analogical, relationship between evolution and thermodynamics, only here it produces a release from the limits defined by both.

In the process, *The World Set Free* redefines the concept of degeneration, converting it from biological into socio-historical signifier: "that same spirit of free-thinking and outspoken publication that in the field of natural science had been the beginning of the conquest of nature, was at work throughout all the eighteenth and nineteenth centuries preparing the spirit of the new world within the degenerating body of the old."[74] The degenerating bodies populating the London slums that seemed, to an earlier generation, threats to the future development of the species, now become mere expressions of an outworn mode of life that is itself giving way. "Degeneration" in this sense is no longer an evolutionary dead-end, but part of a cosmic process of development, in which the old functions as cocoon for the new. The forms through which humans once conceptualized their social, political, and intellectual lives, including the idea of degeneration itself, become vestiges of a passing age, models that need to be shed, rather than implacable pressures structuring the course of future history. Like earlier writers on degeneration, Wells describes a kind of evolutionary energy, one that powers the development of human civilization upwards. But grounded in a material resource base that is now infinite, there is no danger of that energy running out. Instead, it becomes a means to transcending materiality altogether.

We have seen this story before. Just as an earlier generation of productivist writers like Tyndall suggested a world of sun-powered locomotives and self-extracting coal, thereby naturalizing the workings of industry, Wells imagines the use of atomic power as an essentially natural process. He writes that with the use of the new atomic engines came "a gigantic replacement of industrial methods and machinery"[75] – a formulation that suggests "industrial" refers not to a method of production or the large-scale use of machinery to harness energy, but to a social and historical era that has been superseded. *The World Set Free*, like *Heat Considered as a Mode of Motion*, is a fantasy that one can have the industrial without the industrial, the benefits of large-scale energy extraction without any of the ecologically and socially disastrous consequences. The key to the atomic age for Wells is that it is entirely without environmental cost. The new engines have a by-product, but one that few object to: "in both the Dass-Tata and Holsten-Roberts engines one of the recoverable waste products was gold."[76] The "extravagant filthiness" of fossil-fuel-driven machines, the narrator tells us, "still astonish[es] the visitors to the museum of machinery at South Kensington."[77] Pollution, it turns out, was not a product of energy-intensive processes, it was a product of *coal*. Like degeneration, resource scarcity, and other Victorian-era problems, waste is a relic of a benighted era, conquered through techno-evolution. To imagine pollution as a uniquely Victorian signifier is to quarantine it historically, and to imagine that the period's lessons about energy waste and environmental devastation simply do not apply to the new epoch.

The ecological drama, once again, is played out in London, which is no longer "the somber smoke-darkened city of the Victorian time," but a "spotlessly clean" environment.[78] Industrialism without waste, modern urban life without environmental damage – Wells's vision of nuclear energy returns us to Carlyle's productivist dream for Manchester in *Chartism*: "Soot and despair are not the essence of it [the city]; they are divisible from it, – are they not at this hour crying fiercely to be divided?"[79] Carlyle's vision could not stand up to the actual conditions of urban life in mid-nineteenth-century England; as we saw, he had to retreat into dubious metaphysical distinctions between reality and "semblance" in order to make the accumulating city waste disappear. Thanks to vastly improved methods of waste disposal and management, cleaner-burning engines and fireplaces, and city ordinances curtailing the production of smoke, many of the urban waste forms that had troubled Dickens, Ruskin, and other mid-century critics had disappeared from view by the time Wells was writing. The city no longer presented the same spectacle of pollution and disorganization that challenged mid-century productivist fantasy. One could imagine, as Wells did, a future where waste *didn't exist*, since it was already being effectively removed from everyday experience.

In *The World Set Free*, the limits facing humankind are not imposed by nature or the environment; instead, they are internal and self-generated. The novel is, in effect, an evolutionary drama about whether human beings can adapt, can modify their customs and institutions to a pristine new environment of energetic abundance. It is in many ways a fantasy of a "clean slate," powered by nuclear technology, in which the resources of nature are restocked, the environment is restored to its original condition, and the only thing still "dirty" is the capitalist mindset and its economic structures. Indeed, by making gold the by-product given off by the atomic engines, Wells converts pollution from an environmental problem into a social and economic complication. No natural ecosystems are deranged by the sudden pile-up of gold; no disastrous health issues arise. Instead, it shocks the global financial system, since gold, along with coal, oil, and other commodities foundational to the dying "industrial" age, are now worthless. Markets are destabilized and wars break out, but the conflict is conducted entirely within a human sphere in which nature has been bracketed. In fact, since atomic energy has nothing but environmentally advantageous consequences, the human fighting comes to seem only that much more insipid and unnecessary, the product of sclerotic modes of organization whose obsolescence is fully exposed.

The World Set Free recapitulates productivist dreams in another sense: it imagines a world without entropy. Just as productivism found its ultimate expression in popular accounts of the indestructibility of energy and in the consoling notion that no matter what transformations occurred, "the flux of power is eternally the same," (as Tyndall put it), Wells imagines a world so stocked with power that resource waste becomes irrelevant. More significantly, in his vision, the "orderly conquest of nature"[80] made possible by atomic energy refers not simply to the organized application of the scientific method to any and all human problems, but to the development of technologies that create order without any wasteful remainder. The immense expenditure of energy is not matched by an immense production of entropy. In this way, the book is not simply a dream of neutering the pressures of natural selection, it is a dream of overcoming the second law of thermodynamics as well. The heat death of the sun, which punctuates the vision of the future in *The Time Machine*, is nowhere to be found in *The World Set Free*. This is not simply because Wells has shortened his temporal scope in the latter book; it is also because the access to atomic energy and the world of unlimited power and abundance seems to offer a replacement of the sun as humanity's main energy source. This is implicit in the image of the scientist, Holsten, addressing the sun: "'Ye auld thing,' he said, – and his eyes were shining, and he made a kind of grabbing gesture with his hand; 'ye auld red thing ... We'll have ye *yet*."[81] It is an image of outsized ambition, but Wells treats Holsten as a heroic, Promethean figure, making possible the day when nature can be fully commanded and then transcended altogether.

Notes

Introduction

1 Chevron. "Human Energy." TV advertisement (2 October 2007). Available at www.youtube.com/watch?v=-KyjTGMVTkA (accessed January 8, 2014).

2 David Goodstein, *Out of Gas: The End of the Age of Oil* (New York: Norton, 2004), 48.

3 Christopher Herbert, *Victorian Relativity: Radical Thought and Scientific Discovery* (University of Chicago Press, 2001), 35.

4 Thomas Robert Malthus, *An Essay on the Principle of Population*, ed. Philip Appleman, 2nd edn. (New York: Norton, 2004 [1798]), 76.

5 *Ibid.*, 78.

6 In *The Work of the Sun*, Ted Underwood argues that Godwin was a key figure in the late-eighteenth-, early-nineteenth-century productivist redefinition of the word "energy." Godwin, he argues, used the word to signify autonomy, freedom, and a spirit of "production that wells up spontaneously in the worker" (50). In doing so, Godwin sought to decouple power from its traditional roots in the land, and associate middle-class labor with the "spontaneity of natural forces" (54). Malthus, on the other hand, quite clearly wishes to keep energy rooted in the land itself, in the agricultural regions that supply human beings with sustenance. Ted Underwood, *The Work of the Sun: Literature, Science and Political Economy, 1760–1860* (New York: Palgrave, 2005).

7 Kathleen Tobin, *Politics and Population Control: A Documentary History* (Westport, CT: Greenwood, 2004), 1.

8 Lewis Henry Morgan, *Ancient Society; or, Researches in the Lines of Human Progress* (New York: Henry Holt, 1877), 19.

9 William Godwin, *Of Population: An Enquiry Concerning the Power of Increase in the Numbers of Mankind* (London: Longman, 1820), 615.

10 Friedrich Engels, "Outlines of a Critique of Political Economy," in Karl Marx and Friedrich Engels, *Marx and Engels on the Population Bomb*, trans. Ronald Meek (Berkeley: University of California Press, 1971), 63.

11 Malthus, *An Essay*, 90.

12 See Elmar Altvater, "The Social and Natural Environment of Fossil Capitalism," in *Coming to Terms with Nature*, ed. Leo Panitch and Colin Leys, Socialist Register (London: Merlin Press, 2007), 37–71 (37).

13 Michael Perelman, "Marx and Resource Scarcity," in *The Greening of Marxism*, ed. Ted Benton (New York: Guilford, 1996), 64–80 (67). The question of the Malthusian legacy for Marx is a hotly contested subject. See Jonathan Hughes, *Ecology and Historical Materialism* (Cambridge University Press, 2000), 48–54; Ted Benton, "The Malthusian Challenge: Ecology, Natural Limits, and Human Emancipation," in *Socialism and the Limits of Liberalism*, ed. Peter Osborne (New York: Verso, 1991), 241–269 (247).

14 See Samuel Baker's discussion of a "planetary Malthus" in *Written on The Water: British Romanticism and the Maritime Empire of Culture* (Charlottesville: University of Virginia Press, 2010), 136.

15 Malthus, *An Essay*, 22.

16 *Ibid.*, 20.

17 Kenneth Boulding, "The Economics of the Coming Spaceship Earth," in *Valuing the Earth: Economics, Ecology, Ethics*, ed. Herman Daly and Kenneth N. Townsend (Cambridge, MA: MIT Press, 1993), 297–310 (297). It's worth noting that just as Malthusianism was often used to justify economic and social policy that punished the very poor, so could the "spaceship earth" metaphor be used to argue for coercive policy towards the Third World. See Hughes, *Ecology and Historical Materialism*, 40–42.

18 Daniel Hall, *Practical Lessons and Exercises in Heat* (London: Rivington, 1893), 194. Modern physics, in contrast, would define a closed system as that which receives no additional *matter* from the outside, but which can receive energy. See Eric D. Schneider and Dorion Sagan, *Into the Cool: Energy Flow, Thermodynamics, and Life* (University of Chicago Press, 2006), 26.

19 T. E. Young, *On Centenarians; and the Duration of the Human Race: A Fresh and Authentic Enquiry* (London: Charles and Edward Layton, 1899), 125.

20 Schneider and Sagan, *Into the Cool*, 79.

21 See Joe Burchfield, *Lord Kelvin and the Age of the Earth* (University of Chicago Press, 1990 [1975]), 23.

22 Paul Ehrlich, Anne Ehrlich, and John P. Holdren, "Availability, Entropy, and the Laws of Thermodynamics," in Daly and Townsend, *Valuing the Earth*, 69–73 (73).

23 Ilya Prigogine and Isabelle Stengers, *Order out of Chaos: Man's New Dialogue with Nature* (New York: Bantam, 1984), 127.

24 Lynda Nead, *Victorian Babylon: People, Streets and Images in Nineteenth-Century London* (New Haven: Yale University Press, 2000), 15.

25 Richard Lehan, *The City in Literature: An Intellectual and Cultural History* (Berkeley: University of California Press, 1998), 123.

26 William Stanley Jevons, *The Coal Question: An Inquiry Concerning the Progress of the Nation, and the Probable Exhaustion of Our Coal Mines*, 2nd edn. (London: Macmillan, 1866), 178.

27 Nicholas Georgescu-Roegen, *The Entropy Law and the Economic Process* (Cambridge, MA: Harvard University Press, 1971), 294.

28 *Ibid.*, 295.

29 Michel Serres has noted that the advent of the steam engine and the depend-ence upon coal introduce a new relationship to time; *Hermes: Literature, Science, Philosophy*, ed. Josue V. Harari and David F. Bell (Baltimore: Johns Hopkins University Press, 1982), 71.

30 George Levine, *Darwin and the Novelists: Patterns of Science in Victorian Fiction* (Cambridge, MA: Harvard University Press, 1988), 159.

31 John Stuart Mill, *Principles of Political Economy*, 2 vols., Vol. II, 5th edn. (New York: D. Appleton, 1896), 339.

32 John Ruskin, *The Works of John Ruskin*, ed. E. T. Cook and Alexander Wedderburn, 39 vols. Vol. XVII, (London: G. Allen, 1903–1912), 110.

33 Paul Crutzen, "Geology of Mankind," *Nature* 415.6867 (2002): 23.

34 Frederick Charles Krepp, *The Sewage Question: Being a General Review of All Systems and Methods Hitherto Employed in Various Countries* (London: Longmans, 1867), 203.

35 Prigogine and Stengers, *Order out of Chaos*, 116.

36 Ehrlich, Ehrlich, and Holdren, "Availability, Entropy, and the Laws of Thermodynamics," 72–73 (original emphasis).

37 Gillian Beer, *Darwin's Plots: Evolutionary Narrative in Darwin, George Eliot and Nineteenth-Century Fiction*, 3rd edn. (Cambridge University Press, 2009), 10.

38 Patricia Yaeger, "Editor's Column," *PMLA* 126.2 (2011): 303–310 (307).

39 James Mussell, "Science," in *Charles Dickens in Context*, ed. Sally Ledger and Holly Furneaux (Cambridge University Press, 2011), 326–333 (326).

40 Vanessa Ryan, "Living in Duplicate: Victorian Science and Literature Today," *Critical Inquiry* 38.2 (2012): 411–417.

41 Nancy Paxton, *George Eliot and Herbert Spencer: Feminism, Evolutionism, and the Reconstruction of Gender* (Princeton University Press, 1991), 3–14 and *passim*. See also Adelene Buckland's argument for the interchange between literature and geology in *Novel Science: Fiction and the Invention of Nineteenth-Century Geology* (University of Chicago Press, 2013), 15–19 and *passim*.

42 Ryan, "Living in Duplicate," 415–416.

43 Iwan Rhys Morus, *When Physics Became King* (University of Chicago Press, 2005), 55.

44 *Ibid.*, 57.

45 Rick Rylance, *Victorian Psychology and British Culture* (Oxford University Press, 2000), 2.

46 M. King Hubbert, "Exponential Growth as a Transient Phenomenon in Human History," in Daly and Townsend, *Valuing the Earth*, 113–126 (113).

47 Frederick Soddy, *Wealth, Virtual Wealth, and Debt* (London: George Allen, 1983 [1926]), 29–30.

48 A similar dynamic is at play in discussions of an emergent industrial power like China, whose environmental problems have been frequently described as "Dickensian." See for example Keith Bradsher and David Barboza, "Pollution from China Casts a Global Shadow," *The New York Times*, June

11, 2006. Linfen in China was described in *Time* as a "soot-blackened city in China's inland Shanxi province [that] makes Dickensian London look as pristine as a nature park"; Bryan Walsh, "The World's Most Polluted Places," *Time* (September 12, 2007). Available at http://content.time.com/time/ specials/2007/article/0,28804,1661031_1661028_1661016,00.html (accessed January 4, 2014). I don't want to suggest that China's growth hasn't had grave environmental consequences, but the frequent comparisons with nineteenth-century conditions has the effect of suggesting that the West has somehow overcome the environmental problems of the Victorian era.

49 Goodstein, *Out of Gas*, 32.

50 Richard Anthony Proctor, "Britain's Coal Cellars," *St. Paul's* 9 (October–December 1871): 182–194 (194).

51 For an engaging discussion of the "wishful thinking" involved in the quest to build a fusion reactor, see Charles Seife's aptly titled *Sun in a Bottle: The Strange History of Fusion*, 227 and *passim*.

52 Joseph Holdsworth, *On the Extension of the English Coal-Fields* (London: R. Middleton, 1866), 111–112.

53 Clifford Krauss, "Drilling Boom Revives Hope for Natural Gas," *The New York Times*, August 24, 2008, A1.

54 George Basalla, "Some Persistent Energy Myths," in *Energy and Transport: Historical Perspectives on Policy Issues*, ed. George Daniels and Mark H. Rose (London: Sage, 1982), 27–38 (27).

55 *Ibid.*, 28.

1 The city and the sun

1 T. H. Huxley, "On the Formation of Coal," in *Discourses: Biological and Geological* (New York: D. Appleton, 1897 [1870]), 137–161 (158–161).

2 Henry Adams, *The Degradation of the Democratic Dogma* (New York: Macmillan, 1919), 142–143.

3 William Whewell, *Astronomy and General Physics Considered with Reference to Natural Theology* (London: William Pickering, 1833), 289.

4 James Moore, "Theodicy and Society," in *Victorian Faith in Crisis: Essays on Continuity and Change in Nineteenth-Century Religious Belief*, ed. Richard J. Helmstadter and Bernard Lightman (New York: Stanford University Press, 1990), 153–186 (158–159; original emphasis).

5 *Ibid.*, 159.

6 William Buckland, *Geology and Mineralogy Considered with Reference to Natural Theology*, 2 vols., Vol. I (London: William Pickering, 1836), 595–6.

7 *Ibid.*, 131–132.

8 Frank M. Turner, *Contesting Cultural Authority: Essays in Victorian Intellectual Life* (Westport, CT: Greenwood, 2004), 104.

9 Huxley, "On the Formation of Coal," 160.

10 Richard Jones, *An Essay on the Distribution of Wealth and on the Sources of Taxation* (London: John Murray, 1831), xiii.

11 Buckland, *Geology and Mineralogy*, 537–538.
12 Robert Hunt, "British Diamonds," *The St. James's Magazine* 1 (May 1861): 223–234 (231).
13 As Geoffrey Cantor has recently argued, the Great Exhibition of 1851, the showcase of English technology, was framed by many leading religious figures in explicitly "providentialist terms"; "Science, Providence and Progress at the Great Exhibition," *Isis* 103.3 (2012): 439–459 (445).
14 The entropic, anti-Providential historical narrative brought about by the emergence of fossil-fuel culture was famously articulated by Henry Adams in his *A Letter to American Teachers of History* (Washington, DC: J. H. Furst, 1910).
15 Charles Babbage, *An Essay on the General Principles which Regulate the Application of Machinery* (London: W. Clowes, 1827), 7–8.
16 Underwood, *The Work of the Sun*, 172.
17 Babbage, *An Essay*, 8.
18 Charles Babbage, *The Ninth Bridgewater Treatise: A Fragment*, 2nd edn. (London: John Murray, 1838), 34–41.
19 M. Norton Wise and Crosbie Smith, "Work and Waste: Political Economy and Natural Philosophy in Nineteenth Century Britain," *History of Science* 27 (1989): 263–301, 391–449; 28 (1990): 221–261 (27: 429).
20 Brian Wynne argues: "scientific naturalism was … the cosmological back-cloth of industrialization … Destiny was to be placed firmly in human, scientific hands, not in divine ones." "Natural Knowledge and Social Context: Cambridge Physicists and the Luminiferous Ether," in *Science in Context: Readings in the Sociology of Science*, ed. Barry Barnes and David Edge (Cambridge, MA: MIT Press, 1982), 212–231 (218–219).
21 See Peter J. Bowler, *The Non-Darwinian Revolution: Reinterpreting a Historical Myth* (Baltimore: Johns Hopkins University Press, 1988).
22 Anson Rabinbach, *The Human Motor: Energy, Fatigue and the Origins of Modernity* (Los Angeles: University of California Press, 1992), 3.
23 *Ibid.*, 2–3.
24 Underwood, *The Work of the Sun*, 1–2.
25 See Thomas Kuhn, "Energy Conservation as an Example of Simultaneous Discovery," in *The Conservation of Energy and the Principle of Least Action*, ed. I. Bernard Cohen (New York: Arno, 1981), 321–345 (338).
26 See Rhys Morus, *When Physics Became King* (University of Chicago Press, 2005), 123–155.
27 Samuel Smiles, *The Life of George Stephenson and of His Son Robert Stephenson* (New York: Harper, 1868), 468.
28 See, for example, Benjamin Ward Richardson, "Sun Force and Earth Force," *The Popular Science Review* 5 (1866): 327–336 (327), cited in Underwood, *The Work of the Sun*, 183.
29 John Herschel, *A Treatise on Astronomy* (London: Longman, 1833), 211.
30 See Juan Martinez-Alier, *Ecological Economics: Energy, Environment and Society* (Oxford: Basil Blackwood, 1990), 161–162.

31 Smiles, *The Life of George Stephenson*, 468.

32 H. G. Wells, *The World Set Free: A Story of Mankind* (New York: E. P. Dutton, 1914), 25.

33 Balfour Stewart, *The Conservation of Energy* (London: Henry S. King, 1873), 34.

34 For a discussion of this passage of Stewart's, see Philip Mirowski, *More Heat than Light: Economics as Social Physics, Physics as Nature's Economics* (Cambridge University Press, 1989), 132.

35 Quoted in Peter Guthrie Tait, "Energy," *North British Review* 40 (May 1864): 177–193 (181).

36 Quoted in John Masson, *Lucretius: Epicurean and Poet*, 2 vols., Vol. I (London: John Murray, 1907), 139.

37 See Rabinbach, *The Human Motor*, 313.

38 John Tyndall, *New Fragments*, 2nd edn. (London: Longmans Green, 1892), 386.

39 John Tyndall, *Heat Considered as a Mode of Motion* (New York: D. Appleton, 1863), 448.

40 John Tyndall, *Address Delivered before the British Association Assembled at Belfast* (London: Longmans Green, 1874), 64.

41 Tyndall, *Heat*, 449. Although in his own day his perceived materialism made him a controversial figure, Tyndall's conception of matter and energy "held very real pantheistic and transcendental possibilities" in Frank Turner's words; *Contesting Cultural Authority*, 21. Greg Myers discusses the continuities between Tyndall's rhetoric and a traditional religious point of view: "Tyndall's wording is that of an agnostic; the physicist, rather than the creator, breathes life into this world. But the radical new concepts of conserved and trans-formed energy are assimilated into a philosophy dating from *Ecclesiastes*"; "Nineteenth-Century Popularizations of Thermodynamics and the Rhetoric of Social Prophecy," *Victorian Studies* 29.1 (Fall 1985): 35–66 (43).

42 Tyndall, *Heat*, 448.

43 *Ibid.*, 447.

44 Herbert Spencer, *First Principles of a New System of Philosophy* (New York: D. Appleton, 1865), 251.

45 See Mirowski, *More Heat than Light*, 266–267; Underwood, *The Work of the Sun*, 180–181.

46 See Barri Gold, *ThermoPoetics: Energy in Victorian Literature and Science* (Cambridge, MA: MIT Press, 2010), 6–7.

47 See Mirowski, *More Heat than Light*, 35–59.

48 John Tyndall, *The Glaciers of the Alps* (London: John Murray, 1860), 246.

49 Stephanie Pain, "Before It Was Famous: 150 Years of the Greenhouse Effect," *New Scientist* 202.2708 (May 16, 2009): 46–47 (47).

50 Jevons, *The Coal Question*, 2.

51 Smiles, *The Life of George Stephenson*, 495.

52 Although Marx and Engels were, of course, instrumental in theorizing the various mystifications of capitalist productive practices, they were hostile to

any theory of "natural limits." For this reason Marxist scholars like Benton, Kate Soper, and John Bellamy Foster have been working both to uncover the ecological dimensions of Marx's thought, and to visit a "critical transformation" (Ted Benton, "Marxism and Natural Limits," in Benton, *The Greening of Marxism*, 157–186 [157]) on those aspects of his work that are still problems for environmental action and awareness.

53 Thomas Carlyle, *Chartism*, 2nd edn. (London: James Fraser, 1840), 83.

54 Thomas Carlyle, "Signs of the Times," in *Critical and Miscellaneous Essays: Collected and Republished*, 5 vols., Vol. I, 2nd edn. (London: James Fraser, 1840), 262–294 (267).

55 Thomas Carlyle, *On Heroes, Hero Worship, and the Heroic in History* (London: Chapman and Hall, 1840), 11.

56 Thomas Carlyle, *Sartor resartus* (London: Chapman and Hall, 1831), 48.

57 *Ibid.*, 49.

58 *Ibid.*, 48–49.

59 Carlyle, *Chartism*, 36.

60 Thomas Carlyle, *Past and Present* (London: Chapman and Hall, 1843), 37–38.

61 See, for example, U. C. Knoepflmacher, "The Novel between City and Country," in *The Victorian City: Images and Realities*, ed. H. J. Dyos and Michael Wolff, 2 vols., Vol. II (London: Routledge, 1972), 517–536 (530–536).

62 Carlyle, *Chartism*, 83–84.

63 Carlyle, *Past and Present*, 374–375.

64 Carlyle, *Sartor resartus*, 48.

65 Underwood, *The Work of the Sun*, 177.

66 Crosbie Smith, *The Science of Energy: A Cultural History of Energy Physics in Victorian Britain* (University of Chicago Press, 1998), 181.

67 George Levine, "From Know-Not-Where to Nowhere," in Dyos and Wolff, *The Victorian City*, Vol. II, 495–516 (501).

68 Christopher Hamlin, "Providence and Putrefaction: Victorian Sanitarians and the Natural Theology of Health and Disease," *Victorian Studies* 28.3 (Spring 1985): 381–411 (381–382).

69 John Holland, *The History and Description of Fossil Fuel, the Collieries and Coal Trade* (London: Whittaker, 1835), 460.

70 Anon., review of W. S. Jevons, *The Coal Question*, *The Times*, April 19, 1866, 10, cited in *W. S. Jevons: Critical Responses*, ed. Sandra Peart, 4 vols., Vol. I (London: Routledge, 2003), 195–198 (196).

71 Even the most sanguine observers noted this issue. In his preface to *The Life of George Stephenson*, Samuel Smiles remarks on how reliant the metropolis had become on an entire coal-fired infrastructure: "London now depends so much upon railways for its subsistence, that it may be said to be fed by them from day to day, having never more than a few days' food in stock. And the supply is so regular and continuous, that the possibility of its being interrupted never for a moment occurs to anyone" (xxv). Smiles is not interested in ringing alarm bells; instead he takes this dependence as an occasion to

marvel at the vast system of life that the invention of the railway has made possible; nevertheless, the darker implications of this conception of London are readily apprehensible.

72 Jevous, *The Coal Qustion*, 232.

73 *Ibid.*, 157.

74 *Ibid.*, 196–197.

75 William Waterston, "Coal," in *Cyclopaedia of Commerce, Mercantile Law, Finance, Commercial Geography and Navigation* (London: Henry G. Bohn, 1844), 164.

76 Jevons, *The Coal Question*, 160–161.

77 *Ibid.*, 162.

78 *Ibid.*, 371.

79 Grant Duff, "Must We Then Believe Cassandra?," in *Miscellanies, Political and Literary* (London: Macmillan, 1878), 57–93 (65–66).

80 Jevons, *The Coal Question*, 8.

81 Catherine Gallagher, *The Body Economic: Life, Death, and Sensation in Political Economy and the Victorian Novel* (Princeton University Press, 2006), 38.

82 Jevons, *The Coal Question*, 248.

83 *Ibid.*, 358.

84 William Sidney Gibson, *The Certainties of Geology* (London: Smith Elder, 1840), 256.

85 Holdsworth, *On the Extension of the English Coal-Fields*, 111–112.

86 *Ibid.*, 112.

87 *Ibid.* (original emphasis).

88 *Ibid.*, 18.

89 *Ibid.*, 8–9.

90 *Ibid.*, 22.

91 See John Bellamy Foster, *Marx's Ecology: Materialism and Nature* (New York: Monthly Review Press, 2000), 148–149.

92 See *ibid.*, 149–170; Karl Marx, *Capital*, 3 vols., Vol. I, trans. Ben Fowkes (New York: Penguin, 1990), Chapter 15.

93 Richard Anthony Proctor, *The Sun: Ruler, Fire, Light, and Life of the Planetary System* (London: Longmans Green, 1872), 400.

94 Justus von Liebig and Alderman Mechi, "The Sewage of Towns," *The Farmer's Magazine* 17 (1860): 163–165 (164).

95 Marx, *Capital*, Vol. I, 637–638.

96 As Graeme Davidson argues, "Few ideas have exercised as powerful an influence upon students of urban society as the organic or biological conception of the city. From Aristotle's *Politics* to the Chicago School and beyond, social theorists have likened cities to bodies or organisms; dissected them into constituent organs." In "The City as a Natural System: Theories of Urban Society in Early Nineteenth Century Britain," in *The Pursuit of Urban History*, ed. Derek Fraser and Anthony Sutcliffe (London: Edward Arnold, 1983), 349–370 (349).

97 Thomas Hawksley, "The Power for Good or Evil of Refuse Organic Matter," in *The Sewage of Towns: Papers by Various Authors, Read at a Congress on the Sewage of Towns Held at Leamington Spa, Warwickshire*, ed. John Hitchman (London: Simpkin, Marshall, 1866), 3–62 (47).

98 If the perfect economy and conserving order of Providence was to be maintained as a viable idea, then either the city somehow fell outside nature altogether, or else it opened up a problem *within* the natural order that had to be solved. We have already seen how Carlyle attempted to quarantine city waste metaphysically by subscribing to the former option, and how awkward and uncertain this division was. Hawksley, writing some decades later, is in the second camp, and we can see the different kind of awkwardness involved for him.

99 Quoted in Hamlin, "Providence and Putrefaction," 391.

100 Marx, *Capital*, Vol. 1, 638.

101 *Ibid.*, 637.

102 Friedrich Engels, *The Condition of the Working Class in England*, ed. Victor Kiernan (New York: Penguin, 2005 [1845]), 149.

103 Holdsworth, *On the Extension of the English Coal-Fields*, 17.

104 Nead, *Victorian Babylon*, 84–85.

105 Henry Mayhew, *The Criminal Prisons of London and Scenes of Prison Life* (London: Griffin, Bohn, 1862), 29.

106 *Ibid.*

107 *Ibid.*, 39.

108 Lewis Mumford, *The City in History: Its Origins, Its Transformations and Its Prospects* (New York: Harcourt Brace, 1961), 563–567.

109 J. C. Platt and J. Saunders, "Underground," in *London*, ed. Charles Knight, 6 vols., Vol. 1 (London: Charles Knight, 1841), 233.

110 Nead, *Victorian Babylon*, 15.

111 Mayhew, *The Criminal Prisons of London*, 9.

112 *Ibid.*, 9.

113 *Ibid.*, 8–9.

114 *Ibid.*, 9.

115 Nead, *Victorian Babylon*, 97.

116 Blanchard Jerrold, *London: A Pilgrimage* (New York: Anthem, 2005 [1872]), 18.

117 Jerrold, *London*, 18.

118 *Ibid.*, 12.

119 *Ibid.*, 39.

120 *Ibid.*, 21.

121 Nead, *Victorian Babylon*, 29.

2 The heat death of the sun at the dawn of the Anthropocene

1 Gillian Beer, *Open Fields: Science in Cultural Encounter* (New York: Oxford University Press, 1999), 225.

2 *Ibid.*

3 Quoted in Tait, "Energy," 181.

4 Prigogine and Stengers, *Order out of Chaos*, 116.

5 For the conceptual roots of the second law of thermodynamics, and the shift in the governing organizing metaphor – from the timelessness of the balance to the temporal irreversibility of the engine – see Wise and Smith, "Work and Waste," Part II.

6 Anon., "The Place Where Light Dwelleth," *The British Quarterly Review* 51 (April 1870): 409–441 (413–414).

7 Rylance, *Victorian Psychology*, 26.

8 William Thomson, "On a Universal Tendency in Nature to the Dissipation of Mechanical Energy," in *Mathematical and Physical Papers*, 5 vols., Vol. I (Cambridge University Press, 1882), 511.

9 Myers, "Nineteenth-Century Popularizations of Thermodynamics and the Rhetoric of Social Prophecy," *Victorian Studies* 29.1 (Fall 1985): 35–66 (44).

10 William Thomson and P. G. Tait, *Treatise on Natural Philosophy*, 2 vols., Vol. I (Cambridge University Press, 1883), 486.

11 For the influence of natural theology on Thomson's work, see Crosbie Smith, "Natural Philosophy and Thermodynamics: William Thomson and 'The Dynamical Theory of Heat,'" British Journal for the History of Science 9 (November 1976): 293–319; and David Wilson, "Kelvin's Scientific Realism: The Theological Context," Philosophical Journal 11 (1974): 41–60.

12 Balfour Stewart and Peter Guthrie Tait, *The Unseen Universe; or, Physical Speculations on a Future State*, 6th edn. (London: Macmillan, 1876), 209.

13 Georgescu-Roegen, *The Entropy Law*, 9.

14 Mirowski, *More Heat than Light*, 63.

15 Serres, *Hermes*, 72.

16 William Thomson and P. G. Tait, "Energy," *Good Words* 3 (1862): 601–607 (606).

17 Balfour Stewart and Norman Lockyer, "The Sun as a Type of the Material Universe," Parts I and II, *Macmillan's Magazine* 18 (July 1868): 246–257 (319).

18 Balfour Stewart, "What Is Energy?," Parts I–IV, *Nature* 1 (April 28, 1870): 647–648; 2 (June 2, 1870): 78–80, (July 7, 1870): 183–185, (August 4, 1870): 270–271 (Part I, 648).

19 Stewart, *The Conservation of Energy*, 152.

20 Proctor, *The Sun*, 475.

21 F. Max Müller, *Lectures on the Origin and Growth of Religion* (London: Routledge, 1997), 207–208, cited in Beer, *Open Fields*, 224.

22 Stewart, *The Conservation of Energy*, 154.

23 Myers, "Nineteenth-Century Popularizations of Thermodynamics," 55.

24 M. Norton Wise and Crosbie Smith, *Energy and Empire: A Biographical Study of Lord Kelvin* (Cambridge University Press, 1989), 331.

25 Myers, "Nineteenth-Century Popularizations of Thermodynamics," 46.

26 Bruce Clarke, "Dark Star Crashes," in *From Energy to Information: Representation in Science and Technology, Art, and Literature*, ed. Bruce Clarke and Linda Henderson (Stanford University Press, 2002), 59–75 (60).

27 Quoted in Burchfield, *Lord Kelvin and the Age of the Earth*, 79. For a fuller discussion of the conflict between Darwin and Thomson, geology and physics, see Beer, *Darwin's Plots*, 160–163; and Burchfield, *Lord Kelvin and the Age of the Earth*, 70–79.

28 For an excellent discussion of this topic, see Theodore M. Porter, "A Statistical Survey of Gases: Maxwell's Social Physics," *Historical Studies in the Physical Sciences* 12 (1981): 77–116 (100–116).

29 Gaston Bachelard, *The New Scientific Spirit* (Boston: Beacon Press, 1984), 65, cited in Rabinbach, *The Human Motor*, 48.

30 Stewart and Lockyer, "The Sun as a Type," 325.

31 *Ibid.*, 324.

32 *Ibid.*, 326–327. For a discussion of Stewart's "anti-materialist" position, see Graeme Gooday, "Sun-Spots, Weather and the Unseen Universe: Balfour Stewart's Anti-Materialist Representations of Energy in British Periodicals," in *Science Serialized: Representations of the Sciences in Nineteenth-Century Periodicals*, ed. Geoffrey Cantor and Sally Shuttleworth (Cambridge, MA: MIT University Press, 2004), 111–147 (113–114).

33 Perhaps the most well-known instance of this emphasis on mind is Maxwell's famous thought experiment, the "sorting demon" who could theoretically reverse the workings of the second law of thermodynamics. Although Maxwell's demon was offered less as a serious proposition than as a heuristic device, it illustrates the desire to imagine the mind a loophole of sorts in the strict economy of energy.

34 As G. H. Lewes argues: "When you say it is according to a law bodies gravitate, that fluids ascend to their level, or that the needle points towards the north, you are superadding to the *facts* an abstract entity which you believe coerces the facts … What is this law which produces the phenomena, but a more subtle, more impersonal substitute for the Supernatural Power"; *Comte's Philosophy of the Sciences* (London: Bell and Daldy, 1871 [1853]), 52.

35 Levine, *Darwin and the Novelists*, 91.

36 T. H. Huxley, *Evolution and Ethics* (New York: D. Appleton, 1897 [1893]), 83–84.

37 Wise and Smith, "Work and Waste," Part II, 398.

38 M. Norton Wise, "Time Discovered and Time Gendered in Victorian Science and Culture," in Clarke and Henderson, *From Energy to Information*, 39–58 (54–55).

39 Stewart and Lockyer, "The Sun as a Type," 320.

40 *Ibid.*, 319.

41 For a discussion of the way in which the laws of energy served to bolster and reify a conception of causality that positivism had attempted to discredit, see Peter Allan Dale, *In Pursuit of a Scientific Culture: Science, Art, and Society in the Victorian Age* (Madison: University of Wisconsin Press, 1990), 130–136.

42 Stewart and Tait, *The Unseen Universe*, 127.
43 As Beer points out in *Open Fields*, the "cutback" in temporal horizons was part of the thermodynamic physicists' strategy to discredit uniformitarian geology and thus "undermine evolutionary theory" (162). But the extreme bends in time found in Stewart's work, I would argue, also suggest a complex attempt to fashion a fully moral universe from the laws of thermodynamics.
44 While the pro-capitalist ideology behind much mid-century Victorian thermodynamic writing is clear enough – and wonderfully discussed by Myers in his essay – it is worth noting that in his later writing, Thomson made dire predictions about the pace and environmental impact of the fossil-fuel-based manufacturing system. But by and large, especially in the middle decades of the century, it is the case that thermodynamic writing tended to ignore the implications of the second law for terrestrial resource use and instead focused on the "naturalness" of the industrial order.
45 Stewart, *The Conservation of Energy*, 153.
46 Herman von Helmholtz, "On the Interaction of Natural Forces," trans. John Tyndall, in *Popular Lectures on Scientific Subjects* (New York: D. Appleton, 1873), 153–196 (192).
47 George Hodgins, "Energy and Explosives," *Brotherhood of Locomotive Firemen and Enginemen's Magazine* 59 (September 1915): 299–301 (300).
48 Clarke, "Dark Star Crashes," 60.
49 Stewart and Tait, *The Unseen Universe*, 126.
50 Underwood, *The Work of the Sun*, 7.
51 Stewart and Tait, *The Unseen Universe*, 126.
52 *Ibid.*; Myers, "Nineteenth-Century Popularizations of Thermodynamics," 57.
53 R. H. Patterson, "Sensationalism in Science," *Belgravia* 6 (October 1868): 77–81 (77).
54 For a discussion of the "heat death of the sun" and sensationalism, see Alberto Gabriele, *Reading Popular Culture in Victorian Print: Belgravia and Sensationalism* (New York: Palgrave Macmillan, 2009), 63–65.
55 Anon., review of W. S. Jevons, *The Coal Question*, *The Times*, June 26, 1866, cited in *W. Stanley Jevons: Collected Reviews and Obituaries*, ed. Takutoshi Inoue (Bristol: Thoemmes Press, 2002), 93–104 (96).
56 Thomson and Tait, "Energy," 606.
57 Jevons, *The Coal Question*, 164.
58 Anon., review of Jevons, *The Coal Question* (June 26, 1866), 94.
59 George Perkins Marsh, *Man and Nature; or, Physical Geography as Modified by Human Action* (New York: Scribner, 1864), 55.
60 *Ibid.*, 44.

3 Energy systems and narrative systems in Charles Dickens's *Bleak House*

1 See G. K. Chesterton, *Dickens: A Critical Study* (New York: Dodd Mead, 1906), 77–78; J. Hillis Miller, *Charles Dickens: The World of His Novels*

(Cambridge, MA: Harvard University Press, 1958), 86, 90, 137; Alex Woloch, *The One versus the Many* (Princeton University Press, 2003), 144, 175, 185.

2 W. J. Harvey, "The Double Narrative of *Bleak House*," in Charles Dickens, *"Bleak House": A Norton Critical Edition*, ed. George Ford and Sylvère Monod (New York: Norton, 1977), 963–970 (966).

3 V. S. Pritchett, "Dickens," in *The Pritchett Century: A Selection of the Best by V. S. Pritchett* (New York: Modern Library, 1998), 573–579 (577).

4 E. D. H. Johnson, *Charles Dickens: An Introduction to His Novels* (New York: Random House, 1969), 149.

5 Dickens, *Bleak House*, 469.

6 Miller uses the language of energy and entropy without specifically discussing thermodynamics. Wilkinson helped establish the historicist case by reading *Bleak House* alongside scientific lectures and articles on energy in Dickens's journal, *Household Words*. In a chapter of her *ThermoPoetics*, Gold provides a brilliant and thorough exploration of the connection between energy science and Dickens's novel. See J. Hillis Miller, "The World of *Bleak House*," in Dickens, *Bleak House*, ed. Ford and Monod, 947–960; Ann Wilkinson, "*Bleak House*: From Faraday to Judgment Day," *ELH* 34.2 (1967): 225–247; Barri Gold, "*Bleak House*: The Novel as Engine," in *ThermoPoetics*, 187–224.

7 Dickens, *Bleak House*, 52, 306.

8 See Dickens, *Bleak House*, esp. 89–92.

9 Dickens, *Bleak House*, 411.

10 *Ibid.*, 1.

11 *Ibid.*, 445.

12 *Ibid.*, 1.

13 *Ibid.*, 249.

14 *Ibid.*, 250.

15 *Ibid.*, 250.

16 *Ibid.*, 456.

17 Mirowski, *More Heat than Light*, 106.

18 See Gallagher, *The Body Economic*, esp. 35–61.

19 Stewart and Lockyer, "The Sun as a Type," 319.

20 Stewart, *The Conservation of Energy*, 26.

21 Dickens, *Bleak House*, 67.

22 Garrett Stewart, "Dickens, Eisenstein, Film," in *Dickens on Screen*, ed. John Glavin (Cambridge University Press, 2004), 122–144 (129).

23 The epistemological doubts raised in moments like this stand in contrast to the easy correspondence between nature and industry often described in thermodynamic texts. Note Stewart and Tait's comment in *The Unseen Universe*: "The visible universe may with perfect truth be compared to a vast heat-engine, and this is the reason why we have brought such engines so prominently before our readers. The sun is the furnace or source of high-temperature heat of our system, just as the stars are for other systems" (126). Here we see the industrial world naturalized in no uncertain terms, with modern technological processes providing a working model for the operations of the

entire universe. In Stewart's claim of "perfect truth" for his comparison we can see how the distinction between analogy and identity becomes entirely unclear.

24 Dickens, *Bleak House*, 154.
25 *Ibid.*, 254.
26 *Ibid.*, 80, 229.
27 *Ibid.*, 80.
28 *Ibid.*, 577.
29 *Ibid.*, 35.
30 *Ibid.*, 387.
31 See *The Oxford English Dictionary*, 2nd edn. (Oxford University Press, 1989), s.v. "sustainable, *adj*." Available at www.oed.com/view/Entry/195210?redirecte dFrom=sustainable#eid (accessed January 11, 2014).
32 Thomas Malthus, *Additions to the Fourth and Former Editions of "An Essay on the Principle of Population,"* (London: J. Murray, 1817), 35.
33 *OED*, s.v. "sustainable, *adj*."
34 Nicholas Simons, *Cases Decided in the High Court of Chancery by the Right Hon. Sir Lancelot Shadwell*, 17 vols., Vol. XI (London: V. and R. Stevens, 1853), 92.
35 Dickens, *Bleak House*, 67.
36 *Ibid.*, 492.
37 Joseph Meeker, *The Comedy of Survival: In Search of an Environmental Ethic* (New York: Scribner, 1974), 58.
38 Anon., "The Coal Question," *The Examiner*, reprinted *Littell's Living Age* 79 (December 1863): 226–230 (227).
39 Dickens, *Bleak House*, 227.
40 See, for example, Philip Fisher's discussion of the novel in "City Matters, City Minds," in *The Worlds of Victorian Fiction*, ed. Jerome Buckley (Cambridge, MA: Harvard University Press, 1975), 371–389 (386).
41 Dorothy Van Ghent, "The Dickens World: A View from Todgers," *Sewanee Review* 58.3 (1950): 419–438 (426).
42 Stewart and Tait, *The Unseen Universe*, 198.
43 Babbage, *The Ninth Bridgewater Treatise*, 114–119.
44 Thomson, "On a Universal Tendency," 511.
45 As Terry Eagleton argues, "Dickens is forced in his later fiction to use as aesthetically unifying images the very social institutions (the Chancery Court of BH, the Circumlocution Office of LD) which are the object of his criticism"; *Criticism and Ideology: A Study in Marxist Literary Theory* (London: Verso, 2006 [1975]), 129.
46 Tina Young Choi, "Forms of Closure: The First Law of Thermodynamics and Victorian Narrative," *ELH* 74.2 (Summer 2007): 301–322 (312).
47 *Ibid.*, 314.
48 Ken Hiltner, *What Else Is Pastoral? Renaissance Literature and the Environment* (Ithaca, NY: Cornell University Press, 2011), 96.
49 Levine, *Darwin and the Novelists*, 18.

50 Indeed, we might connect this to James Krasner's point about the "entangled bank" image in *On the Origin of Species*: the very distinctness of this metaphor, he argues, makes it an inadequate representation of the fluid, intangible, ever-shifting, unfocused ecological dynamics the book describes (118).
51 Hiltner, *What Else Is Pastoral?*, 123.
52 Dickens, *Bleak House*, 620.
53 *Ibid.*, 621.

4 The renewable energies of *Our Mutual Friend*

1 For a discussion of thermodynamic principles in Spencer, see Gold, *ThermoPoetics*, 72–111.
2 Anon., "Is Heat Motion?," *All the Year Round* 13 (July 1, 1865): 534–538; anon., "Heat and Work," *All the Year Round* 14 (August 5, 1865): 29–33; Edmund Saul Dixon, "Physical Force," *Household Words* (March 12, 1859): 354–359; Edmund Saul Dixon, "Vital Heat," *Household Words* (June 19, 1858): 13–18; anon., "Small-Beer Chronicles," *All the Year Round* 8 (February 14, 1863): 58–62; anon., "Respecting the Sun," *All the Year Round* 13 (April 22, 1865): 297–300.
3 See anon., "How Long Will Our Coal Last?," *All the Year Round* 2 (March 17, 1860): 488–490; anon., "The Coal Question."
4 Tyndall, *Heat*, 448.
5 As Jonathan Smith has argued, the endlessly metamorphic world of *Household Words*, firmly grounded in natural-theological harmonies, gives way to concerns about scarcity and exhaustion in *All the Year Round*. This shift, which Smith locates in 1860, corresponds to the developments we charted in previous chapters: the popularization of thermodynamic ideas, including the "heat death" of the sun, in the 1850s, and rising anxieties about the continued availability of coal and other resources, resulting in Jevons's *The Coal Question* (1865), among other works. See Jonathan Smith, "Heat and Modern Thought: The Forces of Nature in *Our Mutual Friend*," *Victorian Literature and Culture* 23 (1995): 37–69.
6 See, for example, J. Hillis Miller's influential reading: "*Our Mutual Friend* remains true to its rejection of the idea that there is an ideal unity of the world transcending the differences between individual lives, and perceptible from the outside by Providence … here there is no unifying center"; *Charles Dickens*, 292.
7 See Gooday, "Sun Spots," 111–112 and *passim*.
8 Daniel Wise, *The Young Man's Counselor; or, Sketches and Illustrations of the Duties and Dangers of Young Men* (Cincinnati: Poe and Hitchcock, 1860), 88.
9 Thomson and Tait, "Energy," 601.
10 *Ibid.*
11 J. P. Nichol, "Energy," in *A Cyclopaedia of the Physical Sciences* (London: Richard Griffin, 1860), 316–318 (316).
12 Stewart, "What Is Energy?," 78 (original emphasis).

13 Edwin Chadwick, "Opening Address of the President of Section F (Economic Science and Statistics) of the British Association for the Advancement of Science," *Journal of the Statistical Society of London* 25 (1862): 502–524 (509–511).

14 Anon., "National Portraits," *All the Year Round* 9–10 (November 7, 1863): 252–256 (255).

15 Thomson and Tait, "Energy," 605.

16 Ted Underwood, "Productivism and the Vogue for 'Energy,'" *Studies in Romanticism* 34.1 (1995): 103–125 (116).

17 Gallagher, *The Body Economic*, 3; Jules Law, *The Social Life of Fluids: Blood, Milk, and Water in the Victorian Novel* (Ithaca, NY: Cornell University Press, 2010), 3.

18 See Smith, "Heat and Modern Thought," 42.

19 Jules Law, *The Social Life of Fluids*, 10.

20 Rabinbach, *The Human Motor*, 78.

21 Karl Marx, *Capital*, 3 vols., Vol. III, trans. Ernest Untermann (Chicago: Charles Kerr, 1909), 954–955.

22 Some environmentally minded critics have taken Marx to task for this, arguing that, in imagining the transition to socialism, he failed to realize that the entire technostructure would also need to be revolutionized. Otherwise, an ecologically destructive, resource-intensive capitalist mode of production would simply be replaced by an ecologically destructive, resource-intensive socialist mode of production. See, for example, Rudolf Bahro, *Socialism and Survival* (London: Heretic Books, 1982), 27. Other Marxist scholars have identified the ecological ambiguities in Marx's work; Michael Perelman, for example, argues that his ambivalence regarding ecological limits stems from a distrust of any line of thinking that seemed to lend support to the hated Malthusian doctrine ("Marx and Resource Scarcity," 66–67).

23 Chadwick, "Opening Address," 514.

24 "Abel Handy," "Hard-Labour in Store," *Punch* 46–47 (April 9, 1864): 151.

25 *Ibid.*

26 Stewart, "What Is Energy?," 647.

27 Anon., "Up-Hill Work," *All the Year Round* 13 (July 15, 1865): 593–596 (594).

28 Anon., "Heat and Work."

29 George Levine, *Dying to Know: Scientific Epistemology and Narrative in Victorian England* (University of Chicago Press, 2002), 153.

30 Charles Dickens, *Our Mutual Friend* (New York: G. W. Carleton, 1885 [1865]), 53.

31 George Orwell, "Charles Dickens," in *Selected Writings* (London: Heinemann, 1958), 147.

32 Dickens, *Mutual Friend*, 27.

33 *Ibid.*, 67.

34 *Ibid.*, 27.

35 *Ibid.*, 27.

36 Law, *The Social Life of Fluids*, 61.

37 See, for example, Jerrold, *London*. In a brilliant article on thermodynamics in the novel, Jonathan Smith argues that Wrayburn's complaints about energy illustrate the fact that "in *Our Mutual Friend*, both extremes, working frenetically but inefficiently or not working at all, are equally unacceptable"; "Heat and Modern Thought," 57. While I agree with this formulation, I would argue that, for Dickens, locating the middle ground is itself the problem. The extreme division depicted here between a wasteful indolence and a wasteful hyper-kineticism suggests the difficulty of finding a stable territory within which *any* action can be meaningful, at least in the early parts of the novel.

38 Dickens, *Mutual Friend*, 146.

39 Gallagher, *The Body Economic*, 105.

40 See *ibid.*, 35–61.

41 Dickens, *Mutual Friend*, 12.

42 *Ibid.*, 11.

43 *Ibid.*, 173.

44 Andrew Wynter, "The Use of Refuse," *The Quarterly Review* 124 (January and April 1868): 334–356 (337).

45 *Ibid.*, 335.

46 Krepp, *The Sewage Question*, 203.

47 Douglas Strutt Galton, "Report of the Royal Commission on Metropolitan Sewage," *Journal of the Society of Arts* 33 (February 13, 1885): 290–303 (296), cited by Nicholas Goddard, "'A Mine of Wealth'?: The Victorians and the Agricultural Value of Sewage," *Journal of Historical Geography* 22.3 (1996): 274–290 (277).

48 Dickens, *Mutual Friend*, 492.

49 *Ibid.*, 79.

50 *Ibid.*, 171.

51 Wynter, "The Use of Refuse," 336.

52 Nancy Aycock Metz, "The Artistic Reclamation of Waste in *Our Mutual Friend*," *Nineteenth Century Fiction* 34.1 (June 1979): 59–72 (68).

53 Chadwick, "Opening Address," 512.

54 Dickens, *Mutual Friend*, 390.

55 *Ibid.*, 389.

56 *Ibid.*, 290.

57 *Ibid.*, 530.

58 *Ibid.*, 531.

59 *Ibid.*, 678.

60 *Ibid.*, 776.

61 *Ibid.*, 216.

62 *Ibid.*,217.

63 *Ibid.*, 792.

64 *Ibid.*, 791.

65 *Ibid.*, 732.

66 Mary Poovey, *Making a Social Body: British Cultural Formation, 1830–1864* (University of Chicago Press, 1995), 167.

5 John Ruskin's alternative energy

1 Timothy Clark, *The Cambridge Introduction to Literature and the Environment* (Cambridge University Press, 2010), 16.

2 Jonathan Bate, *Romantic Ecology: Wordsworth and the Environmental Tradition* (New York: Routledge, 1991), 58–61.

3 See Martinez-Alier, *Ecological Economics*, 8, 97; Daly and Townsend, *Valuing the Earth*, 18.

4 References to Ruskin's works are taken from *The Works of John Ruskin*, and are indicated by volume and page numbers, thus: III.129.

5 See Stuart Peterfreund, "The Re-Emergence of Energy in the Discourse of Literature and Science," *Annals of Scholarship* 4.1 (1986): 22–53 (35–36).

6 Underwood, *The Work of the Sun*, 34.

7 *Works of John Ruskin*, VI.128.

8 *Ibid.*, IV.133–134.

9 *Ibid.*, XVI.385.

10 For the Romanticist roots of the energy concept, see Kuhn, "Energy Conservation," 338 and *passim*.

11 *Works of John Ruskin*, X.208–209.

12 *Ibid.*, X.192.

13 *Ibid.*, X.240.

14 *Ibid.*, X.214. Unless otherwise noted, all emphases are Ruskin's.

15 *Works of John Ruskin*, X.212.

16 See Thomas Richards, *The Commodity Culture of Victorian England: Advertising and Spectacle, 1851–1914* (Stanford University Press, 1990), 23–24.

17 Regenia Gagnier, *The Insatiability of Human Wants: Economics and Aesthetics in Market Society* (University of Chicago Press, 2000).

18 *Works of John Ruskin*, XVII.212.

19 *Ibid.*, X.193.

20 Dickens, *Mutual Friend*, 18.

21 *Ibid.*, X.18.

22 Quoted in George Herbert Perris, *The Industrial History of Modern England* (New York: Henry Holt, 1914), 546.

23 Patrick Geddes, *John Ruskin, Economist* (Edinburgh: William Brown, 1884), 13.

24 *Works of John Ruskin*, XVII.153.

25 *Ibid.*, XVII.84.

26 J. A. Hobson, *John Ruskin, Social Reformer*, 3rd edn. (London: Allen and Unwin, 1968 [1902]), 138–139.

27 See Gallagher, *The Body Economic*, 35–61.

28 Geddes, *John Ruskin*, 28.

29 *Works of John Ruskin*, XVII.29–30.

30 *Ibid.*, XVII.183.

31 I would add that Ruskin's interest in productivity here is not just a question of metaphysics or ethics. It also contains a significant physical argument,

which is that unfettered competition under a *laissez-faire* economic system is ultimately a wasteful way of using national energy.

32 See James Clark Sherburne, *John Ruskin; or, The Ambiguities of Abundance* (Cambridge, MA: Harvard University Press, 1972), 86–93.

33 *Works of John Ruskin*, XVI.18–19.

34 *Ibid.*, XVII.73.

35 *Ibid.*, XVII.35.

36 *Ibid.*, XVII.77.

37 *Ibid.*, XVII.79.

38 *Ibid.*, XVII.101.

39 Francis Edgeworth, *Mathematical Psychics: An Essay on the Application of Mathematics to the Moral Sciences* (London: Kegan Paul, 1881), 9.

40 Sherburne, *John Ruskin*, 137–138; William Henderson, *John Ruskin's Political Economy* (New York: Routledge, 1999), 142.

41 William Stanley Jevons, *The Theory of Political Economy*, 3rd edn. (London: Macmillan, 1888), 2. Available online at Library of Economics and Liberty, www. econlib.org/library/YPDBooks/Jevons/jvnPE.html (accessed January 7, 2014).

42 Gagnier, *The Insatiability of Human Wants*, 1.

43 Mirowski, *More Heat than Light*, 254.

44 Soddy, *Wealth, Virtual Wealth, and Debt*, 94.

45 Mill, *Principles of Political Economy*, 335.

46 *Ibid.*, 339–340.

47 *Ibid.*, 339.

48 *Works of John Ruskin*, XVI.110.

49 See Sherburne, *John Ruskin*, 122.

50 Mill, *Principles of Political Economy*, 340.

51 *Works of John Ruskin*, XVIII.134.

52 *Ibid.*, XVII.406–407.

53 *Ibid.*, XVII.405.

54 *Ibid.*, XVII.236.

55 Hobson criticizes Ruskin for his unwillingness to take his radical approach to the "costs" of labor – his insight that the value of certain commodities can never make up for the "life" the laborer had to spend in their production – and apply it to his analysis of the economic system; *John Ruskin*, 97–100. But here, I think, we see the reason why: there are some forms of work that cannot be made healthy, but also cannot be dispensed with.

56 *Works of John Ruskin*, XVIII.137. See Philip Mallet's essay "The City and the Self," in *Ruskin and Environment: The Storm Cloud of the Nineteenth Century*, ed. Michael Wheeler (Manchester University Press, 1995), 38–51, which also emphasizes Ruskin's idea of the city as unproductive and "parasitic" (42).

57 *Works of John Ruskin*, XVIII.137.

58 *Ibid.*, XVI.378.

59 *Ibid.*, XVI.378.

60 *Ibid.*, XXXIV.10.

61 *Ibid.*, XXXIV.8.

62 *Ibid.*, XXXIV.9.

63 *Ibid.*, XXXIV.38.

64 *Ibid.*, XXXIV.33.

65 For more on Ruskin's performative science, see Sharon Weltman's terrific *Performing the Victorian: John Ruskin and Identity in Theater, Science, and Education* (Columbus: Ohio State University Press, 2007).

66 Myers, "Nineteenth-Century Popularizations of Thermodynamics," 36. For an excellent analysis of Ruskin's complicated relationship with science and his interest in "the scientific fidelity to natural fact" see Edward Alexander, "Ruskin and Science," *Modern Language Review* 64.3 (July 1969): 408–521 (511).

67 *Works of John Ruskin*, XXXIV.7.

68 *Ibid.*, XXIV.37.

69 *Ibid.*, XXIV.37.

70 Dickens, *Bleak House*, 1.

71 *Works of John Ruskin*, XXXIV.38.

72 Thomas Richards, *The Imperial Archive: Knowledge and the Fantasy of Empire* (New York: Verso, 1993), 86.

73 As Myers notes, Ruskin's quarrel with Tyndall about energy begins with *The Eagle's Nest* (1872), where he dismisses Tyndall's work on the first law of conservation as "commonplace"; Myers, "Nineteenth-Century Popularizations of Thermodynamics," 43. For an extended discussion of Ruskin's disagreements with Tyndall, see Paul Sawyer, "Ruskin and Tyndall: The Poetry of Matter and the Poetry of Spirit," in *Victorian Science and Victorian Values*, ed. James Paradis and Thomas Postlewait (New Brunswick: Rutgers University Press, 1985), 217–246.

74 *Works of John Ruskin*, XXXIV.42.

75 *Ibid.*, XXXIV.61.

76 *Ibid.*, XXXIV.61–62.

77 *Ibid.*, XXXIV.62.

78 Sherburne, *John Ruskin*, 1.

79 *Works of John Ruskin*, XXXIV.40–41.

80 *Ibid.*, XXXIV.62.

81 *Ibid.*, XXXIV.15.

82 *Ibid.*, XXXIV.31.

83 Proctor, *The Sun*, 454.

84 William Crookes, "Some Possibilities of Electricity," *The Living Age* 193 (April, May, June 1892): 93–97 (97).

85 Jonathan Bate also sees in Ruskin's late writings a "familiar and modern" connection between industrial "progress" and changes in global weather patterns; *Romantic Ecology*, 61.

86 Gillen Wood, "Constable, Clouds, Climate Change," *The Wordsworth Circle* 38.1–2 (2007): 25–34 (29).

87 Alan Bewell, "Jefferson's Thermometer: Colonial Biogeographical Constructions of the Climate of America," in *Romantic Science: The Literary Forms of
Natural History*, ed. Noah Herringman (Albany, NY: SUNY Press, 2003),
111–138 (131).

6 Personal fantasy, natural limits: Robert Louis Stevenson's
Dr. Jekyll and Mr. Hyde

1 Stevenson's grandfather Robert, for whom Stevenson College in Edinburgh is
named, was a well-known lighthouse engineer, and Stevenson's paternal uncles
and father, Thomas, all followed in Robert's footsteps. Thomas Stevenson,
bitterly disappointed that his son abandoned his scientific training and the
family calling to pursue literature, was an active participant in the scientific
culture of Edinburgh, ascending to President of the Royal Society in 1884.

2 Robert Louis Stevenson, *On the Thermal Influence of Forests*, Vol XXII of *Letters
and Miscellanies of Robert Louis Stevenson* (New York: Scribner, 1889 [1873]),
611–621 (612).

3 Crosbie Smith, *The Science of Energy*, 103.

4 See Wise and Smith, *Energy and Empire*, 36–38, 101–114.

5 *Ibid.*, 87–88.

6 The *Memoir of Fleeming Jenkin* is almost exclusively interested in its subject as
a personality and social being; there is little engagement with his work as an
engineer.

7 See Robert Louis Stevenson, *The Letters of Robert Louis Stevenson*, ed. Bradford
A. Booth and Ernest Mehew, 8 vols., Vol. V (New Haven: Yale University
Press, 1994–1995), 346.

8 Robert Louis Stevenson, *The Strange Case of Dr. Jekyll and Mr. Hyde* (London:
Longmans Green, 1886), 138, 2.

9 For a valuable modern discussion of irreversibility, see Prigogine and Stengers,
Order out of Chaos, esp. 208–209, 310.

10 Stevenson, *Jekyll and Hyde*, 103.

11 *Ibid.*, 132.

12 *Ibid.*, 137.

13 *Ibid.*, 125.

14 *Ibid.*, 113.

15 *Ibid.*, 30.

16 *Ibid.*, 118.

17 *Ibid.*, 109.

18 *Ibid.*, 117–118.

19 Marina Warner, *Fantastic Metamorphoses, Other Worlds: Ways of Telling the Self*
(Oxford University Press, 2002), 4–5.

20 Stewart and Tait, *The Unseen Universe*, 115.

21 Stewart and Lockyer, *The Sun as a Type*, 320.

22 Warner, *Fantastic Metamorphoses*, 18.

23 Peter Guthrie Tait, *Lectures on Some Recent Advances in Physical Science with a
Special Lecture on Force* (London: Macmillan, 1876), 23, 114.

24 Stevenson, *Jekyll and Hyde*, 8.
25 *Ibid.*, 118.
26 *Ibid.*, 119.
27 *Ibid.*, 97.
28 *Ibid.*, 136.
29 *Ibid.*, 74.
30 Tait, *Lectures*, 20.
31 Everett Mendelsohn, *Heat and Life: The Development of the Theory of Animal Heat* (Cambridge, MA: Harvard University Press, 1964), 5.
32 Tait, *Lectures*, 22–23.
33 *Ibid.*, 69–70. See also Helmholtz, "On the Interaction of Natural Forces," 153–196.
34 Stevenson, *Jekyll and Hyde*, 138.
35 *Ibid.*, 104.
36 *Ibid.*, 15.
37 *Ibid.*, 100.
38 *Ibid.*, 6.
39 *Ibid.*, 37.
40 *Ibid.*, 107. As further evidence that Stevenson had engineering in mind, it is worth noting that the detective assigned to the Carew murder investigation is one "Inspector Newcomen," most likely an allusion to Thomas Newcomen, the celebrated English inventor and "father of the Industrial Revolution."
41 Stevenson, *Jekyll and Hyde*, 118.
42 *Ibid.*, 99–100.
43 The adjective "old" is used again and again in the text, describing the bond between Lanyon, Utterson, and Jekyll nearly every time the topic arises (12, 16, 22, 42, 43, 67); but it is also used to describe the dissecting room (19); the revolver Lanyon readies (71); and, crucially, the chemical that Jekyll can no longer procure ("'For God's sake,' he added, 'Find me some of the old'" [55]).
44 Stevenson, *Jekyll and Hyde*, 116.
45 *Ibid.*, 111–112.
46 *Ibid.*, 116.
47 *Ibid.*, 114.
48 Stevenson, *Letters*, III.221; IV.24.
49 *Ibid.*, VI.71.
50 *Ibid.*, I.374.
51 Stevenson, *Jekyll and Hyde*, 114.
52 Garrett, "Cries and Voices: Reading *Jekyll and Hyde*," in *"Dr. Jekyll and Mr. Hyde" after One Hundred Years*, ed. William Veeder and Gordon Hirsch (Chicago University Press, 1988), 69–72 (64). For other discussions of the metaphor of chemical purification in the novel, see Vladimir Nabokov, *Lectures on Literature*, ed. Fredson Bowers (New York: Harcourt Brace, 1980), 182–184; and Ronald Thomas, "The Strange Voices in the Strange Case: Dr. Jekyll, Mr. Hyde, and the Voices of Modern Fiction," in Veeder and Hirsch, *"Jekyll and Hyde" after One Hundred Years*, 73–93 (79).

53 James Clerk Maxwell, "Address to the Mathematical and Physical Sections of the British Association," *Nature* 3 (September 22, 1870): 419–422 (421).

54 Stevenson, *Jekyll and Hyde*, 137.

55 *Ibid.*, 139.

56 *Ibid.*, 134.

57 *Ibid.*, 134.

58 *Ibid.*, 10.

59 Sir Walter Scott, *Waverley* (London: T. and A. Constable, 1901 [1814]), 382.

60 Stevenson, *Jekyll and Hyde*, 116.

61 Tait, *Lectures*, 71.

62 Robert Louis Stevenson, *Records of a Family of Engineers*, in *"Memoir of Fleeming Jenkin" and "Records of a Family of Engineers,"* Vol. XVIII of *Letters and Miscellanies of Robert Louis Stevenson* (New York: Scribner, 1920), 264.

63 Robert Louis Stevenson, "A Humble Remonstrance," in *Memories and Portraits* (New York: Charles Scribner's Sons, 1898), 275–299 (283).

64 Stevenson, *Records of a Family of Engineers*, 263–264.

65 *Ibid.*, 265–266.

66 For useful descriptions of *Dr. Jekyll and Mr. Hyde* as a kind of mechanism, see Irving S. Saposnik, "The Anatomy of *Dr. Jekyll and Mr. Hyde*," *SEL* 11 (1971): 714–731 (726); and Garrett, "Cries and Voices," 60. Stevenson's text may be a better "engine" than his grandfather's, but as Garrett and others have shown, its effect is to break apart settled categories and raise questions it doesn't answer.

67 Stevenson, *Jekyll and Hyde*, 23.

68 Robert Kiely, *Robert Louis Stevenson and the Fiction of Adventure* (Cambridge, MA: Harvard University Press, 1964), 123.

69 Stevenson, *Jekyll and Hyde*, 118.

70 *Ibid.*, 110. Another key subversion of magic occurs when Hyde offers Lanyon "a new province of knowledge and new avenues to fame and power" (75) if he agrees to behold the transformation. Hyde assumes the role of Mephistopheles in this scene, but Lanyon's curiosity gains him nothing, not even the temporary access to "fame and power" usually granted to participants in such fateful pacts.

71 Stevenson, "A Humble Remonstrance," 283.

72 Stevenson, *Jekyll and Hyde*, 107.

73 Unsurprisingly, the emphasis on the force of psychic states has made the novel an inviting candidate for Freudian interpretation. The focus on energy forms is, in a sense, both a revision and an elaboration of the psychoanalytic point of view, insofar as Freud's understanding of the psychic "mechanism" was profoundly influenced by thermodynamics, especially as described by Herman von Helmholtz. The connection between Stevenson and Freud can be traced back to a shared background in energy science. See Frank Sulloway, *Freud, Biologist of the Mind: Beyond the Psychoanalytic Legend* (New York: Basic Books, 1979), esp. 170, 235.

74 Stevenson, *Jekyll and Hyde*, 116.

75 *Ibid.*, 118.
76 *Ibid.*, 84. Crosbie Smith and his co-authors write on steamship engineers and their financial backers: In all of these cases, capital, in whatever form, could be deployed for the benefit of humankind or for wasteful and extravagant ends. From the perspective of a Christian moral economy, therefore, the parable of the talents treated capital as a gift to individuals, to be used wisely or simply wasted through a lack of use. Sooner or later, however, the individual would have to account for his actions, morally as well as materially, leaving, as Thom had long preached, true waste (manifest as either reckless extravagance or as unwise parsimony) as the ultimate sin of humankind." (Crosbie Smith, Ian Higginson, and Philip Wolstenholme, "'Avoiding Equally Extravagance and Parsimony': The Moral Economy of the Ocean Steamship," *Technology and Culture* 44.3 [2003]: 443–469 [462])
77 *Works of John Ruslin*, XVII.152.
78 Smith et al., 'Ocean Steamship', 443–469 [462].
79 Stevenson, *Jekyll and Hyde*, 19.
80 *Ibid.*, 19.
81 *Ibid.*, 110.
82 *Ibid.*, 50.
83 *Ibid.*, 122.
84 *Ibid.*, 125.
85 *Ibid.*, 140.
86 Stevenson, *Letters*, V.163.
87 Stevenson, *Jekyll and Hyde*, 3.
88 Robert Louis Stevenson, *Treasure Island* (London: Cassell, 1898 [1883]), 115.
89 Stevenson, *Jekyll and Hyde*, 97.
90 See, for example, D. L. Wright, "'The Prisonhouse of My Disposition': A Study of the Psychology of Addiction in *Dr. Jekyll and Mr. Hyde*," Studies in the Novel 26 (1994): 254–267; Joyce Carol Oates, "Jekyll/Hyde," The Hudson Review 40.4 (Winter 1988): 603–608.
91 Malthus, *An Essay*, 79.
92 *Ibid.*, 78.
93 Stevenson, *Jekyll and Hyde*, 126.
94 *Ibid.*, 100.
95 Stephen Arata, *Fictions of Loss in the Victorian "Fin de siècle"* (Cambridge University Press, 1996), 36.
96 Stevenson, *Jekyll and Hyde*, 118.
97 *Ibid.*, 17.
98 *Ibid.*, 98.
99 Stewart and Lockyer, "The Sun as a Type," 324–325.
100 Stevenson, *Jekyll and Hyde*, 97.
101 In *The Revenge of Gaia*, James Lovelock draws upon the Jekyll-and-Hyde myth to discuss the climate-change crisis and the duality of the human approach to the environment; *The Revenge of Gaia* (New York: Basic Books, 2006), 6.

102 Huxley, *Evolution and Ethics*, 83–84.
103 Arata, *Fictions of Loss*, 39.
104 Allan Stoekl, *Bataille's Peak: Energy, Religion, and Postsustainability* (Minneapolis: University of Minnesota Press, 2007), 120.

7 Joseph Conrad: energy, entropy, and the fictions of empire

1 Joseph Conrad to R. B. Cunninghame Graham (December 14, 1897), in *The Letters of Joseph Conrad*, ed. Laurence Davies, Frederick R. Karl, and Owen Knowles, 7 vols, Vol. I, (New York: Cambridge University Press, 1983), 409.
2 Joseph Conrad, *The Secret Agent* (Oxford University Press, 1998 [1907]), xxxvi.
3 Conrad, *Secret Agent*, 214.
4 Stewart, "What Is Energy?," 79.
5 Stewart and Lockyer, "The Sun as a Type," 324.
6 Benjamin Kidd, *Social Evolution* (London: Macmillan, 1894), 317.
7 Benjamin Kidd, *The Control of the Tropics* (New York: Macmillan, 1898), 5–6.
8 Stephen Bunker, *Underdeveloping the Amazon: Extraction, Unequal Exchange and the Failure of the Modern State* (Urbana: University of Illinois Press, 1985), 21.
9 Kidd, *The Control of the Tropics*, 76.
10 Proctor, *The Sun*, 450.
11 *Ibid.* (my emphasis).
12 Joseph Conrad, *Heart of Darkness*, ed. Ross C. Murfin (Boston, MA: Bedford, 1994 [1899]), 21. Subsequent references are included in the text.
13 Alf Hornborg, "Machine Fetishism, Value, and the Image of Unlimited Good: Towards a Thermodynamics of Imperialism," *Man* 27.1 (1992): 1–18 (10).
14 John Herschel to W. S. Jevons (January 8, 1866), cited in Martinez-Alier, *Ecological Economics*, 161–162.
15 Herschel to Jevons (March 8, 1866), cited in *ibid.*, 162.
16 Jevons, *The Coal Question*, 375.
17 Richards, *The Imperial Archive*, 93.
18 Foster, *Marx's Ecology*, 151–154.
19 Henry Charles Carey, *Principles of Social Science*, 3 vols., Vol. II (Philadelphia: J. B. Lippincott, 1860), 215.
20 Justus von Liebig, introduction to *Die organische Chemie in ihrer Anwendung auf Agricultur und Physiologie*, 2 vols., 7th edn. (Braunschweig: Vieweg, 1862 [1840]), 85, translated in Foster, *Marx's Ecology*, 164.
21 Foster, *Marx's Ecology*, 164 (original emphasis).
22 Carey, *Principles of Social Science*, 211, 215.
23 Jevons, *The Coal Question*, 215.
24 See Martinez-Alier, *Ecological Economics*, 8.
25 See Mirowski, *More Heat than Light*, 218–219; 254–262.

26 T. H. Huxley, "Capital: The Mother of Labour," *Nineteenth Century: A Monthly Review* 26 (March 1890): 513–532 (517).

27 *Ibid.*, 515.

28 *Ibid.*, 517.

29 Joseph Conrad, *Nostromo* (New York: Penguin, 1990 [1905]), 66–67.

30 *Ibid.*, 66.

31 Joseph Conrad, *Lord Jim*, ed. Allan H. Simmons (New York: Penguin, 2007 [1900]), 215.

32 Hornborg, "Machine Fetishism," 10 (original emphasis).

33 Even the term "raw materials" is loaded, since it suggests that the products of nature require human industry to achieve their final form.

34 Rosa Luxemburg, *The Accumulation of Capital*, trans. Agnes Schwarzschild (London: Routledge, 2003 [1913]), 397.

35 Conrad, *Secret Agent*, 28, 18.

36 *Ibid.*, 28.

37 *Ibid.*, 32.

38 *Ibid.*, 32.

39 *Ibid.*, 33.

40 *Ibid.*, 30.

41 Joseph Conrad and Ford Madox Ford, *The Inheritors* (New York: Carroll and Graff, 1985 [1901]), 12–13.

42 See Gold's discussion of *The Coming Race* as a thermodynamic text in *Thermopoetics*, 76–100.

43 Conrad, *Secret Agent*, 33.

44 *Ibid.*, 88.

45 *Ibid.*, 18.

46 *Ibid.*, 19.

47 Jevons, *The Coal Question*, 374.

48 Conrad, *Secret Agent*, 11.

49 *Ibid.*, 100.

50 *Ibid.*, 57.

51 Barri Gold, "The Consolation of Physics: Tennyson's Thermodynamic Solution," *PMLA* 117 (2002): 449–464 (452).

52 Conrad, *Secret Agent*, 53.

53 *Ibid.*, 42, 47.

54 *Ibid.*, 48.

55 *Ibid.*, 44.

56 *Ibid.*, 30.

57 *Ibid.*, 264.

58 *Ibid.*, 239.

59 *Ibid.*, 254.

60 *Ibid.*, 259.

61 *Ibid.*, 241.

62 *Ibid.*, 244.

63 *Ibid.*, 260.

64 *Ibid.*, 242–243.

65 Ford Madox Ford, *The Soul of London: A Survey of a Modern City*, ed. Alan G. Hill (London: Everyman, 1995 [1905]), 42.

66 Conrad, *Secret Agent*, 11–12.

67 Conrad, *Nostromo*, 162.

68 Conrad, *Secret Agent*, 33.

69 Wise and Smith, *Energy and Empire*, 723–724.

70 Conrad, *Secret Agent*, 51.

71 Hugh Epstein, "A Pier-Glass in the Cavern," in *Conrad's Cities: Essays for Hans van Marle*, ed. Gene Moore (Amsterdam: Rodopi, 1992), 175–196 (188).

72 Ford, *The Soul of London*, 106–107.

73 Joseph Conrad, "Henry James: An Appreciation," in *Joseph Conrad in Fiction*, ed. Walter F. Wright (Lincoln: University of Nebraska Press, 1984), 82–88 (84).

74 Conrad, *Secret Agent*, 44.

75 *Ibid.*, 227.

76 *Ibid.*, 99–100.

77 Irving Howe, "Conrad: Order and Anarchy," in *"The Secret Agent": A Casebook*, ed. Ian Watt (London: Macmillan, 1973), 140–149 (141).

78 Conrad, *Secret Agent*, 13.

79 Bunker, *Underdeveloping the Amazon*, 15.

80 Hobson, *John Ruskin*, 230.

81 *Ibid.*

82 J. A. Hobson, *Imperialism: A Study*, 3rd edn. (London: Allen and Unwin, 1968 [1902]), 296.

83 Georgescu-Roegen, *The Entropy Law*, 277.

84 Conrad, *Secret Agent*, 27.

85 *Ibid.*, 152.

86 *Ibid.*, 92.

87 Conrad to Cunninghame Graham (January 14, 1898), in *Letters*, II.17.

88 Conrad, *Secret Agent*, 12.

89 *Ibid.*, 44.

90 Joseph Conrad, *The Mirror of the Sea*, in *"A Personal Record" and "The Mirror of the Sea"* (New York: Penguin, 1998 [1912, 1906]), 155.

91 Conrad, "Henry James," 84–85.

92 *Ibid.*, 86.

93 *Ibid.*, 84.

94 Conrad, *The Mirror of the Sea*, 189.

95 Conrad, *Secret Agent*, 18–19.

96 Conrad, *Lord Jim*, 173.

97 *Ibid.*, 127.

98 *Ibid.*, 280.

99 Conrad, *Heart of Darkness*, 31.

100 Joseph Conrad, *Youth: A Narrative* (London: William Blackwood, 1903 [1898]), 34.

101 Conrad, *Secret Agent*, 50.
102 *Ibid.*, 258.

8 Evolutionary energy and the future: Henry Maudsley and H. G. Wells

1 John Edward Morgan, "The Danger of Deterioration of Race from the Too Rapid Increase of Great Cities," in *Transactions of the National Association for the Promotion of Social Science: Sheffield Meeting, 1865*, ed. G. W. Hastings (London: Longmans Green, 1866), 427–449 (442).
2 *Ibid.*, 428.
3 *Ibid.*, 427.
4 *Ibid.*, 434.
5 Daniel Pick, *Faces of Degeneration: A European Disorder* (Cambridge University Press, 1996), 197.
6 Anon., "The Deterioration of Race," *The Lancet* 1 (June 23, 1866): 690–692 (691).
7 Morgan, "The Danger of Deterioration of Race," 444.
8 See Gareth Stedman Jones, *Outcast London: A Study in the Relationship between Classes in Victorian Society* (New York: Pantheon, 1985), 284–285 and *passim*.
9 K. Corbet, "The Degeneration of Race," *The Lancet* 2 (August 17, 1861): 170.
10 *Ibid.*, 691.
11 Jones, *Outcast London*, 313.
12 *Ibid.*, 285.
13 See *ibid.*, 284–285.
14 George Henry Jennings, *An Anecdotal History of the British Parliament from the Earliest History to the Present Time* (London: Horace Cox, 1880), 343.
15 Frederick Webb Headley, *Problems of Evolution* (London: Duckworth, 1900), 279.
16 Samuel Smith, *The Industrial Training of Destitute Children* (London: Kegan Paul, 1885), 11.
17 Henry Maudsley, *The Physiology and Pathology of Mind* (New York: D. Appleton, 1867), 202.
18 For Maudsley's changing understanding of the threat degeneration posed, see Pick, *Faces of Degeneration*, 209.
19 For some of the historical underpinnings of this change of attitude, see Jones, *Outcast London*, 281–314.
20 Maudsley, *Physiology and Pathology*, 73–74.
21 Stewart and Lockyer, "The Sun as a Type," 325.
22 Maudsley, *Physiology and Pathology*, 202.
23 Maudsley, like Morgan, argues that the environment in which the urban poor live produces weakness, illness, and etiolated physiologies, but he also imagines the way those compromised physiologies both reflect and produce

compromised minds and psychologies. The fear of the "vigorous" growth of the weaker classes is a fear of the manifold forms of socially unacceptable behavior that contribute nothing to national productivity or the advancement of the species. This includes the vigorous reproductive habits of the lower classes, whose birth rate, as many commentators noted, seemed to be outpacing that of the middle classes. That reproductive growth, for Maudsley, posed a threat not just to the "decaying reason" of the debilitated individual, but to that of the species more generally.

24 Stewart and Tait, *Unseen Universe*, 126.

25 It is no accident that Francis Galton singles out energy as the prime quality of development: "in any scheme of eugenics, energy is the most important quality to favour; it is, as we have seen, the basis of living action, and it is eminently transmissible by descent"; *Inquiries into Human Faculty and Its Development* (London: Macmillan, 1883), 27. Galton shares with Maudsley an interest in the way energy could be transmitted through reproduction. Eugenics was, in essence, a vast system of evolutionary engineering, designed to manage the energy of the race.

26 Underwood, *The Work of the Sun*, 33–34.

27 Galton, *Inquiries into Human Faculty*, 25.

28 Francis Galton, "Hereditary Talent and Character," *Macmillan's* 12 (May–October 1865): 318–327 (326).

29 *Ibid.*, 319.

30 Jones, *Outcast London*, 304–307.

31 Headley, *Problems of Evolution*, 241.

32 *Ibid.*, 207, 204.

33 *Ibid.*, 249.

34 *Ibid.*, 264.

35 *Ibid.*, 249.

36 *Ibid.*, 276.

37 *Ibid.*, 206.

38 Henry Maudsley, *Body and Will* (New York: D. Appleton, 1884), 322–323.

39 *Ibid.*, 317.

40 Maudsley, Body and Will, 324.

41 Elizabeth Deeds Ermarth, *The English Novel in History 1840–1895* (New York: Routledge, 1996), 46–47.

42 Many critical discussions of *The Time Machine* conflate the evolutionary and thermodynamic trajectories, describing the death of the sun at the end of the novel as the culminating symbol of the degenerative tendencies of human biology. See, for example, John Partington, "*The Time Machine* and *A Modern Utopia*: The Static and Kinetic Utopias of the Early H. G. Wells," *Utopian Studies* 13.1 (2002): 57–68 (62); Robert Philmus, "*The Time Machine*; or, The Fourth Dimension as Prophecy," *PMLA* 84.3 (May 1969): 530–535 (531); Darko Suvin, "'*The Time Machine* versus Utopia' as a Structural Model for Science Fiction," *Comparative Literature Studies* 10.4 (December 1973): 334–352 (343).

43 H. G. Wells, *The Time Machine*, ed. Nicholas Ruddick (New York: Broadview, 2001 [1895]), 92.

44 For a discussion of the way in which *The Time Machine* comments on topical controversies about aestheticism and evolution, see Gowan Dawson's *Darwin, Literature and Victorian Respectability* (Cambridge University Press, 2007), 216.

45 H. G. Wells, "Fiction about the Future," in *H. G. Wells's Literary Criticism*, ed. Patrick Parrinder and Robert Philmus (Totawa: Barnes and Noble, 1980 [1938]), 246–251 (246).

46 Wells, *Time Machine*, 90.

47 Stewart, *The Conservation of Energy*, 154.

48 Wells, *Time Machine*, 111.

49 *Ibid.*, 106.

50 George Howard Darwin, "On the Precession of a Viscous Spheroid, and on the Remote History of the Earth," in *Scientific Papers*, 2 vols., Vol. II (Cambridge University Press, 1908), 36–140.

51 Wells, *Time Machine*, 144.

52 *Ibid.*, 146.

53 *Ibid.*, 147.

54 Maudsley, *Body and Will*, 319–320.

55 *Ibid.*, 319.

56 *Ibid.*, 323.

57 This kind of thinking structured narratives of cultural decline. Oswald Spengler imagined that wildly different accounts of decay and collapse were simply versions of the same master narrative written in different idioms: "what the myth of *Götterdämmerung* signified of old the theory of Entropy signifies today – the world's end as completion of an inwardly necessary evolution"; *Today and Destiny: Vital Excerpts from the Decline of the West* (New York: Knopf, 1940), 290. As J. Edward Chamberlin argues, "the second law of thermodynamics was the most powerful figuration of degeneration that the nineteenth century proposed"; "Images of Degeneration: Turnings and Transformations," in *Degeneration: The Dark Side of Progress*, ed. Chamberlin and Sander L. Gilman (New York: Columbia University Press, 1985), 263–289 (272).

58 H. G. Wells, "The Extinction of Man," in *Certain Personal Matters: A Collection of Material, Mainly Autobiographical* (London: Laurence and Bullen, 1898), 172.

59 T. H. Huxley, "The Struggle for Existence in Human Society," in *Readings from Huxley*, ed. Clarissa Rinaker (New York: Harcourt Brace, 1920), 82–83.

60 Maudsley, *Body and Will*, 320.

61 Richards, *The Imperial Archive*, 103.

62 Huxley, *Evolution and Ethics*, 81.

63 Richard Anthony Proctor, "The Past and Future of Our Earth," *Contemporary Review* 25 (December 1874–May 1875): 74–92 (91).

64 Tyndall, *Heat*, 448.
65 Wells, *Time Machine*, 155.
66 For a discussion of this see Paul Alkon, *Science Fiction before 1900: Imagination Discovers Technology* (New York: Routledge, 2002), 1–6.
67 Maudsley, *Body and Will*, 239.
68 See Robert Weeks, "Disentanglement as a Theme in H. G. Wells's Fiction," *Papers of the Michigan Academy of Science, Arts, and Letters* 39 (1954): 439–444 (440); and John Glendening, "Green Confusion: Evolution and Entanglement in H. G. Wells's *The Island of Doctor Moreau*," *Victorian Literature and Culture* 30.2 (2002), 571–597 (582).
69 Wells, *Time Machine*, 155.
70 Philmus, "*The Time Machine*," 534.
71 Wells, *The World Set Free*, 27. Subsequent references are included in the text.
72 Wells, *Time Machine*, 52.
73 See Morse Peckham, "Darwinism and Darwinisticism," *Victorian Studies* 3.1 (September 1959): 19–40 (20–24). In this shift to Darwinisticism, Wells aligns himself with early-twentieth-century thinkers who subscribed to an evolutionary order not driven by natural selection, including Bergson and Shaw.
74 Wells, *Time Machine*, 144.
75 *Ibid.*, 41.
76 *Ibid.*, 44.
77 *Ibid.*, 57.
78 *Ibid.*, 63.
79 Carlyle, *Chartism*, 52.
80 Wells, *Time Machine*, 21.
81 *Ibid.*, 29.

Bibliography

Adams, Henry. *The Degradation of the Democratic Dogma*. New York: Macmillan, 1919.

A Letter to American Teachers of History. Washington, DC: J. H. Furst, 1910.

Alexander, Edward. "Ruskin and Science." *Modern Language Review* 64.3 (July 1969): 508–521.

Alkon, Paul. *Science Fiction before 1900: Imagination Discovers Technology*. New York: Routledge, 2002.

Altvater, Elmar. "The Social and Natural Environment of Fossil Capitalism." In *Coming to Terms with Nature*. Ed. Leo Panitch and Colin Leys. Socialist Register. London: Merlin Press, 2007. 37–71.

Anon. "The Coal Question." *The Examiner*. Reprinted *Littell's Living Age* 79 (December 1863): 226–230.

"The Deterioration of Race." *The Lancet* 1 (June 23, 1866): 690–692.

"Heat and Work." *All the Year Round* 14 (August 5, 1865): 29–33.

"How Long Will Our Coal Last?" *All the Year Round* 2 (March 17, 1860): 488–490.

"Is Heat Motion?" *All the Year Round* 13 (July 1, 1865): 534–538.

"National Portraits." *All the Year Round* 9–10 (November 7, 1863): 252–256.

"The Place where Light Dwelleth." *The British Quarterly Review* 51 (April 1870): 409–441.

Review of W. S. Jevons, *The Coal Question*. *The Times*, April 19, 1866. 10. Cited in *W. S. Jevons: Critical Responses*. Ed. Sandra Peart. 4 vols., Vol. 1. London: Routledge, 2003. 195–198.

Review of W. S. Jevons *The Coal Question*. *The Times*. June 26, 1866. Cited in *W. Stanely Jevons: Collected Reviews and Obituaries*. Ed. Takutoshi Inoue. Bristol: Thoemmes Press, 2002. 93–104.

"Up-Hill Work." *All the Year Round* 13 (July 15, 1865): 593–596.

Arata, Stephen. *Fictions of Loss in the Victorian "Fin de siècle."* Cambridge University Press, 1996.

Babbage, Charles. *An Essay on the General Principles which Regulate the Application of Machinery*. London: W. Clowes, 1827.

The Ninth Bridgewater Treatise: A Fragment. 2nd edn. London: John Murray, 1838.

Bahro, Rudolf. *Socialism and Survival*. London: Heretic Books, 1982.

Baker, Samuel. *Written on the Water: British Romanticism and the Maritime Empire of Culture.* Charlottesville: University of Virginia Press, 2010.

Basalla, George. "Some Persistent Energy Myths." In *Energy and Transport: Historical Perspectives on Policy Issues.* Ed. George Daniels and Mark H. Rose. London: Sage, 1982. 27–38.

Bate, Jonathan. *Romantic Ecology: Wordsworth and the Environmental Tradition.* New York: Routledge, 1991.

Beer, Gillian. *Darwin's Plots: Evolutionary Narrative in Darwin, George Eliot and Nineteenth-Century Fiction.* 3rd edn. Cambridge University Press, 2009.

Open Fields: Science in Cultural Encounter. New York: Oxford University Press, 1999.

Benton, Ted (ed.). *The Greening of Marxism.* New York: Guilford, 1996.

"The Malthusian Challenge: Ecology, Natural Limits, and Human Emancipation." In *Socialism and the Limits of Liberalism.* Ed. Peter Osborne. New York: Verso, 1991. 241–269.

"Marxism and Natural Limits." In *The Greening of Marxism.* Ed. Ted Benton. New York: Guilford, 1996. 157–186.

Besant, Walter. *The Art of Fiction.* Boston, MA: Cupples, Upham, 1884.

Bewell, Alan. "Jefferson's Thermometer: Colonial Biogeographical Constructions of the Climate of America." In *Romantic Science: The Literary Forms of Natural History.* Ed. Noah Herringman. Albany, NY: SUNY Press, 2003. 111–138.

Boulding, Kenneth. "The Economics of the Coming Spaceship Earth." In *Valuing the Earth: Economics, Ecology, Ethics.* Ed. Herman Daly and Kenneth N. Townsend. Cambridge, MA: MIT Press, 1993. 297–310.

Bowler, Peter J. *The Non-Darwinian Revolution: Reinterpreting a Historical Myth.* Baltimore: Johns Hopkins University Press, 1988.

Bradsher, Keith, and David Barboza. "Pollution from China Casts a Global Shadow." *The New York Times*, June 11, 2006.

Buckland, Adelene. *Novel Science: Fiction and the Invention of Nineteenth-Century Geology.* University of Chicago Press, 2013.

Buckland, William. *Geology and Mineralogy Considered with Reference to Natural Theology.* 2 vols., Vol. I. London: William Pickering, 1836.

Bunker, Stephen. *Underdeveloping the Amazon: Extraction, Unequal Exchange and the Failure of the Modern State.* Urbana: University of Illinois Press, 1985.

Burchfield, Joe. *Lord Kelvin and the Age of the Earth.* University of Chicago Press, 1990 [1975].

Cantor, Geoffrey. "Science, Providence and Progress at the Great Exhibition." *Isis* 103.3 (2012): 439–459.

Carlyle, Thomas. *Chartism.* 2nd edn. London: James Fraser, 1840.

On Heroes, Hero Worship, and the Heroic in History. London: Chapman and Hall, 1840.

Past and Present. London: Chapman and Hall, 1843.

Sartor resartus. London: Chapman and Hall, 1831.

"Signs of the Times." In *Critical and Miscellaneous Essays.* 5 vols., Vol. I. London: James Fraser, 1840. 262–294.

Carey, Henry Charles. *Principles of Social Science.* 3 vols., Vol. II. Philadelphia: J. B. Lippincott, 1860.

Chadwick, Edwin. "Opening Address of the President of Section F (Economic Science and Statistics) of the British Association for the Advancement of Science." *Journal of the Statistical Society of London* 25 (1862): 502–524.

Chamberlin, J. Edward. "Images of Degeneration: Turnings and Transformations." In *Degeneration: The Dark Side of Progress.* Ed. J. Edward Chamberlin and Sander L. Gilman. New York: Columbia University Press, 1985. 263–289.

Chesterton, G. K. *Dickens: A Critical Study.* New York: Dodd Mead, 1906.

Chevron. "Human Energy." TV advertisement. 2 October 2007. Available at www.youtube.com/watch?v=-KyjTGMVTka (accessed January 8, 2014).

Choi, Tina Young. "Forms of Closure: The First Law of Thermodynamics and Victorian Narrative." *ELH* 74.2 (Summer 2007): 301–322.

Clark, Timothy. *The Cambridge Introduction to Literature and the Environment.* Cambridge University Press, 2010.

Clarke, Bruce. "Dark Star Crashes." In *From Energy to Information: Representation in Science and Technology, Art, and Literature.* Ed. Bruce Clarke and Linda Henderson. Stanford University Press, 2002. 59–75.

Conrad, Joseph. *Heart of Darkness.* Ed. Ross C. Murfin. Boston, MA: Bedford, 1994 [1899].

"Henry James: An Appreciation." In *Joseph Conrad on Fiction.* Ed. Walter F. Wright. Lincoln: University of Nebraska Press, 1984. 82–88.

The Letters of Joseph Conrad. Ed. Laurence Davies, Frederick R. Karl, and Owen Knowles. 7 vols. New York: Cambridge University Press, 1983.

Lord Jim. Ed. Allan H. Simmons. New York: Penguin, 2007 [1900].

Nostromo. New York: Penguin, 1990 [1905].

"A Personal Record" and "The Mirror of the Sea." New York: Penguin, 1998 [1912, 1906].

The Secret Agent. Oxford University Press, 1998 [1907].

Youth: A Narrative. London: William Blackwood, 1903 [1898].

Conrad, Joseph, and Ford Madox Ford. *The Inheritors.* New York: Carroll and Graff, 1985 [1901].

Corbet, K. "The Degeneration of Race." *The Lancet* 2 (August 17, 1861): 170.

Crookes, William. "Some Possibilities of Electricity." *The Living Age* 193 (April, May, June 1892): 93–97.

Crutzen, Paul J. "Geology of Mankind." *Nature* 415.6867 (2002): 23.

Dale, Peter Allan. *In Pursuit of a Scientific Culture: Science, Art, and Society in the Victorian Age.* Madison: University of Wisconsin Press, 1990.

Daly, Herman, and Kenneth N. Townsend. *Valuing the Earth: Economics, Ecology, Ethics.* Cambridge, MA: MIT Press, 1993.

Darwin, Charles. *On the Origin of Species by Means of Natural Selection.* New York: D. Appleton, 1864.

Darwin, George Howard. "On the Precession of a Viscous Spheroid, and on the Remote History of the Earth." In *Scientific Papers*, 2 vols., Vol. II. Cambridge University Press, 1908. 36–140.

Davidson, Graeme. "The City as a Natural System: Theories of Urban Society in Early Nineteenth Century Britain." In *The Pursuit of Urban History*. Ed. Derek Fraser and Anthony Sutcliffe. London: Edward Arnold, 1983. 349–370.

Dawson, Gowan. *Darwin, Literature and Victorian Respectability*. Cambridge University Press, 2007.

Dickens, Charles. *Bleak House*. London: Bradbury and Evans, 1853.

Our Mutual Friend. New York: G. W. Carleton, 1885 [1865].

Dixon, Edmund Saul. "Physical Force." *Household Words* 19 (March 12, 1859): 354–359.

"Vital Heat." *Household Words* 18 (June 19, 1858): 13–18.

Duff, Grant. "Must We Then Believe Cassandra?" In *Miscellanies, Political and Literary*. London: Macmillan, 1878. 57–93.

Eagleton, Terry. *Criticism and Ideology: A Study in Marxist Literary Theory*. London: Verso, 2006 [1975].

Edgeworth, Francis. *Mathematical Psychics: An Essay on the Application of Mathematics to the Moral Sciences*. London: Kegan Paul, 1881.

Ehrlich, Paul, Anne Ehrlich, and John P. Holdren. "Availability, Entropy, and the Laws of Thermodynamics." In *Valuing the Earth: Economics, Ecology, Ethics*. Ed. Herman Daly and Kenneth N. Townsend. Cambridge, MA: MIT Press, 1993. 69–73.

Engels, Friedrich. *The Condition of the Working Class in England*. Ed. Victor Kiernan. New York: Penguin, 2005 [1845].

"Outlines of a Critique of Political Economy." In Karl Marx and Friedrich Engels, *Marx and Engels on the Population Bomb*. Trans. Ronald Meek. Berkeley: University of California Press, 1971.

Epstein, Hugh. "A Pier-Glass in the Cavern." In *Conrad's Cities: Essays for Hans van Marle*. Ed. Gene Moore. Amsterdam: Rodopi, 1992. 175–196.

Ermarth, Elizabeth Deeds. *The English Novel in History 1840–1895*. New York: Routledge, 1996.

Fisher, Philip. "City Matters, City Minds." In *The Worlds of Victorian Fiction*. Ed. Jerome Buckley. Cambridge, MA: Harvard University Press, 1974. 371–389.

Ford, Ford Madox. *The Soul of London: A Survey of a Modern City*. Ed. Alan G. Hill. London: Everyman, 1995 [1905].

Foster, John Bellamy. *Marx's Ecology: Materialism and Nature*. New York: Monthly Review Press, 2000.

Gabriele, Alberto. *Reading Popular Culture in Victorian Print: Belgravia and Sensationalism*. New York: Palgrave Macmillan, 2009.

Gagnier, Regenia. *The Insatiability of Human Wants: Economics and Aesthetics in Market Society*. University of Chicago Press, 2000.

Gallagher, Catherine. *The Body Economic: Life, Death, and Sensation in Political Economy and the Victorian Novel*. Princeton University Press, 2006.

Galton, Douglas. "Report of the Royal Commission on Metropolitan Sewage." *Journal of the Society of the Arts* 33 (1884–1885): 290–299.

Galton, Francis. "Hereditary Talent and Character." *Macmillan's* 12 (May–October 1865): 318–327.

Inquiries into Human Faculty and Its Development. London: Macmillan, 1883.

Garrett, Peter. "Cries and Voices: Reading Jekyll and Hyde." In *"Dr. Jekyll and Mr. Hyde" after One Hundred Years*. Ed. William Veeder and Gordon Hirsch. University of Chicago Press, 1988. 59–72.

Geddes, Patrick. *John Ruskin, Economist*. Edinburgh: William Brown, 1884.

Georgescu-Roegen, Nicholas. *The Entropy Law and the Economic Process*. Cambridge, MA: Harvard University Press, 1971.

Gibson, William Sidney. *The Certainties of Geology*. London: Smith Elder, 1840.

Glendening, John. "Green Confusion: Evolution and Entanglement in H. G. Wells's *The Island of Doctor Moreau*." *Victorian Literature and Culture* 30.2 (2002): 571–597.

Goddard, Nicholas. "'A Mine of Wealth'? The Victorians and the Agricultural Value of Sewage." *Journal of Historical Geography* 22.3 (July 1996): 274–290.

Godwin, William. *Of Population: An Enquiry Concerning the Power of Increase in the Numbers of Mankind*. London: Longman, 1820.

Gold, Barri. "The Consolation of Physics: Tennyson's Thermodynamic Solution." *PMLA* 117 (2002): 449–464.

ThermoPoetics: Energy in Victorian Literature and Science. Cambridge, MA: MIT Press, 2010.

Gooday, Graeme. "Profit and Prophecy: Electricity in the Late-Victorian Periodical." In *Science in the Nineteenth-Century Periodical*. Ed. Geoffrey Cantor and Sally Shuttleworth. Cambridge University Press, 2007. 238–254.

"Sun-Spots, Weather and the Unseen Universe: Balfour Stewart's Anti-Materialist Representations of Energy in British Periodicals." In *Science Serialized: Representations of the Sciences in Nineteenth-Century Periodicals*. Ed. Geoffrey Cantor and Sally Shuttleworth. Cambridge, MA: MIT University Press, 2004. 111–147.

Goodstein, David. *Out of Gas: The End of the Age of Oil*. New York: Norton, 2004.

Gose, Elliott. "'Cruel Devourer of the World's Light': *The Secret Agent*." *Nineteenth Century Fiction* 15.1 (1960): 39–51.

Greenslade, William. *Degeneration, Culture and the Novel 1880–1940*. Cambridge University Press, 1994.

Hall, Daniel. *Practical Lessons and Exercises in Heat*. London: Rivington, 1893.

Hamlin, Christopher. "Providence and Putrefaction: Victorian Sanitarians and the Natural Theology of Health and Disease." *Victorian Studies* 28.3 (Spring 1985): 381–411.

Handy, Abel. "Hard-Labour in Store." *Punch* 46–47 (April 9, 1864): 151.

Harvey, W. J. "The Double Narrative of *Bleak House*." In Charles Dickens, *"Bleak House": A Norton Critical Edition*. Ed. George Ford and Sylvère Monod. New York: Norton, 1977. 963–970.

Hawksley, Thomas. "The Power for Good or Evil of Refuse Organic Matter." In *The Sewage of Towns: Papers by Various Authors, Read at a Congress on the Sewage of Towns Held at Leamington Spa, Warwickshire*. Ed. John Hitchman. London: Simpkin, Marshall, 1866. 3–62.

Headley, Frederick Webb. *Problems of Evolution*. London: Duckworth, 1900.

Helmholtz, Hermann von. "On the Interaction of Natural Forces." Trans. John Tyndall. In *Popular Lectures on Scientific Subjects*. New York: D. Appleton, 1873. 153–196.

Henderson, William. *John Ruskin's Political Economy*. New York: Routledge, 1999.

Herbert, Christopher. *Victorian Relativity: Radical Thought and Scientific Discovery*. University of Chicago Press, 2001.

Herschel, John. *A Treatise on Astronomy*. London: Longman, 1833.

Hiltner, Ken. *What Else Is Pastoral? Renaissance Literature and the Environment*. Ithaca, NY: Cornell University Press, 2011.

Hobson, J. A. *Imperialism: A Study*. 3rd edn. London: Allen and Unwin, 1968 [1902].

John Ruskin, Social Reformer. 3rd edn. London: James Nisbet, 1904 [1898].

Hodgins, George. "Energy and Explosives." *Brotherhood of Locomotive Firemen and Enginemen's Magazine* 59 (September 1915): 299–301.

Holdsworth, Joseph. *On the Extension of the English Coal-Fields*. London: R. Middleton, 1866.

Holland, John. *The History and Description of Fossil Fuel, the Collieries and Coal Trade*. London: Whittaker, 1835.

Hope, William. "The Use and Abuse of Town Sewage." *JSA* 34 (1869–1870): 298–304.

Hornborg, Alf. "Machine Fetishism, Value, and the Image of Unlimited Good: Towards a Thermodynamics of Imperialism." *Man* 27.1 (1992): 1–18.

The Power of the Machine: Global Inequalities of Economy, Technology and Environment. Walnut Creek, CA: AltaMira Press, 2001.

Houen, Alexander. "*The Secret Agent*: Anarchism and the Thermodynamics of Law." *ELH* 65 (1998): 995–1016.

Howe, Irving. "Conrad: Order and Anarchy." In *"The Secret Agent": A Casebook*. Ed. Ian Watt. London: Macmillan, 1973. 140–149.

Hubbert, M. King. "Exponential Growth as a Transient Phenomenon in Human History." In *Valuing the Earth: Economics, Ecology, Ethics*. Ed. Herman Daly and Kenneth N. Townsend. Cambridge, MA: MIT Press, 1993. 113–126.

Hughes, Jonathan. *Ecology and Historical Materialism*. Cambridge University Press, 2000.

Hull, Edward. *The Coal Fields of Great Britain: Their History, Structure, and Resources*. 2nd edn. London: Edward Stanford, 1861.

Hunt, Robert. "British Diamonds." *The St. James's Magazine* 1 (May 1861): 223–234.

Huxley, T. H. "Capital: The Mother of Labour." *Nineteenth Century: A Monthly Review* 26 (March 1890): 513–532.

Evolution and Ethics. New York: D. Appleton, 1897 [1893].

"On the Formation of Coal." In *Discourses: Biological and Geological*. New York: D. Appleton, 1897 [1870]. 137–161.

"The Struggle for Existence in Human Society." In *Readings from Huxley*. Ed. Clarissa Rinaker. New York: Harcourt Brace, 1920.

Inoue, Takutoshi (ed.). *W. Stanley Jevons: Collected Reviews and Obituaries*. Bristol: Thoemmes Press, 2002.

Jennings, George Henry. *An Anecdotal History of the British Parliament from the Earliest History to the Present Time*. London: Horace Cox, 1880.

Jerrold, Blanchard. *London: A Pilgrimage*. New York: Anthem, 2005 [1872].

Jevons, William Stanley. *The Coal Question: An Inquiry Concerning the Progress of the Nation, and the Probable Exhaustion of Our Coal Mines*. 2nd edn. London: Macmillan, 1866.

The Theory of Political Economy. 3rd edn. London: Macmillan, 1888. Available online at Library of Economics and Liberty, www.econlib.org/library/ YPDBooks/Jevons/jvnPE.html (accessed January 7, 2014).

Johnson, E. D. H. *Charles Dickens: An Introduction to His Novels*. New York: Random House, 1969.

Jones, Gareth Stedman. *Outcast London: A Study in the Relationship between Classes in Victorian Society*. New York: Pantheon, 1984.

Jones, Richard. *An Essay on the Distribution of Wealth and on the Sources of Taxation*. London: John Murray, 1831.

Kidd, Benjamin. *The Control of the Tropics*. New York: Macmillan, 1898.

Social Evolution. London: Macmillan, 1894.

Kiely, Robert. *Robert Louis Stevenson and the Fiction of Adventure*. Cambridge, MA: Harvard University Press, 1964.

Knoepflmacher, U. C. "The Novel between City and Country." In *The Victorian City: Images and Realities*. Ed. H. J. Dyos and Michael Wolff. 2 vols., Vol. II. London: Routledge, 1972. 517–536.

Krasner, James. "A Chaos of Delight: Perception and Illusion in Darwin's Scientific Writings." *Representations* 31 (Summer 1990): 118–141.

Krauss, Clifford. "Drilling Boom Revives Hope for Natural Gas." *The New York Times*, August 24, 2008. A1.

Krepp, Frederick Charles. *The Sewage Question: Being a General Review of All Systems and Methods Hitherto Employed in Various Countries*. London: Longmans, 1867.

Kuhn, Thomas, "Energy Conservation as an Example of Simultaneous Discovery." In *The Conservation of Energy and the Principle of Least Action*. Ed. I. Bernard Cohen. New York: Arno, 1981. 321–345.

Law, Jules. *The Social Life of Fluids: Blood, Milk, and Water in the Victorian Novel*. Ithaca, NY: Cornell University Press, 2010.

Lehan, Richard. *The City in Literature: An Intellectual and Cultural History*. Berkeley: University of California Press, 1998.

Levine, George. *Darwin and the Novelists: Patterns of Science in Victorian Fiction*. Cambridge, MA: Harvard University Press, 1988.

Dying to Know: Scientific Epistemology and Narrative in Victorian England. University of Chicago Press, 2002.

"From Know-Not-Where to Nowhere." In *The Victorian City: Image and Reality*. Ed. H. J. Dyos and Michael Wolff. 2 vols., Vol, II. New York: Routledge, 1999. 495–516.

Lewes, G. H. *Comte's Philosophy of the Sciences*. London: Bell and Daldy, 1871 [1853].

Liebig, Justus von, and Alderman Mechi. "The Sewage of Towns." *The Farmer's Magazine* 17 (1860): 163–165.

Lovelock, James. *The Revenge of Gaia*. New York: Basic Books, 2006.

Luxemburg, Rosa. *The Accumulation of Capital*. Trans. Agnes Schwarzschild. London: Routledge, 2003 [1913].

Mallet, Philip, "The City and the Self." In *Ruskin and Environment: The Storm Cloud of the Nineteenth Century*. Ed. Michael Wheeler. Manchester University Press, 1995. 38–51.

Malthus, Thomas Robert. *Additions to the Fourth and Former Editions of "An Essay on the Principle of Population."* London: J. Murray, 1817.

An Essay on the Principle of Population. Ed. Philip Appleman. 2nd edn. New York: Norton, 2004 [1798].

Marsh, George Perkins. *Man and Nature; or, Physical Geography as Modified by Human Action*. New York: Scribner, 1864.

Martinez-Alier, Juan. *Ecological Economics: Energy, Environment and Society*. Oxford: Basil Blackwood, 1990.

Marx, Karl. *Capital*. 3 vols., Vol. I. Trans. Ben Fowkes. New York: Penguin, 1990.

Capital. 3 vols., Vol. III. Trans. Ernest Untermann. Chicago: Charles Kerr, 1909.

Masson, John. *Lucretius: Epicurean and Poet*. 2 vols., Vol. I. London: John Murray, 1907.

Maudsley, Henry. *Body and Will*. New York: D. Appleton, 1884.

The Physiology and Pathology of Mind. New York: D. Appleton, 1867.

Maxwell, James Clerk. "Address to the Mathematical and Physical Sections of the British Association." *Nature* 3 (September 22, 1870): 419–422.

"Molecules." *Nature* 8 (September 25, 1873): 437–441.

Theory of Heat. 10th edn. London: Longmans Green, 1891.

Mayhew, Henry. *The Criminal Prisons of London and Scenes of Prison Life*. London: Griffin, Bohn, 1862.

Meeker, Joseph. *The Comedy of Survival: In Search of an Environmental Ethic*. New York: Scribner, 1974.

Mendelsohn, Everett. *Heat and Life: The Development of the Theory of Animal Heat*. Cambridge, MA: Harvard University Press, 1964.

Metz, Nancy Aycock. "The Artistic Reclamation of Waste in *Our Mutual Friend*." *Nineteenth Century Fiction* 34.1 (June 1979): 59–72.

Mill, John Stuart. *Principles of Political Economy*. 2 vols., Vol. II. 5th edn. New York: D. Appleton, 1896.

Miller, J. Hillis. *Charles Dickens: The World of His Novels*. Cambridge, MA: Harvard University Press, 1958.

"The World of *Bleak House*." In Charles Dickens, *"Bleak House": A Norton Critical Edition*. Ed. George Ford and Sylvère Monod. New York: Norton, 1977. 947–960.

Mirowski, Philip. *More Heat than Light: Economics as Social Physics, Physics as Nature's Economics*. Cambridge University Press, 1989.

Moore, James. "Theodicy and Society." In *Victorian Faith in Crisis: Essays on Continuity and Change in Nineteenth-Century Religious Belief*. Ed. Richard J. Helmstadter and Bernard Lightman. New York: Stanford University Press, 1990. 153–186.

Morgan, John Edward. "The Danger of Deterioration of Race from the Too Rapid Increase of Great Cities." In *Transactions of the National Association for the Promotion of Social Science: Sheffield Meeting, 1865*. Ed. G. W. Hastings. London: Longmans Green, 1866. 427–449.

Morgan, Lewis Henry. *Ancient Society; or, Researches in the Lines of Human Progress*. New York: Henry Holt, 1877.

Morus, Iwan Rhys. *When Physics Became King*. University of Chicago Press, 2005.

Mumford, Lewis. *The City in History: Its Origins, Its Transformations and Its Prospects*. New York: Harcourt Brace, 1961.

Mussell, James. "Science." In *Charles Dickens in Context*. Ed. Sally Ledger and Holly Furneaux. Cambridge University Press, 2011. 326–333.

Myers, Greg. "Nineteenth-Century Popularizations of Thermodynamics and the Rhetoric of Social Prophecy." *Victorian Studies* 29.1 (Fall 1985): 35–66.

Nabokov, Vladimir. *Lectures on Literature*. Ed. Fredson Bowers. New York: Harcourt Brace, 1980.

Nead, Lynda. *Victorian Babylon: People, Streets and Images in Nineteenth-Century London*. New Haven: Yale University Press, 2000.

Nichol, J. P. "Energy." In *A Cyclopaedia of the Physical Sciences*. London: Richard Griffin, 1860. 316–318.

Oates, Joyce Carol. "Jekyll/Hyde." *The Hudson Review* 40.4 (Winter 1988): 603–608.

Orwell, George. "Charles Dickens." In *Selected Writings*. London: Heinemann, 1958.

Pain, Stephanie. "Before It Was Famous: 150 Years of the Greenhouse Effect." *New Scientist* 202.2708 (May 16, 2009): 46–47.

Partington, John. "*The Time Machine* and *A Modern Utopia*: The Static and Kinetic Utopias of the Early H. G. Wells." *Utopian Studies* 13.1 (2002): 57–68.

Patterson, R. H. "Sensationalism in Science." *Belgravia* 6 (October 1868): 77–81.

Paxton, Nancy. *George Eliot and Herbert Spencer: Feminism, Evolutionism, and the Reconstruction of Gender*. Princeton University Press, 1991.

Peart, Sandra (ed.). *W. S. Jevons: Critical Responses*. 4 vols., Vol. I. London: Routledge, 2003.

Peckham, Morse. "Darwinism and Darwinisticism." *Victorian Studies* 3.1 (September 1959): 19–40.

Perelman, Michael. "Marx and Resource Scarcity." In *The Greening of Marxism.* Ed. Ted Benton. New York: Guilford, 1996. 64–80.

Perris, George Herbert. *The Industrial History of Modern England.* New York: Henry Holt, 1914.

Peterfreund, Stuart. "The Re-Emergence of Energy in the Discourse of Literature and Science." *Annals of Scholarship* 4.1 (1986): 22–53.

Philmus, Robert. "*The Time Machine*; or, The Fourth Dimension as Prophecy." *PMLA* 84.3 (May 1969): 530–535.

Pick, Daniel. *Faces of Degeneration: A European Disorder.* Cambridge University Press, 1996.

Platt, J. C., and J. Saunders. "Underground." In *London.* Ed. Charles Knight. 6 vols., Vol. I. London: Charles Knight, 1841.

Poovey, Mary. *Making a Social Body: British Cultural Formation, 1830–1864.* University of Chicago Press, 1995.

Porter, Theodore M. "A Statistical Survey of Gases: Maxwell's Social Physics." *Historical Studies in the Physical Sciences* 12 (1981): 77–116.

Prigogine, Ilya, and Isabelle Stengers. *Order out of Chaos: Man's New Dialogue with Nature.* New York: Bantam, 1984.

Pritchett, V. S. "Dickens." In *The Pritchett Century: A Selection of the Best by V. S. Pritchett.* New York: Modern Library, 1998. 573–579.

Proctor, Richard Anthony. "Britain's Coal Cellars." *St. Paul's* 9 (October–December 1871): 182–194.

"The Past and Future of Our Earth." *Contemporary Review* 25 (December 1874–May 1875): 74–92.

The Sun: Ruler, Fire, Light, and Life of the Planetary System. London: Longmans Green, 1872.

Rabinbach, Anson. *The Human Motor: Energy, Fatigue and the Origins of Modernity.* Los Angeles: University of California Press, 1992.

Richards, Thomas. *The Commodity Culture of Victorian England: Advertising and Spectacle, 1851–1914.* Stanford University Press, 1990.

The Imperial Archive: Knowledge and the Fantasy of Empire. New York: Verso, 1993.

Ruskin, John. *The Works of John Ruskin.* Ed. E. T. Cook and Alexander Wedderburn. 39 vols. London: G. Allen, 1903–1912.

Ryan, Vanessa L. "Living in Duplicate: Victorian Science and Literature Today." *Critical Inquiry* 38.2 (2012): 411–417.

Rylance, Rick. *Victorian Psychology and British Culture.* Oxford University Press, 2000.

Saposnik, Irving S. "The Anatomy of *Dr. Jekyll and Mr. Hyde.*" *SEL* 11 (1971): 715–731.

Sawyer, Paul. "Ruskin and Tyndall: The Poetry of Matter and the Poetry of Spirit." In *Victorian Science and Victorian Values.* Ed. James Paradis and Thomas Postlewait. New Brunswick: Rutgers University Press, 1985. 217–246.

Schneider, Eric D., and Dorion Sagan. *Into the Cool: Energy Flow, Thermodynamics, and Life.* University of Chicago Press, 2006.

Scott, Sir Walter. *Waverley.* London: T. and A. Constable, 1901 [1814].

Seife, Charles. *Sun in a Bottle: The Strange History of Fusion and the Science of Wishful Thinking.* New York: Viking, 2008.

Serres, Michel. *Hermes: Literature, Science, Philosophy.* Ed. Josue V. Harari and David F. Bell. Baltimore: Johns Hopkins University Press, 1982.

Sherburne, James Clark. *John Ruskin; or, The Ambiguities of Abundance.* Cambridge, MA: Harvard University Press, 1972.

Simons, Nicholas. *Cases Decided in the High Court of Chancery by the Right Hon. Sir Lancelot Shadwell.* 17 vols., Vol. XI. London: V. and R. Stevens, 1853.

Simpson, J. A., and E. S. C. Weiner (eds.). *The Oxford English Dictionary.* 2nd edn. Oxford University Press, 1989. Available at www.oed.com (accessed January 11, 2014).

Smiles, Samuel. *The Life of George Stephenson and of His Son Robert Stephenson.* New York: Harper, 1868.

Smith, Crosbie. "Natural Philosophy and Thermodynamics: William Thomson and 'The Dynamical Theory of Heat.'" *British Journal for the History of Science* 9 (November 1976): 293–319.

The Science of Energy: A Cultural History of Energy Physics in Victorian Britain. University of Chicago Press, 1998.

Smith, Crosbie, Ian Higginson, and Philip Wolstenholme. "'Avoiding Equally Extravagance and Parsimony': The Moral Economy of the Ocean Steamship." *Technology and Culture* 44.3 (2003): 443–469.

Smith, Jonathan. "Heat and Modern Thought: The Forces of Nature in *Our Mutual Friend.*" *Victorian Literature and Culture* 23 (1995): 37–69.

Smith, Samuel. *The Industrial Training of Destitute Children.* London: Kegan Paul, 1885.

Soddy, Frederick. *Wealth, Virtual Wealth, and Debt.* London: George Allen, 1983 [1926].

Spencer, Herbert. *First Principles of a New System of Philosophy.* New York: D. Appleton, 1865.

Spengler, Oswald. *Today and Destiny: Vital Excerpts from the Decline of the West.* New York: Knopf, 1940.

Stevenson, Robert Louis. "A Humble Remonstrance." In *Memories and Portraits.* New York: Charles Scribner's Sons, 1898. 275–299.

The Letters of Robert Louis Stevenson. Ed. Bradford A. Booth and Ernest Mehew. 8 vols. New Haven: Yale University Press, 1994–1995.

"Memoir of Fleeming Jenkin" and "Records of a Family of Engineers." Vol. XVIII of *Letters and Miscellanies of Robert Louis Stevenson.* New York: Scribner, 1920.

On the Thermal Influence of Forests. Vol. XXII of *Letters and Miscellanies of Robert Louis Stevenson.* New York: Scribner, 1898 [1873]. 611–621.

The Strange Case of Dr. Jekyll and Mr. Hyde. London: Longmans Green, 1886.

Treasure Island. London: Cassell, 1898 [1883].

Stewart, Balfour. *The Conservation of Energy.* London: Henry S. King, 1873.

"What Is Energy?," Parts I–IV. *Nature* 1 (April 28, 1870): 647–648; 2 (June 2, 1870): 78–80, (July 7, 1870): 183–185, (August 4, 1870): 270–271.

Stewart, Balfour, and Norman Lockyer. "The Sun as a Type of the Material Universe," Parts I and II. *Macmillan's Magazine* 18 (July 1868): 246–257; (August 1868): 319–327.

Stewart, Balfour, and Peter Guthrie Tait. *The Unseen Universe; or, Physical Speculations on a Future State.* 6th edn. London: Macmillan, 1876.

Stewart, Garrett. "Dickens, Eisenstein, Film." In *Dickens on Screen.* Ed. John Glavin. Cambridge University Press, 2004. 122–144.

Stoekl, Allan. *Bataille's Peak: Energy, Religion, and Postsustainability.* Minneapolis: University of Minnesota Press, 2007.

Sulloway, Frank. *Freud, Biologist of the Mind: Beyond the Psychoanalytic Legend.* New York: Basic Books, 1979.

Suvin, Darko. "'*The Time Machine* versus Utopia' as a Structural Model for Science Fiction." *Comparative Literature Studies* 10.4 (December 1973): 334–352.

Tait, Peter Guthrie. "Energy." *North British Review* 40 (May 1864): 177–193.
Lectures on Some Recent Advances in Physical Science with a Special Lecture on Force. London: Macmillan, 1876.

Thomas, Ronald. "The Strange Voices in the Strange Case: Dr. Jekyll, Mr. Hyde, and the Voices of Modern Fiction." In *"Dr. Jekyll and Mr. Hyde" after One Hundred Years.* Ed. William Veeder and Gordon Hirsch. University of Chicago Press, 1988. 73–93.

Thomson, William. "On a Universal Tendency in Nature to the Dissipation of Mechanical Energy." In *Mathematical and Physical Papers.* 5 vols., Vol. I. Cambridge University Press, 1882. 511.
"On the Age of the Sun's Heat." *Macmillan's Magazine* 5 (March 1862): 388–393.

Thomson, William, and P. G. Tait. "Energy." *Good Words* 3 (1862): 601–607.
Treatise on Natural Philosophy. 2 vols., Vol I. Cambridge University Press, 1883.

Tobin, Kathleen. *Politics and Population Control: A Documentary History.* Westport, CT: Greenwood, 2004.

Turner, Frank M. *Contesting Cultural Authority: Essays in Victorian Intellectual Life.* Cambridge University Press, 1993.

Tyndall, John. *Address Delivered before the British Association Assembled at Belfast.* London: Longmans Green, 1874.
The Glaciers of the Alps. London: John Murray, 1860.
Heat Considered as a Mode of Motion. New York: D. Appleton, 1863.
New Fragments. 2nd edn. London: Longmans Green, 1892.

Underwood, Ted. "Productivism and the Vogue for 'Energy,'" *Studies in Romanticism* 34.1 (1995): 103–125.
The Work of the Sun: Literature, Science and Political Economy, 1760–1860. New York: Palgrave, 2005.

Van Ghent, Dorothy. "The Dickens World: A View from Todgers." *Sewanee Review* 58.3 (1950): 419–438.

Veeder, William, and Gordon Hirsch (eds.). *"Dr. Jekyll and Mr. Hyde" after One Hundred Years*. University of Chicago Press, 1988.

Walsh, Bryan. "The World's Most Polluted Places." *Time*. September 12, 2007. Available at http://content.time.com/time/specials/2007/article/0,28804,1661031_1661028_1661016,00.html (accessed January 4, 2014).

Warner, Marina. *Fantastic Metamorphoses, Other Worlds: Ways of Telling the Self* Oxford University Press, 2002.

Waterston, William. "Coal." In *Cyclopaedia of Commerce, Mercantile Law, Finance, Commercial Geography and Navigation*. London: Henry G. Bohn, 1844.

Webb, Igor. *From Custom to Capital: The English Novel and the Industrial Revolution*. Ithaca, NY: Cornell University Press, 1981.

Weeks, Robert P. "Disentanglement as a Theme in H. G. Wells's Fiction." *Papers of the Michigan Academy of Science, Arts, and Letters* 39 (1954): 439–444.

Wells, H. G. "The Extinction of Man." In *Certain Personal Matters: A Collection of Material, Mainly Autobiographical*. London: Laurence and Bullen, 1898.

"Fiction about the Future," in *H. G. Wells's Literary Criticism*. Ed. Patrick Parrinder and Robert Philmus. Totawa: Barnes and Noble, 1980 [1938]. 246–251.

The Time Machine. Ed. Nicholas Ruddick. New York: Broadview, 2001 [1895].

The World Set Free: A Story of Mankind. New York: E. P. Dutton, 1914.

Weltman, Sharon. *Performing the Victorian: John Ruskin and Identity in Theater, Science, and Education*. Columbus: Ohio State University Press, 2007.

Whewell, William. *Astronomy and General Physics Considered with Reference to Natural Theology*. London: William Pickering, 1833.

Whitworth, Michael. "Inspector Heat Inspected: *The Secret Agent* and the Meaning of Entropy." *Review of English Studies* 49 (1998): 40–59.

Wilkinson, Ann. *"Bleak House*: From Faraday to Judgment Day." *ELH* 34.2 (1967): 225–247.

Wilson, David. "Kelvin's Scientific Realism: The Theological Context." *Philosophical Journal* 11 (1974): 41–60.

Wise, Daniel. *The Young Man's Counselor; or, Sketches and Illustrations of the Duties and Dangers of Young Men*. Cincinnati: Poe and Hitchcock, 1860.

Wise, M. Norton. "Time Discovered and Time Gendered in Victorian Science and Culture." In *From Energy to Information: Representation in Science and Technology, Art, and Literature*. Ed. Bruce Clarke and Linda Henderson. Stanford University Press, 2002. 39–58.

Wise, M. Norton, and Crosbie Smith. *Energy and Empire: A Biographical Study of Lord Kelvin*. Cambridge University Press, 1989.

"Work and Waste: Political Economy and Natural Philosophy in Nineteenth Century Britain." *History of Science* 27 (1989): 263–301, 391–449; 28 (1990): 221–261.

Woloch, Alex. *The One versus the Many*. Princeton University Press, 2003.

Wood, Gillen. "Constable, Clouds, Climate Change." *The Wordsworth Circle* 38.1–2 (2007): 25–34.

Wright, D. L. "'The Prisonhouse of My Disposition': A Study of the Psychology of Addiction in *Dr. Jekyll and Mr. Hyde.*" *Studies in the Novel* 26 (1994): 254–267.

Wynne, Brian. "Natural Knowledge and Social Context: Cambridge Physicists and the Luminiferous Ether." In *Science in Context: Readings in the Sociology of Science.* Ed. Barry Barnes and David Edge (Cambridge, MA: MIT Press, 1982). 212–231.

Wynter, Andrew. "The Use of Refuse." *The Quarterly Review* 124 (January and April 1868): 334–356.

Yaeger, Patricia. "Editor's Column." *PMLA* 126.2 (2011): 303–310.

Young, T. E. *On Centenarians; and the Duration of the Human Race: A Fresh and Authentic Enquiry.* London: Charles and Edward Layton, 1899.

Index

CAMBRIDGE STUDIES IN NINETEENTH-CENTURY
LITERATURE AND CULTURE

General editor

Gillian Beer, *University of Cambridge*

Titles published

CPSIA information can be obtained
at www.ICGtesting.com
Printed in the USA
LVHW081340270322
714519LV00009B/647